Managing Airports

Managing Airports: An International Perspective

Third edition

Anne Graham

AMSTERDAM • BOSTON • HEIDELBERG • LONDON • NEW YORK • OXFORD
PARIS • SAN DIEGO • SAN FRANCISCO • SINGAPORE • SYDNEY • TOKYO

Butterworth-Heinemann is an imprint of Elsevier

Butterworth-Heinemann is an imprint of Elsevier
Linacre House, Jordan Hill, Oxford OX2 8DP, UK
30 Corporate Drive, Suite 400, Burlington, MA 01803, USA

First edition 2001
Second edition 2003
Third edition 2008

Notice
No responsibility is assumed by the publisher for any injury and/or damage to
persons or property as a matter of products liability, negligence or otherwise, or from any
use or operation of any methods, products, instructions or ideas contained in the material
herein. Because of rapid advances in the medical sciences, in particular, independent
verification of diagnoses and drug dosages should be made

British Library Cataloguing-in-Publication Data
A catalogue record for this book is available from the British Library

Library of Congress Cataloging-in-Publication Data
A catalog record for this book is available from the Library of Congress

ISBN: 978-0-7506-8613-6

Typeset by Charon Tec Ltd., A Macmillan Company.
(www.macmillansolutions.com)

Printed and bound in Hungary

For information on all Butterworth-Heinemann publications
visit our website at elsevierdirect.com

Contents

List of Figures

List of Tables

Preface

When the first edition of this book was published in 2001, the airport industry had received relatively little attention in the published literature and had been very much overshadowed by the airline sector. Hence this was the motivation for writing the book. Shortly after the publication, the airport sector had to cope with the unparalleled consequences of the events of 9/11, the Iraq War, the outbreak of SARS and the continuing threat of terrorism. These were consequently considered in the second edition which was published in 2003. At the time of writing this edition, it was unclear what the longer term impacts of these events would be. Five years on it can be concluded that they have proved to be a significant turning point for the industry and since then it has been operating in a much more volatile and uncertain environment. This is not just directly due to increased security concerns, but also because of changing airline structures, unprecedented fuel price rises and increased environmental pressures.

Whilst in general more has now been written about the airport industry, there is still a comparative dearth of literature which focuses on the current managerial and business aspects of running an airport, rather than taking more of a technical and operation viewpoint. Therefore the aim of this book, as in previous editions, is to provide a comprehensive appreciation of the key management issues facing modern-day airport operators. As well as providing an up-to-date review of all the latest developments and trends, additional coverage is provided on new topics such as the emergence of the financial investor; low-cost airline terminals; security developments post 9/11 and the liquids security scare; technological innovations associated with check-in and biometric identification; and incentives offered to airlines both by airport operators and regional public agencies.

Airports are now complex businesses requiring a range of business competencies and skills. The emphasis here is on the economic, commercial, and planning areas at a strategic level. An international approach has been adopted reflecting the increasingly international nature of the industry. The book uses material from a wide range of airports and has a very practical focus. While most of the case studies are from the developed world, which has witnessed the fastest pace of change, they nevertheless have relevance to airport operators throughout the world. The book provides an overview of all the key management challenges facing airports. By necessity the scope has to be very far-reaching and so it cannot offer an in-depth treatment of every issue. Instead it is intended that the book should enable the reader to acquire a broad and up-to-date insight into the workings of the industry which will meet the needs of anyone who wishes to work, or is already working, in the airport sector.

Acknowledgements

On completion of this third edition, it has become apparent to me that it is now an impossible task to name all the many individuals and organizations who have helped me in writing these books. All my colleagues as usual at the University of Westminster have been extremely tolerant and patient as I struggled to write the book with numerous other deadlines approaching, and have provided much support and encouragement. I have also benefited enormously from discussions from my own students, from participants from airport management training programmes organized by the University and from the large number of industry professionals and other academics who have provided me with invaluable insights into the management of airports. I must also thank all the staff at Butterworth-Heinemann/ Elsevier for their continual support over the years and all the helpful advice and assistance which they have given me.

Finally, I must thank my family and friends for again putting up with the disruption to their lives while I have been writing this book. I am very appreciative of the support from my mother Barbara Miller, who continues to show a keen interest in my work and has provided an invaluable press-cutting service, and from the rest of the Miller family and the Daswanis 'over the road'. Above all, my children, Lorna, Callum, and Ewan, have been very patient with my preoccupation with this book – although they still do not understand, even by the third edition, why anyone would want to write or read about airports! I owe a special debt of gratitude to Ian who has tolerated my unreasonable behaviour but also remains convinced that an airport detective story would be a better read!

Abbreviations

ACCC	Australian Competition and Consumer Commission
ACI	Airports Council International
ACSA	Airports Company South Africa
AdP	Aéroports de Paris
AEA	Association of European Airlines
AENA	Aeropuertos Espanoles y Navegacion Aerea
AGI	Airports Group International
AIA	Athens International Airport SA
AIP	Airport Improvement Program
ANSconf	Conference on the Economics of Airports and Air Navigation Services
APD	Air Passenger Duty
API	Advanced passenger information
ARI	Aer Rianta International
ASAS	Airport surface access strategy
ASQ	Airport Service Quality
ATC	Air traffic control
ATF	Airport transport forum
ATM	Air transport movement
ATU	Airport throughput unit
BA	British Airways
BCBP	Bar coded boarding pass
BCIA	Beijing Capital International Airport
BOOT	Build–own–operate–transfer
BOT	Build–operate–transfer
BRT	Build–rent–transfer
BT	Build–transfer
CAA	Civil Aviation Authority
CAEP	Committee on Aviation Environmental Protection
Capex	Capital expenditure
CDA	Continuous descent approach
CDG	Charles de Gaulle
CIPFA	Chartered Institute of Public Finance and Accountancy
CO_2	Carbon dioxide

CPH	Copenhagen Airport A/S
CRI	Centre for Regulated Industries
CUSS	Common use self service check-in
CUTE	Common use terminal equipment
DAA	Dublin Airport Authority
dB	Decibel
DCMF	Design–construct–manage–finance
DDF	Dubai Duty Free
DEA	Data envelopment analysis
DMU	Decision making unit
EBIT	Earnings before interest and tax
EBITDA	Earnings before interest, tax, depreciation and amortization
ECAC	European Civil Aviation Conference
EDS	Explosive detective system
EEA	European Economic Area
EIA	Environmental impact assessment
EIS	Environmental impact statement
EFQM	European Foundation for Quality Management
EMAS	Eco Management and Audit Scheme
ENEA	Establishing a Network for European Airports
ETRF	European Travel Research Foundation
EU	European Union
EV	Enterprise value
FAA	Federal Aviation Administration
FAC	Federal Airports Corporation
F&B	Food and beverage
GA	General aviation
GDP	Gross domestic product
HTA	Hochtief AirPort
HTAC	Hochtief AirPort Capital
IATA	International Air Transport Association
ICAO	International Civil Aviation Organization
IDFC	International Duty Free Confederation
IPO	Initial public offering
ISO	International Standards Organization
LAGs	Liquids, aerosols, and gels
LAX	Los Angeles International
LCC	Low cost carrier
LCCT	Low cost carrier terminal
LOS	Level of service
LTO	Landing and take-off
MA	Manchester Airport plc
MAG	Macquarie Airports Group
MAp	Macquarie Airports
MAW	Maximum authorized weight
MCT	minimum connect time
MIDT	Market Information Data Tapes

MII	Majority-in-interest
MIS	Management information system
MRTD	Machine Readable Travel Document
mppa	Million passengers per annum
MTOW	Maximum takeoff weight
NRI	Non-resident Indian
NO_x	Nitrogen oxide
OAG	Official Airline Guide
OFT	Office of Fair Trading
PFC	Passenger facility charge
PIATCO	Philippine International Air Terminals Co.
PNR	Passenger name record
PNR	Preferred noise route
POS	Point of sale
ppa	Passengers per annum
QSM	Quality Service Monitor
RAB	Regulated asset base
RDF	Route development fund
RFID	Radio frequency identification
ROCE	Return on capital employed
ROR	Rate of return
ROT	Tehabilitate–own–transfer
SARS	Severe acute respiratory syndrome
SDR	Special drawing right
SLA	Service level agreement
SPA	Strategic partnership agreement
SPT	Simplifying Passenger Travel
TDENL	Total-day-evening-night-level
TFP	Total factor productivity
TJ	Tera Joule
TQM	Total quality management
TSA	Transportation Security Administration
UNWTO	United Nations World Tourism Organisation
VAT	Value added tax
WLU	Work load unit
YVRAS	Vancouver Airport Services

CHAPTER 1

Introduction

Airports are an essential part of the air transport system. They provide the entire infrastructure needed to enable passengers and freight to transfer from surface modes of transport to air modes of transport and to allow airlines to take off and land. The basic airport infrastructure consists of runways, taxiways, apron space, gates, passenger and freight terminals, and ground transport interchanges. Airports bring together a wide range of facilities and services to fulfil their role within the air transport industry. These services include air traffic control, security, fire and rescue in the airfield. Handling facilities are provided so that passengers, their baggage, and freight can be successfully transferred between aircraft and terminals, and processed within the terminal. Airports also offer a wide variety of commercial facilities ranging from shops and restaurants to hotels, conference services, and business parks.

Apart from playing a crucial role within the air transport sector, airports are of strategic importance to the regions they serve. In a number of countries they are increasingly becoming integrated within the overall transport system by establishing links to high-speed rail and key road networks. Airports can bring greater wealth, provide substantial employment opportunities and encourage economic development – these factors can be a lifeline to isolated communities. However, they do have a very significant effect, both on the environment in which they are located and on the quality of life of the residents living nearby. A growing awareness of general environmental issues has heightened the environmental concerns about airports.

The focus of this book is on management issues faced by airport operators. The performance of these operators varies considerably depending on their ownership, management structure and style, degree of autonomy and funding. Typically, the actual airport operators themselves provide only a small proportion of an airport's facilities and services; airlines, handling agents, government bodies, concessionaires, and other specialist organizations undertake the rest of the activities. The way in which operators choose to provide the diverse range of airport facilities has a major impact on their economic and operational performance and on the relationship with their customers.

Thus airport operators will each have a unique identity – but all have to assume overall control and responsibility at the airport. Each airport operator faces the challenging task of co-ordinating all the services to enable the airport system to work efficiently. The service providers are just some of the airport stakeholders, which operators need to consider; others include shareholders, airport users, employees, local residents, environmental lobbyists, and government bodies. A complex situation exists with many of these groups having different interests and possibly holding conflicting views about the strategic role of the airport. All the stakeholder relationships are important but, clearly, the development of a good relationship with the airlines is critical, as ultimately this will largely determine the air services on offer at the airport.

Globally, the airport industry is dominated by North America and Europe in terms of passenger numbers and North America and Asia Pacific in terms of cargo tonnes carried (Figure 1.1). According to the Airports Council International (ACI), North American airports handled 1579 million passengers in 2007, which represented 33 per cent of the total 4645 million passengers around the world. There were 1450 million passengers in Europe, accounting for a further 31 per cent of the total air traffic. As regards air cargo, North America is again the largest market with 32 million tonnes of the global 88 million tonnes representing a market share of 35 per cent (Figure 1.2). Asian Pacific airports have the second highest volume of air cargo with a global share of 33 per cent, reflecting the importance of this area in the global economy.

The importance of the North American region is reflected in the individual traffic figures of the various airports. For example, out of

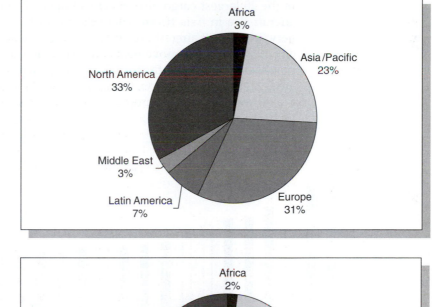

Figure 1.1
Airport passengers by world region, 2007
Source: ACI.

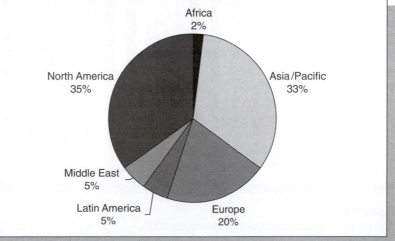

Figure 1.2
Airport cargo tonnes by world region, 2007
Source: ACI.

the 20 largest global airports, 13 are US airports in terms of passenger numbers, 6 in terms of cargo and 14 when air transport movements are being considered (Figures 1.3–1.5). North American airports tend to have a comparatively high number of air traffic movements since the average size of an aircraft tends to be smaller because of competitive pressures and the dominance of domestic traffic. However, when just international air traffic is being examined, the European region's significance becomes much more important (Figure 1.6). Heathrow has the most international air traffic, whereas Atlanta and Chicago have the largest passenger throughput. The largest passenger airport in the Asia Pacific region is Tokyo Haneda, which is dominated by domestic traffic.

Not all the major cargo airports coincide with the major passenger airports. Memphis is the world's largest cargo airport because Federal Express is based here. Similarly, UPS has its base at Louisville. The air cargo market is the largest in the Asia Pacific region where 9 out of the 20 largest cargo airports are situated. The larger than average aircraft size in Asia (from where the majority of orders for the new very large A380 aircraft are coming) means than none of the busiest airports in terms of movements are situated in this region. Dubai airport also makes it into the top 20 airports when cargo is being considered. All the other airports, whether measured in passengers or cargo, are in North America, Europe, or Asia Pacific with none in any other global region.

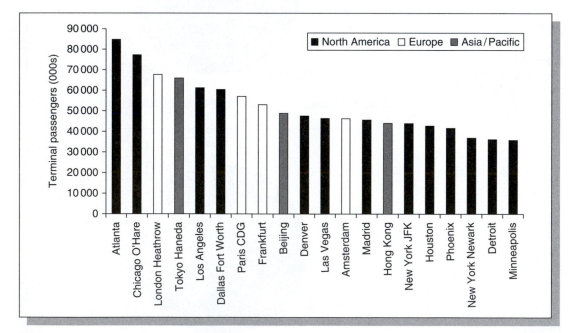

Figure 1.3
The world's 20 largest airports by total passengers, 2006
Source: ACI.

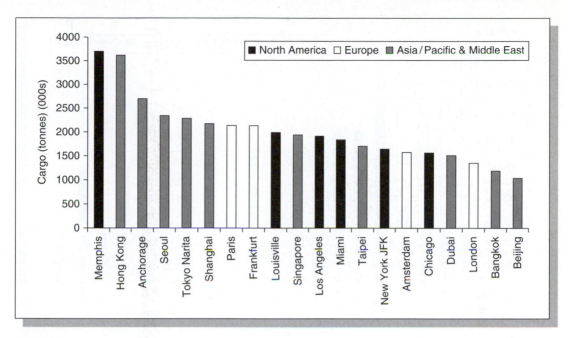

Figure 1.4
The world's 20 largest airports by cargo tonnes, 2006
Source: ACI.

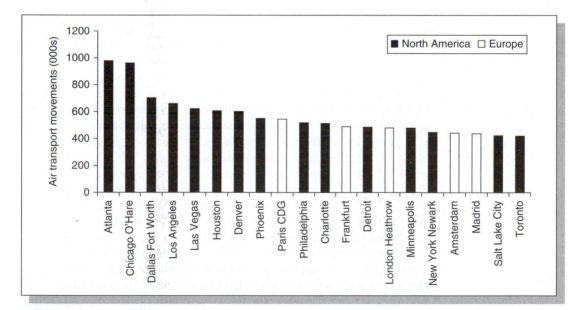

Figure 1.5
The world's 20 largest airports by aircraft movements, 2006
Source: ACI.

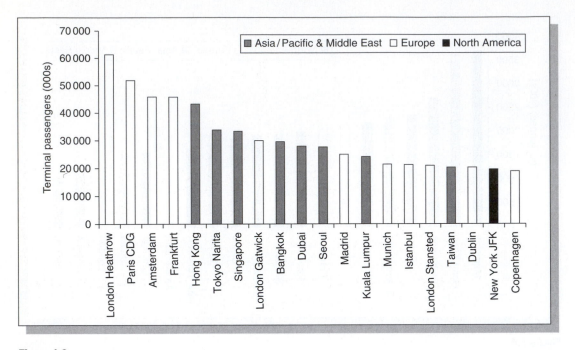

Figure 1.6
The world's 20 largest airports by international terminal passengers, 2006
Source: ACI.

The aviation industry has been growing virtually continuously since the Second World War with periodic fluctuations because of economic recessions or other external factors such as the Gulf War in 1991. However this growth was dramatically halted recently due to the events of 9/11 combined with a global economic downturn. Since then the airport industry has experienced a number of volatile years with further events such as the Iraq war and the outbreaks of SARS in 2003. These events have had different impacts in different regions of the world as illustrated by Figure 1.7 which shows the devastating effect of 9/11 on North American airports and also the very significant influence which SARS had on Asian Pacific air traffic. Table 1.1 shows the growth of passenger number at the major airports of the world since 1990. The average annual growth was 5.1 per cent in the 1990s but was only 2.4 per cent between 2000 and 2005 as airports recovered from these various events. In recent years the market share of US airports has decreased whereas it has risen in the Asia Pacific. This increase in importance of the Asia Pacific region within the global aviation environment seems set to continue, with, for example, very much higher than average growth rates being experienced in India and China.

The growth in demand for air transport has had very significant economic and environmental consequences for both the airline and the airport industries. Moreover, since the 1970s there have been major regulatory and structural developments, which have dramatically affected the way in which the two industries operate. Initially,

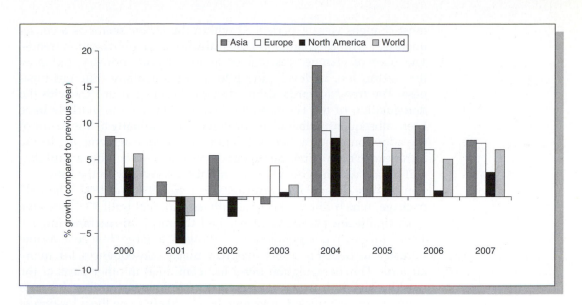

Figure 1.7
Airport passenger growth by main region, 2000–2007
Source: ACI.

Table 1.1 Growth in passenger numbers at the world's 20 largest airports 1990–2006

		1990	2000	2005	2006	Average annual change (%)		
						2000/1990	2005/2000	2006/2005
1.	Atlanta	48 015	80 162	85 907	84 847	5.3	1.4	−1.2
2.	Chicago O'Hare	60 118	72 144	76 510	77 028	1.8	1.2	0.7
3.	London Heathrow	42 647	64 607	67 915	67 530	4.2	1.0	−0.6
4.	Tokyo Haneda	40 188	56 402	63 282	65 810	3.4	2.3	4.0
5.	Los Angeles	45 810	66 425	61 489	61 041	3.8	−1.5	−0.7
6.	Dallas Fort Worth	48 515	60 687	59 176	60 226	2.3	−0.5	1.8
7.	Paris CDG	22 506	48 246	53 798	56 850	7.9	2.2	5.7
8.	Frankfurt	28 862	49 361	52 219	52 811	5.5	1.1	1.1
9.	Beijing	N/A	21 659	41 004	48 654	N/A	13.6	18.7
10.	Denver	27 433	38 752	43 388	47 325	3.5	2.3	9.1
11.	Las Vegas	18 833	36 866	43 989	46 193	6.9	3.6	5.0
12.	Amsterdam	16 178	39 607	44 163	46 066	9.4	2.2	4.3
13.	Madrid	15 869	32 893	41 940	45 501	7.6	5.0	8.5
14.	Hong Kong	18 688	32 752	40 270	43 857	5.8	4.2	8.9
15.	New York JFK	29 787	32 779	41 885	43 762	1.0	5.0	4.5
16.	Houston	17 438	35 251	39 685	42 550	7.3	2.4	7.2
17.	Phoenix	21 718	36 040	41 214	41 437	5.2	2.7	0.5
18.	New York Newark	22 255	34 195	34 000	36 724	4.4	−0.1	8.0
19.	Detroit	21 942	35 535	36 389	35 972	4.9	0.5	−1.1
20.	Minneapolis/ St Paul	20 381	36 752	37 604	35 612	6.1	0.5	−5.3
Average						5.1	2.4	4.0

Source: Airports Council International.

most changes were experienced within the airline sector as a consequence of airline deregulation, privatization and globalization trends. The pace of change was slower in the airport industry, but now this sector, too, is developing into a fundamentally different business. The trend towards airline deregulation began in 1978 with the deregulation of the US domestic market. Many more markets have been subsequently liberalized or deregulated initially as the result of the adoption of more liberal bilateral air service agreements. In the European Union (EU), deregulation was achieved with a multilateral policy, which evolved over a number of years with the introduction of three deregulation packages, in 1987, 1990 and 1993. The 1993 package, which did not become fully operational until 1997, was the most significant package and has had the most far-reaching impact. This European deregulation has allowed a large low-cost airline industry to develop, which has had major consequences for many airports. This deregulation trend has continued in other parts of the world which in turn has encouraged more low-cost airline development. A very significant milestone here is likely to be the adoption of the EU-US open aviation area in 2008.

At the same time as the airline industry has been deregulated, airline ownership patterns have also changed. Most airlines, with the notable exception of those in the United States, were traditionally state owned and often subsidized by their government owners. However, this situation has substantially changed as an increasing number of governments have opted for partial or total private sector airline ownership, primarily to reduce the burden on public sector expenditure and to encourage greater operating efficiency. The other most significant development within the airline industry, partly due to deregulation and privatization trends, is the globalization of the industry and the emergence of transnational airlines. Three major alliance groupings, namely Star, oneworld, and Sky Team, have emerged with global networks. These alliance groupings are dominating the airline business – accounting for over half of all air traffic. Also airline mergers are occurring, for example, with Air France and KLM and with Lufthansa and Swiss.

The airports have now found themselves being caught up in this environment of change. Radical restructuring has occurred, which in many ways mirrors that which has fundamentally changed the airline industry. Three key developments have been witnessed within the airport sector:

1. *Airport commercialization*: Airport commercialization is the transformation of an airport from a public utility enterprise to a commercial enterprise along with the adoption of a more businesslike management philosophy.
2. *Airport privatization*: Airport privatization is the transfer of the management of an airport, and in many cases the ownership as well, to the private sector by a variety of methods. These methods

include share flotations, the adoption of strategic partnerships or the introduction of private management contracts.

3. *Airport ownership diversification*: Airport ownership diversification relates to the emergence of a number of different types of new investors and operators of airports, such as financial investors and infrastructure companies, some of which have interests in an increasing number of airports around the world.

This book discusses the implications of the development of the airport sector, which is moving from an industry characterized by public sector ownership and national requirements into a new era of airport management which is beginning to be dominated by the private sector and global players. Airports are now complex enterprises that require a wide range of business competencies and skills – just as with any other industry. Airports can no longer see their role simply as providers of infrastructure but, instead, as providing facilities to meet the needs of their users.

Chapter 2 describes the trends in ownership and management structures which are taking place. These developments are having a major impact on both economic performance and service provision, which are considered in Chapters 3 and 4. These changes, occurring at the same time as deregulation within the airline industry, mean that the traditional airline–airport relationship has been irreversibly changed. Chapter 5 looks at this, focusing primarily on airport charging, regulation and slots issues.

A major consequence of airport commercialization and privatization trends is that airport operators are devoting much more time and effort to build up the non-aeronautical or commercial areas of the business. Chapter 6 looks in detail at this area of operation. Airport competition, hardly considered to be a relevant issue by many airports just a few years ago, is also becoming increasingly important. Marketing, which for so long has been a basic business competence in most other industries but ignored by many airports, is now a firmly accepted management practice at airports. Chapter 7 considers airport marketing.

The remaining chapters of the book take a broader view of the airport business and consider the role that airports play on the environment and surrounding community. This role needs to be clearly understood if future growth in the airport industry is to continue. Chapter 8 discusses the economic impacts of airports and how airports can act as a catalyst for business and tourism development. Chapter 9 goes on to consider the environmental impacts and ways in which airports are attempting to minimize the adverse effects. Finally, Chapter 10 brings together the key issues of each chapter in order to make predictions for the coming years and to assess the future prospects of the industry.

CHAPTER 2

The changing nature
of airports

Traditional airport ownership and management

The aim of this chapter is to discuss the development of the airport sector as it has moved from an industry characterized by public sector ownership and national requirements into a changed era of airport management, which is beginning to be dominated by the private sector and global players.

Virtually all airports were traditionally owned by the public sector. European airports serving major cities such as Paris, London, Dublin, Stockholm, Copenhagen, Madrid, and Geneva were all owned by national governments, as were many other airports outside Europe such as those in Tokyo, Singapore, Bangkok, Sydney, and Johannesburg. Elsewhere, local governments, either at a regional or municipal level, were the airport owners. This was the situation with most US airports. Regional airports in the United Kingdom also followed this pattern. Manchester airport, for example, was owned by a consortium of local authorities with 55 per cent ownership resting with Manchester City Council and the remaining 45 per cent split evenly among eight councils of other nearby towns. In Germany, Düsseldorf airport was jointly owned by the governments of North Rhine, Westfalia state and the city of Düsseldorf, while the joint owners of Hanover airport were the governments of the state of Lower Saxony and the city of Hanover.

With a number of airports, there may have been both local and national government interest. For example, Frankfurt airport was jointly owned by the state of Hesse (45 per cent), the city of Frankfurt (29 per cent), and the federal government (26 per cent). Similarly, Amsterdam was owned by the national government (76 per cent) and the municipalities of Amsterdam (22 per cent) and Rotterdam (2 per cent). Vienna airport was another example, owned by the Republic of Austria (50 per cent), the Province of Lower Austria (25 per cent), and the city of Vienna (25 per cent). Basel–Mulhouse or EuroAirport, situated on the border between Switzerland and France, was a rather unique airport being jointly owned by the national governments of both Switzerland and France.

It was only in the 1990s that there started to be a significant presence of privately, or partially privately, owned airports. Before this the only privately owned airports were small general aviation (GA) or aeroclub airports, and so the influence of the private sector on the airport industry was very limited. Thus public ownership – either at a local and/or national level – used to be the norm. However, the way in which the government owners chose to operate or manage the airports varied quite significantly and had a major impact on the airport's degree of independence and autonomy. The strictest form of control existed when the airport was operated directly by a government department, typically the Civil Aviation Authority (CAA), Ministry of Transport or, in a few cases, the military. This was the common practice for airports in areas such as Asia, the Middle

East, Africa, and South America. In Canada the State Department of Transport directly operated the 150 commercial Canadian airports. Within Europe, Greece was a good example of a country where airports were effectively run by the CAA.

In other cases, semi-autonomous bodies or companies, but still under public ownership, operated the airports. In some instances, these organizations managed more than one airport, as was the situation in Europe with the British Airports Authority (BAA) and Aer Rianta Irish Airports. There were also airport authorities or companies that operated just one major airport. This was the case at Amsterdam airport and many of the German airports. In the United States, airport authorities also existed for some of the airports, such as the Minneapolis–Saint Paul Metropolitan Airports Commission. In a few cases there were multipurpose transport authorities, such as the Port Authority of New York and New Jersey or Massport in Boston, which operated other transport facilities as well as airports.

There were also a few examples of airports being operated on a concession basis for the central government. At the larger Italian airports (e.g. Venice, Milan), companies with public (usually local) shareholdings and perhaps some private shareholdings as well held the operating concession for a long-term period, such as 60 years at Milan airport. The concession could cover management of the total airport and handling services (e.g. Milan, Turin) or just some of the services such as terminal management and handling (e.g. Palermo). At French regional airports also, the concessions were given to the local chambers of commerce with the national government retaining some control over the airfield facilities. At Zürich airport, the Zürich Airport Authority, which was owned by the Canton of Zürich, was responsible for the planning and overall operation of the airport and the airfield infrastructure, while a mixed public private company, FIG, managed and constructed the terminal infrastructure.

Moves towards commercialization

Attitudes towards these publicly owned, and often strictly controlled, airports was historically that of a public utility with public service obligations (Doganis, 1992). Consequently commercial and financial management practices were not given top priority. In the 1970s and 1980s, however, as the air transport industry grew and matured, and as the first steps towards airline privatization and deregulation took place, views about airport management began to change. Many airports gradually started to be considered much more as commercial enterprises and a more businesslike management philosophy was adopted. Thus 'commercialization' of the airport industry began to take place. The pace of change varied considerably in different parts of the world, with Europe generally leading the way. By contrast airports in areas such as those in Africa and South America generally held on to more traditional attitudes towards airports and experienced less change.

Moves towards commercialization were reflected in a number of different interrelated developments. First, various airports loosened their links with their government owners. This was achieved with the establishment of more independent airport authorities or, in some cases, by corporatization, which involved the setting up of an airport company with public sector shareholders. Such developments generally gave the airports more commercial and operational freedom, and sometimes opened the door to private sector investment and partnerships.

There had always been a number of airports, such as Amsterdam and Frankfurt, which had been run by airport corporations or companies. However, changing attitudes in the 1970s and 1980s led to many more airport authorities and companies being established. For example, in 1972 the International Airports Authority of India was established to manage the country's four international airports, while in 1986 the domestic airports came under the control of the National Airports Authority. These two authorities merged in 1995. In Indonesia, two organizations – Angkasa Pura I and II, in charge of the airports in the east and west of the country, respectively – became public enterprises in 1987 and limited liability companies in 1993. Other examples included the Polish Airport State Enterprise established in 1987, the Federal Airport Corporation of Australia set up in 1988, and Aeropuertos Espanoles y Navegacion Aerea (AENA) in Spain and the Kenya Airports Authority, both formed in 1991. In some cases, such as with Copenhagen airport (1991) or the South African airports (1994), the establishment of an airport corporation was primarily undertaken as an interim step towards airport privatization.

Canada is an interesting example where the management of many of the country's major airports, previously under the direct central control of Transport Canada, was passed over by way of long-term leases to individual non-profit-making authorities in the 1990s. The aim behind this was to improve efficiency and integrate each airport more closely with the local economy. The first airport authorities were set up for Montreal's two airports, Vancouver, Calgary, and Edmonton in 1992. By 2000, control of over 100 Canadian airports had been transferred to local organizations (Caves and Gosling, 1999). In China as well, the central government began on a process of handing over airports to local government control in 1988 with Xiamen airport and by 2004 all airports, with the exception of Beijing and those in Tibet, were operated by local government airport corporations (Zhang and Yuen, 2008).

Greater attention began to be placed on the commercial aspects of running an airport such as financial management, non-aeronautical revenue generation, and airport marketing. The operational aspects of the airport had traditionally overshadowed other areas and most airport directors and senior management were operational specialists.

However, the commercial functions of an airport were gradually recognized as being equally important and, as a result, the resources and staff numbers employed in these areas were expanded. Relatively underused practices, such as the benchmarking of financial performance and quality management techniques, also began to be accepted – albeit rather slowly at the start – by a growing number of airports as essential management tools. In some airports, the typical functional organization structure with different departments for finance, operations, administration, and so on was replaced with departments or business units more focused on customers' needs, such as airline or passenger services.

One of the most visible indications of moves towards commercialization and an increased focus on treating the airport as a business was greater reliance being placed on non-aeronautical or commercial revenues. Aeronautical revenues, such as landing and passenger fees from the airlines, had been traditionally by far the most important source. For a number of airports, notably in Europe, non-aeronautical sources overtook aeronautical sources as being the most important revenue. For instance, this occurred at Amsterdam airport in 1984. This development was primarily the result of greater space being allocated to retail and other non-aeronautical facilities, the quality being improved and the range of commercial activities being expanded.

The airport industry had historically played a rather passive role towards marketing and responded to customer needs only when necessary. A more businesslike approach to airport management, coupled with a more commercially driven and competitive airline industry, encouraged airports to take a much more active and proactive role. In the United Kingdom, for example, many of the airports set up marketing departments, started to use pricing tactics and promotional campaigns to attract new customers, and began to undertake market research (Humphreys, 1999).

In the past, because of government controls, it was sometimes very difficult to obtain financial accounts that gave a true indication of an airport's financial and economic performance. Often an airport would adopt public accounting practices specific to the country and would use public sector rather than more standard commercial procedures. This meant that comparisons with other organizations could not easily be made. Moreover, some of the airports were not considered as a separate accounting unit. This meant that the airport's costs and revenues were treated as just one item within the government department's overall financial accounts and rarely were they matched together to assess the profitability of the airport. In certain cases no separate balance sheet existed for the airport.

An increasing number of airports started adopting more commercial accounting practices in the 1970s and 1980s. This was often the direct result of the loosening of government links with the establishment of an airport authority or corporation. For instance, in the United Kingdom in 1987, all the major regional airports became public limited companies. This meant that the airports adopted commercial private sector accounting procedures. One example of this was that for the first time they showed depreciation as a measure of cost of capital. Similarly, when Geneva airport became an independent authority in 1994 it began to show a balance sheet and asset values in its annual accounts, which had previously been omitted.

Why privatization?

While the 1970s and 1980s were dominated by airport commercialization, the 1990s were the decade when airport privatization became a reality. But what is meant by 'airport privatization'? It can have various meanings. In its broadest sense, it is usually associated with the transfer of the management of an airport, and in many cases the ownership as well, to the private sector.

The theoretical arguments for and against privatization of publicly owned organizations, particularly when a share flotation is being considered, are well known. They have been fiercely debated over the years and are well documented (e.g. see Jackson and Price, 1994; Beesley, 1997). Privatization will reduce the need for public sector investment and provide access to the commercial markets. It will reduce government control and interference and may increase an organization's ability to diversify. It may bring about improved efficiency, greater competition, wider share ownership and provide greater incentives for management and employees to perform well. On the other hand, it may create a private monopoly which overcharges, delivers poor standards of service, invests inadequately and gives insufficient consideration to externalities such as controlling environmental impacts and maintaining social justice. Less favourable employment conditions may be adopted and redundancies may occur.

There were a number of developments in the 1980s and 1990s that occurred within the air transport industry which have specifically strengthened the case for airport privatization in some countries (Croes, 1997; Freathy and O'Connell, 1998. First, the demand for air transport continued to grow and is predicted to grow well into the future. In some markets, notably Europe and North America, deregulation encouraged growth and meant that the existing airport capacity could not cope with this growth. Airport privatization was seen as a way of injecting additional finance into the airport system to pay for the needed future investment. Moreover, one of the major traditional sources of airport financing, namely public sector funds, became increasingly scarce in the modern-day global economic climate as governments strived to reduce their public sector spending or to shift their focus onto non-revenue-earning activities which appeared to be more worthy, such as health and education.

15

From one viewpoint, airport privatization can be seen as just an evolutionary stage of airport development. Airports have evolved from public sector utilities to commercial enterprises and privatization can be considered as commercialization taken to its limits. Increased commercialization has brought about healthy profits and market-oriented management. Airports have shown that they have the proven ability to meet private sector requirements – albeit from a rather protected position in many cases. At the same time, the changes within the airline industry have inevitably had a major impact on the airport sector. The transformation from a predominately publicly owned and state-controlled airline industry to a global competitive business with much more commercial freedom has forced many airports to have a much more customer-focused outlook when coping with their airline customers.

The increasing number of airport privatizations that are taking place throughout the world demonstrate the growing acceptance of this process as a method of tackling some of the challenges that many airports face in the 21st century. However, airport ownership and control is always likely to be a controversial area. For many countries, transferring airports which are considered to be national or regional assets to the private sector remains a politically sensitive policy. The inherently monopolistic position of many airports will also continue to be of concern to politicians and airport users. The fear is that priority will be given to shareholders or investors and that user and community needs will be neglected. To some opponents, the privatization of airports, which is in effect the air transport 'infrastructure', does not make sense. Unlike the situation with the airlines, that is, air transport 'operators', where competition can more easily be encouraged, airports have a greater tendency to be natural monopolies, which cannot be duplicated. Views about privatization vary considerably in different regions of the world, in different countries and even between local and central government bodies in individual countries. As a result, commercialization does by no means always have to lead to privatization and there are a number of examples of airports, such as Manchester in the United Kingdom, which are run on a very commercial basis but have no desire to become totally private organizations.

The evolution of the airport business at Vienna airport

Vienna airport authority was created in 1954 when the airport handled just 64 000 passengers annually. The shareholders were the Federal Republic of Austria (50 per cent), the city of Vienna (25 per cent), and Province of Lower Austria (25 per cent). In the next two decades, the airport embarked on major expansion projects of the runway, passenger terminal, and cargo facilities and by 1978 was handling 2.8 million passengers. During this time, the authority was being run very much as a public utility, making losses, and receiving subsidies from the public sector owners (Gangl, 1995).

Between 1978 and 1985 the airport authority went through a major organizational restructuring which meant that the airport began to be considered much more as a business enterprise. A new functional organization structure with main departments of airport traffic operation, financial/accounting, planning and construction, maintenance and infrastructure services, and administration was set up. New planning and management procedures were introduced and the airport began to proactively market itself to airlines. As a result, the airport made a profit for the first time in 1979 and has remained in profit ever since. By 1985, the airport was handling 3.9 million passengers and had begun to pay dividends to its three public sector shareholders.

In the late 1980s, further commercialization took place with the replacement of the functional organization structure with a new system which allowed the airport authority to respond more effectively to its customers. It set up business units or customer divisions separately for airlines and passengers, and supported these with service divisions (such as construction, maintenance and technical service, safety and security, and finance and accounting) and central offices (such as legal affairs, communications and environment, human resources). The business units were required to make profits while the service units were there to provide services in the most cost-effective manner. Management practices, with greater emphasis on private sector practices in the area of business and strategic planning and cost control, were introduced. A comprehensive management information system (MIS) was launched, and training programmes focused on customer orientation and effective business practices were set up. Attention was also given to developing the non-aeronautical side of the business, such as retail and catering, marketing and service quality provision (Gangl, 1998).

In 1990 it became apparent that a capital expenditure programme of AS8 billion was needed to extend the airport's annual capacity from 6 to 12 million passengers. Eighty per cent of this capital was available through cash flow and retained profits but other sources were needed for the remaining 20 per cent. Budget constraints meant that increasing the equity of the public shareholders was out of the question. The realistic options were either raising the money through loans/bonds or raising equity on the capital markets. At that time, Austrian interest rates for medium- and long-term loans as well as bonds were high. On the other hand, the Vienna stock market, like most others throughout the world, was in a poor trading situation. Eventually, the airport decided on a share flotation for 1992.

This wasprimarily because it did not want the large loan servicing costs right through until the next capacity expansion, which was planned in 2000, and then further debt requirements.

In order to be floated on the stock exchange, the airport authority had to implement a number of very significant changes. This included changing the corporate status from a limited liability company to a joint stock company, and increasing the share capital by 50 per cent. Business appraisals for valuing the company were undertaken and consultations were held with capital market analysts. Employee share-acquisition programmes and investor relations programmes were set up and sales support were undertaken through marketing, advertising, and road shows in areas such as Austria, the United Kingdom, Germany, Switzerland, Japan, and Taiwan. The airport also had to ensure that it developed a private sector and market-oriented management approach with an appropriate corporate culture and image – a process which had begun in the 1980s and was further developed during the privatization process (Gangl, 1994). The organizational structure was further refined to be more customer focused, with aviation units (airside services, airline and terminal services, and handling services) and non-aviation units (consumer services, technical services, land development, and real estate) both being supported by central services.

In spite of the poor stock market conditions, the flotation or initial public offering (IPO) took place in June 1992 and was oversubscribed three times in Austria and five times internationally. The sale brought in AS1.8 billion which was used by the airport company to partly finance its expansion plans. The success of the flotation meant that the Austrian government opted to sell half of its remaining 36.5 per cent stake in the airport in a secondary offering in 1995 – this time retaining the AS2.2 billion proceeds itself. This gave private shareholders 47 per cent of the airport. In 2001, the public shareholding in the company was reduced to 40 per cent, which followed a share buy-back in 2000 that resulted in 10 per cent of shares being placed in an employee foundation. In 1995, Amsterdam airport also bought 1 per cent of the airport with the aim of establishing a strategic alliance to encourage commercial and technical cooperation. However, this arrangement was terminated in 1998 (Figures 2.1–2.4).

Since partial privatization in the early 1990s, passenger numbers have increased by an average annual growth of 6.8 per cent (Figure 2.5). Profitability, in terms of the earnings before interest and tax (the EBIT margin), has fluctuated but in most years has been very healthy at above 20 per cent (Figure 2.6). Like a number of major airports in Europe, the airport has been keen to become involved in international projects. For example,

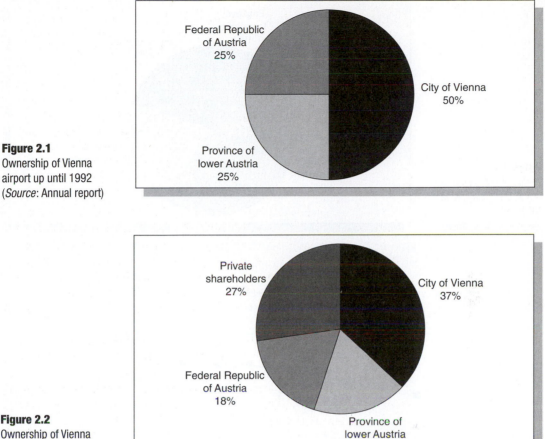

Figure 2.1
Ownership of Vienna
airport up until 1992
(*Source*: Annual report)

Figure 2.2
Ownership of Vienna
airport after IPO in 1992
(*Source*: Annual report)

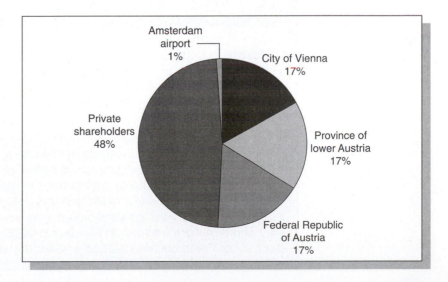

Figure 2.3
Ownership of Vienna
airport after secondary
offering in 1995
(*Source*: Annual report)

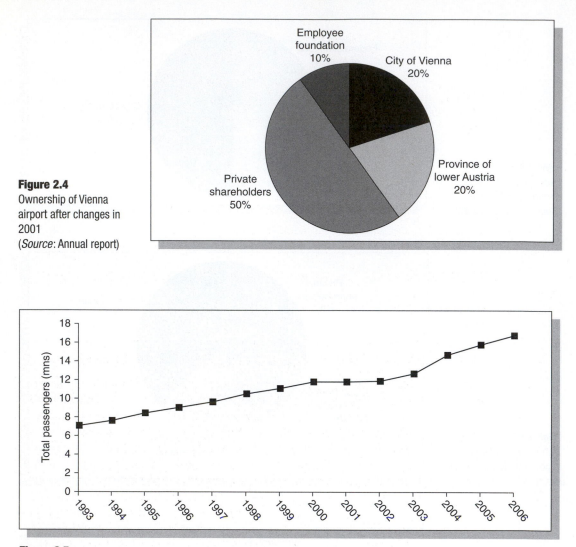

Figure 2.4
Ownership of Vienna airport after changes in 2001
(*Source*: Annual report)

Figure 2.5
Total passengers at Vienna airport, 1993–2006
(*Source*: Annual reports)

it was partly responsible, with other investors, for a new international terminal and car park at Istanbul airport which was opened in 2000. In 2002 a consortium led by Vienna airport bought a 40 per cent stake in Malta airport. Most recently it was a member of the TwoOne consortium which acquired a 66 per cent share of Kosice airport in Slovakia in 2006 and it bought 25 per cent of Friedrichshafen airport in Germany in 2007.

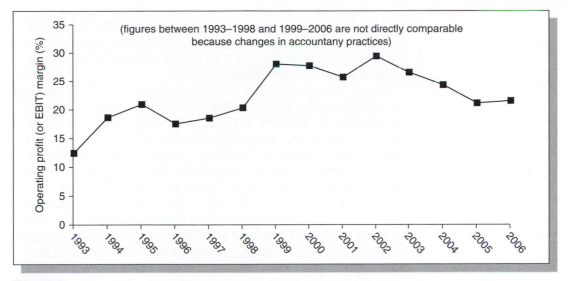

Figure 2.6
Profitability – Vienna airport group, 1993–2006
(*Source*: Annual reports)

French regional airports: preparing for privatization

In contrast to Vienna airport and a number of other European airports, France has been relatively slow in allowing privatization of any of its airports. It was not until 2004 and 2005 when legislation was passed, which cleared the way for the partial privatization of Aéroport de Paris (AdP) in 2006. At the same time a new ownership and management structure for the larger regional airports was agreed, which could ultimately lead to some privatization.

Traditionally, French regional airports have been operated as concessions by the local chambers of commerce and industry with the national government retaining some control over the airfield facilities. The new law of 22 July 2005 divided the regional airports into two groups. First there were the larger 12 major regional airports ranging from Nice with nearly 10 million passengers to Cayenne with less than 400 000 passengers (Figure 2.7). Four of these (Pointe à Pitre, Fort de France, Saint Denis–Réunion and Cayenne) were overseas airports. With all of these the legislation stated that the French government would remain the landowner but private companies would be created and granted a long-term airport concession (of a maximum of 40 years). Initially these private companies would only have public shareholders, namely the French state (60 per cent), local authorities, and the chamber of commerce and industry but there could be the possibility of private investors later. The chamber of commerce employees would be on loan to these new airport companies for a maximum of 10 years. With the remaining 151 airports, the new framework allowed for the inclusion of the local governments and private investors into the capital arrangements but they had to remain under majority public ownership (Feller, 2006).

Already companies have been created at Lyons, Toulouse, and Bordeaux and this will follow soon at Nice and Montpelier. For example, at Toulouse a 40-year concession (until 2046) was agreed in 2006 and the new public limited company has the French Govern- ment, the chamber of commerce and industry, and local authorities as the shareholders (Figure 2.8). At other airports, such as Marseilles, Strasbourg, and Saint–Denis, companies are expected to be set up in 2010 or 2011. Once the companies have been established there are three options available. The public shareholders can remain or the French state can sell a minority interest to private investors and other public shareholders. Alternatively it can sell its majority interest to private investors but only after 2013. A number of these regional airports, as in other European countries such as the United Kingdom and Germany, have good growth prospects and would be attractive to private investors, albeit that there will still be a certain amount of control exercised by the state. Ultimately the timing and any privatization will depend on the individual shareholders although the French government does not generally seem of favour in keeping its majority shares. At the same time the chambers of commerce, who view airports as important for regional development seem more positive about privatization than the local authorities who tend to be more focused on local issues (Guitard and Vernhes, 2007).

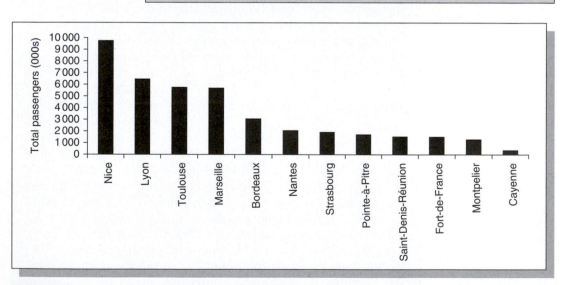

Figure 2.7
Traffic at 'private company' French regional airports 2006
(*Source*: Direction Generale de l'Aviation Civile)

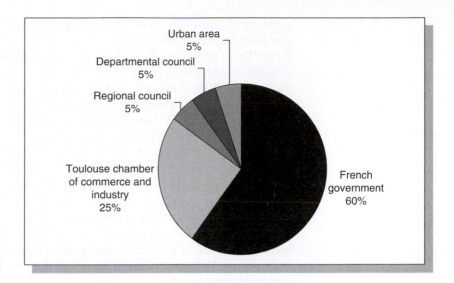

Figure 2.8
Ownership of Toulouse
airport 2007
(*Source*: Airport Website)

The privatization timetable

The first major airport privatization took place in the United Kingdom in 1987. This was the total flotation of shares of BAA which at that time owned three London airports (Heathrow, Gatwick, and Stansted) and four Scottish airports (Aberdeen, Edinburgh, Glasgow, and Prestwick). This successful privatization opened up the debate at many other airports as to whether they too should be privatized. However, in the next few years only a handful of airports were actually privatized. In the United Kingdom, this included Liverpool airport which was partially privatized in 1990, East Midlands which was totally privatized in 1993, and Belfast International which was subject to a management buyout in 1994. Elsewhere in Europe and in other continents there was little evidence of definite moves towards privatization, with the notable exceptions of Vienna and Copenhagen airport. As previously mentioned, 27 per cent of shares in Vienna airport were floated in 1992, followed by a secondary offering of a further 21 per cent in 1996. Similarly, at Copenhagen airport there were share flotations of 25 per cent in 1994 and a further 24 per cent in 1995.

The year 1996 appeared to be a turning point for the airport industry and the following few years saw airport privatization becoming a much more popular option in many areas of the world. In that year, for instance, Bournemouth and Cardiff airports were privatized in the United Kingdom and private involvement in the new Athens airport at Spata was agreed. Airports as diverse as Düsseldorf, Sandford Orlando, Naples, Rome, Birmingham, Bristol, Melbourne, Brisbane, and Perth were partially or totally privatized in 1997. Further privatizations took place in 1998 in Australia as well as in South Africa, Argentina, and other destinations such as Luton, Stockholm, Skavsta, Auckland, Wellington, and Hanover. In 1999 and 2000, a number of airports in central and southern American countries, such as Mexico, the Dominican Republic, Chile, Costa Rica, and Cuba, were privatized. There were also share flotations for Malaysian Airports, Beijing Capital International Airport (BCIA), and Zürich Airport. The first partially private financed Indian airport was opened in Cochin, Kerala in southern India, having been financed 26 per cent from the state of Kerala and the rest from non-resident Indians (NRIs), financial institutions, and airport service providers.

In 2001, privatization occurred at airports as varied as Frankfurt, Newcastle, Seeb and Salahah in Oman, and Sharm El Sheikh in Egypt. However by the end of the year, the events of 9/11, coupled with an economic downturn and airline failures in some areas, meant that airport privatization temporarily became a less attractive option and various privatizations at airports such as Milan, Brussels, and Sydney were postponed or cancelled. As the air transport industry continued to be affected by external events such as the Iraq War and SARS, very few new privatizations took place in 2002 and 2003 – with the notable exception of Sydney and Malta. However by 2004 there were signs that airport privatization was back on the agenda for a number of airports, for example, with the successful privatization of Brussels and with agreements being reached to develop two greenfield airport sites in India, namely Bangalore and Hyderabad, partially through private investment. Further privatizations followed in 2005, for instance in Cyprus (Larnaca and Paphos), Budapest, and Venice. In 2006, a number of other airports such as Paris, Kosice in Slovakia, Varna and Burgas in Bulgaria, and the regional airports in Peru were partially or fully privatized. In the same year, private involvement at the main Indian airports of Delhi and Mumbai was agreed. Most recently in 2007, airport privatization has taken place at Xi'an airport in China, in Pisa, Leeds–Bradford, Antalya and Amman, and it was announced that a new private airport will be built in Murcia in Spain. In addition there was the sale of the first Russian airport, namely Mukhino airport, to foreign investors.

However, not all these privatizations have been successful. This has been due to a number of different reasons such as conflicts that have arisen between governments and the new private operator and the enforcement of the terms of privatization agreements, problems related to the selection of the most suitable investor or inappropriate/ unrealistic estimations of passenger/airline demand and the financial situation. For example, the Frankfurt airport company, Fraport was involved with a privatization project at Manila Airport in the Philippines which has led to a complex and extended dispute with the Philippine government. In Berlin, there were several separate attempts to use private investors to develop a new airport to serve the city until this approach was abandoned following a number of legal challenges between bidders and complaints from local residents. In Argentina, the new airport operator overestimated the profits which could be generated from the airports which eventually meant that the privatization agreement had to be renegotiated. With greater privatization experience, no doubt future airport privatizations processes will become better informed, which should help reduce some of these problems, although clearly other external risks and uncertainties, for instance related to security, traffic growth, airline strategies, airport competition, and general economic/political factors, will still remain whenever any airport is privatized.

Types of privatization

Airports are generally seen as attractive organizations to investors, for a number of reasons. First, the airport industry has strong growth potential. Many of the airports, particularly the major ones, face limited competition, both from other airports and other modes of transport. There are very high barriers to entry within the industry due to the large capital investment needed and the difficulties in finding appropriate, convenient locations where airport development is allowed. However risks clearly exist as well, such as political interference in the form of airport regulation and control over airport development and the changing nature of the airline industry with developments such as deregulation and greater collaboration through alliances.

Airport privatization can occur in different ways (Carney and Mew, 2003). The types of privatization models broadly fall into five categories:

1. share flotation
2. trade sale
3. concession
4. project finance privatization
5. management contract.

The selection of the most appropriate type of privatization involves a complex decision-making process which will ultimately depend on the government's objectives in seeking privatization. For example, is the type of privatization required to lessen the burden on public sector finances, generate funds from the airport sale, increase share ownership or encourage greater efficiency, competition or management expertise within the airport sector? In reaching a decision, factors such as the extent of control which the government wishes to maintain; the quality and expertise of the current airport operators; further investment requirements and the financial robustness of the airports under consideration all have to be taken into account.

Share flotation

The first option is a share flotation or an IPO with the airport company's share capital being issued and subsequently traded on the stock market. Management will usually be given options to acquire shares. To date, the only 100 per cent share flotation which had taken place

Table 2.1 Examples of airport privatization through share flotations

Airport	Date	Type of sale
UK: BAA	1987	100% IPO
Austria: Vienna	1992	27% IPO
	1995	21% Secondary offering
	2001	Further secondary offering[a]
Denmark: Copenhagen	1994	25% IPO
	1996	24% Secondary offering
	2000	17% Secondary offering
Italy: Rome	1997	45.5% IPO
New Zealand: Auckland	1998	51.6% IPO
Malaysia: Malaysia Airports	1999	18% IPO
China: BCIA	2000	35% IPO and trade sale
Switzerland: Zürich	2000	22% IPO and 28% secondary offering
Italy: Florence	2000	39% IPO
Germany: Fraport	2001	29% IPO
China: Hainan Meilan	2002	20% IPO
Italy: Venice	2005	28% IPO
France: Aéroports de Paris	2006	33% IPO
Italy : Pisa	2007	21% IPO

Note: [a]In 2001 at Vienna airport a further sale of shares following a re-purchase of some shares which were transferred to an employee foundation resulted in 40% of the airport remaining under government ownership.
Source: Compiled by author from various sources.

was with BAA in 1987 (now de-listed). Other partially floated airport companies include Vienna airport (Flughafen Wien AG), Copenhagen Airports A/S (now de-listed), Zürich, Auckland Airport, Malaysia Airports (an organization owning 37 airports in the country), Fraport, AdP, Rome (now de-listed), Florence, Venice, Pisa, and Hainan Meilan and BCIA in China (Table 2.1). The BCIA flotation is interesting as it was the first airport where a share flotation came after an initial trade sale to a strategic partner, namely AdP. With this 'cornerstone' approach AdP bought 10 per cent of the airport, ABN Amro Ventures bought another 8 per cent and institutional and retail investors a further 17 per cent – leaving the Chinese government with a 65 per cent share (Beechener, 2000). A number of other Chinese airports (Shanghai, Shenzhen, Xiamen, and Guangzhou) have been listed on the domestic stock exchanges.

With a share flotation, the government owner will give up total or partial ownership, while transferring the economic risks and effective control to the new shareholders. Generally, the stock markets have viewed purchases of shares in airport companies in a favourable light, with positive factors such as strong growth prospects, limited competition because of high barriers to entry and minimal threats of substitutes, and potential commercial opportunities influencing their views.

Total or partial privatization of this type will totally eliminate or certainly reduce the need for state involvement in the financing of airport investment. The proceeds from such a privatization could be used for funding future investment at the airport, as with the IPO of 27 per cent at Vienna airport, or can go directly to the government, as with BAA. Even when total privatization takes place, a degree of government influence can theoretically be maintained by issuing a golden share to the government so that in extreme cases national interests can be protected. To prevent domination by any individual shareholder, limits can be placed on the maximum shareholding. For instance the UK government had a golden share in BAA which gave it the right of veto over undesirable takeovers deemed to be against national interests and capped the amount of shares that any one shareholder can hold at 15 per cent. However, the European Court of Justice declared this type of shareholding to be illegal in 2003 because it prevents capital movements within the EU. When the government maintains a partial share in the business, this will give it some influence over strategic decisions affecting the airport. However this has to be weighed up against the obligations of ownership and any conflicts that may occur with other government roles such as policymaker and regulator.

In order to be floated on the stock market, the airport company will be required to have a track record of minimum profits to make the airport attractive enough to the investors. Airports not performing well would clearly find it hard to be successfully privatized in this way. Fully developed capital markets also need to be in existence, which may not be the situation in certain areas, for example, in South America and Africa. The airport company will have to get used to daily scrutiny of its financial performance by its shareholders and other investors and, as a consequence, may find it hard not to become preoccupied with the share price. However, the existing management will usually be able to remain in control of the company as the investors will tend to have a relatively passive role. Moreover, issuing shares to employees may give them an incentive and make them feel more involved in the affairs of the airport company.

Trade sale

With this option, some parts of the airport or the entire airport will be sold to a trade partner or consortium of investors, usually through a public tender. All the trade sales which took place in the 1990s involved strategic partners rather than just passive investors. This meant that the management and technological expertise of the partners as well as financial capabilities were taken into account while agreeing on a sale.

Table 2.2 Examples of airport privatization through trade sales

Airport	Date	Share of airport sold (%)	Main buyer
UK: Liverpool	1990	76	British Aerospace
UK: Prestwick	1992	100	British Aerospace
UK: East Midlands	1993	100	National Express
UK: Southend	1994	100	Regional Airports Ltd
UK: Cardiff	1995	100	TBI
UK: Bournemouth	1995	100	National Express
UK: Belfast International	1996	100	TBI
UK: Birmingham	1997	51	Aer Rianta/Natwest Ventures (40%) Other investors (11%)
UK: Bristol	1997	51	Firstbus
UK: Liverpool	1997	76	Peel Holdings
UK: Kent International	1997	100	Wiggins
Italy: Naples	1997	65	BAA
Australia: Brisbane, Melbourne, Perth	1997	100	Various
Sanford Orlando	1997	100	TBI
Germany: Düsseldorf	1998	50	Hochtief and Aer Rianta
Skavsta Stockholm	1998	90	TBI
South Africa:ACSA	1998	20	ADRI South Africa consortium (Aeroporti di Roma had 69% share)
Germany: Hanover	1998	30	Fraport
New Zealand:Wellington	1998	66	Infratil
Australia: 15 remaining major Australian airports (except Sydney)	1998	100	Various
UK: Humberside	1999	83	Manchester airport
US: Stewart International	1999	100	National Express
Belgium: Liege	1999	25	AdP
Italy: Rome	2000	51	Leonardo consortium
Italy: Turin	2000	41	Benetton Group consortium
Germany: Hamburg	2000	36	Hochtief and Aer Rianta
UK: Newcastle	2001	49	Copenhagen airport
Australia: Sydney	2002	100	Macquarie/Hochief consortium
Malta	2002	40	Vienna consortium
Budapest	2005	75	BAA
Luebeck	2005	75	Infratil
UK: Exeter and Devon	2006	100	Balfour Beatty consortium
Kosice	2006	66	TwoOne Vienna consortium
UK: Leeds Bradford	2007	100	Bridgepoint
China: Xi'an	2007	25	Fraport
Russia: Mukhino	2007	100	Meinl Airports

Note: The table only shows the first sale that was made. In some case there are now different owners.
Source: Compiled by author from various sources.

The first significant trade sale was in 1990 when 76 per cent of Liverpool airport, previously owned by local government, was sold to British Aerospace (Table 2.2). Subsequently a number of other UK airports, such as East Midlands, Cardiff, Bournemouth, and Southend have been totally sold off to a trade partner. In the case of Birmingham, Newcastle, and Humberside airports, a strategic partner has been brought in through a partial sale. Elsewhere in Europe, Hanover, Düsseldorf, Hamburg, and Naples airports have also been partially privatized through a trade sale. AdP has a 25 per cent share of Liège airport in Belgium, which it has developed as an alternative venue for freight activities. Outside Europe, 20 per cent of the Airports Company South Africa (ACSA) was sold to a strategic partner. The ACSA owns and manages nine South African airports including the three major international airports of Johannesburg, Durban, and Cape Town. Two-thirds of Wellington airport in New Zealand has also been sold through a trade sale. Airports which have been leased on long-term arrangements to strategic partners or consortia can also be included in this category – as effectively all control will be transferred from the publicly owned airport to the trade partner. The most notable example here is the Australian airports, the majority of which have been sold on long-term leases (50 years with a further possible option of 49 years) to different consortia. The privatizations at Budapest and Malta are other examples.

In many of these cases, the strategic partner is an established airport operator or the purchasing consortium will contain a member with airport management experience. For example, BAA was the strategic partner in the Naples airport sale and Vienna airport belongs to the consortium which bought part of Malta airport. With most of the Australian airport sales, there was an airport interest within the successful consortia. Many of the participating airports in these airport privatizations were not actually privatized airports themselves which leads to further complications in the definition of a 'private' airport. For example, the former Aer Rianta Irish Airports, which was a public corporation (now Dublin Airport Authority), had been successfully involved in the partial privatization of Birmingham, Hamburg, and Düsseldorf airports. Similarly the government-owned Schiphol group, which owns Amsterdam airports, has a number of interests in other airports around the world. Privatization has been discussed for both these airport groups but has not yet occurred.

Concession

With this type of arrangement, an airport management company or consortium will purchase a concession or lease to operate the 'privatized' airport for a defined period of time, commonly between 20 and 30 years, again usually through a tendering process. Financial terms and the types of lease will vary but typically this option will involve an initial payment and a guaranteed level of investment and/or payment of an annual fee. Hence this tends to be a more complex approach, which has high transactions costs and needs to carefully designed and implemented to ensure that the private contracts achieve the government policy objectives.

These concession arrangements are the most popular form of airport privatization in developing countries, accounting for more than 40 per cent of airport contracts and 60 per cent of investment commitments in 1990–2005 (Andrew and Dochia, 2006). They were particularly popular in Central and South America in the late 1990s. One of the earliest concession arrangements was agreed in 1997 for the three main airports of Bolivia, namely La Paz, Santa Cruz, and Cochabamba. Airports Group International, the former airport management company (acquired by TBI and then later by Abertis), was awarded the 30-year concession during which time it guaranteed to upgrade the three airports and pay an annual fee of 21 per cent of gross revenues. Another example is the 30-year concession for the 33 Argentinian airports, which was awarded to the consortium, Aeroportuertos Argentinos 2000 (AA2000), which had among its partners, SEA, the Milan airport company, and Ogden, the airport services company. The consortium agreed to pay an annual US$171 million a year for the first 5 years of the agreement and invest US$2 billion. However this concession amount was considered by many, including the International Air Transport Association (IATA), to be totally unrealistic and it proved impossible for AA2000 to pay it all, especially because of the severe political and economic crisis which the country went through after this privatization occurred. Eventually in 2007 it was agreed that the fee would be changed to 15 per cent of revenues (Lipovich, 2008). Another concession agreement was signed between the Peruvian government and the Lima Airport Partners in 2001 (which was a consortium formed by Fraport and Alterra) when 47 per cent of revenues had to be paid to the government and also there were a number of investment obligations in the first 3 years of operation, such as US$1.3 million in the first 180 days (US$3.5 million was actually invested) and US$110 million by 2005 (US$135 million was invested) (Arbulu, 2007). In more recent years concessions have increasingly been used in Eastern Europe and Asia with many involving a public–private partnership (Hooper, 2002).

Generally, with this type of arrangement, the concessionaire will take full economic risk and will be responsible for all operations and future investment. Again as with the trade sales, management and technological expertise will be bought in to run the airport. Since the privatized airport will only be handed over for a fixed period of time, the government owner will have a greater degree of control than with an outright sale and will receive a regular income. This has proved more politically acceptable in some countries, for example, in South America where a number of concession arrangements were negotiated in the late 1990s. Here, traffic growth was predicted to be high but in many cases the infrastructure was inadequate and the governments were unwilling or unable to invest in the airports (Ricover, 1999). At Luton airport in the United Kingdom, a consortium originally consisting of Barclays Investment, Bechtel Enterprises, and Airport Groups International (AGI) (which was subsequently bought by TBI in 1999) was given the 30-year concession to run the airport in 1998. A concessionaire-type arrangement was chosen, rather than a flotation or trade sale, since the local government owners had promised not to relinquish total control of this publicly owned asset to private hands. This arrangement involved paying an initial annual concession fee of US$ 19 million which would increase as passenger traffic grows (Communique Airport Business, 1998). Barclays and Bechtel have subsequently sold off their interest in this airport.

The situation was rather different in Mexico where the country's 58 airports were divided into four groups, namely the North-Central Group (GACN), the Pacific Group (GAP), the Southeast Group (ASUR), and the Mexico City Group (AICM). Each of these groups had at least one large airport (e.g. Mexico City, Cancun, Acapulco) which would make them desirable to private investors but they also had some smaller airports as well. The very small airports were not allocated to any of these groups as, although they were seen as essential for public need, they were not considered to be attractive investments. Concession contracts were awarded for 15 per cent for three of these four groups for an initial 15-year period with an underlying 50-year agreement. There had to be at least one airport operator from another country within each successful consortium to bring international expertise but only 49 per cent could be under foreign ownership and it was also planned that there would be a subsequent flotation of remaining government shares as well. An upfront fee for buying the concession and an annual percentage of revenue had to be paid to the government by the consortia. The concession for ASUR was the first to be awarded in 1998 to a consortium formed by Copenhagen airport and consequently the rest of the shares (except 0.01 per cent which was kept by the government) were sold through flotations in 2000 and 2005. In 1999, 15 per cent of the GAP Group of 12 airports was sold to a consortium with AENA, the Spanish airport group, as a key partner, and then in 2006 the rest of the shares were floated. In 2000, the 15 per cent share of the GACN group was sold to an AdP consortium again with a further flotation of 47 per cent of shares in 2006. The Mexico City group has yet to be privatized because of uncertainty related to a new airport for the capital. Other countries which have had concession agreements for their airports include the Dominican Republic, Chile, Uruguay, Costa Rica, Peru, Tanzania and India (Table 2.3).

Project finance privatization

With this option, a company will usually build or redevelop and then operate an airport or specific facility, such as a terminal, for a certain length of time, typically 20–30 years. This company may be totally private or may be a private–public partnership. At the end of this period, ownership will revert to the government owners. Thus this approach can be viewed as a particular type of concession agreement. Generally such an arrangement will not usually require a large upfront payment but the operating company will bear all the costs

Table 2.3 Examples of airport privatization through concession agreements

Airport	Date	Length of concession (years)	Concessionaire
Columbia: Barranquilla	1997	15	AENA consortium
Columbia: Caratagena	1998	15	AENA consortium
Bolivia: La Paz, Santa Cruz, Cochabamba	1997	25	AGI[a]
UK: Luton	1998	30	AGI[a] Bechtel/Barclays consortium
Mexico: South East Group	1998	15[b]	Copenhagen airport consortium
Mexico: Pacific Group	1999	15[b]	AENA consortium
Argentinean Airport System	1998	33	Aeropuertos Argentina 2000 consortium (including SEA Milan and Ogden)
Tanzania: Kilimanjaro International Airport	1998	25	Mott Macdonald consortium
Dominican Republic: 6 airports including Santo Domingo	1999	20	YVRAS/Odgen consortium
Chile: Terminal at Santiago International Airport	1999	15	YVRAS consortium
Uruguay: Montevideo	1999	25	YVRAS consortium
Costa Rica: San Jose	1999	20	TBI[a]
Columbia: Cali	2000	20	AENA consortium
Mexico: North Central Group	2000	15[b]	AdP consortium
Peru: Lima	2001	30	Fraport/Alterra consortium
Jamaica: Montega Bay	2003	30	YVRAS consortium
Peru: 12 regional airports	2006	25	Ferrovial consortium
India: Delhi	2006	30	GMR/Fraport/Malaysia Airports consortium
India: Mumbai	2006	30	GVK/ACSA consortium
Turkey: Antalya	2007	17	Fraport/IC Holding consortium

Notes: The table only shows the first new operator. In some cases there are now different operators.
[a] AGI was bought by TBI in 1999; Abertis now owns TBI.
[b] Fifteen-year contract but underlying 50-year concession.
Source: Compiled by author from various sources.

of building or re-developing the facility. When it is built, the company will have to cover the operating costs but will also retain most revenues (often after paying an annual fee to the government) until the facility is handed back. Thus, the airport company will take full economic risk for investment and operations. There are a number of project finance privatization methods with the most popular being build–operate–transfer (BOT) when, as the name suggests, the company will build the facility, operate it for a certain length of time and then transfer ownership back to the government. Other similar models include build–transfer (BT), build–rent–transfer (BRT) or design–construct–manage–finance (DCMF). Other options may actually involve the ownership of the facility such as build–own–operate–transfer (BOOT) or rehabilitate–own–transfer (ROT) projects. All these methods, however, are often referred to by the generic term BOT (Ashford, 1999).

This type of arrangement is often used when relatively large investments are needed for totally new airports or perhaps for new passenger terminals or other major facilities. One of the first major projects of this type was Terminal 3 at Toronto's Lester B. Pearson International Airport which was developed as a BOT project by Huang and Danczkay and Lockheed Air Terminals (Ashford and Moore, 1999). The Eurohub at Birmingham airport was built under a BOT-type arrangement by a company comprising Birmingham airport (25 per cent), British Airways (BA) (21.4 per cent), local authorities (14.3 per cent), National Car Parks (21.4 per cent), Forte (6 per cent), and John Laing Holdings (11.9 per cent) (Lambert, 1995). This terminal is now a fully owned and managed facility of Birmingham International Airport plc.

The new Athens airport at Spata Eleftherios Venizelos was built under a 30-year BOT arrangement. The Greek government holds 55 per cent of the shares in the new company, Athens International Airport SA (AIA). The remaining share of 45 per cent share belongs to an international consortium, which is led by the German construction company, Hochtief. Another example of a BOT project was the international passenger Terminal 3 at Ninoy Aquino International Airport in Manila. This was the first project finance model of its kind in the Asia Pacific region but proved unsuccessful after a few years because of a major dispute between the government and the private consortium, the Philippine International Air Terminals Co. (PIATCO), which was led by Fraport. A more recent example is a 25-year BOT project which was agreed in 2007 to develop a new terminal at Queen Alia International airport in Amman in Jordan. Like many of these types of projects, this required an international airport operator to have a share in the winning consortium and in this case this was AdP. The consortium AIG PSC has agreed to pay 54 per cent of gross revenues to the government (Chevallier, 2007).

There are also BOT projects at a number of other airports such as Hyderabad, Bangalore, Tirana, Larnaca, Varna, and Antalya (Table 2.4). Overall new greenfield projects funded in this way have been the second most popular privatization approach in developing countries, accounting for 28 per cent of contracts and more than 20 per cent of investment commitments in 1990–2005 and have been particularly popular in Central and East Asia and Eastern Europe (Andrew and Dochia, 2006).

Table 2.4 Examples of airport privatization through project finance

Airport	Date	Length of agreement (years)	Contractor
Canada: Toronto Terminal 3	1987	Terminated	Lockheed consortium
UK: Birmingham Eurohub	1989	Terminated	Various including Birmingham airport, British Airways,
Greece:Athens	1996	30	Hochtief Consortium
Philippines: Manila International Terminal	1999	Terminated	Fraport consortium
US: New York JFK International Arrivals Terminal	1997	20	Schiphol consortium
Turkey: Ankara	2003	20	TAV
India: Hyderabad	2004	30	Siemens/Zürich airport consortium
India: Bangalore	2004	30	GMR/Malaysia Airports consortium
Albania: Tirana	2005	20	Hochtief consortium
Cyprus: Larnaca and Paphos	2005	25	YVRAS consortium
Bulgaria: Varna and Burgas	2006	35	Fraport consortium
Jordan: Amman	2007	25	Aéroport de Paris consortium

Source: Compiled by author from various sources.

Management contract

The least radical privatization option is a management contract when ownership remains with the government and the contractors take responsibility for the day-to-day operation of the airport, usually for a period of 5–10 years. The government either pays an annual management fee to the contractor, usually related to the performance of the airport, or the contractor will pay the government a share of its revenues. Normally investment will remain the responsibility of the government owner and so the overall economic risk is shared between the owner and the management company. For the government owner this may be politically more acceptable, whereas for the contractor such an arrangement may be attractive in countries where greater financial exposure, through a trade sale, for example, may be seen as too great a risk.

An early example within Europe was Brussels where the terminal was under a management contract to a private company, the Brussels Airport Terminal Company, from 1987. In 1998, however, this company merged with the public company operating the rest of the airport to become the Brussels International Airport Company. More common is for European airports to have management contracts in other areas of the world. For example, the Spanish airport company, AENA, has management contracts for Cayo Coco airport in Cuba whilst Vancouver Airport Services (YVRAS) has contracts with the two main airports on the Turks and Caicos Islands and in the Bahamas. AdP has contracts in Algeria, Egypt, Guinea, Madagascar, and Cambodia. Such arrangements can cover all airport operations or just one aspect, such as retail. BAA, for instance, has a general management contract at Indianapolis airport in the United States and has retail contracts with Pittsburgh, Baltimore, and Boston. Dublin Airport Authority has retail contracts at various airports including in Canada, Russia, Bahrain, Qatar, Kuwait, Beirut, Muscat, Egypt, and Cyprus.

Regulation, competition and efficiency issues

The amount of influence that a government can exert over a private airport clearly depends upon the type of privatization model chosen. A government may hold on to a considerable amount of control if a management or private finance contract is chosen, while very little state influence may remain after an airport company has been floated on the stock market or sold to a strategic partner. In these latter cases it is often feared that the privatized airport will become a private monopoly and will not always operate with the best interests of the airport users in mind by rising charges, reducing the quality of service, and under- or over-investing in facilities. Therefore economic regulation has been introduced at a number of airports when the privatization process has taken place. Chapter 5 explains in detail the type of regulation introduced and the rationale behind it.

There is also another competition issue which has to be taken into account if a group of airports rather than a single individual airport is being considered for privatization: should the airports be sold off together as a group or should they be split up into different companies? This is particularly an issue when the airport group or system may contain a few large international airports which are profitable and a number of smaller regional or local airports which are loss makers. This was the case with the Australian airports and also in a number of South American countries prior to privatization. If the airport group is sold as a single entity, and if generally this group as a whole has a good financial track record, a higher sale price may be achieved primarily because of the lack of perceived competition from other airport operators. In addition, any unprofitable parts of the airport system (usually the smaller airports) will not have to remain under public ownership if the whole group is sold, and raising capital on the commercial money markets for future investments may be easier for a larger company. However, if the group does contain a number of loss making airports this may make the airports group less attractive to investors and the sale price may suffer accordingly. If only the profitable airports are privatized, for example with a concession arrangement, one option would be to use the concession fees to subsidize the smaller airports.

Selling off airports in a group may inhibit competition, although the extent of competition which exists between airports in a group can vary significantly depending on the local situation (see Chapter 7). It is a different situation when the airports have overlapping catchment areas (such as BAA airports in London) compared with serving totally different markets. Airlines tend to be suspicious of airport groups, fearing that they will be paying charges at one airport which will finance the development of another airport, typically in some remote area which they do not use (International Air Transport Association, 2000b). However in response, airports often argue that they achieve economies of scale and are making the best use of resources and expertise by operating as an airport group and that such management enables a strategic and co-ordinated approach to airport development.

In practice in Australia, the government decided on individual privatizations for the major international airports but with packages of some of the smaller ones. Restrictions were imposed to stop the same operator from having overall control at a number of airports. In South America, all 33 Argentinian airports were covered under the same concession agreements, while in Mexico the airports have been divided into four different groups with a mixture of small and large airports in each group. In the United Kingdom, BAA, which is an airport group of seven airports, was privatized in 1987 after much debate as a single entity, but this has remained a controversial issue ever since.

As well as affecting competition between airports, it is often argued that privatization will lead to greater efficiency. To date, there has been only limited and in some cases contradictory research in this area. For example, Parker (1999) investigated BAA before and after its privatization and found no significant variation in performance, and also Hanaoka and Phomma (2004) compared Thai airports under ownership of the Department of Civil Aviation and the more independent Airports of Thailand Public Company Limited (which was partially privatized in 2004) but could not draw any overall conclusions concerning privatization. Moreover Vasigh and Gorjidooz (2006) did not find a significant relationship between efficiency and airport ownership when a sample of 22, both public and private US/European airports, was examined. However, in a very detailed cross-sectional, time series study of 35 European airports Vogel (2006) found that partially and fully privatized airports operated more efficiently than public ones. Within a broader global context, the Air Transport Research Society study of major Asia Pacific, European, and North American airports (see Chapter 3 for further details) also found that there was strong evidence that airports which were majority owned by government departments or were under multi-government ownership were less efficient than airports with a private majority ownership – albeit that this did not seem to be the case for independent publicly owned airport authorities or corporations (Oum *et al.*, 2006).

Understandably the airlines tend to assess the success of airport privatization in terms of service levels and cost-effectiveness rather than by financial gains. Within this context a study of 12 airport privatizations in Europe, Asia, and Latin America was undertaken and from the airlines' viewpoint, some disappointing results were observed (International Air Transport Association (IATA), 2005). Key problems which were identified were the lack of independent or effective economic regulation in some cases (e.g. at Vienna, Zürich, and Auckland airports) or too high concession fees being paid to the government (e.g. in Argentina, at Lima airport in Peru and at Juan Santamaria airport in Costa Rica). Such issues have meant that whilst initially the airline industry was cautiously optimistic about private sector involvement in airports because it would eliminate some of the problems associated with inflexible state-run airports, this no longer seems to be attitude of the airlines (Rowe, 2006).

The United Kingdom: paving the way for airport privatization

The United Kingdom is worthy of special attention when privatization is being considered, not only because the first major airport privatization took place in this country, but also because subsequent privatizations have been quite varied in nature. Airport privatization came about because of a major piece of legislation, the Airports Act that was introduced in 1986. The first part of the Act was concerned with the then government-owned BAA which operated seven UK airports, namely London Heathrow, London Gatwick, London Stansted, and the four Scottish airports of Aberdeen, Edinburgh, Glasgow, and Prestwick. The Act made provision for BAA to become a private company through a subsequent 100 per cent share flotation in 1997. This reflected the overall aim of the conservative Thatcher government of the time to privatize nationalized industries such as utilities and communications, and to increase share ownership among the UK population.

The second part of the Act required all airports with a turnover of more that £1 million in two of the previous 3 years to become companies. Prior to this Act, these airports had been run directly by their local government owners. Sixteen airports were covered by this part of the Act, ranging from Manchester airport, owned by a consortium of local authorities which at that time had a throughput of 9 million passengers, to Southend airport, owned by Southend Borough Council and handling just over 100 000 passengers. The shareholders of these airport companies were initially to be the local government owners but the shares could then be sold off to private investors if desired by the public sector owners. This was the Conservative government's ultimate aim. The Act also introduced economic regulation at these airports which is discussed in Chapter 5 (UK Government, 1986).

BAA was floated in 1987 with £1.2 billion going to the government. This gave BAA the freedom to borrow from commercial markets and diversify into areas of operations such as hotels, property management and hospital shops, which it did in its first few years of operation (Doganis, 1992). BAA subsequently dramatically expanded the retail part of its business and became a global player in airport management by having interests in airports in as diverse areas as Australia, Italy, the United States, Mauritius, and Oman (most of these links no longer exist). Meanwhile, the new situation at the regional airports gave them considerable more opportunity to commercialize their activities. As a result the share of non-aeronautical revenue has increased at the majority of these airports and more resources have been devoted to commercial activities such as marketing (Humphreys, 1999).

The most significant impact of the Airports Act has been the change in ownership patterns which have emerged (Table 2.5). By the early 1990s, the regional airports were finding it increasingly difficult to obtain permission to borrow funds for investment and, in 1993, the government announced that there would be no further spending allocation for airports. The only alternative for airports that wished to invest was privatization, which an increasing number of airports had no choice but to adopt. Political pressures from a Conservative central government, which was very much ideologically attracted to the transfer of public service to the private sector whenever possible, undoubtedly played a major role.

Various airports, such as East Midlands, Cardiff and Bournemouth chose full privatization through a trade sale to a strategic partner. Southend airport was also totally privatized but in this case the sale was undertaken to ensure the survival of the airport rather than to give access to finance for expansion as with many of the other airports (Humphreys, 1999). Some airports such as Newcastle and Norwich have opted for a partially privatized approach which gives them access to finance but also enables some local public control to be maintained. Birmingham airport is an interesting example which initially overcame funding difficulties by establishing a joint venture company to build the additional Eurohub terminal with a BOT project without a change in overall ownership. This solved the short-term problem of funding but subsequent traffic growth meant that there was once again pressure for additional investment and this time the airport opted for a partial privatization.

Table 2.5 Ownership patterns at main[a] UK airports, 2007

Airport	Present ownership	Private interest (%)	Privatization date
Aberdeen	Ferrovial (BAA)	100	1987
Belfast City	Ferrovial	100	N/A
Belfast International	Abertis (TBI)	100	1994
Birmingham	Local authorities/Ontario Teachers' Pension Plan/ Victoria Funds Management Corporation/Employees	51	1997
Bournemouth	Manchester airport	c	1995
Bristol	Macquarie Airports	100	1997
Cardiff	Abertis (TBI)	100	1995
Doncaster (Robin Hood)	Peel Airports	100	N/A
Durham Tees Valley	Local authorities/Peel Airports Ltd	75	2003
East Midlands	Manchester airport	c	1993
Edinburgh	Ferrovial (BAA)	100	1987
Exeter	Balfour Beatty	100	2007
Glasgow	Abertis (BAA)	100	1987
Highlands and Islands Airports[b]	Scottish Office Highlands and Islands Airports Ltd)	0	N/A
Leeds Bradford	Bridgepoint	100	2007
Liverpool	Peel Airports Ltd	100	1990
London City	AIG/GE/Credit Suisse	100	N/A
London Gatwick	Ferrovial (BAA)	100	1987
London Heathrow	Ferrovial (BAA)	100	1987
London Luton	Abertis (TBI)	100[d]	1998
London Stansted	Ferrovial (BAA)	100	1987
Manchester	Local authorities	0	N/A
Newcastle	Local authorities/Copenhagen airport	49	2001
Norwich	Local Authorities/Omniport	80	2003
Prestwick	Infratil Ltd	100	1987
Southampton	Ferrovial (BAA)	100	1961

Notes: N/A not applicable; the table shows the most recent owner, not necessarily the first private sector owner. When there are a number of owners, only the main owners are shown.
[a]All airports with more than 500 000 annual passengers in 2006/2005.
[b]Nine airports including Inverness with over 500 000 passengers.
[c]100 per cent share is held by Manchester airport which is under local authority ownership.
[d]The private investors have a 30-year concession contract. Ownership remains with the local authorities.
Source: Compiled by author from various sources.

A few local authority airport owners remained strongly opposed to privatization moves – arguing that the airport should remain in public sector hands to maintain its role as a regional public asset. Manchester was one such airport and financed the whole of its second runway project from retained profits. Its public sector status, however, meant that it was not free to expand internationally on equal terms with competing private airports. It was involved with the successful consortium in the sale of Adelaide/Parafield and Coolangetta airports in Australia but because of its status could only act on a consultancy basis with no equity share involved. From April 1999, however, this situation changed with legislation introduced to allow for the larger profitable regional airports which were still in local governments hands (Manchester, Newcastle, Leeds-Bradford, and Norwich) to be able to borrow money on the open market (Department of the Environment & Transport and the Regions (DETR), 1998). This enabled Manchester to purchase 83 per cent of the nearby Humberside airport soon afterwards. However by 2007, Manchester airport remained the only major regional airport which was totally publicly owned.

There are also a small number of other airports in the United Kingdom which have had a different history. The relatively newly developed London City airport and Belfast City airport have always been in private hands. Belfast International was privatized by means of a management buyout in 1994 and was subsequently sold to TBI in 1996. Most of the very small regional airports in the United Kingdom remain under public sector ownership. Highlands and Islands Airports Ltd, a state-owned company, operates nine airports in Scotland with the help of a government subsidy. Looking back to 1986 before the Airports Act, it may be seen that a number of airports, such as Exeter, Humberside, Liverpool, London Stansted, Norwich, and Prestwick, recorded a loss before depreciation and interest (results after depreciation charges were not available) (Table 2.6). By 2005–2006, all airports were in a profitable situation with the exception of Durham Tees Valley and the Highland and Islands Airports.

At the time of the privatization of BAA, there were extensive debates as to whether the airports of BAA should be privatized as a group or separately (see Chapter 7). In the end there was group privatization but since then the airline regulatory environment has become progressively more liberal providing more opportunities for airport competition. Consequently there have been various governmental reviews investigating whether BAA should be split up but none have made these recommendations. However the most extensive review to date is now being undertaken by the Competition Commission which could ultimately lead to a demand for BAA to divest in one or more of its airports.

Table 2.6 Traffic and profitability growth at main[a] UK airports, 1987–2006

Airport	Total passengers (thousands)		Profit before depreciation, interest, and tax (× 1000 UK£)[b]		Profit before interest and tax[c] (× 1000 UK£)
	1986–1987	2005–2006	1986–1987	2005–2006	2005–2006
Aberdeen	1452	2954	1500	13092	10944
Belfast International	1882	4823	3935	10637	9436
Birmingham	1725	9386	6781	51989	35477
Bournemouth	137	916	164	3501	2951
Bristol	436	5157	1131	28961	25344
Cardiff	436	1772	689	7220	5953
Durham Tees Valley	297	899	135	−1418	−2715
East Midlands	941	4155	3637	23030	15804
Edinburgh	1756	8507	2800	38716	31381
Exeter	105	874	−59	10151	1019
Glasgow	3200	8830	5500	35309	25789
Highlands and Islands	N/A	1078	N/A	−356	−861
Leeds Bradford	508	2601	2134	4847	1357
Liverpool	263	4654	−2053	18366	N/A
London City	N/A	1998	N/A	8814	7587
London Gatwick	16751	32851	53200	131400	80560
London Heathrow	32092	67437	119000	583600	415100
London Luton	1635	9150	4003	21773	12878
London Stansted	577	22337	−1800	74900	46000
Manchester	7596	27593	18715[d]	130481	71818
Newcastle	1165	5234	3526	28403	19072
Norwich	191	584	−56	1851	563
Southampton	267	1874	N/A	10434	8791

[a] All airports with more than 500000 annual passengers excluding Belfast City, Coventry, Doncaster (Robin Hood), and Prestwick when data was not available.
[b] Also known as Earnings before Interest, Tax, Depreciation and Amortization (EBITDA).
[c] Also known as Earnings before Interest and Tax (EBIT).
[d] 1985–1986 data.
Source: Chartered Institute of Public Finance and Accountancy (CIPFA), Centre for Regulated Industries (CRI), BAA, and annual accounts.

Australia and New Zealand: a phased privatization process

Between 1988 and 1997, most of Australia's airports were operated by the state-owned Federal Airports Corporation (FAC). At the beginning of 1997, the FAC operated 22 airports and handled over 60 million passengers annually. The FAC corporate office undertook various central services and imposed a common charging policy on its airports. Discussions relating to the privatization of the FAC began in the early 1990s, and a firm decision to privatize them was made in 1996. Considerable attention was given to whether the airports should be sold off as a system (as had happened with BAA which was the only other airport group at that time that had been privatized) or to whether they should be sold off individually. Issues relating to the national interest, efficiency and competition were fiercely debated. Political factors played a key role, particularly because government forecasts had shown that separate sales would generate more income (Knibb, 1999). Eventually, it was decided that the airports would be leased off individually on long-term 50-year leases, with a further option for 49 years.

In phase 1 of the privatization process, three airports, namely Melbourne, Brisbane and Perth, were sold in 1997. After Sydney, these three airports were the most profitable airports in the FAC system and they handled most of the traffic. It was the government's intention to bring competition and diversity into the airport system and so there were strict cross-ownership limits associated with the airport sales. Potential buyers had to have a majority Australian interest and airport management experience. As in the United Kingdom, the privatized airports were initially price regulated. In addition, they are required to undertake quality of service monitoring and to provide evidence of this to the regulator. They also had to provide development guarantees by preparing 5-yearly master plans and pledging a certain sum for investment.

A number of airport companies were interested in operating the Australian airports including BAA, Manchester, Vienna, Amsterdam, Aer Rianta, National Express, and AGI. In the end BAA, Amsterdam and AGI were each partners in winning consortia (Table 2.7). The enterprise value to earnings multiples were particularly high for the Australian airports, which was not only due to the fact there were a large number of binders, but also because high growth was being forecast and the infrastructure needs were relatively small.

It was decided that a further group of airports would be privatized in 1998. These 'phase-2' airports included Adelaide which was the largest airport with just under 4 million passengers and GA airports such as Archerfield, Parafield, and Jandakot. Whereas the phase-1 airports had been relatively independent profitable entities, over half of these smaller airports were making losses and were much more reliant on the services of the FAC corporate office. Considerable preparation was therefore involved in getting the airports reading to be stand-alone entities (FAC, 1997). In spite of the fact that these airports

Table 2.7 Privatization details of Australian airports

Airport	Ownership	Privatization date: sale price (million A$)
Brisbane	Brisbane Airport Corporation Ltd (Schiphol Group, Commonwealth Investments, Port of Brisbane, and others)	July 1997: 1397
Melbourne	Australia Pacific Airports Pty Ltd (BAA, AMP, Deutsche Asset Management, and Hastings Fund)	July 1997: 1307
Perth	Westralia Airports Corporation Ltd (AGI, Hastings Fund, Infratil)	July 1997: 639
Adelaide/Parafield	Adelaide Airport Ltd, Parafield Airport Ltd (Unisuper, Macquarie Airport Group, John Laing, Serco, and others)	May 1998: 365
Alice Springs/Darwin/Tennant Creek	Northern Territories Airports Ltd (AGI/Infratil)	May 1998: 110
Archerfield	Archerfield Airport Corporation Ltd (Miengrove Pty)	May 1998: 3
Canberra	Capital Airports Group (local company)	May 1998: 66
Colangatta	Gold Coast Airport Ltd (Unisuper, Macquarie Airport Group, Serco, and others)	May 1998: 104
Hobart	Hobart International Airport Corporation (AGI, Hobart Ports, Hambros)	May 1998: 36
Jandakot	Jandakot Airport Holdings (property investors and former FAC employees)	June 1998: 7
Launceston	Australia Pacific Airports Pty Ltd (BAA, AMP, Deutsche Asset Management, and Hastings Fund)	May 1998: 17
Moorabbin	Metropolitan Airport Consortium (property investors and former FAC employees)	May 1998: 8
Townsville/Mount Isa	Australian Airports Ltd (former FAC CEO and financial investors)	May 1998: 16
Sydney	Southern Cross Airports Consortium (Macquarie Airport Group, Hochtief, and others)	June 2002: 5588

Source: Compiled by author from the individual airport regulation reports and other sources.

were smaller and not in such a healthy position, again there was considerable interest in the sales and relatively high purchase prices were paid. Some airport companies which were involved with the phase-1 airports, such as BAA and AGI, gained further airports under this phase-2 privatization. Former FAC employees also gained interest in a number of airports such as Jandakot, Moorabbin, Townsville, and Mount Isa. Cross-ownership restrictions prevented certain neighbouring airports coming under single ownership. Airlines were also not allowed to have greater than a 5 per cent share in any airport.

Sydney Kingsford airport and the GA airports in the Sydney basin (Bankstown, Camden, and Hoxton Park) were excluded from these two phases of privatization because of unresolved issues related to noise control at Sydney Kingsford airport and continuing controversy over if, when and where a second Sydney airport would be built (Ballantyne, 1997). In 1998, a separate state-owned entity, Sydney Airports Corporation, was established to run the four Sydney airports and Elldeson, the GA airport in Victoria which had been withdrawn from the privatization process. In 2000, plans to develop a second Sydney airport were shelved for at least a decade clearing the way for privatization in 2001. However, the collapse of the Australian carrier Ansett and the events of 11 September 2001 meant that the privatization of Sydney airport was postponed until 2002 when it was bought by a consortium led by the two companies Macquarie Airports and Hochtief Airport.

Unlike in Australia, the airports in New Zealand had always been operated individually and not as a group. The road to airport privatization began in 1985 when the government decided that the airports would become public companies owned by the government and local authorities. This happened at the three largest airports, Auckland, Wellington, and Christchurch in the late 1990s and since then all the other major airports have moved to such a structure. The first airport to be privatized was Auckland in 1998 when the government sold its 52 per cent shareholders through an IPO. This was the first airport in the Asia Pacific region to be floated on the stock exchange. This is still the current ownership structure of the airport although in 2007 the airport was the subject of an attempted takeover bid by Dubai Aerospace Enterprise. Also in 1998, 66 per cent of Wellington's shares were acquired by the utility company Infratil through a trade sale. By contrast, Christchurch airport remains in public ownership, with Christchurch City having 75 per cent of the shares and the central government owning the rest. There is also some partial private ownership at some of the smaller airports but most airports still maintain some local government ownership (Lyon and Francis, 2006).

Both Australia and New Zealand are very reliant on air transport with large distances and poor surface transport, and both countries are politically, culturally and economically fairly similar. They were relatively early in privatizing their airports compared to elsewhere and they did this at a time when other public enterprises in the two countries were being privatized. However the nature of the airport privatization was in some ways quite different. Moreover different approaches to airport regulation were adopted (which will be explored in Chapter 5).

US airports: the slow pace towards privatization

Since the United States has always possessed a private airline industry, it is often assumed that the airport industry must be primarily driven by private sector considerations as well. This is not the case. Nearly all US airports remain under local public ownership – with the pace towards privatization being much slower than in many other parts of the world.

There are two key factors which make US airports unique when possible privatization is being considered. First, US airports enter into legally binding contracts with their airline customers, known as airport use agreements, which detail the charging and conditions for the use of both airfield and terminal facilities. The airports, in reality, operate very closely with the airlines and the airlines have a considerable amount of influence as regards future developments at the airports. Airline approval would be needed, therefore, if privatization were to take place. Second, the airports are funded through a mixture of private and public funds. Most airports, and all the major ones, already have access to private financing through the commercial bond markets, where the airports have tax-exempt status due to their public ownership. Funding is also available from passenger facility charges (PFCs) which are generated by the passengers at individual airports and from grants from the Airport Improvement Program (AIP) which comes from the federal government's Aviation Trust Fund (which also funds air traffic control), financed primarily by a national passenger tax. At major airports tax-exempt commercial bonds and PFCs make up the bulk of the investment funds whereas at smaller airports the AIP funds are proportionally more important (General Accounting Office (GAO), 2007) (Figures 2.9 and 2.10).

For some time there has been a concern that these funds will not be adequate, or are not the most appropriate, to meet future airport (and air traffic control) investment needs and so a number of changes to the PFC and AIP funds have been proposed. This may result in a substantial reduction in money available from the trust fund. Inevitably as elsewhere where airport funding has become an issue, privatization has also been considered as an option. In the United States, though, it is not an easy process. Way back in 1995, the privatization of John Wayne Airport in California's Orange County was discussed as part of the solution to the county's bankruptcy (Poole, 1995). However, the likelihood of litigation by the airlines – who argued that federal law prohibited the use of airport revenues (including sale proceeds) for non-airport purposes (so-called 'revenue diversion') – led to the conclusion that airport privatization was not feasible. This key issue, namely the inability of airport

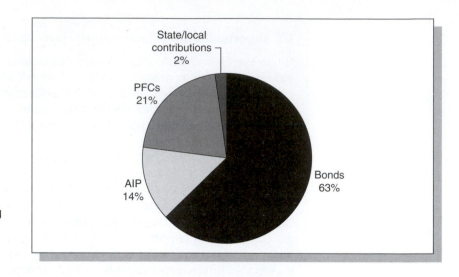

Figure 2.9
External capital funding
at larger US airports in
2001–2005
(*Source*: GAO)

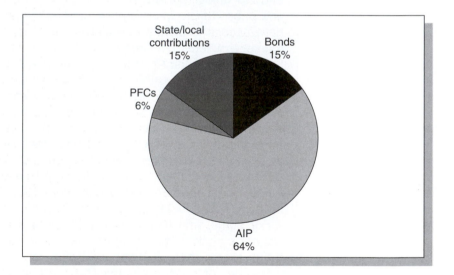

Figure 2.10
External capital funding
at smaller US airports in
2001–2005
(*Source*: GAO)

owners to reap the financial benefits from the airports, is seen as one of the key obstacles to airport privatization in the United States. Many argue that if airport revenues were diverted to other municipal purposes, costs at the airports would rise for both passengers and airlines. Also many local politicians, who hold very powerful positions, do not wish to give up control of their airports. Various other issues would have to be resolved if such privatization were to take place. For example, would private airports survive if they could not use trust fund, PFC, or tax-exempt debt financing? Would they have to pay back the federal grants? At many of the airports, the use agreements with the airlines could mean that the airports could only be privatized as the agreements expire or that privatization would have to be limited within the bounds of the agreement.

There has been some, albeit rather limited, moves towards airport privatization with the introduction of the airport privatization pilot programme in October 1996. This makes provision for five airports to be exempted from some of the legal requirements that impede their sale to private entities (GAO, 1996). For example, the restrictions on prohibiting revenues to be used for non-aeronautical reasons (i.e. general municipal purposes) have been waived. Such privatizations need approval of the 65 per cent of airlines using the airport if the revenues are to be used for other purposes. Under the scheme, there must be a GA airport and only one large hub airport. GA airports may be leased or sold but larger airports can only be leased.

There has been only limited interest in this scheme particularly because of slow and rather complex approval procedures and the majority airline consensus rule. The only airport privatized under the scheme to date is Stewart International Airport in New York, which was given a 99-year lease to the British company, National Express. The airport transferred management in April 2000 (Federal Aviation Administration, 2000; McCormick, 2000). However the airport never received the approval of the required majority of airlines and so the lease payments still had to be used for airport purposes. Then in 2006 the airport lease was sold back to the public body, the Port Authority of New York and New Jersey, as National Express no longer has an interest in operating airports (Poole, 2007). Other airports such as Brown Field (a GA facility in San Diego), Aguadilla in Puerto Rico, and New Orleans Lakefront have also been looked at under the scheme but none have actually been privatized.

The latest airport to be considered is Chicago Midway which the Federal Aviation Administration (FAA) has confirmed as the large hub in the programme. The airport would continue to have access to PFCs and federal grants. The largest airline at the airport, the low-cost carrier Southwest, has signed a new use agreement to take account of this but the programme requires five airlines in total to sign to reach the 65 per cent approval criteria and so the project is still on-going (Iley, 2007). AdP and a number of different private operators with an interest in airports, such as Goldman Sachs, Deutsche Bank, Macquarie Bank and Ferrovial have already expressed an interest in bidding for the lease contract (Momberger Airport Information, 2007).

Meanwhile there have been some proposals to change the privatization programme. The FAA has suggested that it could be increased to 15 airports with a removal of the airline consent. In response the Democratic House proposed a 75 rather than 65 per cent airline approval criterion and the removal of federal grant entitlements for privatized airports (Iley, 2007).

In spite of these developments, more radical privatization still seems fairly remote. However, greater private participation has been achieved with the adoption of management contracts and project finance schemes at some airports. The former company, Airports Group International, had some management contracts before the 1990s, but mostly at small airports with the exception of the international terminal at Atlanta airport. However, in 1995 BAA won the 10-year management contract for Indianapolis airport which was an airport of considerable size at that time with a throughput of 6.7 million passengers. Under the scheme, BAA was not to receive any fixed management fee but would share in the savings it generated. The company guaranteed average annual savings of more than US$3 million (US$32 million over a 10-year agreement) and would not be paid any fees until it produced average annual savings of nearly US$6 million (US$58 million over a 10-year agreement). BAA expected to save the airport $100 million during the 10-year contract by increasing non-aviation revenue and reducing expenditure from energy supply, equipment, and payroll costs. The airport board would continue to set policy enforce agreements and control rates and charges (Ott, 1998). In 1998 an amended new 10-year contract was signed. BAA also has retail management contracts at Boston and Pittsburgh. In another development in 1997, the financing, construction and operation of the international arrivals building at New York JFK airport was handed over to a private consortium (which includes Amsterdam Schiphol airport) for 20 years. There have also been some plans to develop a new airport in Illinois (Abraham Lincoln National Airport) through a public–private partnership where the government would own the land and the private contractor would own and operate the facilities. Generally, however the fiscal and political constraints which exist at US airports have meant that private sector involvement has in some cases been difficult to maintain successfully. The notable example here is the airport of Harrisburg where BAA lost a management contract only after managing the airport for 3 years of the 10-year agreement primarily because the airport's administration changed (Gethin, 2002). The former Wiggins (Planestation) group also withdrew its interest at Smyrna airport near Nashville, Tennessee because of administrative constraints.

India: using privatization to modernize the airport system

The recent development of India's economy, together with a rapidly expanding middle class and a more liberal domestic and international regulatory aviation environment, has resulted in a huge growth in air travel over the last few years, particularly with annual passenger growth exceeding 20 per cent in the last 2 years (Table 2.8). There are many more airlines now serving domestic and international routes and there is a growing Indian low-cost carrier industry. All of this has meant that many of the airports have inadequate and ageing infrastructure and that there is a lack of internationally accepted standards to cope with this increased demand. In the next 10–15 years, it is forecast that passenger traffic will continue to grow annually by 12–15 per cent (International Civil Aviation Organization (ICAO), 2007).

There are 449 airports and airfields in India. Up until recently all major commercial airports in India were managed by the state organization the Airport Authority of India (AAI) which was formed in 1995 with the merging of the National Airports Authority and the International Airports Authority of India. AAI manages 92 airports directly and is also responsible for 28 civil passenger enclaves at defence airfields as well providing all the air traffic control services. Even before the recent traffic boom of the last few years, privatization was being discussed in the late 1990s for the four main international airports (Delhi, Mumbai, Chennai, and Kolkata) but this came to nothing – particularly because no foreign investment was allowed in airports at this time. The first actual privatization project did not occur with these airports but at Cochin, Kerala in southern India where a new airport opened in 1999 having been financed 26 per cent

Table 2.8 Total airport traffic at Indian airports 2002–2007

April–March	2002–2003	2003–2004	2004–2005	2005–2006	2006–2007
Passengers (mns)	44.0	48.7	59.3	73.4	96.4
Freight ('000) tones	982.4	1 068.2	1280.6	1404.0	1553.5
Aircraft Movements ('000)	560.6	638.6	719.1	838.4	1075.5
Growth rates (%)					
Passengers	10.0	10.7	12.8	23.8	31.3
Freight	15.1	8.7	19.9	9.6	10.6
Aircraft Movements	9.9	13.9	12.6	16.6	28.2

Source: Airports Authority of India.

from the state of Kerala and the rest from NRIs, financial institutions, and airport service providers.

After many bureaucratic, legal, and political delays, two 30-year (with another 30-year option) BOT greenfield airport projects were set up in 2004. This was after it was agreed that the AAI could enter into joint ventures with private and foreign investors as long as 26 per cent public ownership was retained. These two airports are in the IT centres of Bangalore and Hyderabad. At Bangalore the private consortium consisted of Siemens, Zürich Airport and the Indian engineering and construction company Larsen and Toubro (L&T) where US$430 million will be spent to produce an airport which will handle 11 million passengers (Brunner, 2007). At Hyderabad the private investors were GMR, a large Indian infrastructure company, and Malaysia Airports Holdings Berhad. In this case US$390 million is being invested on an airport with a 7 million passenger capacity (International Civil Aviation Organization, 2007). Both airports will open in 2008. Then again after many delays and a very lengthy bidding process, private–public joint venture partnerships were eventually agreed for India's two largest airports (accounting for nearly half of total Indian traffic), namely Delhi and Mumbai in 2006 (Jain *et al.*, 2007). These are 30-year concession agreements – again with a possibility of a further 30 years – which aim to upgrade and modernize the two airports. In both cases the AAI has a 26 per cent share in the new airport companies, Delhi International Airport Private Limited (DIAL) and Mumbai International Airport Private Limited (MIAL). The international airport operators Fraport and Malaysia Airports Holdings BhD both have a share in DIAL as well as GMR. The South African airport company ACSA has a stake in MIAL together with a large Indian infrastructure company GVK. DIAL has agreed to pay 46 per cent of revenues to the government and the first stage of development, which will involve upgrading the existing terminal and constructing a new domestic terminal and runway, will cost around US$2 billion. MIAL has agreed to pay 39 per cent of revenues and to invest US$1.6 billion to develop the capacity of the airport from its current 18 million passengers to 40 million. (Centre for Asia Pacific Aviation, 2007a) (Table 2.9).

Attention has now turned to the other two major international airports at Chennai and Kolkata. Whilst similar privatizations models were discussed, local governments' opposition to such proposals has meant that the funding for the modernization of these airports is coming directly from the AAI. Also the AAI has a master plan to develop and modernize 35 non-metro airports and whilst private involvement is being sought for non-aeronautical activities, the aeronautical infrastructure will be funded

Table 2.9   Privatization projects at Indian airports

Airport	Privatization date	Airport partners	Passengers 2006–2007 (millions)	Percentage Share of AAI Traffic
Cochin	1999	26% State of Kerala/74% non resident Indians (NRIs), financial institutions, and airport service providers	2.6	2.7
Bangalore	2004	26% AAI/State of Karnataka 74% Siemens/Zürich Airport/L&T	8.1	8.4
Hyderabad	2004	26% AAI/State of Andhra Pradesh 74% GMR/Malaysia Airports	5.8	6.0
Delhi	2006	26% AAI/74% GMR/Fraport/ Malaysia Airports/other private investors	20.4	21.1
Mumbai	2006	26% AAI/74% GVK/ACSA/other private investors	22.2	23.0

Source: Compiled by the author from various sources.

directly by AAI. In addition there are a number of other green-field sites such as Kannur (Kerala), MOPA (Goa), Chakan (Pune, Maharashtra), Navi (Mumbai) and Noida (Delhi). It is likely that some of these projects will be built through public–private BOT arrangements as with Hyderabad and Bangalore (Ionides, 2007; International Civil Aviation Organization, 2007).

The airport operators and investors

Airport privatization has attracted a variety of different investors and companies who have become interested in making airport purchases. In the early stages of privatization in the 1990s, many of the potential investors were well-established airport companies who welcomed the opportunity to expand beyond previously well-defined national barriers. Many of these companies, for example, BAA, AdP, Aer Rianta (now the Dublin Airport Authority), Schiphol (owners of Amsterdam airport), and Fraport (owners of Frankfurt airport) had already been active in providing consultancy services and running management contracts at other airports and it was a natural evolution of the business to get more heavily involved in other airports. AdP had built a reputation in the management of engineering and construction projects in countries such as China, Vietnam, Cyprus, the Philippines, Indonesia, and the Lebanon. Fraport had been involved with ground-handling contracts and baggage systems in as diverse areas as Spain, the United States, and Kenya. Aer Rianta had mostly specialized in retail contracts.

So privatization increased the opportunities for international expansion for airport companies, particularly because in many cases the potential buyers had to provide evidence of airport management expertise. By 2000, BAA had airport interests in Italy, the United States, Australia, and Mauritius. The Schiphol Group had involvement in other airports in the Netherlands, Australia, and the United States. Other European airports or airport groups with international interests included Rome, Milan, Copenhagen, Fraport, AdP, Vienna, Zürich, AENA (Spain), and Aer Rianta (Ireland). Some of these airports, such as Rome, Milan, and Fraport, also had involvement in other airports in their own country. Outside Europe, international airport companies were less involved, with the notable exception being YVR Airport Services (YVRAS) which is a subsidiary of Vancouver airport, and had interests in a number of South and Central American airports and Sharm El Sheikh airport in Egypt (although the later was subsequently cancelled by the Egyptian government).

Some airport operators, such as Fraport, Zürich Unique, YVRAS, and Vienna, have continued to expand their involvement in other airports and have been joined by more recent players such as Changi airport and Malaysia Airport Holdings Berhad, which reflects the growing importance of Asia within the global airport industry and the increased interest in privatization in the area. Others have reduced their involvement such as the Dublin Airport Authority which has sold its share in Hamburg and Birmingham airports and BAA which disposed of its interest in its Australian airports and Budapest to focus on its core UK activities and to reduce its debt.

There were also a number of property, utility, infrastructure and construction organizations that saw some potential synergies with airport operations and took advantage of the early airport privatizations. One such property developer was TBI which developed its involvement in the airport sector in the mid/late 1990s by acquiring interests in Cardiff in 1995 and Belfast International in 1996 in the United Kingdom, Stockholm Skavsta airport in Sweden (in 1998) and Orlando Sanford International airport in the United States (in 1997). In 1999, it took the decision to concentrate on its airport business and so disposed of all property interests except the Cardiff Hilton Hotel. It subsequently took over AGI and acquired extra interests in Australia, Bolivia, United States, Canada and Luton (although a number of these have now been disposed of). More recently it has been taken over by the Spanish infrastructure company Abertis in 2005 and has expanded further with the Abertis acquisition of Desarrollo de Concesiones Aeroportuarias (DCA) in 2007 which has stakes in 15 airports in Mexico, Jamaica, Chile, and Columbia. This means that the company now has interests in 29 airports in eight countries (Centre for Asia Pacific Aviation, 2007b). Another UK property developer is Peel Holdings which acquired Liverpool airport in 1997, Durham Tees Valley in 2003 and has subsequently gone on to develop Robin Hood Doncaster airport which was previously a military base. Then there is the New Zealand utility company, Infratil which became involved with airports when it purchased two-thirds of Wellington airport in 1998. More recently it has gone on to purchase Prestwick and London Manston airport in the United Kingdom and 90 per cent of Luebeck airport in Germany.

The Spanish infrastructure company Ferrovial has emerged somewhat later as a major player within the airport industry. In the early 2000s it acquired interests in Bristol and Belfast City in the United Kingdom, Niagra Falls in the United States, and Antofagasta in Chile. However it has been its purchase of BAA in 2006 which has transformed Ferrovial into the world's largest airport operator (in terms of passenger numbers). Meanwhile the largest construction company to get involved with airports has been the German company Hochtief. Its early investments included Athens, Hamburg and Düsseldorf and subsequently it has expanded its operations to include Sydney, Tirana in Albania and Budapest. Another construction company is the French company Vinci which has had a close partnership with AdP on international projects. In the past there has also been interest from transport companies, most notably National Express which had stakes in East Midlands, Bournemouth (and Stewart International) until 2001 when it sold its UK airports to concentrate on other transport activities. UK transport operators, Firstgroup and Stagecoach, also owned one UK airport each in the late 1990s but have now sold these airports. This shows that perhaps the synergies from airport operations which these transport operators had hoped for were not as significant as was first thought.

An area of considerable debate is whether airlines should buy and operate airports. In the United States, airlines already partially or totally lease terminals and in Australia some of the domestic terminals are leased to Qantas. This means that the airlines get exclusive rights to parts of the terminal. Elsewhere, however, such practice is not very common. An unusual example was the Birmingham Eurohub which was partially financed by BA. A more recent development was Lufthansa's joint venture partnership with Munich airport in developing its second terminal which opened in 2003. The airport company has a 60 per cent shareholding whilst Lufthansa has a 40 per cent shareholding (Kerkloh, 2007). Also since 2005 Lufthansa has begun to invest in Fraport and now has a 10 per cent stake in the airport. The main reason given for this purchase was to enable Lufthansa to intensify its partnership with Fraport and to strengthen its position at Frankfurt, which is its major hub. Thai Airways and Bangkok Airways have also shown interest in operating airports to achieve greater control, with Thai Airways having a

10-year management contract at Chittagong airport in Bangladesh and Bangkok Airways building and operating three small Thai airports serving tourist destinations. In China too, airlines such as Hainan Airlines, Sichuan Airlines and Shandong have all become involved with airports, primarily to ensure that investment takes place (Centre for Asia Pacific Aviation, 2007a).

If an individual airline or alliance grouping wanted to buy a substantial share of an airport to obtain more control over the facilities and develop a stronger brand presence, there may be a number of regulatory and competition issues which need to be considered to ensure that this does not lead to discriminatory practices. In some cases there may be limits to airline ownership when an airport is privatized. Low-cost carriers particularly have also expressed an interest in running their own facilities in order to keep the service simple and keep down costs. EasyJet, in its early years when it was developing services out of London Luton airport, unsuccessfully tried to buy the airport when it was up for sale. Ryanair has also been unsuccessful in getting approval to build its own low-cost terminal at Dublin which it had been demanding for many years.

More recently there has been a new type of investor who has become interested in airports, namely financial investors, who through private equity and infrastructure funds have been able to raise substantial amounts of capital to purchase stakes, and often controlling interests, in airports. By being able to accept a highly leveraged debt structure, these investors have been able to outbid other competitors at recent airport sales. The first major organization of this type to get involved was the Macquarie Group. In 2006–2007, all the sales at UK airports (excluding BAA), namely at Birmingham, Leeds Bradford, Exeter, and London City, involved financial investors. This increased interest from the capital markets is demonstrated by a substantial number of investors with a private equity background, such as ABN Amro Infrastructure Capital Equity Fund; Credit Suisse and GE Energy Financial Services and GE Commercial Aviation Services; Morgan Stanley; Goldman Sachs; Merrill Lynch; Cathay Securities and DWS Investments, all of whom set up their own airport or infrastructure funds in 2006 (Kalenda 2007).

The success of many past airport privatizations, coupled with high predicted growth patterns and the need for capital investment at many airports, has resulted in more and more investors and companies becoming interested in becoming potential purchasers and the competition has intensified. Also an active secondary market has developed and there are now a number of examples of various privatized airports (such as Rome, Copenhagen, BAA, Budapest, Bournemouth, Prestwick, and Birmingham) where there have been further changes in ownership. CAPA estimate that cashed up investors hold an estimated US$50 billion in funds presently to pursue aviation infrastructure assets primarily in Europe, the Middle East, and Asia. There is an estimated 60 leading (active and potential) global airport investors.

Inevitably, this has led to the purchase prices being pushed up, particularly when financial investors have been involved who are able to accept a much more highly leveraged debt structure. Potential buyers typically will consider the price of the airport (enterprise value, EV) in relation to profit (earnings before interest, tax, depreciation, and amortization, EBITDA or earnings before interest and tax, EBIT) when deciding whether to invest. For earlier IPO privatizations such as BAA, Vienna, Copenhagen, and Auckland, the EV/EBITDA multiples were in the region of five to ten. For the earlier trade sales of the Australian airports and some of the UK regional airports such as Bristol and Cardiff higher multiples in the region of 15 were achieved. However this increased interest in airport privatization and the emergence of the financial investor has meant that there have been some very high values in recent years for trade sales. For example in 2006 the values for trade sales were 28× at London city, 16× for BAA, 29× for Budapest (in 2005) and 23× for an aborted sale at Bratislava (Schrankler, 2006). Over the years on average for flotations or equity offerings the multiple is 8.1× compared with the much higher figure of 16.9× for trade sales (Kalenda, 2007).

Hochtief: From construction services to managing airports

Hochtief is an international construction services company based in Germany which for many years had been involved in the planning, constructing and financing of airports before being active in any privatization developments. Then in 1996 it led the consortium which won the BOT project contract for the new Athens airport. It had responsibilities for developing and financing the airport and when it opened in 2001, Hochtief became an airport operator as well for the first time. Meanwhile in 1997, in response to the growing number of privatization opportunities Hochtief founded the fully owned subsidiary Hochtief AirPort (HTA). HTA's next airport involvement came in 1998 when it formed a consortium with the former Irish airport operator Aer Rianta, to buy 50 per cent of Düsseldorf airport through a trade sale. This was followed by the purchase of another German airport, namely Hamburg airport in 2000, when again it teamed up with Aer Rianta to buy 49 per cent of the airport. In 2002 it was part of the successful Southern Cross Airports Consortium which bought Sydney airport. At this airport HTA operates on the basis of an Airport Strategic Advisory Agreement and has been involved with introducing new organizational structures, implementing cost management programmes and developing new revenues streams. Returning to Europe, in 2005 it led a consortium which won a BOT contract at Tirana airport in Albania. It has a 47 per cent share in the consortium and the project will last until 2025. Then in 2007 it bought a 37 per cent interest in

Table 2.10   Hochtief AirPort portfolio of airports

	Athens	Budapest	Düsseldorf	Hamburg	Sydney	Tirana
Passengers 2006 (mns)	15.1	8.3	16.6	12.0	31.0[a]	0.9
Revenues 2006 (mn €s)	357.5	166.6	303.7	223.1	436.2[a]	19.7
EBITDA[b] 2006 (mn €s)	232.7	76.4	131.1	75.6	351.9[a]	n/a
HTA shareholding (%)	26.7	37.6	20.0	34.8	8.1	47.0
HTAC shareholding (%)	13.3	0.0	10.0	14.2	5.1	0.0
Initial date of HTA involvement	1996	2007	1998	2000	2002	2006

[a]July 2006–June 2007.
[b]Earnings before interest, tax, depreciation, and amortization.
Source: Hochtief website.

the secondary sale of BAA's shareholdings in Budapest airport. So to date, HTA now has a portfolio of six airports which in total handle over 80 million passengers (Table 2.10).

To strengthen its financial position in its involvement in airport projects and to create new sources of capital, in 2005 HTA founded an international airport investment partnership called Hochtief AirPort Capital (HTAC) with Hastings Funds Management Ltd of Australia (50 per cent of partnership), Caisse de depot et placement du Quebec, Canada (40 per cent) and KfW IPEX-Bank, Germany (10 per cent). HTA is responsible for the management of this partnership. Consequently HTA has transferred some of its airport shareholdings of Athens, Düsseldorf, Hamburg and Sydney airports to this partnership. Moreover two of these investors, namely Caisse and KfW, have an additional 20 per cent interest in the airport consortium at Tirana. Overall Hochtief believes that the combination of HTAC capital and HTA airport management know-how has provided it with greater opportunities to successfully buy more privatized airports.

In addition HTA offers services to other airports and related businesses. Since 2002, it has had a 49 per cent shareholding in the British company Transport & Logistics Consultancy Ltd that specializes in the planning, development and implementation of processes and facilities, especially at airports, to optimize operational procedures. More recently in 2006 Hochtief AirPort Retail (HTAR) was set up to sell HTA's retail know-how to third parties, with the first client being Tirana airport where it has a retail concession up to 2014. In summary therefore, HTA now has three interrelated business areas, namely the management of its airport portfolio, the management of the HTAC investment partnership and the selling of its special know-how to the third parties (Figure 2.11).

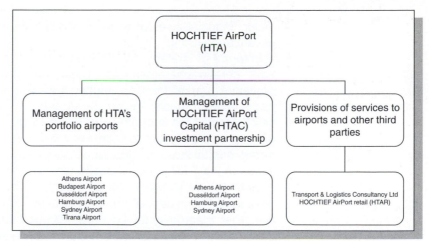

Figure 2.11
Structure of HTA
(*Source*: Hochtief website)

Macquarie: The emergence of the airport financial investor

The Macquarie Group is a very large Australian company offering a wide range of international banking, financial, advisory and investment services. In recent years, it has developed a very broad range on infrastructure, real estate and private equity investment funds in Australia and other countries. The group's first involvement with airport privatization was in the United Kingdom when the private equity investment fund Macquarie Airports Group (MAG) acquired shares in Birmingham and Bristol airport in the United Kingdom. Then in 2002 the special purpose investment fund Macquarie Airports (MAp) was founded and listed on the stock exchange. The first major involvement of MAp was with Sydney airport in 2002 which was a much more complex acquisition than the UK regional airports because of the size of the airport and because it was also subject to economic regulation. This was followed by Rome airport in 2003, Brussels airport in 2004 and Copenhagen airport in 2005. In most cases funding has not only come from MAp but also other Macquarie funds – for instance at Brussels airport with the Macquarie European Infrastructure Fund and the Macquarie Global Infrastructure Fund. In tendering for these airports, MAp not only had an attractive financial offer with its highly leveraged debt structure but was able to offer in-house operational expertise, since the specialist airport consultancy, the Portland Group, had came under Macquarie ownership in 2000. Hence MAp grew very quickly to become the second largest private owner operator after BAA/Ferrovial and the first major financial investor to have a major involvement in airport privatization (Smith, 2006).

In terms of strategy, MAp chooses to invest in airports which have certain characteristics. These characteristics include a dominant market position; higher than average growth potential; surplus capacity; under-developed commercial opportunities; potential for economies of scale to drive earnings margin growth; and potential to increase returns to investors by optimizing capital structure (Macquarie Airports, 2007; Frank-Keyes, 2006). In 2007 MAp also chose to withdraw from its involvement in Birmingham airport to focus on other activities and to withdraw from Rome airport, primarily because of disagreement with the other main investor Leonardo about future investments at the airport. In this later case €480 million was paid in 2003 for the 45 per cent stake in the airport which was sold for almost three times as much (€1237) in 2007. This means that MAp currently has an interest in four airports which handle over 70 million passengers (Table 2.11). In addition in 2007 MAp made a long-term strategic investment in Japan where there are likely to be other privatization opportunities in the future. It has a 14.9 per cent interest (overall Macquarie managed funds have a 19.9 per cent interest) in Japan Airport Terminal which is a private company which owns, manages and operates the three passenger terminals at Haneda airport and operates retail and catering businesses at Narita and Kansai airport.

Table 2.11 Macquarie airport portfolio of airports

	Bristol	Brussels	Copenhagen	Sydney
Passengers 2006 (mns)	5.2[a]	16.6	18.9	31.0[b]
Revenues 2006 (mn €s)	72.9[a]	347.1	387.5	436.2[b]
EBITDA[c] 2006 (mn €s)	42.6[a]	183.1	209.6	351.9[b]
Macquarie managed funds ownership interests	100.0	75.0	53.4	78.7
MAp ownership (%)	32.1	62.1	53.4	72.1
Initial date of Macquarie involvement	2001	2004	2005	2002

[a] April 2005–March 2006.
[b] July 2006–June 2007.
[c] Earnings before interest, tax, depreciation, and amortization.
Source: Macquarie website and annual accounts.

The consequences of privatization and internationalization of the airport industry

Airport privatization and the emergence of new international airport operators has major implications for the airport industry. With the increased number of potential airport investors, there has been considerable debate as to which type of investor is likely to be the most successful and most appropriate for the long-term development of the airport industry. The traditional airport companies have core skills and competencies related to both the operational and business aspects of managing an airport, which they have already gained through airport management in the home country, and which have been used to grow their business. In the early stages of privatization, purchasing other airports was viewed by some as a natural progression for airport companies that had gone through the processes of commercialization and then privatization. Once privatization had proved to be successful, it seemed quite logical that the commercially minded airports might next seek to acquire other interests to expand and add value to their company. Moreover for such airport companies there may be distinct advantages in expanding internationally if their own core infrastructure (e.g. terminal or runway) is physically or environmentally constrained, as is the situation at a number of European airports. Financial growth in the home market may be hindered by a regulatory system which may limit the amount of revenue generated from aeronautical sources, such as with BAA. In addition, international expansion can provide the much needed finance for development in the home market and may safeguard the success of the core business.

However, it was not just the privatized or partially privatized airports (such as those of BAA, Copenhagen, and Vienna) which sought to become international companies. There were also companies such as AdP, Milan, and AENA, which were not responsible to private shareholders, but were just as keen to acquire other airports. The motivation for such expansion was less clear – though it is true that such airports, too, were increasingly under greater pressure to perform well and many were expected to be privatized eventually. Perhaps for some airports there may also have been an element of fear of being left behind in the race to become international airport operators.

Internationalization strategies for airport companies, however, have changed since these early 'gold rush' years in the late 1990s. A more volatile aviation industry, coupled with more experience of international operations has meant that generally airports have become more cautious in their approach and a number of companies, such as AdP and Fraport, have reassessed their international expansion ambitions. There is now far more focus on considering whether the investment will make strategic sense or will really add value. This has also resulted in a number of airports pulling out from some of their international projects. For example, Aeroporti de Roma which sold its share in the Airports Company of South Africa in 2005 and in AdP disposed off its share of BCIA in 2007. Similarly Copenhagen airport sold its interest in Hainan Meilan in 2007.

The successful airport companies are the ones which also become competent in bid and project management and in developing new skills in change management and business development to cope with the opportunities arising from the new investments. Some of the utility, property and construction companies which already have a number of these skills and which started in airport operations primarily because of the synergies with existed with their businesses, have developed very proficient skills in operating and management airports. Hochtief is a very good example of this. There are also some new airport companies, for example Meinl Airports, Tepe Akfen Ventures (TAV) and Dubai Aerospace Enterprise who see their strength in specializing in a certain geographical area such as Eastern/Central Europe for Meinl and Turkey and the surrounding area for TAV.

As with many other industries, growing the business through mergers and acquisitions can produce higher returns and increased shareholder value. Also risks may be reduced by going global, thereby placing less relevance on any one national economy and lessening exposure to downturns in individual economies. However there does not seem to be such obvious synergies in controlling a global group of airports as there are, for example with airlines, particularly when the airports are operating in different regulatory environments. Whilst airline alliances are primarily being driven by a need to expand networks and increase market accessibility, most of the potential benefits of operating a group of airports appear to come from shared knowledge, expertise and financial resources rather than marketing opportunities.

Airport groups can potentially reduce costs through bulk buying and joint purchasing in some areas. For example, cost reductions could be achieved with joint purchasing of equipment such as ramp buses and fire engines, and through negotiation of more favourable insurance policies. Costs could also be saved by having a single head office and through centralizing many functions such as accounting and information technology. Joint training programmes could be arranged and there may be cost advantages through combined marketing. Standard commercial contracts could be agreed with core partners at the airports. In addition, the advantages of being 'big' could help the airport company keep up-to-date with technology developments and the latest airport management tools and techniques around the world.

A key issue is whether the new financial investors are adequately suited to be long-term airport investors. They arrived relatively late at airports because traditionally they have much more short-term horizons than airport operators and expect to add value by selling the business after a few years. In addition they like to have a controlling majority which was not offered at a number of possible privatizations which were designed to run in partnership with public authorities. However the growing number of privatizations allowing total or majority private sector ownership together with the emergence of secondary market with airports has made the airport industry a more attractive option. Moreover aviation growth and the increasing opportunities for privatization worldwide, as well as the restricted funds which are now available to some of the traditional airport operators since they already reached the limits of their financial capabilities with international projects, has created many more chances for these new sources of capital. However it can be argued that financial investors may not have the appropriate know-how and understanding of the complexity of the airport business and the range of interests, such as passengers, airlines, employees, concessionaires, visitors, neighbours, and perhaps public shareholders, which have to be taken into account. This together with a lack of a long-term commitment and often highly geared operations makes the success of such investments much more uncertain.

For all airport investors there are a number of important considerations which need to be taken into account to minimize the risk of any specific project. For example, often a local partner will be required in the purchasing consortia and the appropriate choice here will be crucial. Likewise the financial structure related to the consortium partners and their exact roles needs to be considered as do any cultural differences or communication problems between the consortium partners and local staff. All this means that the contractual framework and choice of partners for any project will be very important. There will also be political risks which the investor may have very limited control over. For example, even if a government has relinquished all effective control of an airport to a private operator, a change in the air transport regulatory system or the introduction of more stringent environmental legislation or different planning regulations could have a fundamental impact on the way in which the airport operates. Also the extent of any political instability and the general political and legal situation needs to be considered, as well as the government relationship with the other stakeholders such as the airlines and the border control and immigration agencies. These risks and others may be reduced by carrying out a comprehensive due-diligence assessment of all areas of the airport business.

Koch and Budde (2005) identify the most important success factors for international airport companies as the availability of capital resources, personnel resources and know-how (such as operational expertise, international know-how, and an efficient organizational structure), a management approach with a focus on value creation, and international experience. Feldman (2006) argues that successful international airport investors/managers need to have both strong financial resources but also established credibility. Currently with the exception of Macquarie Airports the financial investors have the financial resources but not the credibility. On the other hand they are many airport groups such as Vancouver, Vienna, and Fraport which have high credibility but now have very limited funds. The two airport groups, identified as having both high credibility and financial resources are Hochtief and Ferrovial.

It is certainly true that the emergence of the financial investors has changed the nature of airport privatizations. It may well be that in the future that different investors will focus on different types of airports. 'Mature' airports in developed countries may be sold using an IPO, as long as the level of local public demand is seen as strong, or may be sold to current and new financial investors. In these cases bringing in operational expertise will be less of a priority. The same will be true of secondary transactions which are also likely to be attractive to the financial markets. Elsewhere, however, in more developing areas, for example India and China, it may very well be that the airport sales will continue to go to the established airport groups (or at least in partnerships with financial investors), whether they are construction or property or traditional airport companies groups, where both new infrastructure and international operational expertise is needed.

One of the major advantages of internationalization or globalization for airlines and other companies is the advantage of being able to sell one common product or one global brand to the customer. For international airport companies, branding could involve the use of similar signposting, colour schemes and interior design for the entire airport. Examples of this have existed for many years with national airport groups. For example, BAA has traditionally used a common and constant brand image for its seven UK airports. The merits of branding within the airport industry are, however, very questionable (see Chapter 7). Most passengers, particularly leisure passengers who travel infrequently, would probably not be aware of any common branding and would find it very difficult to define any distinguishing features of a certain airport brand.

On the other hand, there could be benefits to an individual airline or airline alliance in operating out of more than one airport which is owned by an international airport company. For example, standard contracts could be agreed for the whole airport network, quantity discounts on charging could be negotiated and there could be common agreements on the use of gates and other facilities. This was the idea behind the Wiggin's Group expansion into airports; the company's overall objective was to develop a global network of over 20 regional airports under its so-called PlaneStation concept. Wiggins believed that the power of the PlaneStation brand would significantly benefit the airports within this network and would bring the resources needed to improve their performance which have previously been unavailable under individual, public ownership. Wiggins therefore had a very different strategy to most of the other emerging global airport companies that tend to buy up airports which already are successful or appear to have great potential. Wiggins claimed that common standards and processes at all the network airports along with one single administrative system provided the potential for improving the quality and effectiveness of the facilities offered to the airline operators and logistic organizations who planned to operate from a number of airports in the network. There would also be scope for the building of close relationships with airlines and other operators with, for example, risk sharing, simplified negotiation, and common tariffs (Lewin, 2002). However Wiggins/Planestation went out of business in 2005 primarily because of the financial failure of its main airline at Manston airport, namely the low-cost carrier EUjet, which the airport company had invested in when the financial problems of the airline became evident.

Clearly the main driving force behind the internationalization of the airport industry has been airport privatization which has enabled a growing number of airports to be purchased outright or at least managed on a long-term basis by an external airport operator. However this internationalization could also occur as a result of greater co-operation between airport operators or through the establishment of airport alliances. Unlike airline co-operation, which is primarily driven by a need to expand networks and increase market accessibility, airport co-operation is likely to be encouraged by a desire to benefit from shared knowledge, expertise and financial resources. In the late 1990s, there was considerable discussion about the possibility of the development of airport alliances particularly in the light of increased competition in the airline industry and the emergence of their global alliances. This had meant that airports themselves faced increased competition and were under greater pressure to reduce costs, improve quality, and add value to their organizations – all of which, theoretically, could have be helped by airport co-operation. In late 1999, the Schiphol–Fraport 'Pantares' alliance was agreed which was the first, and to date the only major alliance agreement witnessed by the airport industry. Schiphol and Fraport believed that there was scope for co-operation because the two airports were both European hubs but serving different airlines alliances; they had complementary competencies, they were at similar levels of globalization and they shared the same strategic approach. They identified seven areas where co-operation seemed possible (Endler, 2000; Verboom, 2000):

1. *Aviation ground services*: Ground and cargo handling logistic systems; bidding for international projects.
2. *Retail and passengers*: Retail business at home and international airports; e-business and intermodal strategies.
3. *Facility management*: Purchasing, project management and technical services; standardization of equipment and technology.
4. *Real estate*: Site development at home and other airports, marketing, bidding for international projects.
5. *Information technology*: System and equipment standardization; product and technology development; marketing.

6. *International projects*: Privatization projects; project management; financial risk sharing.
7. *Other*: Marketing, research, training and recruitment, environmental issues.

As part of the alliance partnership, the airports agreed not to compete against each other on international contracts. Since Pantares was established, Fraport has taken a share in Brisbane airport, and the alliance is operating a new logistics centre, Tradeport, at Hong Kong airport. The companies also formed a joint venture company, Pantares Systems to serve the information technology and communications needs of the two organizations and to offer related services outside the alliance. However in the end there were very few benefits which were achieved with this alliance.

With only one such example it is difficult to determine whether this disappointing result was due to some unique factors related to the two airport groups or more fundamentally whether airport alliances are not likely to succeed. Within the airline industry it is the regulatory framework which has traditionally limited merger and acquisition activities and encouraged alliances, whereas in the airport industry similar constraints do not really exist. Nevertheless there do seem to be areas in airport operations where co-operation can bring benefits, but perhaps this is better organized on an ad-hoc basis rather then through a general all-encompassing alliance agreement. One such example is a joint venture company called AirportSmart which was founded by AdP, BAA and Copenhagen, and has the custom of other airports. Its aim is to maximize the benefits offered by trading on the Internet for both the airports and the suppliers and to manage joint purchasing arrangements. All this helps demonstrate how the airport industry has fundamentally changed from being operated primarily within a national environment to now being a totally international business.

References and further reading

Andrew, D. and Dochia, S. (2006). The growing and evolving business of private participation in airports, *Public-Private Infrastructure Advisory Facility (PPIAF) Note*, 15, September, available from www.worldbank.org. (accessed 16 October 2007)

Arbulu, J.D. (2007). From Peru to the world. *International Airport Review*, 2, 88–89.

Ashford, N. (1999). Experiences with airport privatization. In: Ashford N. (Ed.), *Airport 2000: Trends for the New Millennium*. Sovereign.

Ashford, N. and Moore, C. (1999). *Airport Finance, 2nd edn*. Loughborough Airport Consultancy.

Ballantyne, T. (1997). Sydney syndrome. *Airline Business*, October, 58–61.

Beechener, J. (2000). Beijing rides market downturn. *Jane's Airport Review*, June, 8–9.

Beesley, M.E. (1997). *Privatization, Regulation and Deregulation, 2nd edn*. Routledge.

Brunner, A. (2007). Bangalore International Airport: India's largest private sector Greenfield airport. *Journal of Airport Management*, *1*(3), 226–231.

Carney, M. and Mew, K. (2003). Airport governance reform: A strategic management perspective. *Journal of Air Transport Management*, *9*, 221–232.

Caves, R. and Gosling, G. (1999). *Strategic Airport Planning*. Elsevier.

Centre for Asia Pacific Aviation (2007a). *Global Airport Privatization Report* (second edition). CAPA.

Centre for Asia Pacific Aviation (2007b). Is airport privatization running out of steam? In Airports Council International, *ACI Airport economics survey 2007*.

Chevallier, J. (2007). *Global Airport Development Conference*, Queen Alia International Airport, Amman, Jordan, November.

Communique Airport Business (1998). Our best deal ever – AGI and London Luton. November/December, 28.

Croes, H. (1997). Airport privatization: cleared to take off. *Aerlines*, Winter, 28–30.

Department of the Environment, Transport and the Regions (DETR) (1998). *A New Deal for Transport*. HMSO.

Doganis, R. (1992). *The Airport Business*. Routledge.

Endler, J. (2000). Global alliances and privatization. *Tenth ACI Europe Annual Assembly*, Rome, June.

Federal Airports Corporation (FAC) (1997). *Annual Report 1997*. FAC.

Federal Aviation Administration (2000). *Fact sheet: Stewart International airport privatization*, 21 March.

Feldman, D (2006). Managing airports for value after the deal gets done, *Global Airport Development Conference*, November.

Feller, G. (2006). Paris goes private. *Airports International*, *39*(7), 24–27, October.

Frank-Keyes, J. (2006). Mather and the Macquarie investment model. *Communique Airport Business*, May, 7–13.

Freathy, P. and O'Connell, F. (1998). *European Airport Retailing*. Macmillan.

Gangl, S. (1994). Financing a partially-privatized airport. *Airports as Business Enterprises Conference*, April.

Gangl, S. (1995). Going to market – Vienna Airport's share flotation. In: Amkreutz J. (ed.), *Sources of Finance for Airport Development in Europe*. ACI Europe.

Gangl, S. (1998). Experiences of privatization. *University of Westminster/Cranfield University Airport Economics and Finance Symposium*, London, March.

Gangl, S. (2002). The globalization of airport companies. *University of Westminster/Cranfield University Airport Economics and Finance Symposium*, March.

General Accounting Office (GAO) (1996). *Airport Privatization: Issues Related to the Sale or Lease of US Commercial Airports*. GAO.

General Accounting Office (GAO) (2007). *Airport Finance: Preliminary Analysis Indicates Proposed Changes in the Airport Improvement Program May Not Resolve Funding Needs for Smaller Airports*. GAO.

Gethin, S. (2002). BAA faces a profit squeeze. *Jane's Airport Review*, July–August, 10–11.

Guitard, J.-F. and Vernhes, J.-M. (2007). What's in the deal pipeline? How are the French regionals preparing for their pending privatization? *Global Airport Development Conference*, November.

Hanaoka, S. and Phomma, S. (2004). Privatisation and productivity performance of Thai airports, *Air Transport Research Society Conference*, Istanbul, July.

Hooper, P. (2002). Privatization of airports in Asia. *Journal of Air Transport Management*, 8, 289–300.

Humphreys, I. (1999). Privatization and commercialization changes in UK airport ownership patterns. *Journal of Transport Geography*, 7, 121–134.

International Air Transport Association (IATA) (2005). *Airport privatization*, IATA economic briefing, IATA

International Civil Aviation Organization (ICAO) (2007). Development of airport infrastructure in India, *Assembly – 36th session Working Paper 141*, ICAO

Iley, P (2007) Chicago Midway update and potential implications for US Pilot Programme, *Global Airport Development Conference*, November.

Ionides, N. (2007). Catching up. *Airline Business*, December, 54–57.

Jackson, P.M. and Price, C.P. (eds.) (2007). *Privatization and Regulation*. Longman.

Jain, R., Raghuram, G. and Gangwar, R. (2007). Airport privatization in India: Lessons from the bidding process in Delhi and Mumbai, *Air Transport Research Society Conference*, Berkeley, July.

Kalenda, R. (2007). What significance does the capital market attach to airports, *10th Hamburg Aviation conference*, February.

Kerkloh, M. (2007). Munich airport's terminal 2: A successful airport–airline collaboration. *Journal of Airport Management*, 1(4), 330–337.

Knibb, D. (1999). Australia's road to privatization. *Airline Business*, August, 40–41.

Koch, B. and Budde, S. (2005). Internationalization strategies in airport companies. In: Delfmann W., Baum H., Auerbach S. and Albers S. (eds.), *Strategic Management in the Aviation Industry*, Ashgate.

Lambert, R. (1995). Birmingham's public–private finance partnership. In: Amkreutz J. (ed.), *Sources of Finance for Airport Development in Europe*. ACI Europe.

Lewin, R. (2002). Developing a global network of airports. *University of Westminster/Cranfield University Airport Economics and Finance Symposium*, March.

Lipovich, G. (2008). The privatization of Argentine airports. *Journal of Air Transport Management*, 14(1), 8–15, forthcoming.

Lyon, D. and Francis, G. (2006). Managing New Zealand's airports in the face of commercial challenges. *Journal of Air Transport Management*, 12, 220–226.

Mather, K. (2006). Macquarie Airports – A fund or operator? *Global Airport Development Conference*, November.

Macquarie Airports (2007). *Macquarie Airports Fact Sheet*, available from www.macquarie.com/map (accessed 3 December 2007).

McCormick, C. (2000). Private partners. *Airports International*, March, 36–41.

Momberger Airport Information (2007). Airport development news, April, available from www.airports.org (accessed 20 November 2007).

Ott, J. (1998). Indianapolis serves as a privatization testbed. *Aviation Week and Space Technology*, 14 December, 52.

Oum, T., Adler, N. and Yu, C. (2006). Privatization, corporatization, ownership forms and their effects on the performance of the world's major airports. *Journal of Air Transport Management*, 12(3), 109–121.

Parker, D. (1999). The performance of BAA before and after privatization: A DEA study. *Journal of Transport Economics and Policy*, 33(2), 133–146.

Poole, R.W. (1995). *How to privatize Orange County's Airports, Policy study 194*. Reason Foundation.

Poole, R.W. (2007). *Annual Privatization Report*. Reason Foundation.

Ricover, A. (1999). Airport privatization of Latin American airports. In: Ashford N. (ed.), *Airport 2000: Trends for the New Millennium*. Sovereign.

Rowe, R. (2006). Private persuasion. *Airline Business*, December, 40–46.

Schrankler, R. (2006). Current trends in equity finance and its consequences for project finance, *Global Airport Development Conference*, November.

Smith, P. (2006). Big Mac gets bigger. *Airfinance Journal*, 292, 34–35.

UK Government (1986). *Airports Act 1986*. HMSO.

Vasigh, B. and Gorjidooz, J. (2006). Productivity analysis of public and private airports: A causal investigation. *Journal of Air Transportation*, 11(3), 144–163.

Verboom, P. (2000). Schiphol Group: creating airport cities. *Tenth ACI Europe Annual Assembly*, Rome, June.

Vogel, H.-A. (2006). Impact of privatization on the financial and economic performance of European airports. *The Aeronautical Journal*, 110(1106), 197–213.

Wang, X. and Seiden, E. (2007). Aviation infrastructure investment in China: Great needs, great opportunities and great challenges. *Journal of Airport Management*, 1(3), 232–241.

Zhang, A. and Yuen, A. (2008). Airport policy and performance in mainland China and Hong Kong. In: Winston C., and de Rus G. (Eds.), *Aviation Infrastructure Performance*. Brookings Institution Press.

CHAPTER 3

Airport economics and performance benchmarking

Industry profit levels

This chapter considers the economics of the airport industry. The modern-day commercial and business pressures being placed on most of the airports mean that a thorough understanding of the economics of airports is now, more than ever before, a fundamental prerequisite for all airport managers. The chapter begins by looking at profit levels within the industry and describing the revenue and cost structures. It then goes on to discuss some of the key factors which influence the economics of airports. This leads to a discussion of how economic performance can be measured and the alternative methods which are currently being used to benchmark airport performance.

Table 3.1 shows the profit levels at fifty of the largest airports or airport groups in the world in 2006/2007. Nearly all the airports produced an operating profit (i.e. profit before interest and tax) with the exception of the North American airports of Toronto, Los Angeles, and Dallas/Fort Worth. The operating profit margin, that is profit as a percentage of revenues (also known as the earnings before internet and tax (EBIT) margin), for most airports was above 10 per cent and at a number of airports that margin was substantially greater than this.

Overall for the 100 leading airport groups in 2006/2007 an average operating margin of 16 per cent was recorded. In comparison, the 150 major airlines experienced a profit margin of 4 per cent, and similar differences were experienced in previous years (Figure 3.1). There are a number of reasons for why this so-called 'profitability gap', which is frequently a bone of contention between the airlines and airports, exists. First although airports are increasingly facing much greater competition than before, the airlines generally face much stiffer competition which particularly puts pressure on them to reduce their fares. Secondly in a number of countries there tends to be a shortage of airport capacity which can push up prices whilst in many airline markets there tends to be overcapacity which has the opposite effect. In many cases, the airports have a more diverse customer base than airlines which means that they have less exposure to downturns in individual markets. Thirdly not all the airport revenues (e.g., landing charges, rents) are directly related to passenger numbers, unlike the airlines, which means that fluctuations in passenger numbers generally have less of an impact on airports. Finally on the cost side, airports have less dependence on fuel prices which is a key input cost for airlines over which they have very little control.

However when profitability is related to the investment at the airport, for example, by looking at return on capital employed (ROCE), the differences between the airports and airlines are not so significant which reflects the more capital intensive nature of airport operations. For example, Airports Council International (ACI)-Europe quotes an average figure produced by McKinsey of around 10 per cent for

Table 3.1 Profitability for 50 major airport operators, 2006/2007

No.	Airport operator	Total revenues (million US$)	Operating profit (million US$)	Operating margin (%)
1.	Ferrovial	5200.0[a]	N/A	N/A
2.	AENA Spanish Airports	3331.7	161.7	4.9
3.	Fraport AG	2838.9	416.8	14.7
4.	Aéroports de Paris	2620.1	493.2	18.8
5.	Port Authority of New York and New Jersey	1777.1	367.6	20.7
6.	Narita International Airport Corp	1579.4	286.1	18.1
7.	Schiphol Group	1308.3	398.7	30.5
8.	Hong Kong International	994.4	339.1	34.1
9.	Flughafen Munchen	950.0	N/A	N/A
10.	Avinor Norway	943.6	119.4	12.7
11.	Greater Toronto Airports Authority	941.2	−69.8	−7.4
12.	Infraero Brazil	937.7	225.6	24.1
13.	Kansai International Airport Company	905.9	220.3	24.3
14.	Seoul Incheon International	903.8[a]	N/A	N/A
15.	Luftfartsverket Sweden	815.7	100.9	12.4
16.	Airports Authority of India	788.0	272.9	34.6
17.	Dublin Airport Authority	745.8	107.2	14.4
18.	Manchester Airports Group	733.1	142.6	19.5
19.	Aeroporti di Roma S.p.A.	715.7	184.3	25.8
20.	Turkey State Airports Authority	713.3	365.4	51.2
21.	Civil Aviation Authority of Singapore	705.4	236.3	33.5
22.	City of Chicago Department of Aviation	651.5	19.6	3.0
23.	Miami Dade County Aviation Dept	642.2	182.3	28.4
24.	Los Angeles World Airports	620.7	−10.8	−1.7
25.	SEA Aerporti di Milano	614.8	162.4	26.4
26.	Flughafen Wien AG	602.2	130.8	21.7
27.	Unique Zürich Airport	590.1	287.3	48.7
28.	City and County of Denver Aviation Dept	500.8	101.2	20.2
29.	Southern Cross Airports Corp Holdings Australia	492.1	279.1	56.7
30.	Copenhagen Airports A/S	487.9	208.8	42.8
31.	Dallas/Fort Worth International	485.5	−64.0	−13.2
32.	Flughafen Düsseldorf	475.7	N/A	N/A
33.	Metro Washington Airports Authority	471.2	48.1	10.2
34.	San Francisco International	455.3	22.5	4.9
35.	Brussels Airport Company	453.2[a]	N/A	N/A
36.	Athens International	451.0	N/A	N/A
37.	Airports of Thailand	418.1	175.9	42.1
38.	Massachusetts Port Authority	403.8	178.0	44.1
39.	Beijing Capital International Airport Group Co.	397.1	205.0	51.6
40.	Houston Airport System	393.9	57.2	14.5
41.	Chiang Kai-Shek International Airport Taiwan	390.0	N/A	N/A
42.	Airports Company South Africa	365.4	167.5	45.8
43.	Abertis	353.5	N/A	N/A
44.	Vancouver International Airport Authority	348.1	N/A	N/A
45.	Aeroportos de Portugal, SA	347.3	82.2	20.8
46.	Port of Seattle	337.5	72.1	21.4
47.	Finavia Finland	336.7	29.4	8.7
48.	Flughafen Koln-Bonn	327.5	27.4	8.4
49.	Polish Airports State Enterprise	322.8	104.6	32.4
50.	Malaysia Airports Holdings Berhad	310.0	72.0	25.0

[a] Estimates.

Source: Airline Business.

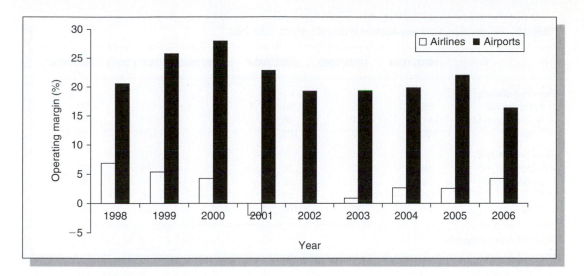

Figure 3.1

Operating margin of world airlines (top 150 airlines) and airports (top 50/100 airports, depending on year) 1998/1999–2006/2007. Source: Airline Business

Table 3.2 Airport operating revenue sources

Aeronautical	Non-aeronautical
Landing fees	Concessions
Passenger fees	Rents
Aircraft parking fees	Direct sales (shops, catering and other services
Handling fees (if handling is provided by the airport operator)	provided by the airport operator)
	Car park (if provided by the airport operator)
Other aeronautical fees (air traffic control, lighting, airbridges, etc.)	Recharges (for gas, water, electricity, etc.)
	Other non-aeronautical revenue (consultancy, visitor and business services, property development, etc.)

airports compared with 6 per cent for airlines (ACI-Europe, 2005). Moreover in a more recent detailed study of European airports, it has been estimated that the average return on capital is only 4.6 per cent and hence it is argued that the airport users, such as airlines, are not actually paying the full cost of the infrastructure that they use (SH&E, 2006).

Revenue and cost structures

Airport revenue is usually classified into two main categories: aeronautical (or aviation) and non-aeronautical (or commercial) revenues (Table 3.2).

Table 3.3 Average revenue and cost structures at European airports, 1983–2007

	1983/1984	1988/1989	1993/1994	1998/1999	2003/2004	2006/2007
Revenue shares (%)						
Aeronautical	59	56	54	50	51	52
Non-aeronautical	41	44	46	50	49	48
Total	100	100	100	100	100	100
Cost shares (%)						
Labour	46	43	39	35	33	33
Depreciation	18	21	22	19	22	20
Other	36	36	39	46	45	47
Total	100	100	100	100	100	100

Source: Annual reports.

Aeronautical revenues are those sources of income which arise directly from the operation of aircraft and the processing of passengers and freight. Non-aeronautical revenues are those generated by activities that are not directly related to the operation of aircraft, notably income from commercial activities within the terminal and rents for terminal space and airport land. The International Civil Aviation Organization (ICAO) has a long list of activities which can be classified as non-aeronautical including cattle farming, concrete-post manufacturing, baseball training camps, mannequins and models show, and pipeline inspection shows (ICAO, 1991)! Then there are a few categories of income that can be classified as either type of revenue. For example, handling revenues are usually treated as aeronautical revenues unless handling is undertaken by handling agents or airlines when the associated revenue (rent or fee based on turnover) is included under rents or concession revenue items. Income received by the airport from aircraft fuel companies or from airlines as a fuel throughput fee could be regarded as directly related to aircraft operations and hence an aeronautical revenue. Alternatively, this income could be considered as commercial income and hence a non-aeronautical revenue. Overall, landing and passenger fees are by far the most important aeronautical revenue sources. Most of the non-aeronautical revenue comes from concessions and rents. Revenues, such as interest received and income earned from subsidiary companies, are usually included under a different 'non-operating' revenue category.

A breakdown of revenues for a sample of European airports is shown in Table 3.3 for the period 1983–2006. The dominant trend up until 1998 was a decline in the importance of aeronautical revenues with a subsequent increase in reliance on non-aeronautical sources. This reflected not only pressures from airlines and regulatory bodies to keep airport charge increases to a minimum but also the increased focus being placed on commercial activities. At some airports, the increase in the proportion of non-aeronautical revenue over the 15 years from 1983 to 1998 had been considerable − for example, at Copenhagen airport the share increased from 41 to 54 per cent and at Geneva airport it rose from 40 to 51 per cent. One of the most notable increases in commercial revenues has been with BAA airports − Chapter 6 outlines how this was achieved. This trend was halted in 1999 because of the impact of the abolition of EU duty- and tax-free goods in this year and since then the share of revenue from aeronautical and non-aeronautical sources has remained fairly equal. The annual economics survey of ACI, which has a much larger sample of airports, reported almost identical results with aeronautical revenue representing 50 per cent of total revenue in 1998 and 48 per cent in 2006 (ACI, 2000; 2007).

Unlike with revenues, there is no industry standard for the reporting of airport operating costs. From published accounts, however, it is usually possible to identify the three separate cost items associated with labour, capital, and other operating costs. Within Europe, labour costs account for an average 33 per cent of total costs with depreciation representing a further 20 per cent. Over the years the labour costs have decreased in importance (Table 3.3). In part this is due to more outsourcing being undertaken by airport operators, particularly in the handling area and in some cases a more productive labour force. However airport operators do seem generally to have less opportunities to reduce staff costs compared with some industries, such as the airline sector, as the majority of staff functions tend to be related to the essential safety and security aspects of operating an airport.

These average values for Europe hide the variation between individual airports which in some cases is quite considerable. Table 3.4 shows these values for a number of European airports. The revenue figures reflect differences in strategies towards aeronautical and commercial activities and also differences in the functions carried out by the airport operator itself. For example, many of the German, Italian and Austrian airports are involved in providing their own handling services. In contrast the London airports, with their aeronautical charges regulated, are much more dependent on commercial activities. Dublin Airport Authority has the highest non-aeronautical share because it operates the duty-free shops itself. The labour costs also vary quite considerably at airports. At Vienna and Frankfurt, labour costs account for around half the total costs, again reflecting their heavy involvement in the labour-intensive handling activity. In contrast, airports such as Basel-Mulhouse, Amsterdam, London Heathrow, and Oslo which are not involved with so many activities, have much lower staff costs.

In the United States, airports tend to use a different breakdown of their activities and revenues, by splitting them into aviation and non-aviation sources. Aviation revenues include not only the aircraft landing fees and the fuel charges but also the rents and the lease revenues from land, terminal, and other buildings or hangars used by airlines. The remaining non-aviation revenues are the same as commercial or

Table 3.4 Revenue and cost structures at a selection of European airports, 2006/2007

Airport	Revenue shares (%)			Cost shares (%)			
	Aero	Non-aero	Total	Labour	Depreciation	Other	Total
Amsterdam	61	39	100	20	21	59	100
Basel-Mulhouse	47	53	100	21	30	49	100
Birmingham	56	44	100	32	23	45	100
Berlin	64	36	100	39	16	45	100
Cologne	73	27	100	39	15	46	100
Copenhagen	50	50	100	51	20	30	100
Dublin	37	63	100	36	12	52	100
Florence	75	25	100	44	19	37	100
Frankfurt	62	38	100	56	13	31	100
Geneva	48	52	100	41	18	40	100
Glasgow	54	46	100	34	17	49	100
London Gatwick	43	57	100	28	18	54	100
London Heathrow	48	52	100	23	22	55	100
London Stansted	43	57	100	34	22	44	100
Manchester	50	50	100	25	27	48	100
Milan	58	42	100	32	28	40	100
Oslo	46	54	100	20	28	52	100
Paris	60	40	100	37	16	47	100
Rome	59	41	100	35	24	41	100
Salzburg	77	23	100	42	19	39	100
Vienna	76	24	100	53	18	29	100
Zürich	52	48	100	33	20	47	100

Note: The data may also include other airports when the airport operator owns more than one airport, but most of it is associated with the major airport shown.
Source: Annual reports.

non-aeronautical revenues. Generally the proportion of revenue from airport charges is low compared to elsewhere because the airports do not charge a passenger charge (although there is a passenger facility charge, this is treated as non-operating revenue – see Chapter 4 for details). They also do not get involved in providing services such as air traffic control or handling. On the contrary the revenue from the rentals is higher because of the greater amount of space and facilities which are rented or leased to the airlines. In terms of costs, the staff costs tend to be low by other international standards – again because these airports tend to get involved in very few additional services which are usually more labour intensive. These characteristics are illustrated in Table 3.5 which shows the revenue and cost structures for a number of US airports. For most of these airports, the airport

Table 3.5   Revenue and cost structures at a selection of major US airports, 2006/2007

Airport	Revenue shares (%)				Cost shares (%)			
	Landing fee	Other[a] aviation	Non-aviation	Total	Labour	Depreciation	Other	Total
Atlanta	10	23	68	100	29	21	50	100
Baltimore	23	31	46	100	14	38	48	100
Boston	20	33	48	100	25	35	40	100
Chicago O'Hare	29	33	38	100	24	29	47	100
Dallas/Fort Worth	40	14	46	100	25	39	36	100
Detroit	28	15	58	100	23	37	40	100
Houston	25	45	30	100	22	42	37	100
Indianapolis	20	22	58	100	28	45	27	100
Las Vegas McCarren	8	33	58	100	34	20	45	100
Los Angeles	27	21	52	100	45	13	43	100
Memphis	36	34	30	100	18	50	32	100
Miami	16	56	28	100	33	24	43	100
Minneapolis-St Paul	17	22	61	100	24	50	26	100
New York JFK	28	41	31	100	16	18	66	100
New York La Guardia	35	25	40	100	25	12	63	100
New York Newark	25	40	35	100	18	25	57	100
Orlando	8	25	67	100	19	35	46	100
Philadelphia	24	45	32	100	22	32	46	100
Phoenix Sky Harbor	13	24	63	100	22	27	51	100
Seattle	14	42	44	100	25	39	35	100
Washington Dulles	14	34	52	100	24	33	43	100
Washington Reagan	17	35	48	100	31	29	40	100

[a] Mostly airline rents.
Source: FAA.

charges represents less than 30 per cent of revenues and the staff costs are also less than 30 per cent of total costs.

Elsewhere in the world where data is readily available, the situation is more mixed (Table 3.6). The Australian and New Zealand airports tend to generate just less than half their revenues from aeronautical sources whereas the Mexican airports are very reliant on this source. The share of staff costs for most of the airports tends to be comparatively low relative to European airports which reflects both minimum involvement in additional activities (e.g. the Australian airports) and lower local labour costs (e.g. in Mexico).

Table 3.6 Revenue and cost structures at a selection of other airports, 2006/2007

	Aero	Non-aero	Total	Labour	Depreciation	Other	Total
New Zealand							
Auckland	48	52	100	29	35	35	100
Christchurch	49	51	100	30	38	32	100
Australia							
Melbourne	47	53	100	28	48	24	100
Perth	41	59	100	19	65	16	100
Sydney	49	51	100	11	35	54	100
Airports of Thailand	67	33	100	16	43	41	100
Hong Kong	48	52	100	20	41	39	100
PT Angkasa Pura II (Indonesia)[a]	80	20	100	46	12	42	100
Mexico							
ASUR	71	29	100	19	35	46	100
GAP	81	19	100	18	40	42	100
OMA	81	19	100	13	59	28	100
Airports Company South Africa	55	45	100	30	39	32	100

[a]2005 data.
Source: Annual reports.

Factors influencing costs and revenues

There are many factors that affect an airport's level and structure of costs and revenues. Some of these are more easily influenced by airport management than others. First, the volume and nature of the traffic, which the airport operator only has limited control over, can have a major impact on the airport's economic performance. As airports increase their traffic throughput, the costs per unit of traffic, or unit costs, decline. Studies of British airports in the 1970s showed that unit costs, measured in costs per passenger handled or per work load unit (a WLU is equivalent to one passenger or 100 kg of freight), fell dramatically as total traffic increased to around 1 or 1.5 million passengers or WLUs. Then at a traffic level of around 3 million passengers or WLUs, the unit costs tended to flatten out and ceased to exhibit a strong relationship with airport size (Doganis and Thompson, 1973). Early studies of Australian and Spanish airports produced similar findings (Assaily, 1989; Doganis *et al.*, 1995). In 1999 an ICAO airport economics study found that costs per WLU or unit costs for airports of less than 300 000 WLUs averaged US$15 were US$9.4 for airports with WLUs between 300 000 and 2.5 million WLUs and were US$8.00 for airports between 2.5 million and 25 million (ICAO, 2000). It is likely that for small airports there will be certain fixed costs associated with the provision of infrastructure and services which will be incurred at the airport irrespective of the traffic levels which will push up the unit costs. More complex analyses also suggest that airports experience economies of scale — with the effects being most significant for smaller airports (Gillen and Lall, 1997; Pels *et al.*, 2001).

There is also very limited evidence (e.g. Murillo-Melchor, 1999) that as airports get large they start to experience diseconomies of scale. This suggests that there might be an optimal size of airport in economic terms (Pels *et al.*, 2001). This may be because the airport system will become more complex, for example with a number of different terminals, which will involve more co-ordination and duplication of services and facilities. Surface access expenditure and costs to alleviate the greater environmental damage will also grow significantly as the airports become large. Moreover it has also been suggested by Kamp *et al.* (2007) that the costs might rise because of more expensive labour costs (due to higher unionization and using staff from farther distances) and the scarcity of cheap land but as yet the evidence regarding diseconomies of scale is far from conclusive.

However larger airports are normally in a better position to provide a greater range of commercial facilities for passengers and other consumers and therefore tend to have a greater reliance on non-aeronautical revenues. The ICAO survey found that on average airports with more than 25 million passengers generated 58 per cent of their revenue from non-aeronautical sources compared with the sample average of 36 per cent. Evidence at a more disaggregate level also exists. For example in 2005, airports of less than 4 millions passengers in Germany, Italy and the United Kingdom generated 31, 33 and 44 per cent of their revenues, respectively from non-aeronautical sources, whereas figures for airports of greater than 10 million passengers were 39, 46 and 57 per cent (Graham, 2006).

Costs associated with international passengers tend to rise as this type of traffic requires more space in the terminal for customs and immigration, and in effect these passengers have to spend longer time in the terminal. International passengers also have more luggage. For example, in Heathrow's Terminal 1 it has been estimated that international passengers on average have 1.3 bags compared with 0.5 for domestic passengers. BAA has estimated that for a hypothetical terminal of 8 million passengers capacity, the cost associated with an international passenger is likely to be 1.62 times greater than the cost of domestic passengers. The cost multiple for EU passengers is less, namely 1.36, which gives a cost multiple between international and EU traffic of 1.20 (Toms, 2000). However, international passengers tend to spend more money at the airport on commercial facilities such as retail and catering which will push up unit revenues – particularly if they have access to duty- and tax-free shopping. This is another reason why large airports tend to be more reliant on non-aeronautical revenue as they often have a higher share of international traffic.

Low cost and charter passengers will not usually need certain facilities such as airline lounges which will influence the airport's cost and revenue levels. They also have different spending patterns to traditional scheduled terminal passengers as do transfer passengers at hub airports (a more detailed description of different spending patterns is given in Chapter 7). Moreover, hub airports with a true 'wave' pattern of flights will have well defined peaks and troughs of traffic which will be more costly to handle than a more evenly spread distribution of flights. Likewise, airports serving holiday destinations may have a problem with peakiness and uneven capacity utilization which may push up costs.

Airports operators are relatively free to choose their own physical and service standards which are considered desirable to provide an acceptable level of service to passengers although in practice many of the standards at airports are fairly similar. Nevertheless, if an airport does decide to aim, say, for a more exclusive product, as with the business airport London City which put leather seats in the departure lounge, it will clearly have resource implications. At the other extreme, there are a few airports such as Singapore Changi, Kuala Lumpur, Marseille, and Budapest which offer a dedicated low cost terminal which again has implications for the cost levels of the airport (see Chapter 4).

There is no 'typical' airport when it comes to looking at the services and facilities that an airport provides. Beyond the basic operational functions, different airports have little in common. Some airport operators will provide activities such as security, air traffic control, handling, car parking, duty-free shops, cleaning, and heavy maintenance, while others will contract these out. In the extreme case, terminals may also be leased as is the situation in the United States. All this will impact on both cost and revenue levels. For example, Vienna airport generates over 30 per cent of gross revenues from handling. This is very different from airports such as London Heathrow or Amsterdam Schiphol which generate a relatively small amount of revenues from this activity in the form of rents and concession fees paid by the airlines and handling agents. In some cases, the situation may be even more complicated as the government may choose to pay for the provision of certain services, as is typically the case with the provision of policing, security, or fire and rescue.

Economic comparisons in any industry have to acknowledge the accounting policies adopted by individual operators. Particularly within the airport industry accounting procedures vary quite considerably since some airports adopt government or public authority accounting methods rather than commercial practices. With government-owned airports it is possible, for example, to find that the airport's land will not be considered to be an airport's asset and hence will not appear in any balance sheet. Views related to how assets should be depreciated differ. For example, Zürich depreciates buildings for 40 years, Amsterdam for 20–40 years, whereas it is 80 years at Copenhagen. Likewise at Dublin runways are depreciated for 10–50 years, at Amsterdam for 15–60 years and at Copenhagen for 80 years. The ICAO 1999 economic survey found that one-third of airports did not show realistic costs associated with depreciation and interest. Moreover, airports will be subject to different taxation regimes, with many public sector airports, for instance those in the United States, being exempt from most business taxes. This will have an impact on any comparative analysis of net profit levels.

The ownership patterns can also influence other factors such as funding arrangements and the cost of capital. In addition, an airport's performance is likely to depend very much on where it is positioned in the investment life cycle, since investment at airports tends to be large and 'lumpy' rather than continuous and gradual. When major developments have taken place, capital costs are likely to be high and poor utilization may push up the operating costs. Later in the cycle, the capital costs will reduce and utilization will hopefully improve. If an airport is congested, it may not be very attractive to its customers but from an economic viewpoint it may perform relatively well.

There are many other factors dependent on an airport's location and geographic situation which, to a large extent, will be beyond the airport operator's specific control. For instance, weather-related expenses, such as snow removal and deicing facilities, will only be incurred at certain airports. Location is also likely to influence the actual layout and design of the airport and the positioning of both airfield and terminal facilities. For example, an airport may require two or more runways not to meet traffic needs, but because of wind conditions or some other particular climatic or geographic characteristics. Environmental limits, imposed to reduce noise or other adverse impacts of air transport, may also mean that the airport cannot make the most efficient use of all resources. An airport may be forced to close at night even if there is sufficient demand to make night flying feasible. In a more general sense, locational factors may also affect the cost and quality of labour and the availability of capital for investment.

Measuring economic performance and efficiency

Growing interest in performance assessment and benchmarking

Until the 1980s, the systematic monitoring and comparing of airport economic performance was not a widely practised activity within the airport industry. This can largely be attributed to insufficient commercial and business pressures for airports and the general lack of experience of benchmarking techniques within the public sector as a whole. The difficulties involved with producing meaningful comparisons, such as varying involvement in airport activities and different accounting policies, only further discouraged most airports from seriously attempting to analyse their comparative performance.

With airport commercialization and privatization has come a marked interest in performance comparisons and benchmarking. As airports have become more commercially oriented, they have been keen to identify the strong performers in the industry and adopt what are seen as best practices. Senior managers can use performance measures to help them define goals and targets. Comparative performance analysis can also give valuable insight into issues such as whether privatized airports are more efficiently run than public sector airports, what is the best organizational framework for an airport and whether airports operated as part of national networks or systems perform better than individual airports. There is, thus, a growing recognition of the value of continuous performance appraisal within the airport industry.

Many other organizations external to the airport sector are also showing a keen interest in using performance measures to compare achievements between airports. Such organizations will have a different ultimate objective for comparing performance and, hence, are likely to view the findings from a different perspective. Investors and bankers, who are traditionally much more used to using financial ratios and other benchmarking techniques than airport operators are anxious to identify possible business opportunities and to ensure that their chosen airport investments continue to perform well. Airlines, now operating in a much more cost-conscious and competitive environment, have an interest in identifying which airports are being inefficiently managed – particularly to add substance to any lobby against increases in user charges. Economic regulators of privatized or autonomously managed airports also have good reasons to monitor airport performance to ensure that users are being fairly charged and that the airports are run efficiently and increasingly a number of regulators have commissioned airport benchmarking studies (e.g. see National Economic Research Associates, 2001; Irish Commission for Aviation Regulation, 2001, 2005; CAA, 2002; see also Chapter 5). Finally local communities may also be anxious to ensure that the airport is being run in an efficient manner to ensure that they can benefit fully from the economic benefits, such as tourism and inward investment, which the airport can bring.

Analysing an airport's economic performance has therefore become an important task for many of those involved, directly or indirectly, with the airport industry. Economic performance appraisal is, of course, only one aspect of airport performance which needs to be assessed (Humphreys and Francis, 2002; Graham, 2005). There are a wide range of operational activities which need to be monitored by looking at measures relating to airside delays, baggage delivery, terminal processing times, equipment availability and so on. In addition consumer satisfaction levels also need to be assessed, typically through passenger surveys. Moreover with the growing concern for the environment there is an increasing use of environmental indicators at airports. These areas are considered in detail in other chapters but the inter-relationships between these different aspects of performance must be recognized. Clearly any decision on service levels or operational procedures will greatly influence an airport's cost and manning levels and vice versa.

Related to this, it should also be noted that there is a growing area of performance measurement which is involved with measuring the detailed processes which the airport undertakes to understand why certain levels of performance exist. This is called bottom-up or process benchmarking, but clearly has large demands on the data which needs to be gathered (Jacobs Consultancy, 2007). As an example, in the UK Civil Aviation Authority's recent review of BAA, consultants were commissioned to do process benchmarking to investigate various aspects of operational performance such as central security search, trolley management and the management of check-in infrastructure and baggage systems.

Performance concepts

Performance measures analyse the relationship between inputs and outputs at an airport. This relationship can be expressed in both financial and physical terms. As with other businesses, labour and capital are the major inputs of the airport system. The simplest physical measure of the labour input is the total number of employees. Any part-time and temporary staff should be converted to full-time equivalents. To capture the effect of the cost of labour as well as productivity per head, the labour input can also be measured in financial terms, namely employee wages and salaries.

Determining a reliable measure of the capital input is much more difficult. In physical terms, capital input is measured by the production capability or capacity of the system. At an airport this cannot be assessed by one measure. The capacity of the runways, terminal, gates and so on have to be considered. Capacity can be measured on an hourly, daily, or annual basis. Depreciation or asset values can be used to measure the financial capital input. These will, however, reflect the accounting policies of the specific airport and may not always be closely related to its economic production capability.

The financial measurement of output is relatively straightforward and can be measured by considering the total revenues generated. Physically, the output of an airport can be assessed in three ways: in terms of quantities of aircraft, passengers, and freight. These measures do not cover all aspects of an airport, for example, its role as a retail facility, but they do capture the key outputs. The use of aircraft movements is not ideal as such measures will not differentiate between different sizes and different types of aircraft. Since most airports handle both passengers and freight, this suggests the use of an output measure which combines the two, such as the WLU. The WLU originated from the airline industry and uses a weight criterion for combining these two types of traffic (i.e. one WLU = one passenger or 100 kg of freight). Some argue, however, that the focus should be on passenger numbers since freight handling at airports is very much an airline activity and has little impact on an airport's economic performance.

The WLU, although probably the most widely accepted aggregate measure, is a rather arbitrary method of linking the two outputs since the same weight of passengers and freight does not involve using the same resources. Ideally, the WLU formula should, therefore, reflect the relative importance or value of the different outputs and, perhaps, include an aircraft movement element. Costs or employee numbers associated with the different outputs could theoretically be used to determine the scaling factor but there is the major problem of joint costs or joint tasks undertaken by the staff. An alternative scaling parameter is the relative prices of the outputs but this assumes a close relationship between price and cost which is not usually the case because of market imperfections, regulation and government interference and, sometimes, cross-subsidies between different traffic. There is the additional problem that there are even different costs and revenues associated with different passenger types, the most notable examples being international and domestic passengers and terminal and transfer passengers.

There has been some research undertaken in this area to investigate whether a more appropriate output measure can be found which takes into account all three key outputs of an airport, namely aircraft movements and size, passengers, and freight (Vallint, 1998). The Transport Research Laboratory which at this time was producing an annual global benchmarking study started using the airport throughput unit (ATU) which combines output measures of WLUs per ATM and WLUs and is defined as:

$$\text{ATUs} = \frac{(\text{WLUs})^2}{\text{ATMs}} = (\text{WLUs}) \times \frac{(\text{WLUs})}{\text{ATMs}}$$

However it can be argued that WLUs per ATMs ratio is actually a productivity measure as the use of a large aircraft compared to a smaller one (or a full plane compared to a partially full plane) is making more efficient use of airfield facilities. Hence this ATU value which is intended to be a measure of output actually also has a component which is productivity related. Therefore a different measure of ATUs is now used by Jacobs Consultancy which has currently undertaken the benchmarking study:

$$\text{ATU} = \text{Passengers} + 10 \times \text{freight tonnes} + 100 \times \text{ATMs}$$

It thus keeps the WLU relationship of 1:10 between passengers and freight but also includes an aircraft movement component. The value of 100 was derived by looking at past studies and determining that handling one ATM requires approximately the same effort as handling one hundred WLUs. The Spanish airports operator AENA uses a slightly different unit of airport activity (UAA) which includes an additional output unit to take account principally of general aviation movements so that it can compare its performance with airports that have very little commercial traffic. Hence the definition is (Jacobs Consultancy, 2007):

$$UAA = \text{Commercial passengers} + 10 \times \text{freight tones} + 100 \times \text{commercial ATMs} + 5 \times \text{other types of transport}$$

To summarize, performance measures or indicators are all about relating one or more of the outputs to one or more inputs. By using a number of these indicators, an airport can assess different aspects of its performance and identify where its strengths and weaknesses lie. These indicators can be grouped into certain categories such as cost efficiency, labour and capital productivity, revenue generation and commercial performance and profitability. In addition to these input: output ratios, a few other key measures such as the share of revenue from aeronautical sources or the percentage of costs which are allocated to staff can give further insights into comparative performance. There are around fifteen to twenty indicators which are commonly used (Doganis, 1992; Ashford and Moore, 1999; Humphreys and Francis, 2000). Table 3.7 presents the most popular indicators. Some of these have been used for the analysis of specific markets such as France (Assaily, 1989) and Australia (Doganis *et al.*, 1994) or more generally to compare airport performance within Europe (Doganis and Graham, 1987; Doganis *et al.*, 1995; Graham and Lobbenberg, 1995) or around the world (Jacobs Consultancy, 2007). In 2000, a survey of 200 of the world's largest airports was undertaken by Loughborough University and the UK Open University to investigate how airports themselves were measuring their performance (Francis *et al.*, 2001). Some of the most popular measures used were found to be cost per passenger and total, aeronautical and non-aeronautical revenue per passenger whilst revenue per WLU, for example, was a less used indicator. The airport organization, ACI also collects data related to some of the indicators. For example, ACI-Europe has a database which contains around 30 economic indicators for 30 airport companies whereas ACI-North America has a macro-benchmarking survey which looks at five key indicators as well as having a more detailed 'Airport Initiative in Measurement Benchmarking Study (AIM)' which looks at 52 indicators (ACI, 2006).

While airport managers will be very keen to understand how efficiently the airport is using its infrastructure and how cost effectively it is doing so, the financial sector will be more focused on ratios related to the business potential of the airport such as profit levels, liquidity ratios and capital expenditure levels. In the international financial markets, profit excluding depreciation is known as earnings before interest, tax, depreciation and amortization (EBITDA) and profit including depreciation is known as EBIT. Another indicator which can be used is the EBITDA or EBIT margin which is the earnings expressed as a percentage of revenue. Operating profit:total

Table 3.7 Performance indicators commonly used to assess economic performance

1. Cost efficiency
    Costs excluding depreciation per WLU
    Costs including depreciation per WLU
    Depreciation costs per WLU
    Labour costs per WLU
    Depreciation share of operating costs
    Labour share of operating costs
2. Labour productivity
    WLU per employee
    Revenues per employee
3. Capital productivity
    WLU/total assets
    Revenues/total assets
    Total assets per employee
4. Revenue generation
    Revenues per WLU
    Aeronautical revenues per WLU
    Non-aeronautical revenues per WLU
    Aeronautical share of total revenues
5. Commercial performance
    Concession plus rental revenues per passenger
    Concession revenues per passenger
6. Profitability
    Operating margin
    Operating profit excluding depreciation per WLU
    Operating profit including depreciation per WLU
    Operating profit including/excluding depreciation/total assets
    Net retained profit after interest and taxation per WLU

Notes: Only operating revenues and costs have been included (i.e. interest, extraordinary items, taxation, and dividends are excluded) with the exception of last indicator (net retained profit after interest and taxation per WLU). Some analysts use passenger numbers rather than WLUs and may include aircraft movements as an airport output measure as well.

assets is commonly referred to as ROCE or return on assets. Putting the traditional indicators in these financial terms enables comparisons to be easily made with other business sectors. Other standard financial ratios such as the interest cover (EBIT:interest) the dividend cover (post-tax profit/dividends), or gearing (debt as a share of shareholders funds) can be used to assess the financial well-being and capital structure of the airport company. Capital expenditure (Capex) per WLU or passenger, employee, or revenues can also give an indication as to the amount of investment which is taking place (Vogel and Graham, 2006).

For the publicly quoted airport companies such as Fraport and Vienna, additional indicators associated with the value of the company can be used. A number of these ratios relate the enterprise value

(EV), which shows the market value of the company's core businesses, to sales, earnings, or throughput (e.g. EV:total revenues; EV:EBITDA; EV:EBIT; EV:WLU). Reference has already been made to these 'value' ratios in Chapter 2 when privatization trends were considered. The price earnings ratio (PER), which shows the relationship between the price of the share and earnings attributable to that share, can also be used (e.g., see Credit Suisse, 2006).

Inter-airport performance

Producing meaningful inter-airport performance indicators is fraught with difficulties because of serious problems of comparability – particularly due to the varying range of activities undertaken by airport operators themselves. Comparing indicators from the raw data can give misleading impressions as airports involved with more activities would inevitably have higher cost and revenues levels and poorer labour productivity.

This problem can be overcome by standardizing or normalizing the airport data so that each airport's performance is presented as if it undertook a uniform set of activities by taking into account the typical profit margins associated with each separate airport activity. For example, if an airport operator undertakes ground handling activities itself, the assumed costs, revenues, and staff numbers associated with this can be deducted in order to make the data more comparable with airports that have no involvement with this activity. A hypothetical concession income from handling agents can then be added to the airport's revenues. Similar adjustments can be made for car parking and other commercial activities. This is the approach used by Jacobs in their airport benchmarking work (Jacobs Consultancy, 2007). In the United States there is also a comparability problem because in some cases the airlines have developed and operated the terminals. One option here which has been used in benchmarking studies is to add in the relevant airline data to ensure that more 'like-with-like' assessments are being made (ACI, 2006). However there will obviously be an element of subjectivity in any assumptions which are used when making adjustments. Moreover making such adjustments will inevitably mean that there is a movement away from reality – which may be less helpful for the airports concerned – and the complementarity of the different activities or the reasons why the airport chooses to provide certain services may be ignored. Ideally, the accounts of each airport could also be adjusted to conform to a common treatment of depreciation, asset values and so on as well, but normally this is too difficult a task. Another way to overcome some of these comparability problems is to aim to choose a set of airports which are as similar as possible but this is often a very difficult task given the multi-dimensional nature of airport operations and data limitations.

Another issue to be faced in comparing airport performance is the difference in cost of living between countries. Official exchange rates may not be a close reflection of relative prices at different airports in different countries. This problem can be addressed by using purchasing power parity exchange rates, rather than market exchange rates. Purchasing power parity exchange rates are calculated by dividing the cost of a given basket of goods in one currency by the cost of the same basket of goods in another country. So, effectively, they convert currencies on the basis of equalizing buying power rather than on the basis of prevailing market conditions. They also overcome problems of currency fluctuations during the period under investigation. Alternatively the special drawing right (SDR) which is a basket of four currencies (the euro, the US dollar, pound sterling and the yen) weighted according to the relative importance of the currency in international trade and finance can be used to overcome the currency fluctuation problem.

Figure 3.2 presents sample indicators, namely total costs per 1000 ATUs from the Jacobs Consultancy benchmarking study which adjusts the data to produce a standardized airport. Forty four airports from the study have been selected from North America, Europe and Asia Pacific. The figure shows quite clearly how the Asian Pacific airports (except Toyko Narita) and the North American airports (except San Francisco and Toronto) have a cost advantage over the European airports.

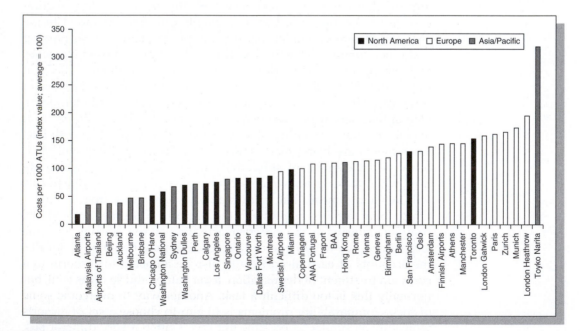

Figure 3.2
Total costs per 1000 ATUs for world airports 2005/2006
(*Source*: Jacobs).

Overall efficiency measures

The performance measures in Table 3.7 are partial measures in that they give an indication of performance which relates specifically to the inputs and outputs that have been chosen. These measures usually require limited data only (unless the data is being adjusted), are relatively easy to compute, and are intuitively simple to understand. They can highlight strengths and weaknesses in certain areas and indicate to management where specific improvements can be made but they cannot give an overall picture or identify the 'best in class'. By definition, they only give a 'partial' and rather disjointed diagnosis of the situation and can be misleading if only selected indicators are chosen. Moreover these measures cannot take account of factor substitution, for example if one airport uses an employee to undertake a specific task whilst another may use a machine.

These shortcomings can be overcome by investigating the relationship between the combined inputs and combined outputs to produce a single or an overall efficiency measure. In contrast to other transport operations and public sector organizations there was little exploration of the use of such methodologies until the 1990s, with the airport sector preferring to concentrate mostly on partial measures (Lemaitre, 1998). Since then there has been growing interest in these alternative measures and a considerable number of efficiency studies have been undertaken for various countries and regions of the world (see Table 3.8), albeit that many of these have focused on technical or operating efficiency and productivity analysis rather than purely financial or economic performance – primarily due to the data problems associated with the financial data (Vogel and Graham, 2006).

There are a number of different ways in which overall efficiency or total factor productivity (TFP) can be assessed (CAA, 2000). A parametric or statistical approach can be adopted by using a production or cost function which recognizes several variables influencing performance. For example, the cost function expresses cost as a function of outputs, input prices and other factors, such as traffic characteristics, which may influence output or input. This function can be estimated by using regression analysis (ordinary or corrected least squares) or by the stochastic frontier method which involves the estimation of a 'frontier' and the airport is only efficient if it operates on the frontier. These models can be used to investigate factor substitution, the impact of variations of input and output prices and to test for economies of scale. Examples include an assessment of the performance of BAA (Tolofari, 1989), 40 Spanish airports (Martin-Cejas, 2002) and a cross-sample of 34 European airports (Pels et al., 2001). However this approach has detailed data requirements and has not been used very often for airports.

Alternatively, a non-parametric index numbers method, such as the Tornqvist total factor productivity, can be used. This requires the aggregation of all outputs into a weighted outputs index and all inputs

Table 3.8 Examples of airport efficiency studies

Authors	Date of publication	Methodology	Coverage
Tolofari	1989	Parametric TFP	BAA UK airports
Prices Surveillance Authority	1993	Index number TFP	6 Australian airports
Gillen and Lall	1997	DEA	US 23 airports
Hooper and Hensher	1997	Index number TFP	6 Australian airports
Graham and Holvad	1997	DEA	25 European/12 Australian airports
Parker	1999	DEA	BAA and 16 other UK airports
Murillo-Melchor	1999	DEA/Malmquist index	33 Spanish airports
Salazar de la Cruz	1999	DEA	16 Spanish airports
Jessop	1999	DEA/Multi-attribute assessment	32 major international airports
Nyshadham and Rao	2000	Index number TFP	25 European airports
Sarkis	2000	DEA	44 US airports
Pels *et al.*	2001	DEA/Parametric TFP	34 European airports
Gillen and Law	2001	DEA/Malmquist index	22 US airports
Martin and Roman	2001	DEA	37 Spanish airports
Abbott and Wu	2002	DEA/Malmquist index	12 Australian airports
Martin-Cejas	2002	Parametric TFP	40 Spanish airports
Pacheco and Fernandes	2002	DEA	33 Brazilian airports
Bazargan and Vasigh	2003	DEA	45 US airports
Holvad and Graham	2003	DEA	21 UK airports
Barros and Sampaio	2004	DEA	13 Portuguese airports
Sarkis and Talluri	2004	DEA	44 US airports
Yoshida	2004	Endogenous weight TFP	30 Japanese airports
Hanaoka and Phomma	2004	DEA	12 Thai airports
Kamp and Niemeier	2005	DEA/Malmquist index	17 European airports
Vogel	2006	DEA	35 European airports
Vasigh and Gorjidooz	2006	Index number TFP	22 US and European airports
Barros and Dieke	2007	DEA	31 Italian airports
Fung *et al.*	2007	DEA/Malmquist index	25 Chinese airports

Source: Author.

into a weighted input index with no assumptions or estimates of the parameters of the underlying production or cost functions having to be made. The outputs are weighted by revenue shares and the inputs are weighted by input cost shares. Such a technique has been used to assess the performance of Australian airports (PSA, 1993; Hooper and Hensher, 1998), 25 European airports (Nyshadham and Rao, 2000) and 22 US and European airports (Vasigh and Gorjidooz, 2006).

A third TFP approach is the endogenous-weight TFP (EW-TFP) method. Unlike the index number TFP, detailed cost or revenue data is not needed for this approach. A multi-input/multi-output production function is specified instead and then physical and financial

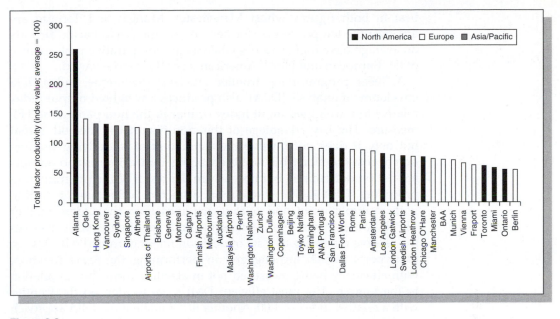

Figure 3.3
Total factor productivity (net variable factor measure) for world airports 2005/2006
(*Source*: ATRS).

input and output data is used to estimate it. This method has been applied to Japanese airports (Yoshida, 2004).

One of the most comprehensive studies of TFP in the airport sector is contained in the Global Airport Benchmarking Report which is produced annually (since 2002) by the Air Transport Research Society (ATRS, 2007). The 2007 report looked at 142 airports and 14 airport groups in Asia Pacific, Europe and North America. It considered various partial measures of performance but unlike the Jacobs' global study it did not adjust the data to take account of different involvement in activities. The TFP method that was adopted as an index number approach using revenue shares as weights for the outputs (aircraft movements, passengers, cargo and other revenue) and cost shares as weights for the inputs (labour, other non-capital inputs, runways, terminals, gates). The capital input was excluded in most measures because of the difficulties in obtaining accurate, comparable data for this. Two overall TFP measures were produced – the 'gross' value and the 'net' value. The net value had the effect of certain factors which were considered beyond management control removed, such as airport size, the share of international and cargo traffic and capacity constraints, in order to leave a measure which was more likely to reflect managerial efficiency. This value is shown in Figure 3.3 for the same 44 airports which were included in Figure 3.2 – the higher the score, the better the performance. Whilst different methodologies and data sets have been used to produce the measures in both these figures, it is interesting to observe that Atlanta performs best in both figures whilst Manchester, Munich and Toronto are amongst the ten poorest performers. Again the Asian Pacific airports on average have higher values whereas the comparative performance of the European and North American airports is more varied.

A linear programming frontier efficiency technique, called data envelopment analysis (DEA), also produces a weighted output index relative to a weighted input index similar to the non-parametric TFP measure. The key advantage of this non-parametric method is that not only it does not involve the estimation of underlying production or cost functions, but also the weights for the inputs and outputs are not predetermined but instead are the result of the programming procedure. DEA is therefore a more attractive technique for dealing with multiple input and output activities than the index number TFP because it has less demanding data requirements. It assesses the relative efficiency of a set of decision making units (DMUs), such as airports, which are engaged in performing the same function, with efficiency being measured not in absolute terms but in relation to the sample. The most efficient DMUs are located on the frontier with a relative index of 1.00. Another advantage of the DEA approach is that it can be used to measure scale effects on airports as there are both constant and variable returns to scale models. However a key limitation of DEA is its sensitivity to outliers and parameter selection and the results may be very different if the input and output selection is different. Moreover if the combined number of inputs/outputs is large relative to the DMUs, DEA tends to overstate performance and leads to many DMUs achieving a maximum efficiency value of 1. DEA produces relative rankings but does not by itself explain the observations. This can be partially overcome with the application of the Malmquist index which when used with DEA is a useful way of identifying the sources of productivity differences over a certain time period as this index allows productivity change to be decomposed into technical changes gained from adopting new technologies and efficiency changes (which in turn can be decomposed into gains from utilizing scale and gains from reducing inefficiency).

DEA and Malmquist techniques have been the most popular method used to assess airport efficiency. In the United Kingdom, Parker (1999) assessed the performance of BAA airports whilst Holvad and Graham (2003) investigated a wider sample of UK airports. Gillen and Lall (1997, 2001), Sarkis (2000), Sarkis and Talluri (2004) and Bazargan and Vasigh (2003) have all investigated the performance of US airports. Performance of airports in other countries has also been examined, for example in Spain (Murillo-Melchor,1999; Salazar de la Cruz, 1999; Martin and Roman, 2001), Portugal (Barros and Sampaio, 2004), Italy (Barros and Dieke, 2007) Germany (Kamp and Niemeier, 2005), Australia (Abbott and Wu, 2002), Brazil (Pacheco and Fernandes, 2003), Thailand (Hanaoka and Phomma, 2004) and China (Fung et al., 2007). Broader regional studies have also been undertaken when for example Graham and Holvad (1997) compared the performance of European and Australian airports, or when Pels *et al.* (2001) and Vogel (2006) assessed comparative European performance.

Finally a multi-attribute approach has also been considered to assess airport performance but has not been widely used. This combines a number of partial performance measures as a weighted sum of inputs. For each measure airports are measured according to how they perform relative to other airports – with a score of 1 for best performer and 0 for worst performer. The weighted sum of these scores gives an overall unitless summary efficiency measure. These weights are assigned to the ratios according to the analyst's preference which can result in different estimates of performance for different analysts. Alternatively equal weights can be applied or the probability distributions for the value of each weight can be used. Decisions also have to be made as to which partial measures are included. This method has been used with a sample of around 35 global airports with six performance measures, namely: EBITDA, concession revenues per passenger, aeronautical revenues per ATM, ATUs per unit of asset value, ATUs per employee, and operating costs per passenger (Jessop, 1999; TRL, 2002).

In summary, over the last decade or so there has been an increasing number of performance techniques which have been applied to the airport industry and this has helped to raise the understanding of comparative airport performance which was previously very limited. Each of these methods have their own advantages and disadvantages, covers various aspects of performance and requires different data and assumptions. The majority of studies have been confined to one specific country, because of the problems of obtaining detailed and comparable data for a number of different countries, although some cross-country research has also been attempted. Moreover the shortcomings of the partial performance measures have suggested that it might be useful to consider the relationship of the combined inputs with the combined output produced, when the difficult task of interpreting a varied set of partial indicators is spared and in some cases influencing variables, such as economies of scale can be taken into account. However with such an aggregate overall efficiency value it may not always be apparent what this it is measuring and thus it may not be very informative for management action unless more additional research to explore the observed differences is undertaken. Nevertheless it does seem now that airport benchmarking has generally been accepted as a useful exercise to undertake. With continuing research hopefully some of the shortcomings of the current approaches may be overcome.

References and further reading

Abbott, M. and Wu, S. (2002). Total factor productivity and efficiency of Australian airports. *The Australian Economic Review*, 35(3), 244–260.

Airport Council International (ACI) (2000). *ACI Airport Economics Survey 1998.* ACI.

Airports Council International (ACI) (2006). *Airport Benchmarking to Maximize Efficiency.* ACI.

Airport Council International (ACI) (2007). *ACI Airport Economics Survey 2006.* ACI.

ACI-Europe (2005). *Building for the Future: Paying for the Airports of Tomorrow.* ACI-Europe.

Air Transport Research Society (ATRS) (2007). *Global Airport Benchmarking Report.* ATRS.

Ashford, N. and Moore, C. (1999). *Airport Finance,* (2nd edn.) Loughborough Airport Consultancy.

Assaily, C. (1989). *Airport Productivity.* Institute of Air Transport.

Barros, C. and Sampaio, A. (2004). Technical and allocative efficiency in airports. *International Journal of Transport Economics,* 31(3), 355–377.

Barros, C. and Dieke, P. (2007). Performance evaluation of Italian airports: A data envelopment analysis. *Journal of Air Transport Management,* 13, 184–191.

Bazargan, M. and Vasigh, B. (2003). Size versus efficiency: A case study of US commercial airports. *Journal of Air Transport Management,* 9, 187–193.

Civil Aviation Authority (CAA). (2000). *The use of benchmarking in airport reviews.* Consultation paper. CAA.

Civil Aviation Authority (CAA) (2002). *Manchester Airport's price cap, 2003–2008: CAA recommendations to the Competition Commission.* CAA.

Credit Suisse. (2006). *European airports: No rush to board.* Credit Suisse.

Doganis, R. (1992). *The Airport Business.* Routledge.

Doganis, R. and Graham, A. (1987). *Airport management: The role of performance indicators.* Transport Studies Group Research Report 13, University of Westminster (formerly Polytechnic of Central London).

Doganis, R., Graham, A. and Lobbenberg, A. (1994). *A Comparative Study of Value for Money at Australian and European Airports.* Cranfield University.

Doganis, R., Graham, A. and Lobbenberg, A. (1995). *The economic performance of European airports.* Department of Air Transport Research Report 3, Cranfield University.

Doganis, R. S. and Thompson, G. F. (1973). *The economics of British airports.* Transport Studies Group Research Report 1, University of Westminster (formerly Polytechnic of Central London).

Francis, G., Fry, J. and Humphreys, I. (2001). *An international survey of performance measurement in airports.* Open University Business School Working Paper 01/4, Open University.

Fung, M., Wan, K., Hui, Y. and Law, J. (2007). Productivity changes in Chinese airports. *Transportation Research Part E,* 44(3), 521–542.

Gillen, D. and Lall, A. (1997). Developing measures of airport productivity and performance: An application of data envelopment analysis. *Transportation Research*, 33E(4), 261–274.

Gillen, D. and Lall, A. (2001). Non-parametric measures of efficiency of US airports. *International Journal of Transport Economics*, 28(3), 283–306.

Graham, A. (2005). Airport benchmarking: A review of the current situation. *Benchmarking: An International Journal*, 12(2), 99–111.

Graham, A. (2006). Assessing the economic challenges facing regional airports in today's environment: Turning these challenges into opportunities, *Global Airport Development Conference*, Rome, November.

Graham, A. and Lobbenberg, A. (1995). Benchmarking European airports. *Airports International*, May, 12–14.

Graham, A. and Holvad, T. (1997). Efficiency variations for European and Australian airports. *EURO XV/INFORMS Joint International Conference*, Barcelona, July.

Hanaoka, S. and Phomma, S. (2004). Privatisation and productivity performance of Thai airports. *Air Transport Research Society Conference*, Istanbul, July.

Holvad, T. and Graham, A. (2003). Efficiency measurement for UK airports: An application of data envelopment analysis. *VIII European Workshop on Efficiency and Productivity*, Oviedo, September.

Hooper, P. and Hensher, D. (1998). *Measuring total factor productivity of airports – An index number approach*. Institute of Transport Studies Working Paper ITS-WP-98-2, Monash University.

Humphreys, I. and Francis, G. (2000). *Traditional airport performance indicators*. Transportation Research Board, no. 1703.

Humphreys, I. and Francis, G. (2002). Performance measurement: A review of airports. *International Journal of Transport Management*, 1, 79–85.

International Civil Aviation Organization (ICAO) (1991). *Airport economics manual*. ICAO, Doc. 9562.

International Civil Aviation Organization (ICAO). (2000). *Financial situation of airports and air navigation services*. ANSConf Working Paper No. 3, ICAO.

Irish Commission for Aviation Regulation (2001). *Report on the reasons for the determination*. Irish Commission for Aviation Regulation.

Irish Commission for Aviation Regulation (2005). *The performance of Dublin Airport: The findings of the comparative reports of the TRL and the ATRS*. Irish Commission for Aviation Regulation.

Jacobs Consultancy (2007). *Airport performance indicators 2007*. Jacobs.

Jessop, A. (1999). A multiattribute assessment of airport performance. *Twenty-fifth Euro Working Group on Financial Modelling of the Institut für Finanzierung und Finanzmarkte*, Vienna, November.

Kamp, V. and Niemeier, H.-M. (2005). Benchmarking of German airports – Some first results and an agenda for further research, *Air Transport Research Society Conference*, Rio, July.

Kamp, V., Niemeier, H.-M. and Mueller, J. (2007). What can be learned from benchmarking studies? Examining the apparent poor performance of German airports. *Journal of Airport Management*, 1(3), 294–308.

Lemaitre, A. (1998). The development of performance indicators at airports. *Air Transport Research Group Conference*, Vancouver, July.

Martin, J. and Roman, C. (2001). An application of DEA to measure the efficiency of Spanish airports prior to privatisation. *Journal of Air Transport Management*, 7, 149–157.

Martin-Cejas, R. (2002). An approximation to the productive efficiency of the Spanish airports network through a deterministic cost frontier'. *Journal of Air Transport Management*, 8, 233–238.

Murillo-Melchor, C. (1999). An analysis of the technical efficiency and productive change in Spanish airports using the Malmquist Index. *International Journal of Transport Economics*, 26(2), 271–291.

National Economic Research Associates (2001). *The Application of Benchmarking to Airports Phase 1: Date Collection and Assessment*. NERA.

Nyshadham, E. and Rao, V. (2000). Assessing efficiency of European airports. *Public Works Management and Policy*, 5(1), 106–114.

Pacheco, R. and Fernandes, E. (2003). Managerial efficiency of Brazilian airports. *Transportation Research*, 37A(4), 667–680.

Parker, D. (1999). The performance of BAA before and after privatization: A DEA study. *Journal of Transport Economics and Policy*, 33(2), 133–146.

Pels, E., Nijkamp, P. and Rietveld, P. (2001). Relative efficiency of European airports. *Transport Policy*, 8, 183–192.

Pilling, M. and O'Toole, K. (2002). Airports: Gloves off. *Airline Business*, December, 38–39.

Prices Surveillance Authority (PSA) (1993). *Inquiry into the aeronautical and non-aeronautical charges of the Federal Airports Corporation*. PSA.

Salazar de la Cruz, F. (1999). A DEA approach to the airport production function. *International Journal of Transport Economics*, 26(2), 255–270.

Sarkis, J. (2000). An analysis of the operational efficiency of major airports in the United States. *Journal of Operations Management*, 18, 335–351.

Sarkis, J. and Talluri, S. (2004). Performance based clustering for benchmarking of US airports. *Transportation Research*, 38A, 329–346.

SH&E (2006). *Capital needs and regulatory oversight arrangement: A survey of European airports*. SH&E.

Tolofari, S.R. (1989). *Airport cost and productivity analysis: Summary of research results*. Department of Transport Technology, Loughborough University.

Toms, M. (2000). Critique of cost benchmarking. *CAA Workshop on Benchmarking of Airports: Methodologies, Problems and Relevance to Economic Regulation*, London, September.

Transport Research Laboratory (TRL) (2000). *Airport performance indicators 2000*. TRL.

Transport Research Laboratory (TRL) (2002). *Airport performance indicators 2002*. TRL.

Vallint, J. (1998). *The suitability of the work load unit as a measure of airport output*. Unpublished MSc transport thesis, University of Westminster, Westminster.

Vasigh, B. and Gorjidooz, J. (2006). Productivity analysis of public and private airports: A causal investigation. *Journal of Air Transportation*, 11(3), 144–163.

Vogel, H. (1997). *Privatization of European commercial airports: motivations, valuations and implications*. Unpublished MBA thesis, Emery-Riddle University, FL.

Vogel, H. (2006). Airport privatisation: Ownership structure and financial performance of European commercial airports. *Competition and Regulation in Network Industries*, 1(2), 139–162.

Vogel, H. and Graham, A. (2006). A comparison of alternative airport performance measurement techniques: A European case study. *Journal of Airport Management*, 1(1), 59–74.

Yoshida, Y. (2004). Endogenous-weight TFP measurement: Methodology and its application to Japanese-airport benchmarking. *Transportation Research*, 40E, 151–182.

CHAPTER 4

Airport operations and service quality

In recent years, structural changes such as commercialization, privatization, and globalization, together with increased competition between airports, have encouraged airports to place more emphasis on quality. Airports which have become regulated in their post-privatization stage, such as at the London airports have also found that their service quality has been the subject of increased scrutiny by the regulators. Moreover airlines have been more anxious to ensure that they get 'value for money' for their fees which they are paying whilst pressure is also coming from the travelling public who are becoming more experienced and demanding consumers of the airport product.

At the same time there have been some major developments in the way that some key processes at airports are provided. This has been partly due to legal and regulatory changes, particularly in the area of security and border control, as the industry has had to adjust to new risks and threats to the business. It has also been as the result of technological innovations that have been applied not only to security and border control but also to other areas, particularly check-in. All of this is having major impacts on the provision of service quality at the airports – even though in many cases the airport operator itself will not be directly involved in the provision of these processes. These effects are extensive, influencing space allocation and efficiency whilst at the same time having an impact on both aeronautical and non-aeronautical revenue generation.

Thus this chapter aims to consider these key issues relating to airport operations and service quality. However the airport business is a very complex one that involves many different processes and activities which would not be possible to cover in a single chapter. Hence the emphasis is on areas where very significant changes have occurred and which have already, or have potential in the future, to produce far reaching impacts on service quality and other aspects of airport management.

Differentiation of service levels

Traditionally most airports and their airline customers offered a common set of services and facilities in trying to serve passengers with different expectations with very little segmentation taking place at the airports. The most notable differentiation was separate check-in for economy and business class passengers and remote stands rather than airbridges for passengers travelling on charter airlines. This level of segmentation was then increased with businesses travellers having access to 'fast-track' systems which guide them swiftly through various processes such as immigration and customs. At the same time the use of airline and airline alliance lounges for premium class and frequent flying passengers expanded rapidly and has now become the norm. However it is not just the business passengers who can now benefit from specialist services. At some airports, such as

London Stansted airport, any passenger can have access to a lounge if they pay for it. At other airports there may be special lounges for babies and children, such as the Babycare Lounge at Amsterdam airport, which has seven semi-transparent cubicles each with a little bed where the baby can sleep. Other facilities include seating for the rest of the family, baby baths, baby changing tables, play areas, and microwaves. Moreover in a few places there has been an attempt to introduce differentiated services elsewhere. A controversial example here is Liverpool airport, which has introduced a £2 security fast lane ticket that is available for all passengers.

The needs and requirements of airline alliance customers are different since they want to be able to share and get cost economies and brand benefits from operating joint facilities at airports. This is very different from when many airports in operation today were built when airlines were usually grouped together according to their type of traffic, such as domestic, short-haul, and long-haul. Whilst new terminals can be built with these different demands in mind, there is always the potential problem that alliance membership may change. Also when an airport has to be redesigned to cope with alliance wishes, it could be particularly difficult to ensure that no one alliance group is at a disadvantage. A notable example here is Heathrow airport after the opening of the new terminal five. This has given British Airways (BA) access to many new facilities and has meant that terminals one and two will now be redeveloped into 'Terminal East' to provide equivalent facilities for members of the Star alliance.

Airlines and passengers have not generally been in the position to unbundle the overall package of airport services and only pay for what they want. However the emergence of the low cost carrier (LCC) industry has created new challenges for airports in this area and is causing a number of airports to consider splitting up their services and to offer a differentiated product to different airline types. This is because LCCs have very different needs from the conventional carriers to ensure that they have quick turnaround times, can raise productivity, and can cut down costs. Moreover their focus on point-to-point services means that more complex passenger and baggage handling systems can be avoided (Table 4.1). These desires relate solely to the terminal and ramp operations, as obviously in terms of airfield operations the requirements have to be the same for all types of airlines to conform to international operational and safety standards and regulations.

For small regional airports, the arrival of LCCs has often been useful to fill up under-utilized existing infrastructure whilst at the same time the airlines have benefitted from uncongested facilities which help them achieve their fast turnarounds. However such a strategy may run into problems if demand grows to such a level that new facilities are needed and the airport charges (which will often be reduced to encourage LCC use) and the non-aeronautical revenues will not be sufficient to fund further investment. Nevertheless

Table 4.1 LCC needs and requirements of airport terminals

Service/facility	LCC needs and requirements
Overall terminal design	Simple, functional with low construction/operating costs
Check-in	Fewer desks than full service airlines (queues may be longer but an increasing number of LCCs are using web and self-service check-in)
Airline lounges	Not needed
Security	Efficient processes so that they do not delay aircraft boarding
Transfer facilities	Not needed (No transfer desks or handling systems for transfer baggage)
Airbridges	Preference for steps for quicker boarding and disembarking (with front and back steps)
Airfield buses	Preference for passengers to walk to/from aircraft if possible to save costs
Office accommodation	Simple and functional

there are many examples of regional airports, such as Liverpool and Prestwick in the UK, which have decided to focus purely on serving the LCC market and have subsequently developed the simplified facilities that these airlines require. Other examples include Finland, where Finavia, the governing body of the Finnish airports, introduced a 'low cost concept' at the small airport of Tampere–Pirkkala airport in 2003 and has decided to do the same in Turku. Outside Europe, this practice is generally not so common. Avalon near Melbourne in Australia is a rare example of an airport that has been developed for the operations of the LCC Jetstar.

In some cases, old disused military airports have been developed primarily to serve the LCC sector. This has been the case of London Manston airport (although currently unused by LCCs) and Robin Hood Doncaster airport in the UK. Frankfurt–Hahn, a former US airbase, is another example where initially the passenger terminal was a converted officers' club. Ryanair began services from the airport in 1999 and then in 2002 it set up a base there. Ryanair now offers its services to 27 destinations and in addition the airport is served by three other LCCs, namely Blue Air, Iceland Express, and Wizz Air. The passenger numbers have gone from just 90 000 passengers in 1999 to over 4 million in 2007. During this time the airport authorities have invested €17 million to give the airport a capacity of 5 million passengers. This is equivalent to an investment cost per passenger of €3.50 compared to €18.25 at Hamburg, €32.40 at Cologne–Bonn, and €60.00 at Munich. Rental space has increased from 180 square metres in 2002 to 3300 in 2005, whilst parking spaces have risen from 3433 to 9736. This means that non-aeronautical revenue now accounts for 35 per cent of all revenues. The airport does not charge a landing fee to airlines with fast turnarounds to minimize the fixed cost per turnaround and the passenger charge varies between € 5.35 for less than 100 000 passengers and €2.48 for 2 to 3 million passengers. There are further discounts beyond 3 million passengers. The airport offers a turnaround time of 25 minutes (Schumacher, 2006; Jacobs Consultancy 2007).

When an airport serves both full service and LCCs, it is a difficult task to meet the different and often conflicting needs of these two types of airlines. One option which is growing in popularity is to develop a specialized low cost facility or terminal. These have a simple design with lower service standards than expected in conventional terminals. Certain costs, for example those associated with the runway, navigational equipment, fire/rescue, and security, will be no different for airlines using the low cost terminals and so landing charges and security charges tend to be the same for all. However within the terminal the simpler design and lack of sophisticated equipment and facilities, such as airbridges, escalators, complex baggage systems, and airline lounges usually result in the airlines that use the terminal being charged a lower passenger charge. An alternative approach to handling LCC traffic is to have a competing terminal. The most notable case here is Ryanair that has lobbied unsuccessfully for a separate terminal for its operations in Dublin for many years. Then there is another option when two or more airports are under the same ownership. In this case one specific airport can deal with the low cost traffic as is the case with Hahn airport in Frankfurt (Fraport owns the main Frankfurt airport and Hahn), Ciampina in Rome (Aeroporti di Roma owns Fiumicino and Ciampina), and London Stansted (and more latterly Gatwick) in London (BAA owns Heathrow, Stansted and Gatwick).

Table 4.2 gives details of some presently existing low cost terminals and facilities. Some of these are refurbished existing facilities and some are dedicated new terminals. For example, Amsterdam airport has built Pier H&M (H for non-Schengen traffic, M for Schengen traffic) at a cost of around €30 million which has a simple design with no airbridges and functions within a 20-minute turnaround time. The passengers use the normal departure lounge with all the commercial facilities before proceeding to the pier. Marseilles has had a separate low cost terminal (MP2) that has been operational since 2006 and was converted from an old cargo facility at a cost of €16.4 million. Ryanair was the first airline to use MP2 when it established Marseille as its first base in France. Elsewhere in Europe, Budapest has also developed an LCC terminal at the cost of around €35 million, particularly to accommodate Wizz Air and Sky Europe who have bases there, and in 2004 Warsaw airport opened its Etiuda terminal, which originally had been an arrivals hall but more recently was used as a supermarket, furniture shop, and storage space. At all these airports, the

Table 4.2 Examples of LCC facilities and terminals

Airport	Date of opening	Type of terminal	Passenger capacity	Gross area (m²)	Airport charges policy	Airline users
Kuala Lumpur	2006	New terminal	10	35290	Cheaper passenger charges	Air Asia, Cebu Pacific Air, Tiger Airways
Singapore	2006	New terminal	2.7	25000	Cheaper passenger charges	Tiger Airways Cebu Pacific Air
Marseille	2006	Refurbished cargo terminal	3.5	7532	Cheaper passenger charges	Bmibaby, EasyJet, Flybe, Myair, Ryanair
Amsterdam	2005	Piers off existing terminal	4	6150	Cheaper landing charge for no airbridges	Various European LCCs
Budapest	2005	Refurbished old terminal	N/A	7990	Cheaper passenger charges	Wizz Air, Sky Europe, EasyJet, Germanwings, Norwegian, Sterling, Jet2.com
JFK	2008	New terminal incorporating old TWA terminal	15	58,000	No difference	JetBlue

Source: Jacobs Consultancy (2007) and airport websites.

passenger charge is lower for the low cost facility except at Amsterdam where there is a differential landing charge depending on whether an airbridge is used or not. In Lyon, in France, a new low cost terminal, which has involved refurbishing an existing charter facility, will be opened in 2008 at a cost of €1.2 million. It will be a base for easyJet (Falconer, 2006). Brussels airport is also planning to open an LCC facility in 2009.

There are also two main LCC facilities in South East Asia, at Singapore airport (the Budget Terminal) and Kuala Lumpur airport [the Low Cost Carrier Terminal (LCCT)], both opened in 2006. At both the airports, the passenger charges for the low cost terminal are lower and the rental charges at Singapore are also claimed to be half of those charged in the main terminal. There have also been discussions about providing similar facilities in Bangkok (maybe on the site of Old Don Muang airport), the Philippines, Indonesia, Dubai, and Delhi (Centre for Asia Pacific Aviation, 2007). In Mexico, at Monterrey airport, Terminal C is an LCC terminal. Southwest in the US already has low cost facilities at Baltimore–Washington, and at JFK airport in New York, the airport owners (the Port Authority of New York and New Jersey) are investing US$ 795 million in a new low cost terminal for JetBlue which will incorporate Eero Saarinen's iconic 1962 TWA terminal and will have an annual capacity of 20 million passengers. JetBlue will cover this investment with lease payments for 30 years and in addition has directly invested $80 million (Blacklock, 2006; Studness, 2007). Another interesting example is Austin–Bergstrom airport in Texas where a low cost terminal is being built and managed by the private aircraft leasing company GECAS primarily because of interest from the Mexican LCC VivaAeroBus that wants to launch cross border services from Austin (Rowe, 2007a).

Whilst these low cost terminals have generally been welcomed by the LCCs, the same has not always been true of the full service airlines. The latter often argue that these terminals are discriminatory against carriers that operate in the main terminals and that airports must ensure that all airlines have access to the new terminals. This does assume that all airlines would want to move to the new terminal, which is a debatable point given the lower service standards that they offer. Also the airlines maintain that airports should be focusing on the reduction of costs for all its airline customers and there should not be differential pricing. If there has to be differential pricing, these must be clearly justified by demonstrating the differential costs that exist so that the full service airlines do not end up subsidizing the LCCs (International Air Transport Association, 2007a). This is particularly relevant as there will be some costs for processes such as security which will be difficult to reduce in the low cost terminals. These concerns mean that the airlines have made a number of legal challenges. For example, at Geneva airport where easyJet is a major airline, there were plans to convert an old terminal into a low cost terminal but Air France-KLM objected and claimed that the lower passenger charge would give the LCCs a competitive advantage. The Swiss Federal Court rejected this but nevertheless Geneva has abandoned its low cost terminal development project. At Marseilles airport, Air France-KLM claimed that the differential charges between the main terminal and the low cost terminal were unreasonable. This has resulted in Marseilles airport discontinuing its separate charges in the main terminal and adopting a single €3.54 fee which is nearer to the €1.22 fee of the low cost terminal (Rowe, 2007a). At Amsterdam, Air France-KLM has also opposed the differential pricing, particularly as there is only a separate pier and not a separate terminal and so as a result many of the main terminal facilities are used by the LCC airlines and their passengers.

For airports, LCC terminals may be an effective and a cost-efficient way of coping with increasing demand, if the current terminal capacity is already well utilized. However if there is still spare capacity in the main terminal, the more favourable option must be to try to get the airlines to use this terminal. The worse case scenario would be when a significant amount of traffic just shifts from the old terminal to the new terminal, leaving the original terminal under utilized at a time when overall costs have increased because of the additional investment, and when aeronautical revenues have dropped with reduced charges for the new terminal. There is also a more general issue related to non-aeronautical revenues. Although most of the low cost terminals have commercial facilities, the revenue from these may be lower than what would have been generated in the main terminal because of a more limited retail offer and also because the basic terminal may not create the right atmosphere and experience to encourage travellers to shop.

At the same time that some airports have been developing terminals and facilities designed to meet the specific demands of the LCCs and their passengers, there has also been increased interest in the development of dedicated terminals for premium travellers at airports. Frankurt airport was one of the first airports to have such a terminal, which was opened by Lufthansa for its first class passengers in 2004. This terminal, which used to be an employee car park, offers upper range catering, showers, entertainment, personal and business facilities and allows a fast track through the security, immigration, and customs processes. Subsequently Qatar Airways opened a business and first class terminal in Doha in 2006, and in 2007 the former premium airline Silverjet opened its own terminal at Luton airport. In the same year Lufhansa opened another terminal in Munich, and in 2008 its subsidiary Swiss will open a similar terminal at Zürich airport (Sobie, 2007). There are also a few examples of whole airports being designed with the premium passengers in mind, such as London City, but these are relatively rare although elsewhere there are smaller private jet facilities also aimed at this market.

The LCCT at Kuala Lumpur

Kuala Lumpur airport is owned by Malaysia Airports Holdings Berhad. This company operates 5 international airports, 16 domestic airports, and 18 rural airports. It was listed on the Kuala Lumpur stock exchange in 1999. Kuala Lumpur airport opened in 1998 and since then passenger numbers have grown from 13 million to 25 million. The LCCT was designed for Air Asia whose total traffic for all operations has increased rapidly from just 611 000 passengers in 2002–2003 to over 5 million in 2006–2007. In both Malaysia and Thailand, Air Asia has the second largest domestic market share after Malaysia Airlines and Thai Airways International, respectively. Overall in 2006, 18 per cent of all passengers and 22 per cent of all movements were related to LCCs (Figure 4.1).

Work began on the LCCT in June 2005 which has a total area 35 290 square metres and a capacity of 10 million passengers. The construction work was fast-tracked and the terminal opened on 23 March 2006, costing in total RM106 million (€23 million). It is on a single floor and has a very simple design with no air-bridges, travellators or escalators, and basic baggage handling system. A number of commercial facilities are also provided (Table 4.3). There are no transfer facilities and therefore, if passengers

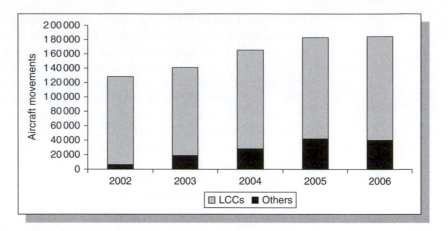

Figure 4.1
Aircraft movements at
Kuala Lumpur airport
2002–2006
(*Source*: Murad, 2007).

Table 4.3 Physical details of the LCCT at Kuala Lumpur

Check in	2650 m^2
	72 desks
Departure halls	International: 3240 m^2
	Domestic: 4430 m^2
	20 gates
Arrival halls	International: 4340 m^2
	Domestic: 1900 m^2
	7 gates
Public concourse	Main Area: 4355 m^2
	International Arrivals: 325 m^2
Common, ramp, and circulation	6760 m^2
Parking bays	30
Commercial facilities	2 Duty free outlets, 4 F&B outlets, 4 retail outlets, 1 foreign exchange

Source: Murad (2007) and airport website.

need to change flights with other carriers they have to travel the 20 km by road to the main terminal, although a rail link has been proposed. Currently Air Asia is the main airline using the terminal although Cebu Pacific Air and Tiger Airways also have some very limited services. There has also been some discussion about Jetstar Airways and Jet Airways using this facility in the future. As with other low cost terminals, all airlines pay the same landing charge but there is a reduced international passenger charge, namely RM 35 (€7.61) compared to RM 51 (€11.09). For a typical operation with an Airbus 319 or Boeing 737-800, this means that total charges paid for operating out of LCCT are about 70 per cent of those for the main terminal (Jacobs Consultancy,

2007). There is scope for expanding the terminal to a capacity of 15 million passengers, but the poor location of this facility, plus the growing LCC demand, has resulted in the airport proposing a total new 30 million annual passenger LCCT.

Service quality

Measuring the level of service

Irrespective of which airlines or passengers the airport's services and facilities are designed for, it is very important to measure the quality of service that is provided. With most service industries there is a particular problem with measuring the quality of service because of the characteristic uneven spread of demand. With many airports, for instance, a terminal will look and feel very different on a quiet Tuesday in winter compared to a busy summer Saturday during the school holidays. Likewise, passenger flows in the early morning or evening at an airport dominated by short-haul business traffic will be considerably greater than at other times of the day. This is bound to play a major role in influencing the passenger's perception of the quality of service provided.

Airports have the additional issue that the overall service is produced as a result of the combined activities of various organizations such as airlines, handling agents, customs and immigration officials, concessionaires, and so on. These different bodies may have different ultimate objectives and conflicting views on what determines satisfactory or good service. In effect, the airport operator only has partial control of all the processes which make up the final product. Areas of responsibility, therefore, have to be very clearly identified and the airport operator must define a common goal for all regarding the service quality. A further problem is that at many airports the airport product has to appeal to a very heterogeneous range of passengers unless they develop specialized terminals as discussed. Some passengers may want to get through the airport as quickly as possible with a minimum of distractions while others enjoy the opportunity of being able to shop and take refreshments. Business and leisure passengers may also have very different needs.

Airports have both objective and subjective measures of service quality. Objective indicators measure the service delivered and can cover areas such as flight delays, availability of lifts, escalators and trolleys, and operational research survey factors such as queue length, space provision, waiting time, and baggage reclaim time. To be accurate, these measures need to be collected regularly and at varying time periods when different volumes and types of passengers are being processed through the airport. The advantages of these are that they are precise and easy to understand (Maiden, 2000). They can also be linked to the passenger service and planning standards such as those devised by International Air Transport Association (IATA) in its airport development manual. This contains established level of service (LOS) parameters for airport planning, although principally only relating to the queuing and waiting standards in the main processing areas, which are in widespread use in the airport industry. There are six levels: A (Excellent), B (High), C (Good), D (Adequate), E (Inadequate), and F (Unacceptable) and typically most airports design facilities to operate at level C in the peak. For example, in the holding areas, this assumes that there is $1.7\,m^2$ for a sitting passenger and $1.2\,m^2$ for a standing area. At level C the maximum occupancy rate will be 65 per cent, whilst it decreases to 40 per cent at level A and increases to 95 per cent at level E. Likewise in the baggage claim areas it assumes that 40 per cent of passengers have trolleys with space allocations of $2.6\,m^2$ per passenger for level A, $1.7\,m^2$ per passenger for level C, and only $1.0\,m^2$ for level E. Whilst C is generally the industry standard, some of the low cost terminals and facilities have a lower design LOS, for example, E at Marseille and Hahn and D/E at Kuala Lumpur and Amsterdam (Jacobs Consultancy, 2007).

Many airports also define their own specific service standards. For example, at Manchester airport there are space standards related to various areas, such as the queuing and holding areas, seating standards in the concourse (25 per cent of passenger to have a seat), departure (75 per cent) and gate lounge (70 per cent), and queue lengths for different processes. With check-in for scheduled services this is less than 3 minutes for 95 per cent of passengers, or in peak periods less than 5 minutes for 80 per cent of the passengers (Competition Commission, 2002). There will also be standards covering first bag and last bag reclaim, for example at Hong Kong this is 20/40 minutes, at Inchoen Seoul 15/37 minutes and at Kuala Lumpur 25/40 minutes. These individual standards are set and revised in the light of customer levels of satisfaction by surveying passengers to find out, say, when they become dissatisfied with the waiting time that they experience. Direct observations or camera shots can also be used to assess real-life situations when queue lengths start to have a negative impact on passenger behaviour. As with all the service measures, the airport is faced with the dilemma that not all types of passenger groups will have the same expectations and so a compromise in the standard in most cases has to be reached.

The objective measures of service quality can only cover a limited range of issues and service dimensions. For instance, while they can measure the reliability of equipment, they cannot tell whether consumers feel safe, assured, and satisfied with their use of the equipment. Similarly, a passenger's perception of the time that they have spent waiting in a queue may be very different from the actual waiting time. Subjective measures, such as looking at passenger satisfaction ratings, are also needed. These measures will enable the quality of service to be assessed through the eyes of users rather than the airport management. There are number of different types of subjective measures with the two key methods being comment/complaints cards and customer surveys. In addition there is the opportunity to analyze routine complaints that are received by the airport operator, by phone, by post, or by e-mail. Focus groups may also be used to investigate important or topical issues in greater detail and there can be 'mystery shoppers' who sample the airport product by anonymously pretending to be passengers.

As regards the benefits of comment cards they are cheap and immediate. If the comments are favourable they may provide a positive public relations opportunity. The airport operator, however, has very little control over this type of feedback. The comments will not come from a representative sample of travellers at airports and will usually only record extreme views since customers will not be motivated to comment unless they feel very strongly about their experience at the airport. While such a system may be able to identify a weakness that can be rectified swiftly, it is not systematic enough to be used for quality improvement programmes or target setting.

In this case consumer surveys are more suitable. Typically such surveys will ask passengers about their usage of facilities and services and their opinion of them in terms of comfort, congestion, cleanliness, value for money, and so on. Also, if passenger profile information is collected, the survey findings can be used to investigate relationships between usage and satisfaction of services with demographics, attitudes, and experiences of travellers. Clearly consideration has to be given to the sample size, interview time, and most appropriate place to survey. Departing passengers may be keen to participate while waiting in their departure lounge having completed all the major essential processes, but tired arriving passengers may be less co-operative, being anxious to find their luggage and return home. The main drawback of surveys is, of course, their high cost. The results are also not so immediate as comment cards and may require careful interpretation.

In 1998, Airports Council International (ACI) investigated quality of service measurement at airports through a survey of its members (Airports Council International, 2000). One hundred and twenty airports responded with the sample ranging from large airports such as Cairo, Johannesburg, Copenhagen, Paris, Frankfurt, Rome, Amsterdam, Dallas, Houston, Chicago, Sydney, Hong Kong, and Tokyo to some very small regional airports. All geographical regions were fairly well represented except for South America. Forty-three per cent of respondents said that they used objective criteria, while 62 per cent used subjective criteria. Both criteria were adopted by 32 per cent of all the airports. Some of the most popular objective measures were related to the availability of trolleys, lifts, escalators, moving walkways, conveyors, and taxi services. The assessment of waiting time and queue length at check-in, security, and immigration was a fairly common practice. Baggage delivery was also measured by a large number of airports, as was cleanliness. Analysis of complaints and comments was viewed as important as well. The subjective measures that were identified considered overall satisfaction with all the general processes at the airport together with more detailed measurements looking at specific service dimensions (Table 4.4). More recently ACI has identified the four key areas of passenger satisfaction that needs to be measured as being related to the experience of coming to the airport, the passenger processing, the commercial services, and the physical facilities (Airports Council International, 2006a).

As with economic performances, airports are now acknowledging that it is equally important to make international comparisons and to benchmark themselves against other airports as well as with

Table 4.4   Criteria most frequently used to measure quality of service at ACI airports

Airport process	Objective criteria	Subjective criteria
General	Response to/analysis of complaints/mail comments Availability of lifts, escalators, moving walkways, etc. Availability of trolleys Cleanliness	Overall customer satisfaction in terms of Attractiveness, convenience, quality
		Quality of public announcements Terminal atmosphere/temperature Availability/quality of trolleys Cleanliness (especially toilets) Seating areas Telecommunication facilities Security/airport safety
Flight information displays, information desk/telephone service		Overall satisfaction
Check-in	Waiting time/queue	Overall satisfaction
Security check	Waiting time/queue	
Immigration	Waiting time/queue	
Catering		Overall satisfaction Quality of goods Value for money Choice
Shops, commercial services (banks, post offices, etc.)		Overall satisfaction Range of goods
		Value for money Staff courtesy
Baggage delivery	Delivery time	Overall satisfaction Waiting/delivery time
Ground access	Taxi availability/waiting time	Overall satisfaction: ground access/public transport

Source: Airports Council International (2000).

their past performances. Such an exercise is particularly problematic because of the lack of consistency or common format of each airport's consumer survey. Also certain airports such as small airports and single terminal airports tend to inherently perform better in quality of service surveys. This is not just because smaller airports seem more personal but also because they are usually served by smaller national or regional populations which may view their airport as a local asset and have a greater pride in it. Some passenger types are likely to complain more than others. For example, in the United Kingdom, business travellers, frequent travellers, and male passengers tend to be far more critical than foreign leisure travellers, first time users, and female passengers (Maiden, 2008).

Since 1993, there has been a major quality of service survey of passengers at sample airports around the world. This was initially undertaken by IATA with its Global Airport Monitor which had just 30 airports and a sample size of 80 000 in its first year. In 2004 and 2005, IATA and ACI joined forces to produce similar research called the ALTEA survey but from 2006 this survey, now called the Airport Service Quality (ASQ) programme has been undertaken solely by ACI. The 2007 survey covered over 90 airports and nearly 200 000 passengers who were surveyed at the departure gates on a quarterly basis. Thirty-four key service areas were investigated (Airports Council International, 2008). Seoul Incheon achieved the overall highest ranking in the survey followed by Kuala Lumpur and Singapore Changi. The best performing airports in different world regions and also by size were also identified (Table 4.5). The regularity with which the survey has been undertaken has meant that it has been generally accepted within the industry. Hong Kong airport, like many other airports, uses the ASQ to complement its annual in-house customer satisfaction survey and its even more detailed service quality focus groups (Wong, 2007). The ASQ's role in airport marketing has also become important with airports which perform well using the findings to publicize and sell their airport to their customers.

There are a number of other surveys which consider passenger satisfaction levels at airports. The largest of these is the Skytrax World Airport on-line survey. The sample size is very large (the 2006–2007 survey covered over 7.8 million completed questionnaires and over 170 airports) although clearly it is more difficult to ensure accurate and unbiased results when an on-line survey such as this is undertaken. However, it is interesting that the top eight airports, namely Hong Kong, Seoul Incheon, Singapore, Munich, Kuala Lumpur, Zürich, Amsterdam, and Vancouver, all appeared in the top five in at least one of the ASQ categories (Skytrax, 2008). In North America there is also the North American Airport Satisfaction study that has been undertaken for a number of years and is based on over 17 000 evaluations of airports and 10 000 passengers (J.D. Power and Associates, 2008).

Table 4.5 Overall passenger satisfaction levels: best performing airports from ACI's 2007 ASQ survey by airport size and region

Africa	Asia Pacific	Europe	Latin America & Caribbean	Middle East	North America
1.Johannesburg	1. Seoul Incheon	1. Oporto	1.Guayaquil	1.Tel Aviv	1. Dallas Fort Worth
2. Cape Town	2. Kuala Lumpur	2. Zürich	2. San Jose	2. Doha	2. Halifax
3. Durban	3. Singapore	3. Helsinki	3. Mexico City	3. Abu Dhabi	3. Ottawa
4. Nairobi	4. Hong Kong	4. Munich	4. Port of Spain	4. Muscat	4. San Diego
	5. Central Japan (NGO)	5. Southampton	5. Curacao		5. Detroit
<5 million passengers	**5–15 million passengers**	**15–25 million passengers**	**25–49 million passengers**	**>40 million passengers**	
1. Halifax	1. Central Japan (NGO)	1. Kuala Lumpur	1. Seoul Incheon	1. Hong Kong	
2. Ottawa	2. Tel Aviv	2. San Diego	2. Singapore	2. Dallas Fort Worth	
3. Guayaquil	3. Auckland	3. Zürich	3. Detroit	3. Denver	
4. Porto	4.Christchurch	4. Vancouver	4. Minneapolis St Paul	4. Houston	
5. Cairns	5. Adelaide	5. Melbourne	5. Munich	5. Amsterdam	

Source: Airports Council International (2008).

Most comparative studies of airport quality look at quality from a passenger's point of view (Lemaitre, 1998). Research into the airlines' point of view is less common. One rare example was a study undertaken by Alder and Berechman (2000) that looked at airline factors such as delays, runway capacity, cost of local labour force, and the reliability of air traffic control for a sample of 26 airports in Western Europe, North America, and the Far East. The information obtained from the airlines was used in a data envelopment analysis to rank airports relative to their quality level. An indication of the comparative situation from the airline viewpoint can also be gained from the Eagle Awards that are annually given to airports that airlines consider provide value for money and a good quality of service. In 2007 this was awarded to Vancouver airport which also performs well in the ASQ and Skytrax surveys (International Air Transport Association, 2007b).

In addition to taking into account airlines' and passengers' views of quality of service, airports need to consider their other customers as well. For example, Amsterdam airport surveys three key customer groups. It undertakes a passenger survey of around 3500 arriving,

Table 4.6 Key service quality indicators for airport customers at Amsterdam airport 2006

Customer	Definition of key indicator	Target for 2006	Achieved in 2006
Passenger Arriving (A)	Percentage who answered 'excellent' or 'good' in response to 'What is your overall assessment of Amsterdam Airport Schiphol?'	A: 92%	A: 93%
Departing and transferring (D)		D: 92%	D: 93%
Airlines and handling agents	Percentage who rated Amsterdam airport as 'excellent' or 'good' in the client satisfaction survey	48%	60%
Tenants	Average mark awarded by tenants for the rented space and associated facilities (10 is maximum)	7	6.8

Source: Schiphol Group (2007).

Table 4.7 Key service quality indicators for passengers at Amsterdam airport 2006

Service feature	Target for 2006 (%)	Achieved in 2006 (%)
Convenient layout of terminal	85	A: 84, D: 77
Waiting facilities near gates/ check-in waiting times	69%/77%	A: 60, D: 77
Price/quality of 'See Buy Fly' airside shopping	56	55
Atmosphere in lounges	83	83

Source: Schiphol Group (2007).

departing, and transfer passengers every two months. It also undertakes a customer satisfaction survey with its airlines and handling agents. Moreover every two years it carries out a survey of all the different companies who rent offices and businesses premises – the 2006 survey covered 187 of these (Schiphol Group, 2007). Tables 4.6 and 4.7 show the key indicators related to these surveys and the corresponding targets that were set. In general the satisfaction rates are far higher with passengers than airlines and handling agents. If such surveys are undertaken they will normally complement more informal assessment undertaken by many airports with airlines and other service providers at the airport, which can be carried out in this way because of their relatively small numbers compared with passengers. For example, Kuala Lumpur has a facilitation committee that meets quarterly which is attended by all service providers and sets service standards and targets and reviews airport performances. The airport operator also has periodic meetings with other committees such as handling, flight operations, ramp safety, and security to discuss service performance and action plans for improvements (Murad, 2007).

Level of delays

A crucial measure of airport performance for airlines and passengers, that airport operators often prefer not to focus on, is the level of delays. This is often because there are many factors that lead to flights being delayed which are outside the airport operator's remit (e.g. en route air traffic control, bad weather or technical problems with the aircraft). It is therefore inevitable that aircraft will deviate from the published schedule, which adds an unpredictable element to the time at which any given flight will wish to use the runway. Maximum runway throughput can only be achieved with queuing of aircraft (on the ground for departing flights or through speed control and 'stacks' in the air for arriving flights) so that there is always an aircraft ready to use the runway. Airports that are operating close to their runway capacity are therefore likely to impose additional delays on flights and exacerbate delays originating from other causes. An airport with spare runway capacity has more scope to accommodate delayed aircraft without disrupting other flights and may be able to avoid queuing aircraft in most cases.

Shortcomings in terminal capacity can also delay aircraft. If there are insufficient stands available, arriving aircraft may be held on the taxiways or apron before they are able to unload. At the day-to-day level, this may be an airline operational decision to await the availability of a preferred gate or avoid bussing passengers from a remote stand. In the longer term, however, airports have the opportunity to expand or upgrade facilities to address these problems. Congestion within the terminals may lead to passengers who have checked in failing to reach the aircraft in time, thus delaying departure; flights may also be held because of awaiting crew or transfer passengers, creating a knock-on of delays from one flight to another. In the United States, it is common practice for the last flight of the day from a hub to be held much longer than earlier ones as it does not present reactionary problems for subsequent flights and enables as many passengers as possible to get home that night.

The airlines can take account of expected queuing times related to shortages of airport runway capacity in planning their schedule. This enables them to maintain a similar level of punctuality performance at congested airports, but at the expense of longer scheduled flight times and the resultant increase in costs from poorer utilization of aircraft and crew. Considering the Amsterdam – London Heathrow

Table 4.8 Schedule time: Amsterdam–London 1985–2007

From	To	Year	Depart	Arrive	Aircraft type	Sector time (hours:minutes)
Amsterdam (AMS)	London (LHR)	1985	1200	1200	DC9	1:00
Amsterdam (AMS)	London (LHR)	2007	1205	1230	B737	1:25
Amsterdam (AMS)	London (LCY)	2007	1020	1035	F50	1:15
Amsterdam (AMS)	Amsterdam (STN)	2007	1245	1245	A319	1:00

Source: OAG Flight Guide/ABC World Airways Guide.

routes it can be seen that a morning flight from Amsterdam to Heathrow, scheduled for 1 hour in 1985 had increased to 1 hour 25 minutes by the year 2007 (Table 4.8). At the less congested airports of London City and Stansted the scheduled flight times were less. Airlines thus include a contingency allowance for delays in their schedule. This means that published comparisons of schedule performance tend to understate the total time wasted compared with the theoretical minimum journey time and airlines can improve their punctuality performance by extending their scheduled journey times. Comparisons between airports and airlines, therefore, have to be treated with caution. Table 4.9 shows delay figures for 2007 and it was the fourth successive year that punctuality deteriorated on intra-European flights. The worst affected airports were London Heathrow and Gatwick with around one third of flights significantly delayed. Rome, Dublin and Paris CDG airports came next. Frankfurt and Copenhagen were better with less than one quarter of flights delayed more than 15 minutes. On average 42 per cent of the delays occurred in the pre-flight preparing phase because the aircraft was not ready whilst 58 per cent were because of delays due to weather conditions, airport congestion or because departure clearance was not given by air traffic control (Association of European Airlines, 2008). However it is much more difficult to measure the extent to which the airport operator played a role in these delays.

Service quality and regulation

When the British airport regulatory system was established following the privatization of BAA in 1987, there was no formal regulation

Table 4.9 Delays at major European airports on intra-European scheduled services, 2007

Airport	Departures delayed more than 15 minutes (%)	Arrivals delayed more than 15 minutes (%)
London LHR	35.5	32.4
London LGW	30.2	31.8
Rome	30.1	24.9
Dublin	28.1	28.7
Paris CDG	27.3	20.9
Madrid	26.5	30.5
Athens	26.4	26.7
Larnaca	26.1	36.6
Frankfurt	24.3	23.9
Barcelona	24.2	23.3
Lisbon	24.1	25.7
Manchester	23.4	21.3
Copenhagen	22.7	22.0
Istanbul	22.6	32.2
Munich	22.6	17.8
Stockholm	22.5	24.2
Helsinki	21.7	20.0

Source: Association of European Airlines (2008).

related to quality of service – although it was clearly recognized that a price cap could produce a strong incentive to cut service levels. During each five yearly regulatory review of BAA London airports and Manchester airport, service quality came under close scrutiny and, for example in the reviews undertaken in 1996–1997, it was recommended that the airports should look at service level agreements as a means to improve their quality of service. However, it was not until 2003 that formal quality of services requirements linked to pricing was introduced with a system of rebates to the airlines being agreed for the next regulatory period (2003–2008) if the airports did not meet certain targets or standards. These targets were based on measures of quality of service to airlines and to passengers (Table 4.10). The services to airlines measures were largely related to existing service level agreements, with the passengers services were based on BAA's Quality Service Monitor (QSM). This survey is undertaken at all BAA airports, covers a sample of over 80 000 passengers and uses a rating scale that gives a value of 5 for an excellent score and 1 when the aspect of service is considered extremely poor. It was also decided that regular independent audits of the QSM should be undertaken to ensure that the methodology was in accordance with best market practices and that representative samples were used.

Table 4.10 Service quality elements included in the regulation of Heathrow and Gatwick airports

	Performance measure	Heathrow standard	Gatwick standard	Changes since 2003–2008
Airline facing services				
Stands	% of time available	99%	99%	Standard raised from 98%
Jetties	% of time available	99%	99%	Standard raised from 97%
Pier service	% of passengers pier served	Linked to expected level of service in each terminal	Linked to expected level of service in each terminal	Replaces a 90% standard
Fixed electrical ground power	% of time available	99%	99%	Standard raised from 98%
Transit system	Cars available (normal/peak)	99%/97%	99%/97%	Unchanged except LHR T5 added
Passenger facing services				
Departure lounge seat availability	Monthly QSM score	3.8	3.8	Standard raised by 0.2
Cleanliness	Monthly QSM score	3.9	4.0	Standard raised by 0.2
Way finding	Monthly QSM score	4.0	4.1	Standard raised by 0.2
Flight information	Monthly QSM score	4.2	4.2	Standard raised by 0.2
Security queues	Waiting time <5 minutes	95% Additional test 99% ≤10 minutes	95% Additional test 98% ≤15 minutes	Standard raised from <10 minutes; new second test
Arrivals reclaim	Baggage carousel serviceability	99%	99%	Standard raised from 98%
Passenger-sensitive equipmenta (general and priority)	% time available	99%	99%	General standard raised from 98%. New priority standard
Aerodrome congestion delay				
Deferment loss of movements	Material events causing deferment/ loss of movements (from BAA Superlog)	0–3 cumulative movements deferred (For 4 or more a increasing scale of rebates exists)	0–3 cumulative movements deferred (for 4 or more a increasing scale of rebates exists)	Unchanged (was not introduced until 2006)

Note: In addition in 2008–2013 there were new airline facing standards related to stand entry guidance, transfer search, staff search, and control posts search.
ᵃ Escalators, people movers, and lifts.
Source: Civil Aviation Authority (2006), Civil Aviation Authority (2008).

This was because the suitability of BAA using its own survey to give an independent and unbiased measure of its performance was questioned by many, especially the airlines. At the same time a system of rebates at Manchester airport were agreed which were based on the Generic Service Standards (GSSs) that the airport operator had developed in consultation with its users.

When the service quality conditions were introduced at Heathrow and Gatwick in 2003, it was decided that at some later date after a period of consultation with the airlines and BAA, a measure should be included to assess aerodrome congestion delay. This was postponed because of the difficulties in finding an acceptable measure of congestion, which relates only to factors that are under the control of the airport operator (as opposed to weather, airline operational factors, etc.). This measure was finally introduced in 2006 when it was decided that rebates would be payable to airlines when 'material events' occurred which were the responsibility of the BAA or of its contractual agents (including NATS that provided air traffic control) and which caused a 'material' or significant operational impact in terms of the number of movements lost or deferred. Material events included events such as industrial action, closure of runways or other areas; failure of equipment, and when bad weather had been forecast and materialized but relevant bad weather equipment (e.g. related to fog, ice, or snow) had not been used. A material operational impact was defined as causing a deferment (or loss) of more than four cumulative movements. In order to measure this BAA was required to keep a 'superlog' which records all the events that have a material effect and which is available for review by the airlines on a weekly basis. The maximum impact of these aerodrome rebates was 1 per cent of the regulated airport charge as compared to 1.5 per cent for the airline related measures and 0.5 per cent for the QSM measures, which meant that in total the rebates were limited to 3 per cent of the charges.

Overall in the period 2003–2008, BAA exceeded the majority of its targets related to these quality performance indicators. In reviewing the situation, the regulators therefore generally thought that there was scope for enhancing the incentives on BAA to maintain and improve the service quality. The main exception was security queuing. When new security regulations were introduced in August 2006 as the result of the liquids security scare, the lengths of security queues increased very significantly. Consequently the security queuing element was actually suspended from the rebates scheme from August to December for Heathrow, and August to October for Gatwick. However security queue performance continued to be below targets even after the suspension period finished (and before it for the case of Heathrow in the first quarter of 2006).

When the new regulation system came into force in April 2008, the range of service measures that were subject to financial incentives was broadened and the target performance levels (particularly for passenger security) were raised (Table 4.10) The maximum level of performance was increased from 3 per cent to 7 per cent of charges (3 per cent for passenger facing and airline facing services, 1 per cent for aerodrome congestion), and in addition positive financial incentives in the form of bonuses of up to 2.25 per cent were introduced for consistently excellent performance across all passenger facing measures and all terminals (Civil Aviation Authority, 2008).

Another airport group that has quality monitoring built into the regulatory process is Aéroports de Paris. This was set up when the airport was partially privatized in 2006. There are 10 indicators which were chosen because they covered areas where the airport company had considerable control and responsibility. There are five related to availability of equipment, three related to passenger satisfaction, and two other miscellaneous measures. These cover responses to complaints and the number of aircraft in contact with the terminal (Table 4.11). A number of the measures are similar to those at Heathrow and Gatwick and as with the new BAA system there are penalties and bonuses. For nine out of the ten indicators these are 0.05 per cent of the price cap and for the parking stands indicator the bonus/penalty is a larger $+/-0.5$ per cent of the price cap (Aéroports de Paris, 2006). In order to monitor passenger satisfaction a new survey called the 'Passenger Observatory' has been set up which is undertaken every three months, both on arrival and on departure.

When the Australian airports were privatized in 1997 and 1998 (see Chapter 2), a regulatory framework comprising a package of measures was introduced. This covered aeronautical charges and financial accounting reporting. It also made specific quality reporting requirements, unlike the UK situation immediately after privatization. The quality monitoring programme in Australia was introduced to assist in the review of prices at the airports, to improve transparency of airport performance, and to discourage operators from abusing their

Table 4.11 Service quality elements included in the regulation of Paris airports

Availability of equipment	Passenger satisfaction	Miscellaneous
Aircraft parking stands	Cleanliness in terminals	Responses to complaints
Airbridges	Direction signs and	Number of parking stands
Electro-mechanical	information on flights	in contact with terminal
equipment	Availability of luggage	
Luggage carousels	trolleys	
Flight information		
systems		

Source: Aéroports de Paris (2006).

market power by providing unsatisfactory standards. The Airports Act 1996 provided for the regulator, the Australian Competition and Consumer Commission (ACCC), to monitor the quality of services against criteria defined by the ACCC. It stipulated that records had to be kept in relation to quality of service and that the ACCC should publish the results of the quality of service monitoring exercise. When price regulation was replaced with price monitoring at the major airports (Sydney, Brisbane, Melbourne, Perth, Adelaide, Canberra, and Darwin) in 2002 it was decided that the monitoring process of the ACCC should continue to complement the price monitoring. This measuring of the quality of service along the lines of the ACCC monitoring can be incorporated into the airport–airline agreements which have been developed since price monitoring replaced formal regulation.

The ACCC reports on a selection of 'static' or objective measures such as the number, availability, and adequacy of particular facilities. In addition certain airports such as Brisbane, Melbourne, Perth, and Sydney are required to provide more detailed subjective satisfaction ratings by passengers. Also the ACCC surveys airlines for their views and obtains information from the Australian Customs Surveys and Airservices Australia, the air traffic control agency. By way of illustration, the summary results of this quality assessment for Brisbane airport in 2005–2006 is presented in Tables 4.12 and 4.13. It was apparent that passengers were least satisfied with the kerbside space and car parking and most pleased with the baggage trolleys! The airlines were least happy with the gate availability in the international terminals.

Quality management at airports

At an increasing number of airports, measuring quality of service is just part of the overall quality management system which has become all about the continuous process of identifying customers needs, assessing their level of satisfaction and taking corrective action when necessary. All employees and all processes are considered to contribute to the long-term success of this system. Effective total quality management is now considered to be the key element in many services businesses and is viewed as giving companies a competitive edge and a way to increase customer confidence. Potential benefits include increased employee motivation, enhanced communication and teamwork within the organization and increased productivity and efficiency. Theoretically, the 'cost of quality' does not have to be expensive as good quality management through quality appraisal and prevention schemes aim to minimize the costly situation when the service is unacceptable and has to be rectified.

In some cases, airports have chosen to certify their quality management system and gain external recognition by using the International

Table 4.12 Objective 'static' quality indicators for the international terminal at Brisbane airport, 2005/2006

Indicator	Value
% of arriving passengers using an airbridge	100
% of departing passengers using an airbridge	100
% of hours with more than 80% check-in desks in use	1
No of arriving passengers per inbound immigration desk during peak hour	55
No of arriving passengers per baggage inspection desk during peak hour	51
No of departing passengers per outbound migration desk during peak hour	55
No of departing passengers per security clearance system during peak hour	110
No of departing passengers per seat in gate lounges during peak hour	0.7
No of departing passengers per sq metre of lounge area during peak hour	0.1
Average throughput of outbound baggage system, bags per hour	404
No of passengers per baggage trolley during peak hour	1.6
No of passengers per flight information display screen during peak hour	12
No of passengers per flight information point during peak hour	26

Source: ACCC (2006).

Table 4.13 Passenger and airline quality survey results at Brisbane airport

Average score (1 = very poor, 5 = excellent)	Passenger ratings of international terminal facilities	Airline ratings of airside facilities
3.0–3.5		Gates availability
3.5–4.0	Car parking: standard Car parking: availability Kerbside space: congestion	Runways availability Runways standard Taxiways availability Taxiways standard Aprons availability Aprons standard Gates standard Ground service sites availability Ground service sites standard
4.0–4.5	Check-in: waiting time Immigration area (inbound): waiting time Baggage inspection (inbound): waiting time Security clearance: quality of search process Gate lounges: seating quality/availability Gate lounges: crowding Baggage reclaim: waiting time Baggage reclaim: information display Baggage reclaim: circulation space Flight information display screens Signage and way finding Washrooms: standard Car parking: time taken to enter Kerbside drop-off/pick-up facilities Taxi facilities: standard	
4.5–5.0	Baggage trolleys: findability	

Source: Australian Competition and Consumer Commission (2006).

Organization for Standardization's (ISO) 9000 family of standards. Up until 2000 there were three key standards namely ISO 9001 which was the most comprehensive standard that covered quality assurance in design, development, production, installation, and servicing, ISO 9002 which did not include the design requirements and ISO 9003 which had the least requirements as it concentrated very much on the final inspection and test (ACI, 2000). However after a review in 2000, the three standards were combined into one called ISO 9001 which is now generally more flexible and takes better account of the needs of service companies. Overall the ISO standard does not tell the airports how they should set up their system but simply gives guidance on the elements which should be included. Certification involves inspection by an independent registration body.

One of the first airports in the world to obtain ISO recognition was Aer Rianta (now the Dublin Airport Authority), which received ISO 9002 certification for airport operations, maintenance, emergency services, health and safety, retail, administration, and human resources in 1993. Then Vienna airport was the first airport to receive ISO 9001 accreditation for the total organization in 1995. Now in Europe there are many airports that have ISO certification for some or all of their activities, although practice varies from country to country. For example in France a number of airports such as Lyon, Bordeaux, Nantes, Nice, Montpelier, Marseille, and Strasbourg have ISO 9001 certification whereas in countries such as the UK and Germany, this is much less common.

Elsewhere in 1997 Infraero in Brazil became the first airport group in the Americas to obtain ISO 9001 certification for a significant number of services at the airport. Then in 2000 John C Munro airport in Ontario, Canada, and Teterboro airport in New Jersey, USA became the first North American airports to receive ISO 9002 certification for a number of different activities. In the Middle East in 2002, most of the departments in Sharjah received ISO 9001 recognition and now other airports such as Abu Dhabi also have similar certification. Airports in Asia such as Kuala Lumpur, Singapore and Incheon Seoul and Calicut in India have also sought ISO 9001 recognition.

In the ACI survey of quality of service, airports were asked whether they had any ISO certification for their services. Out of 120 airports, only 17 had ISO certified services – 10 of which were in Europe. However this was undertaken nearly 10 years ago and a further 24 airports were planning to be certified in the future (Airports Council International, 2000). There are also awards given by external bodies in recognition of their approach to quality management such as the European Foundation for Quality Management (EFQM) excellence awards, for example awarded to Strasbourg and Athens airports, and the Malcolm Baldridge Award in North America. Another survey of the top 200 busiest passenger airports found a fairly similar result to the ACI one, namely that 23 per cent of the airports had quality certification and 5 per cent participated in the Malcolm Baldridge awards scheme (Francis *et al.*, 2003). However it must be borne in mind that both these studies are rather old now and a number of airports have subsequently sought certification.

Security issues

Having investigated in detail the provision of service quality at airports, this chapter now focuses on some key processes which have a major impact on the way airports are operated. There are a number of different activities at airports involved with the protection and well-being of passengers, airlines and other relevant bodies. Within this context, airport security needs to be differentiated from airport safety. Airport security is concerned with the prevention of illegal activities, such as terrorism, as opposed to airport safety which is related to ensuring that the aircraft are safe, for example by not allowing dangerous goods on board and that there are no hazards on the runway. Only airport security is considered here, as this is where there have been very significant changes in recent years. Table 4.14 summarizes the main activities associated with airport security.

Pre-9/11 common minimum standards for airport security were set by International Civil Aviation Organization (ICAO) in Annex 17. In some parts of the world these were also incorporated into regional standards, as was the case in Europe with the European Civil Aviation Conference (ECAC) and its so-called document 30. However the problem with these standards was that there was no binding mechanism to ensure that they were implemented properly and consequently the level of security that was offered at airports throughout the world varied enormously. After the Lockerbie disaster of 1988

Table 4.14 Main security activities at airports

Badge regime
Reliability check on applicants for obtaining badge
Checks on access of staff to restricted areas
Checks on passengers and hand baggage
Baggage reconciliation
Checks on hold baggage
Checks on cargo/airmail
Armed protection landside
Armed protection airside
Protection on parked aircraft
Video supervision

Source: ACI-Europe (2003).

improved measures such as 100 per cent hold baggage screening and baggage reconciliation had been recommended but since these were not mandatory requirements they again were not adopted everywhere. The turning point, however, for many countries came after 9/11 when much more binding legislation was introduced.

9/11 Impacts

Whilst security at airports has always been a very important aspect of operations, the events of 9/11 led to it coming under even closer scrutiny with many additional security measures being introduced. Suddenly, particularly in the United States, it became a national concern and high profile issue that received a considerable amount of media attention. Globally the most immediate effect was the adoption by ICAO in 2002 of an Aviation Security Plan of Action. In this 3-year programme it was agreed that regular and mandatory audits would be conducted of member states to identify and correct deficiencies in the implementation of ICAO security-related standards. In addition, new mandatory security standards were agreed ranging from locking flight deck doors, sharing information about potential security risks, and ensuring that the security measures were implemented in a non-discriminatory manner (Jane's Airport Review, 2002).

The most sweeping changes occurred in the United States where traditionally security measures were relatively lax compared with the rest of the world. Congress quickly developed the Aviation and Transportation Security Act (ATSA) that was signed by President Bush on 19 November 2001. This set a number of important deadlines regarding security that had to be met by the end of 2002 and transferred direct responsibility for security to the Federal Government with the setting up of the Transportation Security Administration (TSA). Then in 2003, overall control was moved from the Department of Transportation to the Department of Homeland Security which had been set up to co-ordinate all security measures in the US. Previously, security at airports had been undertaken by private security company staff who were often underpaid and poorly qualified but the Act provided for these to be replaced by a federal workforce of initially 28 000 properly trained staff who had a mandatory requirement to be a US citizen (Bacon, 2002). There are now around 43 000 TSA staff at US commercial airports.

The new security policies received considerable criticism from the airline and airport industries in terms of the practicalities of introducing enhanced security measures, the feasibility of meeting the tight deadlines and in relation to how the measures would be financed. One of the major areas of discontent was the deadline for all checked baggage to be screened for explosive detective systems (EDSs) by the end of 2002. There were numerous complaints that the new security procedures and rules were inconvenient for passengers and that this significant 'hassle' factor was putting passengers off flying or encouraging them to travel by different modes of transport (Rossiter and Dresner, 2004).

Such fundamental changes to the country's airport security system were costly to implement. The security costs incurred by the airports rose from US$ 556 million in 2000 to US$ 619 million in 2001, an increase of 11 per cent. They were estimated to have increased to US$ 853, a massive 38 per cent rise in 2002. The ATSA authorized US$ 1.5 billion for 2002 and 2003 to allow airports to meet Federal Aviation Administration (FAA)-mandated security expenses. A US$ 2.50 per sector security fee was also introduced to cover some of the costs of the TSA (Field, 2002; Ghobrial and Irvin, 2004). Moreover, the Act gave airports the flexibility to use public money that was obtained from passenger taxes for airport investment [so-called Airport Improvement Program (AIP) funds – see Chapter 5 for details] to pay for any additional security-related activity required. In 2002 the FAA authorized US$ 561 million of these funds to airports for security projects related to the events of 9/11 (General Accounting Office, 2002). Additionally a number of US airports had to redesign many of their commercial facilities in order to conform with the new security measures, which led to a decline in non-aeronautical revenues. For example, new restrictions on the movements of meeters and greeters limited their access to certain retail and catering outlets and a number of car parks had to close.

Outside the United States, much attention was also paid to improving security methods at airports and numerous changes were made. An ACI study undertaken shortly after 9/11 attempted to quantify the security costs directly attributable to the terrorist attacks and found, for example, that Paris CDG airport estimated this to be US$ 20 million, Munich airport provided a figure of US$ 5.3 million, Nairobi US$ 3.4 million, and Toyko Narita US$ 2.6 million. In Europe specifically post-9/11, there was general agreement that security measures should be harmonized throughout the region and in 2003 Regulation 2320/2002 (based on the recommendations outlined in the ECAC document 30) and various complementary implementing regulations came into force (European Commission, 2002). This covers common security rules and the appropriate compliance monitoring mechanisms. The measures include unannounced airport inspections by independent European Union inspectors, 100 per cent staff searches in restricted areas, improved staff background checks, and more stringent baggage screening methods such as limiting personnel 'screen-time'. Each state has to have a national security programme in place (although in most countries these already existed as a result to Lockerbie).

In January 2008, draft regulation was approved within Europe with the aim of clarifying, simplifying and further harmonizing the existing rules of the 2320/2002 legislation. This was thought necessary because it was generally agreed that the original legislation was produced under great political and time pressure in response to the 9/11 events and could have been more flexible and less heavy handed. Also since 9/11 technology has moved on considerably and more understanding of the nature of terrorism threats has been developed. One of the key features of the new legislation is the establishment of the principle of 'one-stop security'. This means that transfer passengers arriving from non-EU countries will no longer have to be re-screened if their security regimes are recognized by the EC to be equivalent to European standards (Falconer, 2008).

Hence in Europe there is a general consensus as to what types of security measures should exist, but a much more controversial area is how security should be funded. The airports and airlines have persistently called for the governments to pay, arguing that since terrorist acts are targeted at states it is the responsibility of states to finance countermeasures to protect the travelling public. They also argue that the inconsistent approach to security provision in funding, which is the situation in Europe, distorts competition. For example, the airport operator designs the security measures at airports such as Athens and Helsinki, whereas this is done by the government in Amsterdam and Lisbon, and is shared between these two and the airlines in Munich. As regards the provision of the security services, virtually all terminal protection is provided by the government through the police, whilst in many cases checks on passengers and luggage are under the control of the airport operators. However, for other security activities, such as staff access checks/badge control, aircraft protection, and cargo checks, a wide range of different organizations such as the airport operator, the airline, the police, or a subcontractor may play a role (ACI-Europe, 2003). The situation may well vary between airports in the same country as well. For example in a sample of 22 main airports in the UK 11 airport operators provided some or all passenger checks, 9 did the hold baggage checks and 9 the access control. Elsewhere these services were outsourced (Centre for the Study of Regulated Industries, 2008). At some airports the security costs are borne by the government that is paid for in many cases by a security tax, or otherwise out of general taxation. Elsewhere, security is paid for by the airport operator through normal airport charges or special security fees usually based on passenger numbers. Often there may be a combination of these different these types of funding.

A study by the Irish Aviation Authority/Aviasolutions (2004) described how European airports (15 EC states and plus Switzerland, Norway, and Iceland) whilst having a mix of different security providers could be categorized overall into two basic models. There is a centralized model when most of the main security activities are the responsibility of the state via a government body [such as the Civil Aviation Authority (CAA), Ministry of Transport or police force] or a decentralized model when most of the activities are provided by the airport operator under the supervision of a relevant government body such as the CAA. In this case they may be provided direct or outsourced to a third party.

Table 4.15 Models of European airport security provision 2002

	Centralized model	Decentralized model
	Austria, Finland, Germany, Iceland, Italy, Luxembourg, Netherlands, Norway, Portugal, Spain, Sweden, Switzerland	Belgium, Denmark, France, Greece, Ireland, UK
Countries with separate security taxes	Austria, Germany, Iceland, Italy, Netherlands, Portugal, Spain	Belgium (nominal tax €0.15), France (estimated 22% of Civil Aviation Tax goes towards security)
Countries with specific security charge	Luxembourg, Sweden, Switzerland, Germany, the Netherlands	Belgium, France, Greece, Ireland, UK (not BAA)

Note: In 2003, the Netherlands shifted to a decentralized approach.
Source: Irish Aviation Authority/Aviasolutions (2004).

Table 4.15 shows which countries fall into each category. It is more common to have security taxes for the centralized model, which overall contributed to 65 per cent of the income generated to cover security. At the Austrian, Italian, and Portuguese airports some of the tax money is shared with the airport operators to cover the services which they provide, whereas at Madrid there is no specific tax but half of the income from the charges goes to the government to cover security. The majority of airports in both groups have specific security related charges. However with both models the passenger is ultimately the main financier of security, either through the taxes or through the charges.

The airlines and airports often compare this inconsistent situation in Europe, where in many cases the air transport industry and its customers bear the majority of the security costs, with the US case. For example, in the US in 2003, only around one-third of the TSA funding was estimated to be generated from the security taxes (Irish Aviation Authority/Aviasolutions, 2004) and generally in Europe considerably more of the security costs are met by the industry than in the US. This is a major problem because it has been estimated that in Europe security costs for the airport operators in Europe have increased from 5–8 per cent of operating costs before 9/11 to around 25 per cent. At many airports, airport staff numbers have increased substantially, for example, Copenhagen airport has increased its security staff from 350 to 750. However this funding issue is not confined to Europe and in other countries, such as Australia and New Zealand, there has also been pressure on the government to cover more of the increased security costs (Association of European Airlines/ACI-Europe, 2006; Rowe, 2007b).

The liquids problem

Since 9/11 there have been a number of terrorist threats which have impacted on airport security, for example, the attempted shoe bomb incidence in 2001 that led to the removal of shoes at passenger screening; but by far the most significant development has been the changes to the liquid, aerosols, and gels (LAGs) regulations. This has happened after 10 August 2006 when the security levels at all UK airports was raised to critical because of an alleged terrorist plot involving the detonation of liquid explosives carried onto as many as 10 transatlantic services sports drinks bottles. At that time all hand baggage became prohibited and 100 per cent passenger searches were undertaken. This led to considerable delays and cancellations at UK airports. Then as the security position changed over subsequent weeks some of the restrictions and rules were relaxed. First on 14 August, passengers were allowed a small bag (up to 45 cm long, 35 cm wide and 16 cm deep), laptops and electronic devices were permitted, but no LAGs were allowed, except those bought in the airside departure lounge. Then on 22 September international agreed hand baggage size (56 cm by 45 cm by 25 cm) was allowed again but still no LAGs could be taken on board (The rules for US flights remained more restrictive).

Whilst these developments were occurring in the UK, a number of other countries particularly in Europe and North America, also placed restrictions on LAGs and hand baggage but overall there was no consistent approach. However by October 2006, the EC agreed European wide rules which came into force in the beginning of November (European Commission, 2006). This allowed passengers to carry on board LAGs again as long as they were in containers no larger than 100 ml and in a clear plastic bag. Duty-free purchases could continue to be taken on board if they were in standard tamper-evident bags (STEBs) but only from an EU or European Economic Area (EEA) airport.

Meanwhile ICAO, in consultation with the EU and US security authorities, has also been working towards a globally acceptable framework that will harmonize all the restrictions on LAGs and agree standards on tamper evident bags. In December 2006 it sent a letter to all states recommending implementation of LAGs restrictions, as in Europe, by March 2007. Whilst many countries (such as South Africa, Australia, New Zealand, Hong Kong, Indonesia, Malaysia, China, and Vietnam) have implemented such restrictions, they vary from country to country since ICAO only provided guidelines. For example for travellers bound for Australia, any LAG items over 100 ml in hand baggage will be removed at the last boarding point which effectively means EU travellers should not make purchases of these in the duty free shops. However this is not the case with New Zealand, and in Hong Kong and Korea the purchases can be kept if they are in a tamper evident bag from a country which has LAG restrictions (Jane's Airport Review, 2007). Then in March 2007 ICAO sent another letter providing additional guidance on the LAG restrictions and with details of the universal specifications for STEBs and supply chain security to ensure secure passage of liquids to the shops. This has the aim of tightening overall security and reducing some of the inconsistencies which existed (Bradbrook, 2007).

The most difficult area to reach any kind of global agreement is in persuading countries to recognize, and have confidence in, the security arrangements which take place elsewhere. If this could happen, then transfer passengers would be allowed to take their purchased goods in STEBs onto their next flight. This does not currently occur in the EU which means that many unsuspecting transfer passengers are having their duty free purchases confiscated (see Chapter 6). However instead in July 2007 the EC introduced regulation 915/2007 (European Commission, 2007) which gives unilateral recognition to non-EU countries that have implemented the ICAO guidelines on LAG restrictions, supply chain security and STEBs. To date only Singapore has been approved, which means that transfer passengers from this country do not have their liquid purchases over 100 ml confiscated, but other countries are now applying for this recognition. The EU and US authorities are also working on harmonizing restrictions across the Atlantic. New technology, which will be able to screen liquids is considered by many to be the ultimate solution to this security problem, but in the meantime the airports have had to bear the additional security costs. For example, BAA spent £27 million on security between January–September 2007 and recruited many more staff because of the new rules that had been introduced (BAA, 2007a).

Passenger profiling

The security measures that have been discussed operate on the principle of using the same processes for all passengers using the assumption that they all pose a similar security risk. Hence the security resources are evenly distributed across all passengers. There is an alternative approach, namely passenger profiling, where passengers of higher risk are identified and then more of the resources and security attention is directed at these. There has been considerable debate as to the merits and effectiveness of passenger profiling techniques to improve the security at airports. Experience is limited with the most widespread use in Israel where it has been implemented for many years.

Passenger profiling can be undertaken in a number of ways. This can be done through interview techniques that allow the profiler to screen the passenger's personality, background, and various details of their journey. It can also be undertaken through behaviour pattern techniques when the profiler will detect suspicious people by observing any irregular behaviour or unusual body language of the passengers. Then there is passenger profiling which can be based on databases of passenger information but this raises personal data protection issues (Airports Council International, 2006b). Overall whilst passenger profiling has the potential of making screening more effective than using the same process for all passengers, it remains very controversial because of issues related to possible discriminatory treatment or violation of passenger privacy rights.

Border control can use data collected by airlines to identify passengers worthy of special attention. This includes passenger name records (PNRs) which contain basis information on the passenger and iternary but may also contain additional information concerning passenger frequent flyer membership and preferences for certain services. There is also advanced passenger information (API) which contains details such as date of birth, nationality, gender, and address in the destination country. Since 2003 the United States (and in Canada since 2006) has required both types of data to be sent in advance which has been very controversial within Europe again because of privacy and data protection concerns. Other countries, such as Australia, New Zealand, Mexico, Korea, and China require API data (Association of European Airlines, 2006). The EU is also proposing a similar system to that of the US.

Check-in processes

Another key process at the airport is check-in. There are now a number of ways that passengers can check in for their flight apart from using the traditional check-in desk. First came the self-service check-in kiosks at airports and then remote methods such as mobile phones and the internet (Sigala, 2008; Field, 2008).

As regards the check-in kiosks, these started appearing about 10 years ago at airports. They were primarily installed by the airlines for their own use – the so-called dedicated or proprietary kiosks. This was an inevitable development as the airline industry saw how self-service technologies in other industries, such as banking, had lowered costs, increased productivity, and reduced customer waiting time. At the same time, better use of the scarce space at airports could be made. This was followed by the development of the common use self-service check-in (CUSS) kiosks which allowed the airlines to share self-service resources. There had been a similar trend with the traditional check-in desks when common use terminal equipment (CUTE) had been introduced in the early 1980s. The earliest CUSS kiosks were installed at Vancouver and Narita airport in 2002. In 2006 around 29 per cent of all passengers used some type of self-service kiosk and this is expected to rise to 49 per cent by the end of 2008. Usage varies considerably though, with 58 per cent of American using this self-service method, whilst equivalent use in the Middle East and Africa is only 10 per cent and just 7 per cent in Latin America (Baker, 2007).

Initially the airlines (and later the airline alliances) developed the dedicated desks to differentiate themselves from others and to give themselves competitive advantage – particularly to their frequent flyers. The kiosks were branded with their name and identity. However there was no common standard for these dedicated kiosks and so the investment and maintenance costs proved to be high – particularly when the airport being served was not a major base for the airline.

Hence the CUSS kiosk was developed. This allows the costs to be shared between different airlines and less airport counter staff are required. However the airlines lose individual influence over the check-in process and the costs which they incur, and are no longer able to differentiate this aspect of their product.

For the airports, the CUSS system provides more flexibility – just as the CUTE system did when it was introduced – and allows for terminal space to be used more efficiently. This may enable a higher volume of passengers to be handled without the necessity of expanding the terminal. The check-in facilities can be placed in the most convenient places in the terminals and spread out if needs be to avoid crowding. In theory space no longer needed for check-in can also be used for retail opportunities although this may well require considerable reconfiguration of the overall space to place these new facilities in an appropriate location. In most cases it is the airport which owns the CUSS kiosks and then charges the airlines (or includes CUSS use in other charges such as for CUTE facilities) but in rare cases it may be the airlines themselves (e.g. Mumbai, Budapest, Frankfurt, Beijing) or the handling agents (e.g. Singapore, Basel, Oslo) (International Air Transport Association, 2008).

For the passenger both types of kiosks provide the opportunity of easier and faster check-in, but the CUSS system gives them more flexibility to check in anywhere regardless of their airline and can thus eliminate any confusion of multiple dedicated terminals. IATA estimates that the average check-in time is 3.5 minutes but with self-service kiosks it is 2.5 minutes or even 1.5 minutes if there is no hold baggage. Kiosks can be placed not only in the traditional check-in areas but also within other places in the terminal and off terminal sites such as car parks, train stations, car rental return facilities, hotels, and cruise ships which can reduce check-in queues in the actual terminal and gives passengers extra convenience and control. Las Vegas airport is an interesting example here. It first launched its CUSS programme 'Airport SpeedCheck' in 2003, but has subsequently developed this to include remote check-in as well ('Airport SpeedCheck Advance'). It has a goal of having 10 per cent of passengers with bags checking in remotely. It has kiosks in two hotels, the convention centre, and rent-a-car centre, which can handle hold baggage. Another example is Hong Kong where there are already two downtown check-ins and three at the SkyPier ferry ports (Ingalls, 2007).

In February 2004 there were only 10 airports using CUSS kiosks but by February 2008 this had increased to 86. This is expected to increase to 130 airports by the end of 2008. Currently the largest number of CUSS kiosks are in Europe (Table 4.16). Trends in the use of dedicated versus CUSS kiosks can be observed from the airport trends IT survey (Figure 4.2). In 2005 only 9 per cent of the airports in the survey had CUSS kiosks compared to half the airports having dedicated kiosks. By 2007 this had increased to 27 per cent with very little change in the use of dedicated kiosks. This higher growth in CUSS

Table 4.16 Use of CUSS kiosks as of February 2008

Region	No of airports using CUSS kiosks	Airports with the most CUSS kiosks
Africa	4	Tambo/Johannesburg (20), Cape Town (10)
Asia Pacific	8	Toyko Narita (174), Seoul Incheon (39)
North Asia	13	Hong Kong (40), Beijing (22)
CIS	1	Moscow Sheremetievo (9)
Europe	34	Amsterdam (157), Manchester (78), Madrid (52), Copenhagen (48), Vienna (47)
Middle East/North Africa	2	Amman (10)
US	11	Las Vegas (180), Dallas Fort Worth (52), San Francisco (35)
Americas (excluding US)	13	Toronto (120), Vancouver (100), Calgary (84)
World	86	

Source: International Air Transport Association (2008).

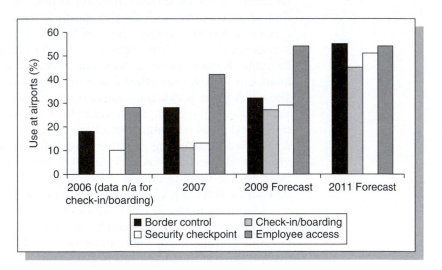

Figure 4.2
Airport use of biometric identification
(*Source*: Airport IT trends survey).

kiosks is forecast to continue into the future and in 5 years around three quarters of the airports are expected to have some type of self-service kiosk with the CUSS method being more popular. The use of CUSS terminals off airport is also forecast to grow.

Increasing the use of CUSS kiosks is one of the aims of IATA's 'Simplifying the Business' initiative which was launched in 2004 to use technology to streamline processes and reduce complexity and

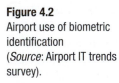

cost. In addition to CUSS kiosks, the other five focus areas were electronic ticketing, bar-coded boarding passes (BCBPs), radio frequency identification (RFID) for baggage management and paperless cargo movements. More recently two other initiatives related to reducing the number of mishandled baggage rates and to encourage 'fast travel' through different self-service processes have also been launched (International Air Transport Association, 2008).

The most basic self-service kiosks will verify the passenger identity (usually with the credit card) and print the boarding pass. Some may allow for meal and seat choices to be made, some may also read travel documents such as passports or visas, whilst others such as at Amsterdam airport can cope with transfer flights. However one of the key issues with the self-service options is coping with hold baggage check-in. Indeed in a survey of passengers in 2006, it was found that baggage was the number one reason passengers listed for not using available self-service options (SITA, 2007). Often once self-service check-in is completed, passengers have to queue up at individual airline desks to check in their luggage. Some machines overcome these problems by being able to print baggage tags so that passengers themselves can tag their baggage and drop them off at a common baggage drop. However this is not allowed in all countries and in 2007 (according to the airport IT trends survey) only 18 per cent of airports offered a common bag drop location. However another 34 per cent planned to introduce such facilities in the next 2 years.

In more recent years personal computer and mobile check-in has become an alternative. This costs even less for the airlines as they do not need to install kiosks and/or use CUSS and the passengers print their own boarding passes in the case of PC check-in using their own paper. IATA's corporate travel survey 2008 showed that 56 per cent had used internet check-in as opposed 69 per cent who had used self-service kiosks (Bruyere, 2008). With mobile phones a BCBP is sent to the display on their phones. Fifty-three per cent of airlines now offer web check-in and a further 36 per cent expect to offer it over the next 2 years. Twenty per cent offer mobile phone check-in with a further 56 per cent in the next 2 years (Baker, 2007). There is the issue of checked baggage with these check-in methods as well and some airlines, for example easyJet, only make it available if there is no hold baggage.

There is currently a very active debate as to whether self-service kiosks have only been an interim solution to improving the check-in process and that eventually they will not be needed as checking in remotely using PCs or mobiles is cheaper for airlines and more convenient for passengers (Jarrell, 2007). However such remote technology is not always available to travellers – particularly if they are away from home. Moreover using such systems are not totally seamless or without cost as security and gate staff have to have the appropriate technology and resources to scan the bar code for the PC boarding card or mobile message. Additionally the self-service kiosks do have opportunities to streamline passenger flows and enhance operational efficiency by being integrated with the other passenger processing technologies involved with the security and border control activities. For example they could scan biometric data to check the traveller's identity against the data which is stored on travel documents or secure databases. If all this technology becomes a reality, the advantages of self-service kiosks over on-line/mobile check-in are likely to increase since the kiosks will provide the opportunity to streamline the repetitive checks of passengers and their documents which the online options will not allow as only some of the processes will be covered.

There is considerable interest in this idea of using the evolving self-service technology to change the current passenger processing model from a series of discrete processes to an integrated model which is more efficient and allows different stakeholders to share information. This will reduce costs, be more efficient, and improve the passenger experience. A notable initiative here is the Simplifying Passenger Travel (SPT) programme which was set up in 2000 and has the participation of airlines, airports, handling agents, government authorities, and technology providers. A concept called the ideal process flow has been developed which combines self-service check-in, new generation passports, biometrics, secure databases, and other technological advances to facilitate automatic authentication of a passenger's identity whenever this is required at different stages in the travel process. The focus is on the end-to-end journey rather than the individual stages or processes (SPT, 2006).

Biometric identification and registered passenger schemes

In parallel with these developments to enhance security procedures, various organizations have begun using new types of security measures such as biometric identification. These use unique physical characteristics to ensure that a passenger or member of staff is known and is allowed to proceed, for example, through a gate or door. Such techniques can be as simple as a specialized identity card or as sophisticated as the recognition of retina or iris patterns, finger prints, or speech. Therefore, this technology concentrates on the individual themselves rather than the more traditional approach of focusing much more on the passenger's baggage. The industry has been developing the technology needed for such biometric processes for some time with the aim of speeding up processing times as well as improving security, but the terrorist attacks of 9/11 and subsequent recent events have made the case for using such measures that very much more convincing.

There are two types of biometric identification, namely physiological biometrics (which relies of recognition, e.g., of finger prints, retina, or iris patterns) and behavioural biometrics (which is associated with aspects of behaviour such as signature and voice). Using biometrics for security or border checks can increase the efficiency of the process, save time and enhance customer service. Also there is no risk of losing, copying, forgetting or having the biometrics stolen. An important use for biometrics is in Machine Readable Travel Documents (MRTDs) such as passports and visas. A biometric passport or ePassport has the passport's critical information stored on a tiny computer chip. In the last few years many countries have issued ePassports with most having passenger information and a digital photo stored on the chip as this facial recognition was the global standard that ICAO agreed to adopt in 2003 (along with voluntary additional fingerprint or iris recognition). By the end of 2007, over 45 countries were issuing ICAO standard ePassports (Siciliano, 2007).

Biometrics can also be used for other processes at the airport as well as border control. It can be used with check-in and boarding to ensure that the passenger boarding the aircraft is the same person as the one who checked in. It can also be used at the security checkpoint to confirm the identity of the passenger. Moreover it can be used for employees as well, particularly to check the identity of those who are entering sensitive and restricted areas (Airports Council International, 2005). Currently this is the most popular use of biometric identification at airports. In the future use of biometrics identification is forecast to increase in all these areas (Figure 4.3).

Some passengers can volunteer (sometimes at a cost) to provide their personal and biometric information to be included in a 'Registered Passenger' or 'Registered Traveller' or 'Trusted Traveller' scheme. A number of these, which are most suitable for frequent flyers have been trialled or are already operational. They are designed to reduce delays at the airport, to enhance the passenger experience by allowing certain processes to be expedited and to maintain or increase levels of security and border control. The passengers' background is investigated and if they are approved they will usually receive a Smart Card which contains their biometric information for use at the airport. According to the 2007 airport IT trends survey, currently

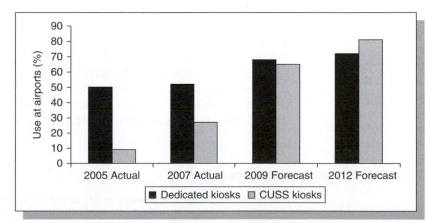

Figure 4.3
Airport use of self-service kiosks
(*Source*: Airport IT trends survey).

14 per cent of airports have registered traveller programmes and a further 23 per cent plan to introduce them in the next 2 years. Many of these current schemes such as the IRIS scheme (Iris recognition) in the UK, the IACS scheme (fingerprint recognition) in Singapore and the Pegase trial (fingerprint) in France have focused on immigration whilst the US Registered Traveller Programme is concerned with passengers who are low risk from a security viewpoint (Accenture, 2007). Then there are other schemes which offer additional perks such as the Privium scheme at Amsterdam airport. This scheme, which uses iris recognition, offers three types of membership. There is Privium Plus which is €119 per annum and provides fast-track border control plus other enhancements such as priority parking, valet parking, and business class check-in. Premium Basic (€99) just offers the expediated border control whereas Premium Partner (€55) is available to partners or dependent children.

Some of the registered passenger trials have been linked into the Simplying Passenger Travel (SPT) initiative. For example in 2007, frequent flyers at Hong Kong airport participated in the SPEED trial which was jointly conducted by the airport, immigration department and Cathay Pacific. Participants received a SPEED card which had fingerprints for biometric identification. The benefits included enhanced internet check-in, dedicated baggage drop, and dedicated channels for airside access, immigration control, security clearance, and aircraft boarding. They were automatically eligible to enroll in the UK Iris's immigration system. Also at Heathrow airport in 2006–2007 there was a trial jointly conducted by BAA, the Border and Immigration Agency, five technology partners and Cathay Pacific and Emirates to test the principles of the ideal process flow of the SPT initiative. This miSense scheme had 1007 participants and collected 13 pieces of biometric information (two iris patterns, ten finger/thumb prints, and one facial image) which were stored on a smart card. The feedback afterwards showed that 72 per cent of users thought that faster journey times was the most important benefit. Moreover 81 per cent said the service was good or excellent and 89 per cent said they would recommend it to a fellow traveller (BAA, 2007b).

Whilst a number of these registered traveller schemes have proved successful, one of the major problems is that different airports across the world are unilaterally adopting different biometric schemes. Unlike with ePassports, there is no industry standard and there is no common consensus as to which technique is most effective. Hence there is a need for the industry to work more together to prevent global technological fragmentation in this situation (Thorn, 2007).

References and further reading

Accenture (2007). *Facilitation of Aviation Security: Feasibility Study of 'Registered Passenger' Concept*. Accenture.

ACI-Europe (2003). *Financing Civil Aviation Security Costs in Europe.* ACI-Europe.

Aeroports de Paris (2006). *Presentation of the economic regulation agreement,* available from www.aerportsdeparis.fr (accessed 30 January 2008).

Airports Council International (ACI) (2000). *Quality of Service at Airports.* ACI.

Airports Council International (ACI) (2005). *The Application of Biometrics at Airports, Position Paper.* ACI.

Airports Council International (ACI) (2006a). *Airport Benchmarking to Maximize Efficiency.* ACI.

Airports Council International (ACI) (2006b). *The Pre-departure Screening Process: A Strategy for Improvement, ACI Position Paper.* ACI.

Airports Council International (ACI) (2008) *Airport Service Quality Awards* 2007, Press release, 25 February.

Alder, N. and Berechman, J. (2000). Measuring airport quality from the airlines' viewpoint. *Fourth Air Transport Research Group Conference,* The Netherlands, July.

Association of European Airlines (AEA) (2006). *Background information on passenger data transfer,* Position paper.

Association of European Airlines (AEA) (2008). *European airlines' 2007 delays highlight the need for ATM reform,* Press release, 19 February.

Association of European Airlines/ACI-Europe (2006). *European Commission report confirms the need for public funding of security,* Press release, 7 August.

Australian Competition and Consumer Commission (ACCC) (2006). *Quality of service – price monitored airports report 2005–06.* ACCC.

BAA (2007a). *BAA results for the nine months to 30 September 2007,* Press release, 14 November.

BAA (2007b). *miSense: Biometrically enabled access control trial at Heathrow airport 2006/07,* Summary report. BAA.

Bacon, J. (2002). *The Aviation and Transportation Security Act: The law and its implementation,* AAAE/ACI-NA Legislative affairs issue brief.

Baker, C. (2007). Checking in, *Airline Business,* July, pp. 38–40.

Blacklock, M. (2006). JetBlue builds at JFK. *Airports International, April,* 22–23.

Bradbrook, C. (2007). Security update, Airport World, April–May, 31.

Bruyere, P. (2008). Extending self-service. *International Airport Review,* 1, 53–55.

Centre for Asia Pacific Aviation (2007). *Global airport privatization report,* Second Edition.

Centre for the Study of Regulated Industries (2008). *Airport statistics 2006/2007,* University of Bath.

Civil Aviation Authority (CAA) (2006). *CAA Decision: Revised statement of standards and rebates for Heathrow and Gatwick airports.* CAA.

Civil Aviation Authority (CAA) (2008). *Economic regulation of Heathrow and Gatwick airports*: CAA decision. CAA.

Competition Commission (2002) *A report on the economic regulation of Manchester airport Plc,* The Stationery office.

European Commission (2002). *Regulation (EC) No 2320/2002 of the European Parliament and of the Council of 16 December 2002 establishing common rules in the field of civil aviation security,* OJ L 355, 30 December.

European Commission (2006). *Regulation (EC) No 1546/2006 amending Regulation (EC) No 622/2003 laying down measures for the implementation of the common basic standards on aviation security,* OJ L 286, 17 October.

European Commission (2007). *Regulation (EC) No 915/2007 amending Regulation* (EC) No 622/2003 *laying down measures for the implementation of the common basic standards on aviation security,* OJ L 200, 1 August.

Falconer, R. (2006). The low-cost challenge for airports, *Communique Airport Business,* June–July 21–22.

Falconer, R. (2008). Revised EU regulatory framework for aviation security agreed, *Communique Airport Business,* March, 22.

Field, D. (2002). US security: Uncertain world. *Airline Business,* June, pp. 46–8.

Field, D. (2008). Remote control, *Airline Business,* January, pp. 45–47.

Francis, G., Humphreys, I. and Fry, J. (2003). An international survey of the nature and prevalence of quality management systems in airports. *TQM and Business Excellence,* 14(7), 819–829.

General Accounting Office. (2002). Using airport grant funds for security has affected some development projects, GAO.

Ghobrial, A. and Irvin, W. (2004). Combating air terrorism: Some implications to the aviation industry. *Journal of Air Transportation,* 2004, 9(3), 67–86.

Ingalls, S. (2007). McCarran International airport: A case study in enhancing processing efficiency. *Journal of Airport Management,* 1(4), 338–347, July–September.

International Air Transport Association (IATA) (2007a). *Low cost facilities and services,* Position statement.

International Air Transport Association (IATA) (2007b). *Eagle awards for DGAC Chile and Vancouver Airport Authority,* Press release, 4 June.

International Air Transport Association (IATA) (2008). *Simplifying the Business project update,* February 2008, available from www.iata. org/stbsupportportal (accessed 4 February 2008).

Irish Aviation Authority/Aviasolutions (2004). *Study on civil aviation financing (summary of final report),* Irish Aviation Authority/Aviasolutions.

Jacobs Consultancy (2007). *Review of Dedicated Low-Cost Airport Passenger Facilities.* Jacobs.

Jane's Airport Review (2002). ICAO set new security standards. April, 18.

Jane's Airport Review (2007). Duty-free industry fears security restrictions pose risk to revenues. May, 4.

Jarrell, J. (2007). Self-service kiosks: Museum pieces or here to stay? *Journal of Airport Management*, 2(1), 23–29.

J.D. Power and Associates (2008). *Satisfaction with baggage claim declines considerably as airport security regulations ... drive higher volumes of checked baggage*, Press release, 22 May.

Lemaitre, A. (1998). The development of performance indicators for airports: A management perspective. *Eighth World Conference on Transport Research*, Antwerp, July.

Maiden, S. (2000). Measuring service quality at airports. *University of Westminster/Cranfield University Airport Economics and Finance Symposium*, London, March.

Maiden, S. (2008). How BAA uses its market research. *University of Westminster Marketing and Market Research Seminar*, London, February.

Murad, A. (2007). KL International Airport – How airports carry out service activities for their customers. *2nd ACI Asia-Pacific Regional Assembly, Conference and Exhibition*, Seoul, May.

Rossiter, A. and Dresner, M. (2004). The impact of the September 11th security fee and passenger wait time on traffic diversions and highway fatalities. *Journal of Air Transport Management*, 10, 227–232.

Rowe, R. (2007a). Budget buildings, *Airline Business*, December, pp. 40–44.

Rowe, B. (2007b). Relief effort, *Airline Business*, June, pp. 52–54.

Schumacher, J. (2007). The latest business model for low-cost airports: The case of Frankfurt-Hahn airport. *Journal of Airport Management*, 1(2), 121–124.

Schiphol Group (2007). *Corporate social responsibility report 2006*, Schiphol Group.

Skytrax (2008). *World airport awards*, available from www.worldairportawards.com (accessed 15 February 2008).

Siciliano, M. (2007). ePassports: Examining the benefits. *International Airport Review*, 4, 73–77.

Sigala, M. (2008). Applications and implications of information and communication technology for airports and leisure travelers. In Graham, A., Papatheodorou, A. and Forsyth, P. (Eds.), *Aviation and Tourism: Implications for Leisure Travel*. Ashgate.

SITA (2007). *SITA 2006 Passenger self-service survey*, SITA.

SPT (2006). *SPT: Ideal Process Flow v2*, available from www/spt.aero (accessed 20 February 2008).

Sobie, B. (2007). Stress free, *Airline Business*, December, pp. 47.

Studness, L. (2007). The role of the airport in the JetBlue business model. *Journal of Airport Management*, 1(2), 118–120.

Thorn, S. (2007). Biometric bandwagon, *Airports International*, September, pp. 28–29.

Wong, Y. (2007). Total airport experience at Hong Kong International airport. *2nd ACI Asia-Pacific Regional Assembly, Conference and Exhibition*, Seoul, May.

CHAPTER 5

The airport–airline relationship

The relationship between the airport operator and the airline is clearly fundamental to the success of any airport business. The sweeping changes which have occurred within the airline industry have meant that airlines, more than ever before, are trying to control their costs in order to improve their financial position in an ever increasing competitive and deregulated environment. At the same time, carriers have been facing unprecedented increases in the price of fuel over which they have had very little control. All this is having an impact on the aeronautical policies of airports. In addition to these problems, an ongoing problem is that demand is outstripping capacity at a growing number of airports and so the traditional mechanism for allocating slots has had to be revisited. These issues are considered in this chapter.

The structure of aeronautical charges

Traditionally, aeronautical charging has been relatively simple with most revenue coming from a weight-based landing charge and a passenger fee dependent on passenger numbers. Many airports still generate their aeronautical revenue in this way. At other airports, charging practices have become more complex and more market based. This reflects the increasingly commercial and competitive airport environment and the contemporary challenges faced by airports such as the growing pressure on facilities, environmental concerns, and rising security costs.

Landing charges

Most airports have a weight-related landing charge based on maximum takeoff weight (MTOW) or maximum authorized weight (MAW). The simplest method is to charge a fixed amount unit rate (e.g. US$X per tonne) regardless of the size of the aircraft. A fixed unit rate will favour smaller aircraft types since tonnage tends to increase faster than aircraft capacity or payload. It will also benefit airlines which have high load factors or seating capacities. This simple method is used at many airports throughout the world including the United States, many of the German airports, and Copenhagen. Some airports have a unit landing charge which declines as the weight of the aircraft increases such as at Oslo airport. Manchester and Brussels airports have a maximum charge for large aircraft whereas at Copenhagen half the tonne charge is levied for aircraft over 200 tonnes. At other airports, for example, at Paris and at the Indian and Spanish airports, the unit rate increases for larger aircraft. At Athens, the rate increases after 55 tonnes but then reduces after 120 tonnes.

This charging mechanism uses the 'ability to pay' principles, since airlines using larger aircraft are in a better position to pay higher charges. Some costs such as runway wear and tear do increase with weight and also larger aircraft require vortex separations, which can reduce the number of aircraft movements during a certain period. Overall, however, there is not a strong relationship between aircraft weight and airfield cost. A flat rate landing charge for all aircraft types may be more appropriate, particularly at congested airports. This is because the cost of occupying the congested runway is movement related and independent of aircraft size. Each aircraft movement will consume the same resource.

Very few airports have adopted a movement-related charge which will clearly tend to be very unpopular with airlines flying small aircraft types. Notable exceptions are Heathrow where there is a fixed runway charge for all aircraft above 16 tonnes. A similar charge exists at Gatwick, although in this case these are differentiated between the peak and off-peak periods. Other airports have not gone this far but some have attempted to charge the smallest aircraft more to particularly encourage the general aviation traffic to move away from congested major airports with for example Frankfurt airport having a minimum landing charge set at 35 tonnes. Elsewhere other airports have differential landing charges by time of day (such as Manchester) to reflect the peaking of demand.

Sometimes charges for air traffic control (ATC) or terminal navigational facilities are incorporated into the landing charge. At other airports, the airport operator may levy a separate charge. Typically this charge will be, like the landing charge, related to the weight of the aircraft. Clearly, there is no logical cost rationale for this since each aircraft movement, regardless of the size of the aircraft, imposes the same costs on the ATC infrastructure. Alternatively, the airline will directly pay the ATC agencies and the airport operator will not be involved in the financing of ATC services at all.

At some airports, domestic or short-haul services have traditionally paid a reduced landing fee. This is not a cost-related charge since the cost to land an aircraft is independent of its origin. Instead, it tends to exist to support local and regional services, which are comparatively expensive to operate. Sometimes such services will have a social role in linking together regional communities and so in effect, the discount will be an unofficial subsidy. The European Commission is against landing charge differentials for domestic and intra-EU traffic, claiming that they are contrary to the principles of the Single Market and most EU airports have now abandoned such a policy.

A growing number of airports have noise-related surcharges or discounts, associated with their landing charges, as a result of increasing concerns about the environment. Some of these are based on airport or country specific aircraft acoustic group classifications, as is the case with airports in Spain, Switzerland, and France. Elsewhere, more standard ICAO 'chapter' classifications are used. (These classifications are based on the level of noise that aircraft make and the areas on the ground which are affected by the aircraft noise. There are currently four classifications: chapter 1 aircraft which were banned from airports in 1990, chapter 2 aircraft which were banned in 2002 from most countries, chapter 3 aircraft and the quietest aircraft which are chapter 4, see Chapter 9.) Airports may adopt different sub-classifications within these groups, for example, at London there are 'minus', 'base', and 'high' categories whereas Düsseldorf airport has a 'bonus' list for the quieter aircraft. At many airports such as Brussels, Oslo, Amsterdam, and those in Germany, the landing charges are higher at night. Night charges for noisy aircraft can be very high; for example, at Munich airport, airlines can end up paying three times as much.

In addition to noise disturbance effects, there are increasing concerns about the impact that aircraft emissions are having on the environment (see Chapter 9 for a complete discussion). As yet this has not been reflected in many airport charges, with the notable exception of Zürich and Geneva airports in Switzerland and the Stockholm airports of Arlanda and Bromma which introduced emissions charges in the late 1990s. Heathrow and Gatwick airports also now have emissions charges (since 2004 and 2005, respectively) and Munich and Frankfurt airports introduced them in 2008.

Passenger charges

Passenger charges are the other main source of aeronautical revenue. These charges are most commonly levied per departing passenger. At most airports, there tends to be a lower charge for domestic passengers to reflect the lower costs associated with these types of passengers. The French airports have four types of charges, namely domestic, Schengen-EU, non-Schengen-EU, and international whilst London Heathrow has charges for domestic, Irish and other international passengers. As with the landing charge in some cases, there may be political or social reasons for keeping down the cost of domestic travel as well. Historically, such policies are often maintained to subsidize the national carrier, which has a large domestic operation. It can be argued, however, that domestic passengers have less potential for generating commercial revenues and hence do not justify the lower passenger charge. A number of airports, particularly in Europe, charge a smaller fee for transfer passengers (e.g. Amsterdam, Dublin, Frankfurt, Helsinki, Vienna, Paris, Zürich, Munich, and Copenhagen) (ACI-Europe, 2003a, b). Elsewhere some airports waive the fee completely (e.g. Dubai and Seoul). A lower transfer charge can be justifiable on cost grounds as such passengers will have no surface access requirements, will not have associated meeters and greeters, and very often will not need check-in, security, and immigration facilities either. However, transfer passengers still require facilities such as baggage handling and may require special facilities in order that a rapid transfer is achieved. Some other airports also have differential charges to reflect peaking, such as East Midlands and Glasgow airports. At Zürich airport there is even a noise charge related to passengers!

An interesting recent development at some of the German airports, such as Düsseldorf and Frankfurt is a fee cap related to passenger charges. This means that a refund is provided for all passengers when the load factor exceeds 80 per cent, provided that the airline has maintained load factors above 80 per cent throughout the year.

Security charges

The responsibility for the provision and financing of airport security varies considerably from country to country. The provision of security services may be performed by the airport's own employees, or by a private company under contract to the airport, the airlines, or a government agency. In many cases, responsibility may be shared between these different bodies. This results in different systems being in place to finance the security measures. The government through general taxation or through a special government departure tax may pay for the security measures. In some countries, security costs are financed directly by the airport operator who will have a special security charge or include it in the passenger charge. Sometimes there is a security charge based on passengers and aircraft tonnes as at Frankfurt. Since 9/11, the whole issue of airport security has become a top priority and many airports throughout the world have been enhancing security levels. In the United States, the responsibility for airport security has passed from private security contractors to federal employees with a US$2.50 tax per passenger to cover some of the costs (see Chapter 4 for more details).

Other charges

There are also a number of other charges which tend to be fairly small compared with the landing and passenger fees. First, there is the parking charge which is usually based on the weight of the aircraft or, sometimes, on aircraft wingspan as found in the case of Malta, Singapore and Malaysia, and some US airports. The parking charge might also be based on the size of parking stands as at Frankfurt or Shannon airports, or as a percentage of the landing fee as at Vienna. There is normally an hourly or daily charge with, perhaps, a rebate for using remote stands. Most airports have a free parking charge, typically ranging from 1 to 4 hours to allow the airline to turnaround at the airport without incurring any charges. A few airports, such as BAA's London airports and Frankfurt have no free parking charge to encourage the airlines to minimize turnaround time. BAA's airports charge per quarter hour and during peak times each minute counts as three. For those airports which have a 24-hour charge, such as Amsterdam, Malta, and Düsseldorf, there is clearly no incentive for airlines to make the most effective use of the apron space. Other airports such as Paris and Frankfurt differentiate between different areas of parking and between night and day.

There may be other charges for certain facilities or services which airports choose to price separately rather than include in the landing or passenger charge. For example, there is a lighting charge at the Paris airports. At other airports such as Dublin there may be an airbridge fee, typically charged per movement, or based on the length of time that the airbridge is occupied. Alternatively, there may be different charges depending on whether the service is 'connected' or not to the gate as at Amsterdam and Frankfurt. Sometimes, similar to the passenger charge, there are cargo charges based on the weight of loaded or unloaded cargo as at the Rome airports. There may be a lower fee for all-cargo aircraft, case at Amsterdam, Frankfurt, Paris, or Manchester airports whereas at some airports, such as Belfast International, the landing charge for such aircraft is higher. There may be additional charges related to services such as fire fighting, storage facility, hangar use, and other airport specific activities.

In 2007, charges at a sample of 70 international airports were investigated which provide a good overview of the charging structures used by different airports (Saounatsos, 2007). As regards the landing charge, 82 per cent of all airports in North and South America used a fixed weight whereas in Europe and other areas this was less common (35 and 14 per cent, respectively). Less than a third of all airports had landing charges that differed by origin or charged peaked prices. Seventy-three per cent of European airports applied a noise charge (with 35 per cent of the airports incorporating the noise charge into the landing charge) but this was far less common at American and other airports. Only a few airports had emission charges, mostly in Europe.

Ground handling and fuel charges

Airlines incur three types of charges when they use an airport. First, they pay landing and passenger fees, and, sometimes other airport fees, which have already been discussed. Then there are ground handling fees which the airport operator may levy if it chooses to provide some of these services itself rather than leaving it to the handling agents or airlines. Finally, there are the fuel charges that are levied by the fuel companies which are normally independent of the airport operator. There are a few notable exceptions, such as certain Middle Eastern airports like Abu Dhabi where the fuelling is provided by a government agency. Hence, all services at the airport can be offered to the airline in one overall package.

It is rare to find published data relating to handling and fuel charges. These are usually negotiable and the agreed prices will depend on various factors such as the size of the airline, the scale of its operation at the airport in question and whether the same handling and fuel companies serve other airports used by the airline. Further complexities occur since there are a variety of ways of charging for activities such as ramp handling, passenger handling, apron buses, aircraft cleaning, ground power, pushback, and so on. In some cases, there may be just one or two charges that cover everything, whereas elsewhere there may be a multitude of individual fees.

Government taxes

There is one final charge which airlines or their passengers often experience at an airport – government taxes (see Table 5.1) (International Air Transport Association (IATA), 2006a; Baker, 2006). This income does not directly go to the airport operator but adds to the overall cost of the 'turnaround' from an airline's point of view. For the passenger, it is very difficult to distinguish between the taxes that go to the government and the airport passenger charges which represent revenue for the airport as both are usually shown as a single 'airport taxes and charges' item on the ticket. Sometimes these taxes may pay for some airport service or investment project, as with a number of taxes in the United States. At Athens airport, there is a government airport development fund and some of this is paid to the airport operator. In Portugal the taxes pay for the provision of some security services or for noise management projects at Amsterdam. Mexico City has a tourist tax on international arriving passengers and a number other countries such as Denmark, Hong Kong and Australia impose a tax on departing passengers.

Table 5.1 Main aeronautical charges at airports

Charge	Common basis for charging	Income to airport operator?
Landing	Weight of aircraft	Yes
Terminal navigation	Included in landing charge or based on weight of aircraft	Sometimes
Airbridge	Included in landing charge or based on aircraft movement	Yes
Passenger	Departing passenger	Yes
Security	Included in passenger charge or based on passenger numbers	Yes
Parking	Weight of aircraft per hour or 24 hours after free period	Yes
Ground handling	Different charges for different activities	Sometimes
Fuel	Volume of fuel	No
Government taxes	Departing passenger	No

In the United Kingdom, a departure tax called the Air Passenger Duty, which goes directly to the Treasury, was introduced in 1994. This was greeted with considerable opposition, especially from the new breed of low-cost carriers who complained that it was too large in proportion to the fares that are being offered. As a compromise, in 2001, a differential tax system, with different amounts for economy and business-class passengers, was introduced. Since then it has increased substantially to reflect the environmental costs of the flight (see Chapter 9 for further details), with the lowest rate being £10 for economy class domestic/EU flights and the highest rate being £80 for premium class long-haul flights. In France, in 2006, a 'solidarity tax' of €1 (economy) and €10 (premium) for European passengers and €4/€40 for intercontinental passengers was introduced to fund development aid in poorer countries. In July 2008, the Dutch government is due to introduce a passenger tax of €11 for European travel and €45 for long-haul travel (transfer passengers are exempt) which has been bitterly opposed by the airlines.

Table 5.2 shows that in Europe taxes account for 16 per cent of the total charges whereas in the United States, they represent over a half of the charges (a full discussion of US charging is provided at the end of this chapter). In most areas except in the United States, passenger charges account for a large share of the total revenues, namely, 36 per cent in Europe and 50 per cent elsewhere. In general there has been a trend towards giving greater relative importance to the passenger fee as compared to the landing fee as airlines tend to prefer passenger fees because passenger numbers help to drive their own level of revenues – although this charging is more risky for the airport operator.

Table 5.2 Relative importance of different aeronautical charges and taxes by world region (%) 2007

	Europe	Australasia, Middle East, and Africa	Americas
Landing	24	29	11
ATC	6	2	2
Passenger	36	50	11
Security	10	4	5
Other[a]	7	8	16
Taxes	16	8	56
Total	100	100	100

Notes: Numbers may not add up to 100 because of rounding. Based on a sample of 70 airports and Boeing 777-200 aircraft.
[a] Includes parking and terminal use fees.
Source: Adapted from Saounatsos (2007).

Also as passenger charges are shown separately on the ticket under airport charges and taxes, this can have a marketing advantage as it will have the effect of apparently reducing the overall fare (excluding charges and taxes) that the airline charges.

The level of aeronautical charges

It is very difficult to compare the level of charges at different airports because of the varied nature of the charging structures. To overcome this problem, comparisons have to be made by examining the representative airport charges for an Airbus A319 on a regional cross border service (Figure 5.1). A sample of 18 airports from around the world has been chosen. The costs are divided between aircraft-related costs which include landing charges as well as ATC and airbridge charges, if these exist; passenger-related costs which include passenger charges and any security charges; and government taxes. The data was not sufficient to allow ground handling and fuel costs to be added. Only published charges were used, so the figures do not take account of any discounts that may be available.

There is a wide spread of charges (excluding taxes) ranging from less than €1000 at Dubai and Mumbai airport to over €3000 at Zürich, London Heathrow, and Amsterdam. Dubai has not increased its charges for many years and even reduced them after 9/11. Singapore and Kuala Lumpur airports which are in direct competition with each other have very similar and relatively low charges in spite of both

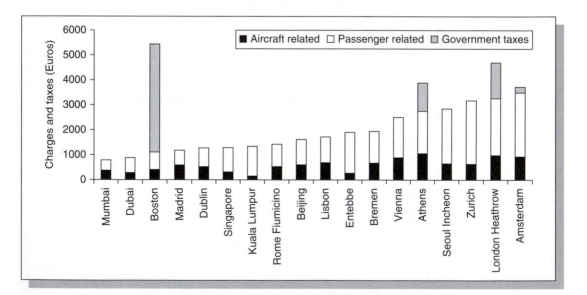

Figure 5.1
Aeronautical charges and taxes for a regional cross-border A319 turnaround in 2007 at world airports.
(*Source*: Cranfield University.)

having a good reputation for a high quality service. The situation changes somewhat when government taxes are included when Boston becomes the most expensive and Heathrow and Athens also become more costly to use. In nearly all cases (except Mumbai) the passenger-related charges are more than the aircraft-related fees. The Jacobs Consultancy undertakes an annual comparison of airport charges and similar relative positions of airports such as Athens, Dubai, Mumbai, and Kuala Lumpur have been observed in these studies.

The impact of aeronautical charges on airline operations

In recent years, airport charges have become increasingly subject to scrutiny from the airlines. A more competitive airline environment and falling yields has forced airlines to focus on major cost-saving initiatives such as outsourcing, reductions in staff numbers, and pegging the level of wages. These are all internal costs over which the airlines have a considerable degree of control. However, airlines have also been looking at their external costs such as airport charges, and demanding that airports adopt cost-cutting and efficiency saving measures themselves, rather than raising their charges (Doganis, 2006). For example, IATA claimed that between 2001 and 2005, airlines reduced their non-fuel costs by 13 per cent whilst at the same time their costs at airports went up by 11 per cent (Citrinot, 2006). The existence of the profitability gap (which was discussed in Chapter 3) as the result of airports generally achieving much higher profit levels than airlines has also contributed to this friction between airports and airlines which has been experienced at some airports. Notable airports where there have been recent disagreements about fees include Paris Charles de Gaulle, Athens, Auckland, Wellington, Sydney, Toronto, and Newark. For a number of years Tokyo Narita was also the subject of much criticism from the airlines until it agreed an average 22 per cent reduction in charges in 2005 (Sobie and Thompson, 2006).

In spite of this growing concern over the level of charges, airport costs generally represent a relatively small part, on average around 4 per cent of an airline's total operating costs. They are least important when long-haul operations are being considered, since the charges are levied relatively infrequently. Airport charges are the most significant for the charter and low-cost carriers as these airlines have minimized or completely avoided some of the other costs which traditional scheduled airlines face. Most low-cost airlines operate short sectors which means that they pay airport charges more frequently. Therefore, it is hardly surprising that it is this type of airline which has been most active in attempting to bring down their airport costs by negotiating incentive deals at airports or operating out of secondary or regional airports which have lower charges.

Accurate international figures illustrating this are difficult to obtain because many airlines do not now report the passenger fee as an airport charge and very often the airport charges may be combined with some other cost item. Figure 5.2 does, however, show the situation for UK airlines. Only landing and passenger charges are shown and so these figures do not represent the total turnaround costs for the airlines. British Airways, with a mix of long- and short-haul flights, has the lowest share of costs at around 3 per cent. For Virgin as well, which only has long-haul flights, airport charges are relatively small. This share is much larger for British Midland, which has a range of domestic and European services with just a very few longer haul flights and Flybe which operates very short sectors. Overall easyJet and MyTravel have very low costs which means that the charges represent quite a significant part (17 per cent) of these costs.

As discussed, peak charges have been introduced by some airports to make the airlines, which are generating the peak demand, pay for the peak capacity infrastructure costs. They have also been used with the intent of shifting some of the peak operations into the off-peak. This is unlikely to occur unless the differential between peak and off-peak pricing is much higher than the current practice. Airline scheduling is a complex task which has to take into account factors such as passenger demand patterns, airport curfews and environmental restrictions, crew availability, peak profiles at other airports, and so on. If the airline were to shift operations to outside the peak period, this could well mean that the peak is merely shifted to another time. In effect, these schedule constraints coupled with the fact that charges make a relatively small contribution to airline total costs, means that demand is fairly inelastic to changes in airport fees. Most peak pricing has very little impact on airline operations other than making it more expensive for airlines to operate in the peak. (The same is probably true of noise and emission charges where maintenance costs and fuel burn considerations are generally likely to have a far greater impact on aircraft renewal strategies than increased airport charges).

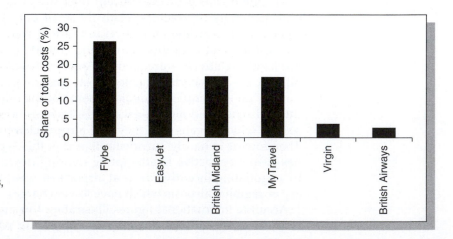

Figure 5.2
Landing and passenger charges as a share of total costs for UK airlines, 2005/06.
(*Source*: CAA airline statistics.)

BAA is one of the few airport operators that developed a peak pricing charging system based on a detailed assessment of marginal costs. In theory, marginal cost pricing leads to the most efficient allocation of resources as only the users, who value a facility at least as much as the cost of providing it, will pay the price for using it. In practice, such pricing policies are complex and very difficult to implement. In the 1970s, BAA introduced a peak surcharge on runway movements on certain summer days, and a peak passenger and parking charge based on marginal cost principles at Heathrow and Gatwick airports. It proved to be ineffectual in shifting any demand largely because of the scheduling problems already described, but also because the charging system was so complex that it was very difficult for the airlines to react. While BAA has retained the peak landing charge (only at Gatwick – Heathrow is full most of the time) and peak parking charges, it has abandoned the more complex peak passenger charges. The airport operator faced widespread opposition from the airlines, particularly the US carriers, to its peak charges, which were considered discriminatory. BAA and the US airlines finally resolved their differences through international arbitration which required BAA to phase out the peak passenger charges. In reality, the airports are now effectively full in most hours and so the concept of the peak hour has become less relevant.

An airport charging policy probably has its greatest impact on airline operations when new routes are being considered – especially when being operated by low-cost airlines or on short regional sectors. This is due to the existence of airport incentive schemes or discounts. These are most likely to be offered at smaller airports that want to encourage growth and provide inducements to airlines which might otherwise not choose to use the airport. Such discounts have, in many cases, been a critical factor when low-cost carriers are selecting suitable airports for their operations (in addition to sufficient demand and fast turnaround facilities). This has been particularly the case when there have been a number of neighbouring or equally suitable airports from which to choose. These discount schemes are discussed in more detail in Chapter 7.

The airport facilities and services that are considered when the airport prices are being set is a major concern of all airlines. There are two alternative approaches, namely the single till approach when all airport activities are included and the dual till approach when just the aeronautical aspects of the operation are taken into account. With the single till concept growth in non-aeronautical revenue can be used to offset increases in aeronautical charges. Within the airport industry single till practices, traditionally were widespread and were accepted by ICAO in its charging recommendations (International Civil Aviation Organization, 1992). The rationale for the single till is that without the aeronautical activities, there would be no market for the commercial operations and hence it is appropriate to offset the level of airport charges with profits earned from non-aeronautical facilities. This is the key justification which the airlines use in favouring such a system which is clearly likely to bring the lowest level of actual charges for them.

However, major concerns about this approach have been voiced (e.g. see Starkie, 2001). As traffic increases, the single till principles will tend to pull down airport charges. This may encourage growth and have the effect of increasing congestion and delays at the airport. The busiest, most congested airports are likely to be in the best position to significantly offset commercial revenues against airport charges. Yet it is these airports which need to manage their limited capacity the most. Bringing down the airport charges for such scarce resources makes no economic sense. In addition, it can be argued that using commercial revenues to offset aeronautical fees prevents these revenues from being used to help finance capital investment, or to aid the development of better commercial facilities. There is thus less incentive to develop commercial operations to their full potential.

By contrast, the dual till concept treats the aeronautical and non-aeronautical areas as separate financial entities, and focuses on the monopoly aeronautical airport services. This is a difficult task because of having to allocate many fixed and joint costs between the aeronautical and the non-aeronautical areas. At the London airports it was calculated some time ago that the transfer from a single till to a dual till approach could mean that airport charges would have to be increased by 35 per cent (Monopolies and Mergers Commission, 1996). The method does, however, provide airports with incentives to develop the commercial side of their business which is effectively uncontrolled, unlike with the single till approach when any development in the commercial areas may well be accompanied by a reduction in aeronautical charges. Clearly there is a major logical argument for not including commercial activities within any regulatory framework since they cannot be considered as monopoly facilities. Moreover, a further argument in favour of the dual till is that it can provide better incentives for aeronautical investment. The reason is that apart from gaining from additional aeronautical revenues if there is aeronautical investment, the airport can benefit from increased unregulated commercial revenues which would have been generated because of the additional passenger volumes. The counter argument here, however, is that with a dual till the incentives to invest on the aeronautical side might be worse as in this case commercial investment might be favoured over aeronautical investment.

As a result of the fierce debate of the merits of the single versus dual systems in recent years, ICAO amended its guidelines on charging in 2001 and the guidelines now state that it may not always be appropriate to use commercial income to offset airport charges (International Civil Aviation Organization, 2004). Currently within Europe a study of 50 major airports found that the single till was used by 42 per cent, the dual till by 29 per cent and a further 25 per cent adopted a hybrid approach (SH&E, 2006). Examples of countries where the major airports use the single till include the United Kingdom, Ireland, France, and Portugal whereas in the Netherlands, Germany (only Frankfurt and Hamburg), Denmark, and Australia a dual till is used. Brussels is aiming to move from a single till to dual till approach in the future (Gillen and Niemeier, 2008). Aéroports de Paris has also indicated that it may not stay with the single till that it now uses. There has been considerable discussion in the United Kingdom about the merits of shifting from a single till to a dual till, but no change has yet occurred. In a theoretical assessment of the different approaches on social welfare, Lu and Pagliari (2004) concluded that the dual till is desirable when aeronautical capacity is fully utilized or already over-utilized, whilst the single till method is preferable where excess capacity exists. Moreover in a study of 60 airports from all over the world, it was concluded that dual till regulation is better than single till regulation in terms of economic efficiency, especially for large and busy airports. (Oum et al., 2004).

Another area of concern for airlines as regards charging policies is cross-subsidization within an airport group under common ownership. This typically occurs when a large international airport provides financial support for a smaller airport, usually serving primarily domestic services. Operators of airport groups argue that the individual airports need to operate as a system to make the most efficient use of resources and to produce cost savings. The airlines tend to be strongly opposed to such cross-subsidizing and argue that if the smaller airports really need financial help for social or economic reasons, they should be supported by government funds instead. There can also be a similar issue when a system approach to pricing is used to fund investment at one particular airport in the system, which it is argued, will bring benefits to the whole system. The notable case here is the BAA London airports where past investment at Stansted airport was cross-subsidized with profits from Heathrow and Gatwick.

A further important airport–airline issue is the pre-financing of future airport infrastructure through airport charges. Pre-financing has traditionally not been an acceptable principle for a number of reasons. First, there is no guarantee that the airlines paying the charges will actually be the airlines which will benefit from the new infrastructure. Also, there may be no certainty that the airport charges will be efficiently spent to provide new facilities. Moreover, the airlines tend to be fearful that they will pay twice for the infrastructure, both before it is built and once it is operational (International Air Transport Association, 2000). However, in spite of these airline concerns, some airports have fees for pre-financing purposes. The most notable example is the United States where Passenger Facility Charges (PFCs) go towards future development projects. A similar situation exists at some Canadian airports. In Greece, higher passenger fees were levied, in spite of airline opposition, to pay for the financing of the new Athens airport. Elsewhere, for example, in the United Kingdom, the regulator takes into account the fact that some pre-financing will take place when setting the appropriate level of charges.

Airports argue that pre-financing in certain circumstances can provide a useful, cheaper source for funding investment in addition to loans and equity which can also be used as security for raising extra finance (Airports Council International, 2000). Airports claim that pre-financing also avoids large increases in airport charges when the infrastructure comes on stream as was experienced at Narita and Kansai airports in Japan or was initially proposed at the new Chek Lap Kok airport in Hong Kong, but was not fully implemented because of fierce opposition from the airlines. As regards the ICAO view, a long established cost recovery policy in the ICAO guidelines on airport charges was that charges should not be levied for any facilities until they become operational. However in recent years, ICAO has acknowledged that, with the growing commercialization within the industry and diminishing dependence on government sources for financing, pre-funding could perhaps be considered, but only in specific safeguarded circumstances. This was therefore incorporated into the amended charging guidelines in 2001.

The airport regulatory environment

Airports are subject to a number of different regulations at both international and national level. Many of these are technical regulations related to the operational, safety and security aspects of managing an airport. Airports are also increasingly becoming subject to environmental regulations which may, for example, restrict aircraft movements due to noise considerations or limit airport infrastructure development. These environmental issues are discussed in detail in Chapter 9. Then there is economic regulation with the main focus being on charge or tariff control. Other economic aspects of operation such as handling activities and slot allocation are also regulated in some areas of the world. Overall, the economic regulatory interest in airports seems to be increasing at a time when, ironically, the airlines business is being progressively deregulated.

On a worldwide basis, the 1944 Chicago Convention, which established an international regulatory air transport system, provides a basis for airport charging. Article 15 gives international authority for the levying of charges by ICAO member states and specifies that there shall be no discrimination between users, particularly from different countries. ICAO produces more detailed guidelines which have an overriding principle that charges should be cost related. They also recommend that the charging system should be transparent and that consultation should take place between airport operators and their customers if changes are proposed (International Civil Aviation Organization, 2004). Such principles were revised in 2001 to take account of new views on issues, such as the single till and pre-financing, which have already been discussed. They are only guidelines and are open to different interpretations, but have generally led to fairly similar overall pricing regimes being adopted by most airports, being broadly related to average cost pricing combined with some market or ability-to-pay pricing. Airport charges can also be subject to the international obligations of bilateral agreements, although this is becoming much less common now. For example, the old UK/US bilateral air service, Bermuda 2 (which was replaced in 2008 by the EU–US Open Skies agreement) stated that airport charges must be related to costs and should allow only reasonable profits. This resulted in a lengthy dispute over Heathrow charges in the 1980s and the 1990s between the US and the UK governments with an eventual agreement in 1994 which provided for a compensation of nearly $30 million in settlement (Competition Commission, 2002).

At a regional level, for many years the European Commission has been proposing the introduction of an airport charges regulatory framework for the whole EU. The first proposal appeared in 1985, and there have been several other attempts to seek approval for such legislation. In January 2007, the European Commission published its most recent proposals. These were based on ICAO principles of non-discrimination, consultation and transparency, but went further by suggesting specific regulations for all EU airports of over 1 million passengers. The proposals recommended the setting up of an independent national regulator in each country and detailed the level of consultation which should take place between airlines and airports. As regards transparency it proposed that airports should supply financial information to the airlines concerning the method of the calculation of charges and the cost structure of the airport, whilst the airlines should provide the airports with information on their traffic forecasts and requirements at the airport. Service level agreements between the airports and their airlines to be decided every 2 years were also proposed. In addition the proposals allowed for differentiation of charges, for example, providing tailored services in dedicated parts of a terminal for additional fees, and they stated that if there were security charges they should be set exclusively to meet security costs (European Commission, 2007a). In January 2008, the proposal received its first reading in the European Parliament where the most significant change was in altering the threshold size for airports which the directive applied to from 1 to 5 million passengers which would reduce the number of regulated airports from 144 (180 in 2011) to 55 (70 in 2011).

Various interested parties have different views about these proposals (European Commission, 2007b). The airlines have generally argued the case for the introduction of the directive and have welcomed the proposals. However members of the Association of European Airlines (AEA) (2008) are disappointed that the directive does not prohibit pre-financing and would generally like more specific provisions to make the airports more cost efficient. Likewise the low cost airlines do not want any pre-financing and would like the directive to stipulate the use of the single till (European Low Fare Airline Association, 2008). However, the airports feel that even the more restrictive 5 million passenger threshold means that too many airports, which do not necessarily have substantial market power, will be regulated unnecessarily and also that the directive does not do enough to incentivise airports to investment (ACI-Europe, 2008). The UK Civil Aviation Authority which has the longest experience in Europe of formally regulating airport charges, also feels that the regulation could be burdensome and should only apply to airports with substantial market power (Civil Aviation Authority, 2007).

Regulation of individual airports

The basic principles

At a national or individual airport level, the degree of government control varies considerably. Many airports under public sector ownership usually need to seek government approval before changing their charging level or structure. In some cases, this may be just a formality. At the other extreme, it may be the government's responsibility to set charges, perhaps after receiving recommendations from the airports. In some countries, particularly where there has been privatization, there may be a more formal economic regulation system. In 1999, ICAO reviewed the situation at 76 member countries throughout the world. Fifty-seven per cent of countries stated that the airport operator with government approval determined charges, and a further 16 per cent of the airport operators determined their charges independently. For the remaining countries, the government was directly responsible for setting the level of fees to be charged (International Civil Aviation Organization, 2000). In a more recent study of 50 major European airports in 2005, it was found that only 5 per cent needed no government approval and 10 per cent had automatic approval. A further 52 per cent had approval (often against transparent criteria) following negotiation, and 31 per cent had their charges set more formally with an agreed formula (SH&E, 2006). Countries in Europe where government approval is sought include Belgium, Cyprus, Czech Republic, Estonia, Italy, Latvia, Lithuania, Poland, Portugal, Slovakia, Spain, and Switzerland.

A more formal regulatory system is often established when there are serious concerns that airports with considerable market power will abuse this situation. This is particularly relevant when airports are privatized and a number of new regulatory frameworks have been set up in countries where privatization has occurred. This has involved using regulatory authorities which are already in existence (as in the United Kingdom) or creating new bodies specifically for this purpose (as in Ireland). Although the regulatory systems at different airports vary, their common purpose is to allow the regulated airports a reasonable rate of return (ROR) on capital while providing the correct incentives for an efficient operation and an appropriate investment policy. In choosing the most suitable regulatory system, consideration has to be given as to the best incentives to encourage appropriate investment, the treatment of commercial revenues, and the maintenance of standards of service. A suitable review process also has to be established.

In general, there are three key ways in which organizations with monopolistic characteristics can be regulated:

1. rate of return regulation
2. price cap regulation
3. reserve regulation.

The ROR mechanism, or so-called cost-based or profit control regulation, is the traditional mechanism which has been used extensively, for example, in the United States and Australia, to regulate natural monopolies. The aim is to prevent regulated companies from setting prices that bear no relation to costs. A certain ROR is established and price increases can only be justified when an increase in costs is incurred. Although such a system can ensure that the prices are related to costs, it provides no incentives to reduce costs. The operator will be guaranteed a certain ROR irrespective of efficiency. Cost inefficiencies might be built into the cost structure which could be passed on to the consumers through increased prices. Such a system can also encourage over investment. To ensure that this does not occur, the regulator has to scrutinize carefully the financial operations and development plans of the regulated companies.

To overcome these shortcomings, alternative regulatory systems have been sought. In the 1980s, price cap regulation began to be used, for example, in the United Kingdom, where a number of the state utilities such as gas and electricity were privatized (Helm and Jenkinson, 1998). This type of regulation, often called incentive regulation, was considered to be more favourable as it can provide the regulated company with incentives to reduce costs while simultaneously controlling price increases. It works by establishing a formula which provides a maximum price that can be set. Typically, the formula will be adjusted for inflation and an efficiency factor:

$$\text{Price cap} = \text{CPI} - X \text{ or RPI} - X$$

where CPI is the consumer price index, RPI the retail price index, and X the efficiency gain target. Costs which are beyond the control of the company can be excluded from the regulation:

$$\text{Price cap} = \text{CPI} - X + Y$$

where Y is the external costs.

Since there is no cap on the profit levels, unlike the ROR method, any efficiency gains which the regulated company can make in excess of the required X will directly benefit the company. Such a method tends to be simpler to administer as companies can change their level or structure of prices as long as they still conform to the price cap without any justification from the regulator – which would be the situation with the ROR system. However there is an issue that the price cap may give inadequate incentives to investment because of the focus on short-term operational efficiency gains within each relatively small price control period combined with the lumpiness and long-lead time of investments.

However, it has also been argued that price cap regulation is not actually an effective alternative to cost-based regulation since the regulator will take into account the ROR of the company, as well as other factors such as operational efficiency, planned investment and the competitive situation, when setting the price cap. For example, in United Kingdom, in order to calculate the total revenue required a regulated asset base (RAB) is defined and valued at the beginning of the price control period and then consequently enlarged to take account of the projected capital expenditure. A cost of capital allowance and depreciation allowance based on the RAB is then added to the projected level of operating expenditure (which will have taken account of any feasible improvements in efficiency) to arrive at the total revenue requirement. The RAB valuation and the cost of capital assumptions are therefore key in determining the maximum level of prices that are allowed. Thus, the regulated company may still have an incentive to overstate the capital expenditure needed, which will only be discouraged by careful scrutiny of the regulator. In spite of these shortcomings, price cap regulation has been the most popular approach adopted for privatized airports.

A further type of regulation is the 'light-handed' approach or 'trigger', 'reserve', 'shadow', or 'conduct' regulation. Here the regulator will only become involved in the price-setting process if the airport's market power is actually abused or if the company and its customers cannot reach agreement. In this case it is the threat of regulation, rather than actual regulation, which is used to provide an effective safeguard against anti-competitive behaviour (Toms, 2003). Sometimes, with reserve regulation, there may be a predetermined regulatory model which will become effective at this stage.

With regulated airports, decisions have to be made as to which airport facilities and services are to be considered under the pricing regime, that is, whether a single till or dual till should be used. In addition if a price cap is used, the regulator must also decide how the 'price' element of the formula is to be set. The main choice is whether to use a revenue yield or tariff basket methodology. The revenue yield formula means that the predicted revenue per unit (usually passengers, in the case of airports) in the forthcoming year will be allowed to increase by the CPI − X or RPI − X percentage. With the tariff basket definition, the weighted average price of a specified 'basket' of tariffs or charges will be allowed to be raised by CPI − X.

Both methods have their drawbacks, and their relative strengths have been fiercely debated by regulators and the industry. The tariff basket approach tends to be simpler since it operates directly on charges and is independent of any forecasts. Companies might, however, be encouraged to put the largest increases on the faster growing traffic since the weights used in the tariff basket are from a previous period. With the revenue yield methodology, an artificial incentive may be created to increase passengers to inflate the denominator in the definition. This could lead to the setting of some charges below the marginal costs of the corresponding services. In general the tariff basket approach is usually considered to give airports greater incentives to move to a more efficient pricing structure. Within Europe over half (59 per cent) the airports with a price cap use the tariff basket approach as opposed to 41 per cent who use the revenue yield method (SH&E, 2006).

It is a common practice to set the price cap in relation to the average costs, which would include consideration of any proposed investment programme, additional costs related to improvements in the quality of service and a reasonable ROR. There has been some debate, however, as to whether industry benchmarking could have a much more active role in this process (Civil Aviation Authority, 2000). Industry best practice could, in theory, replace an assessment of accounting costs as the basis for setting the price cap. This has already been used by the utility regulators for both England and the Netherlands (Burns, 2000). This would mean that the regulatory control would be independent of any company action inappropriately influencing the key variables used in the regulatory formula, such as inflating the asset base. Alternatively, benchmarking could be used much more as a crosscheck to internal methods of setting the price, estimating investment costs or assessing the scope for efficiency and service quality improvements.

The adoption of such 'regulatory benchmarking' is fraught with difficulties because of the extensive problems of comparability associated with such an exercise, the subjective nature by which some of the associated problems are overcome and the lack of general consensus as to the optimal method of benchmarking (see Chapter 3). There is also the fundamental issue that such an approach assumes high costs are, in fact, the result of inefficiency, whereas in reality they may be due to a number of other factors. Only a very detailed assessment of the benchmarking data may be able to identify these factors (Shuttleworth, 2000). Overall all these difficulties have meant that benchmarking has yet to play a major role in setting the overall price although it has increasingly been used to investigate an airport's performance in certain specific areas when the regulatory review is being undertaken.

Another area of major concern within any regulatory framework is often the quality of service (as discussed in Chapter 4). When the regulation does not formally establish service standards or require an appropriate quality monitoring system, there may be little incentive for the airport operator to optimize quality. In reducing the service standards at the airport, the operator could be able to soften the blow of the price control. This could be overcome, in theory, by ensuring that there are measures of congestion and delays to assess the adequacy of the airport facilities and by assessing passenger and airline feedback to determine the operational efficiency of the airport. In practice, as outlined in Chapter 4, defining service dimensions and attempting to adopt a standardized quality level is extremely difficult – particularly given the different expectations of different types of airlines and passengers. In Australia, the initial regulatory framework which was set up when the airports were privatized included some formal service quality monitoring and reporting. At BAA airports service quality came under close scrutiny during the review process, although there were no explicit regulations until 2003.

Regulation examples

In the United Kingdom, both BAA London and Manchester airports have been subject to single till price cap regulation since 1987 (although this is currently under review). The other smaller regional airports do not have direct price control as they are not considered to have sufficient market power to warrant this. The price cap is reviewed every 5 years after an extensive assessment of the airport's operations, financial performance and future plans has been undertaken. Over the years, the approach has tended to drift much more closely to an ROR method with very detailed consideration of the RAB and cost of capital – which as discussed tends to be one of the shortcomings of the price cap approach. The revenue yield method has been adopted at these airports.

Initially the price cap was the same at all airports, being RPI-1 (Table 5.3). During the second 5-year review period in the early 1990s, the price cap was far more restrictive, particularly for the London airports. For the year 1997–2002, the London airport formula did not take account of the loss of EU duty- and tax-free sales

Table 5.3 The 'X' value used for the UK airport price caps

Airport	1987–1991	1992–1993	1994	1995–1996	1997–2002[a]	2003–2008
Heathrow	−1	−8	−4	−1	−3	+6.5
Gatwick	−1	−8	−4	−1	−3	0
Stansted	−1	−8	−4	−1	+1	0
	1988–1992	**1993–1994**	**1995**	**1996–1997**	**1998–2002**	**2003–2009**
Manchester	−1	−3	3	−3	−5	−5

[a] The normal 5-year charging period was extended to 6 years because of the timing of decisions related to the development of Terminal 5 at Heathrow.
Source: Centre for the Study of Regulated Industries.

in 1999. Instead, a compensatory 15 per cent increase in charges over 2 years following abolition of sales was allowed. At Manchester, the abolition was considered when setting the value of X. These airports could allow most increases in security costs to be passed straight through to the airline. Initially 75 per cent of costs were permitted to be passed through with this percentage rising to 95 per cent after the first 5-yearly review. A major impact of this single till regulation at the London airports has been that the commercial aspects of the business have been considerably expanded which has simultaneously led to a substantial reduction in real charges to airline users. This was until 2003–2008 at Heathrow airport when the price cap was set at RPI +6.5 per cent to take account of £7.4 billion investment needs (particularly Terminal 5). At Gatwick and Stansted, it was set at equal to RPI whereas at Manchester there was a price cap of RPI –5 (Civil Aviation Authority, 2003a, b). It was also decided that there should be rebates for users if certain service quality standards were not achieved (see Chapter 4 for details).

The regulation process is somewhat complex because there are two regulators involved (Graham, 2008). There is the sector regulator with detailed knowledge of the aviation industry, namely the Civil Aviation Authority (CAA), and the Competition Commission (previously known as the Monopolies and Mergers Commission) that is a very experienced more general trading regulator. It is the Competition Commission that undertakes the detailed review of the airports' operations every 5 years which then offers advice to the CAA concerning the most appropriate level of price control. The CAA then makes the final decision on the price cap after consultation with the industry and other interested parties. Whilst the skills of these two regulators should be complementary, the two bodies have not always been in agreement. For example, in the 1991 review of BAA they had very different views on assumptions concerning the cost of capital which led to substantially different values of 'X' in the pricing formula being suggested until a compromise was eventually reached (Toms, 2004). Also in the review for the years 2003–2008, the CAA favoured a shift to the dual till whilst the Competition Commission wanted the retention of the single till. In the end the single till was kept (Civil Aviation Authority, 2003a).

In the latest review for 2008–2013, a price cap of +23.5 and +21.0 per cent will be applied for Heathrow and Gatwick respectively for 2008–2009, followed +7.5 per cent and +2.0 per cent for the other 4 years (Civil Aviation Authority, 2008). These positive values of X are to take account of the increases in costs of security and recent and new investments – particularly at Heathrow with Terminal 5 and Heathrow East – but the scale of increases have been very unpopular with the airline industry. Also the incentives for improving service quality have been strengthened as have the capital investment incentive triggers which had been originally introduced in 2003. Manchester airport is no longer price regulated as after a review by the government it was decided that the airport did not have enough market power to warrant this (Department for Transport, 2008a). Stansted was also investigated but in this case the price cap was kept (Department for Transport, 2008b). This will be applied from 2009.

Other countries that have adopted a similar single till price cap regulatory mechanism when they were privatized include South Africa where charges are determined for a period of 5 years but this time with a 2 year overlap – so in effect it is applied every 3 years. In Ireland also, single till price cap regulation, with different limits related to off-peak periods and cargo, was introduced in 2001. These airports are owned by the public sector Dublin Airport Authority company that has considerable market power and handles over 97 per cent of all passenger traffic in Ireland. Two airports recently privatized, namely Malta and Budapest also have price cap regulation but in these cases related to a dual till. Amsterdam airport, where proposals to privatize are yet to be realized, is one of the few major airports in Europe to use a ROR dual till method. At Vienna airport, a slightly different approach has been adopted taking into account both inflation rates and traffic growth patterns. The regulation is applied directly to the charges. There is a sliding scale which protects revenues when there is slow growth, while requiring productivity gains to be made when traffic growth is high (ACI-Europe, 2005). Hamburg airport also uses a sliding scale related to traffic growth with a dual till price cap regulatory system (Niemeier, 2002).

The initial regulatory framework for the privatized Australian airports was fairly similar to that adopted by the UK airports, in that there was a CPI – X formula which also had a security element – but in this case 100 per cent of the charges were allowed to be passed through to the airlines. There was also a dual till rather than a single till. The Australian airports used the basket tariff rather than the revenue yield approach. As in the United Kingdom, the price cap was set for an initial 5 years, but the Australian regulatory framework had more formal conditions relating to airport access and quality of service monitoring which did not apply to the UK airports. The problems of inadequate investment under such regulation were also recognized and so provision was made for an upward adjustment to the price cap if the approved investment was undertaken. The only major airport that was not controlled in this way was Sydney airport, which was not privatized when this regulation was introduced and was subject to a ROR type of regulation which just involved the surveillance or monitoring of prices rather than more restrictive price control (Forsyth, 2004).

This price regulation of Australian airports was identified as causing a number of problems, particularly the requirement of detailed and cumbersome regulatory intervention if investment was planned and overall profit volatility. These problems became acute with the events of 9/11 and the collapse of Ansett, Australia's second largest domestic airline. As a consequence in October 2001, the Australian government suspended the price regulation at all but the four largest airports. Price surveillance was maintained at Sydney airport and at Melbourne, Perth, and Brisbane the price caps were adjusted upwards which allowed the airports to substantially increase their charges. Under the regulatory system, the Australian Productivity Commission was required to undertake a review after it had been in force for 5 years. The final report of the Commission was published in 2002 (Productivity Commission, 2002). It was recommended that price regulation should be replaced by a much more light-handed price monitoring or surveillance and although the price control could be re-introduced if the airports abused their pricing freedom. Amongst some of the arguments used to support this change in regulatory approach (i.e. reserve regulation) was the fact that the price cap system had been costly to administer, had produced poor financial results for the airports, and was unnecessary as commercial pressures would ensure that the airports would not abuse their market power (Forsyth, 2002). The temporary relaxation of the pricing controls was subsequently made permanent and the airports have moved to this reserve regulation system. In 2006 a further review was undertaken by the Productivity Commission which recommended a continuation of the current system for a further 6 years and the government accepted this recommendation (Forsyth, 2008). Elsewhere, the BAA Scottish airports in the United Kingdom is another example of reserve regulation practice.

There has been considerable debate within the airport sector over the last few years as to which is the most optimal method of economic regulation to use (e.g. see Forsyth *et al.*, 2004). Whereas the European Commission and a number of airlines are favouring more regulation, others (e.g. Starkie, 2002, 2005) have argued that given the fact that airports are operating in an increasingly competitive environment that they should no longer be considered as monopoly providers and consequently in the future more governments should move towards a more reserved or light-handed approach. It is argued that most of the current regulatory systems are time-consuming, bureaucratic, and costly and that in most cases litigation or national competition law can cope with any abuses of market power. Moreover, it is asserted that economic regulation can bring its own economic distortions with the problems, for example, of using a single till approach at congested airports which may well give wrong pricing signals or with the difficult cost allocation decisions that have to be made should the dual till approach be adopted.

Related to this is the case of New Zealand where the two main airports of New Zealand, namely Auckland and Wellington, were partially privatized in 1998. The privatization legislation allowed for these airports and Christchurch airport to review their charges every 3 years but they were not subject to any formal price regulation. The legislation also called for the regulator to conduct periodic reviews to assess whether price controls were necessary. This light-handed approach led to much conflict between the airport operators and users regarding the level of charges particularly at Auckland airport and in 2002 it was recommended by the Commerce Commission that price control should be introduced at Auckland airport. This was not recommended for Christchurch and Wellington, however, where the abuse of market power was not considered to be an issue. In spite of this in 2003 the Commerce Minister announced her decision on these recommendations and decided that there would be no controls on any of the three airports (Mackenzie-Williams, 2004).

Another alternative to formal economic regulation can be some kind of recognized agreement between the airlines and airports. Traditionally, the normal contract between an airline and an airport is the published airport conditions of use, which describes the services provided in exchange for the aeronautical fees. This is not a formalized relationship as it does not identify the rights and obligations of both parties. For example, there is no agreement as regards the standard of services to expect and no process is identified should disputes between the airlines and airports arise. The only major country which has the rights and obligations clearly defined and incorporated into a legally binding contract is the United States. These use and lease agreements concentrate on the fees and rentals to be paid, the method by which these are calculated and the conditions of use of the facilities. Service standards are not usually incorporated into these agreements.

However there have been some cases of a more formalized airline–airport relationship emerging. For example, the low cost airlines, such as Ryanair and easyJet, have sought more long-term deals at airports which they have chosen as bases when both fees and service levels are considered. Elsewhere some airports have voluntarily agreed charge levels directly with their airline customers rather than having to go through a regulator. For example at Copenhagen, the airport operator, Danish airlines and IATA representing foreign airlines have established 3-year agreements concerning airport charges. Between 2003 and 2005, it was agreed that charges would increase by 2.75 per cent annually. For 2006–2008, it was decided that charges would increase by 3 per cent in 2006, and 1 per cent in 2007 and 2008. Simultaneously, incentives for passenger growth and the use of large aircraft were introduced, and the security charge was reduced (Copenhagen Airport, 2005). The government only regulates the airport (with a dual till price cap) if the airport and airlines cannot reach an agreement. Likewise in Australia, the movement from price regulation to price monitoring, has encouraged the airports and the airlines to reach 5 year agreements which cover charges and service. Even in the United Kingdom, where a more heavy-handed price cap regulation exists, during the review for the price cap for 2008–2013 the airports and the airlines were encouraged for the first time to enter into a much more direct dialogue (called 'Constructive Agreement') to try to reach an agreement on investment levels, service quality and traffic forecasts – which was successful in some but not all areas.

The initial airport–airline agreement at Frankfurt airport in 2002 went further than all these others. It was a 5-year agreement with Lufthansa, the German Airline Association and the board of airline representatives in Germany (BARIG) that represents airlines flying to Germany and was a risk sharing model which linked airport charges to traffic growth. The 2001 ratio of airports charges to the number of departing passengers was used as a reference ratio for this model. It was agreed that if the passenger forecast figures were reached then the reference ratio would be increased by about 2 per cent annually. If the passenger traffic grew faster than expected then the airlines would receive one-third of this additional revenue due to the unplanned passenger numbers and two-thirds would go to Fraport. Conversely, the airlines would bear one-third of the risk associated with the passenger traffic if it fell below the levels which were planned.

The agreement was validated by public law and if any disputes occurred the Hesse State could intervene and impose dual till ROR regulation. There was a Special Review Board that had representatives from the airlines, Fraport and local government which had four meetings a year to discuss issues arising from the agreement and to swap information. The deal also secured the financing of a 76 million Euro noise protection programme for the local residents. Under the agreement, the airlines waived their right to take legal action against the level of charges whilst Fraport made commitments not to cut costs by reducing service standards and to undertake investment projects which were planned. (Fraport, 2002; Klenk, 2004). Düsseldorf airport also has had a revenue sharing agreement since 2005.

Overall, a study of 50 major airports in Europe in 2005, found that 51 per cent used a price cap formula but only 14 per cent used a ROR formula – with the single till being the most popular approach (SH&E, 2006). A single till price cap is what is favoured by IATA in Europe (International Air Transport Association, 2006a). Table 5.4 compares the formal economic regulation systems that exist at major European airports.

Slot allocation

The rise in air traffic in recent years has put increased pressure on airport capacity, particularly runway capacity, throughout the world. Although, theoretically timely capacity addition might provide a solution to this problem, in many cases environmental, physical or financial constraints have meant that in practice this has not been a feasible or desirable option. Instead, attention has been focused on more short-term solutions to provide some relief for the shortage of capacity both by consideration of capacity or supply-side approaches and by the assessment of demand management options. In a climate

Table 5.4 Examples of formal economic regulation at major European airports

Airport	Type of regulation	Single or dual till
Amsterdam	Rate of return	Dual till
Budapest	Price cap	Dual till
Copenhagen[a]	Price cap	Dual till
Dublin	Price cap	Single till
Frankfurt[a]	Rate or return with revenue sharing	Dual till
Hamburg	Price cap with sliding scale related to passenger growth	Dual till
Malta	Price cap	Dual till
London Heathrow, Gatwick, Stansted	Price cap	Single till
Paria	Price cap	Single till
Vienna	Price cap with sliding scale related to passenger growth	Single till

[a] At Frankfurt and Copenhagen the level of charges are agreed between the airport operator and airline and the economic regulation will only be used if an agreement cannot be reached.
Sources: Compiled by the author from various sources.

of growing environmental opposition to new developments, such solutions may be politically more acceptable. Supply-side options aim to make more efficient use of existing capacity by improving ATC services and ground-side facilities, and thus provide for incremental increases in traffic. Demand management techniques consider the most appropriate mechanisms for allocating airport slots. Airport slots are usually defined as an arrival or departure time at an airport, typically within a 15- or 30-minute period. They are different from ATC slots which are takeoff and landing times assigned to the airline by ATC authorities.

Alternative slot allocation procedures have to be considered at airports because the pricing mechanism fails to balance demand with the available supply. As already discussed, the current level of charges at airports and peak/off-peak differentials when in existence have a relatively limited impact on airline demand. Peak charges would have to be considerably higher to ration demand or to be the equivalent to the market-clearing price needed to match supply and demand or 'clear the market'. This is obviously not helped by the acceptance at many airports of the single till concept which can pull down the level of charges to below that of the cost of supply.

Currently, in all parts of the world except the United States, the mechanism for allocating slots is industry self-regulation by using IATA Schedule Co-ordination Conferences or Committees. These voluntary conferences of both IATA and non-IATA airlines are held twice a year for the summer and winter season with the aim of reaching consensus on how schedules can be co-ordinated at designated capacity-constrained airports. These airports are designated at two levels:

1. *Schedules facilitated (level 2) airports:* demand is approaching capacity but slot allocation can be resolved through voluntary co-operation. These are known as level 2 airports.
2. *Fully co-ordinated (level 3) airports:* demand exceeds capacity and formal procedures are used to allocate slots. The most important of these procedures is 'grandfather rights'. This means that any airline which has operated a slot in the previous similar season has the right to operate it again. This is as long as the airline operates 80 per cent of the flights – the so-called slot retention requirement or 'use it or lose it' rule. The airline does not, however, have to use its slots for the same services each year and can exchange them, for example, between domestic and international routes. Preference is also given to airlines that plan to use a slot more intensively to make the most effective use of the capacity. For example, priority would be given to an airline which plans a daily service rather than one which is less than daily or a service which operates throughout the season rather than only in the peak.

There are also level 1 airports which are non-co-ordinated airports where supply exceeds demand and slot allocations can be decided with simple discussions between the airline, handling agent (if relevant), and airport. Each of the fully co-ordinated or level 3 airports has an airport co-ordinator, traditionally the national airline of the country, which manages the slot allocation process. Between 1990 and 1999, the number of fully co-ordinated airports increased by 18 per cent, while for the schedules facilitated or level 2 airports there was a higher growth of 63 per cent. In 1999, there were 120 fully co-ordinated airports with more than 10 others being fully co-ordinated in the summer months only. Around 80 airports were schedules facilitated. By 2007 there were 139 fully co-ordinated airports and 87 schedules facilitated airports (International Air Transport Association, 2007). Many US airports are also capacity constrained but do not come under the IATA Scheduling Committee mechanism.

In 2007, there were 46 schedules facilitated and 92 fully co-ordinated airports in Europe (Table 5.5). Within the EU, slot allocation comes under the regulation number 95/93 which was introduced in 1993. While the IATA co-ordination system is voluntary, the EU rules are a legal requirement. The IATA system developed primarily as a process to co-ordinate schedules and to avoid unnecessary congestion, whereas the EU regulation had other key objectives such as making the most efficient use of capacity and encouraging competition. However, many of the IATA features have been incorporated into the European law (Table 5.6). An important difference with the European regulation is that the co-ordinator must be independent of all airlines at the airport, thus enabling the process to be more transparent and

Table 5.5   Slot co-ordination status of European airports in 2007

Country	Fully co-ordinated airports (level 3)	Schedules facilitated airports (level 2)
Austria	Vienna	Graz, Innsbruck, Klagenfurt, Linz, Salzburg
Belgium	Brussels	
Bulgaria		Sofia
Cyprus		Larnaca, Paphos
Czech Republic	Prague	
Denmark	Copenhagen	
Finland	Helsinki	
France	Lyon, Paris (Charles de Gaulle, Orly)	Nice
Germany	Berlin (Schoenefeld, Templehof, Tegel) Düsseldorf, Frankfurt, Munich, Stuttgart	Bremen, Cologne, Dresden, Erfut, Hamburg, Hannover, Leipzig, Muenster, Nuremberg, Saarbuecken
Greece	Athens, Chiania, Chios, Corfu, Heraklion, Kalamata, Karpathos, Kavala, Kefallinia, Kos, Lemnos, Mikonos, Mytilene, Paros, Patras, Preveza/Lefkas, Rhodes, Samos, Skiathos, Skiros, Thessalonika, Thira, Zakinthos	
Hungary		Budapest
Iceland	Reykjavik	
Ireland	Dublin	
Italy	Cagliari, Catania, Florence, Lampedusa, Milan (Malpensa, Linate, Orio al Serio), Naples, Palermo, Pantelleria, Rome (Fiumcino, Ciampino), Turin, Venice	Bologna, Pisa
Luxembourg	Luxembourg	
Malta		Luga
Netherlands	Amsterdam, Eindhoven, Rotterdam,	
Norway	Oslo, Stavanger	Bergen
Poland		Gdansk, Katowice, Krakow, Poznan, Rzeszow, Szczecin, Wroclaw
Portugal	Faro, Funchal, Lisbon, Porto	Ponta Delgada
Spain	Alicante, Almeria, Barcelona, Bilbao, Fuerteventura, Gerona, Gran Canaria, Ibiza, Lanzarote, Madrid, Malaga, Menorca, Palma, Reus, Seville, Tenerife (Norte, Reina Sofia), Valencia	La Coruna, Santiago de Compostela, Vitoria, Zaragoza
Sweden	Stockholm (Arlanda, Bromma)	Gothenburg
Switzerland	Geneva, Zürich	Basel-Mulhouse
United Kingdom	London (Heathrow, Gatwick, Stansted), Manchester	Aberdeen, Birmingham, Bristol, Edinburgh, Glasgow, London City, London Luton, Newcastle

Source: International Air Transport Association (2007).

Table 5.6 Key features of the 1993 EU slot allocation regulation

Slots are allocated on basis of historical precedence or 'grandfather rights'
Airlines must use slots of 80% of time – 'use it or lose it' rule
There is a slot pool for new or returned slots
Fifty per cent of slots in the pool are allocated to new entrants
Certain slots can be ring fenced if they are vital for social or economic reasons
Airports are non-co-ordinated, co-ordinated (schedules facilitated) or fully
   co-ordinated
Co-ordination status is defined after capacity review and consultation
An independent co-ordinator supervises the allocation of slots

Source: European Commission (1993).

impartial. In order for an airport to become co-ordinated, the legislation requires that a thorough capacity analysis and consultation process must take place.

The European legislation aims to encourage new entrants, which are clearly disadvantaged by the grandfather rights system, by giving them preference of up to 50 per cent of any new or unused slots. New entrants were initially defined as airlines with less than 4 per cent of daily slots at an airport or less than 3 per cent of slots in an airport system, such as the London airports. They were also airlines which have requested slots for a non-stop intra-EU service where two incumbent airlines already operate. Under certain conditions, slots may be reserved for domestic regional services or routes with public service requirements, so-called 'ring-fencing'.

The grandfather rights system is used with an 80 per cent slot retention requirement although this 'use it or lose it rule' was temporarily suspended after 9/11 since airlines dropped routes because of the sudden downfall in traffic but did not want to lose their historical slots. This was permitted as the result of an amendment in 2002 which states that in certain exceptional circumstances air carriers will not lose their grandfather rights to slots. Airlines are also allowed to exchange slots with other airlines but not to trade slots. In reality, however, a 'grey market' in slot trading, particularly in the United Kingdom, has developed (see discussion below).

The European Commission undertook a review of this slot allocation process and found that there was little evidence that it had encouraged competition or lessened the influence of the major flag carriers at the airports. This is hardly surprising given that the European regime largely maintained the grandfather rights system. At the same time, delays and congestion at many European airports have increased. After a long period of further review and consultation, the European Commission put forward some new proposals in 2001. The proposals were divided into two parts: first, some immediate technical amendments to the existing regulation (which

Table 5.7 Key features of the 2004 amendments to the 1993 EU slot allocation regulation

The co-ordinator is financially independent
The legal status of a slot is a permission not entitlement or property
There is a broader definition of a 'new entrant'
At a local level the rules can be linked to aircraft size for environmental reasons
At a local level the rules can be linked to other transport modes
There are improved enforcement and monitoring procedures

Source: European Commission (2004).

were adopted in 2004) and second some more long-term aims concerned with structural changes to the actual system of allocation.

The technical amendments (793/2004) covered a number of different areas primarily to make the system more flexible and to strengthen the co-ordinator's role (Table 5.7). They stated that there should be financially independent co-ordinators at each airport and that there should be better enforcement and monitoring of the slot rules. An attempt was made to clarify the legal status of slots by defining them as 'entitlements' or 'rights of usage' rather than property to be owned. This was by far the most contentious issue. There was the retention of grandfather rights and the 'use it or lose it' rule but the new entrant threshold was raised to 7 per cent. Another new feature was consideration of environmental constraints with the possibility of higher priority being given to larger aircraft size or lower priority to services where surface alternatives existed.

In the longer term the European Commission is looking at more radical changes to the current process (Kilian, 2008; Sorensen, 2008). In 2004 a report considering market oriented slot allocation mechanisms and their feasibility was completed for the EC (NERA Economic Consulting, 2004). This led to a period of consultation in 2004 and was then followed by a second study in 2006 which focused on secondary trading in more detail, including an assessment of the full economic impacts (Mott MacDonald, 2006). Further consultation took place and most recently the EC published a communication in 2007. This concluded that the regulation amendments had brought about significant improvements aimed at making better use of scarce slots. However there was a need for better implementation in a number of areas (such as functional and financial independence of the co-ordinator and transparency of schedule data) and also more clarification of certain provisions (such as the new entrant rule and the definition of local rules and guidelines) as a number of countries had interpreted the regulations in different ways. The EC therefore stated that it would be focusing its attention on these issues and in April 2008 it adopted a communication related to these (European Commission, 2008). Most importantly for the first time this accepted secondary trading of slots.).

Alternative slot allocation mechanisms

The current scheduling committee system is widely accepted and has succeeded in providing a stable environment for allocating slots. However, there is considerable concern that as pressure on runway capacity continues, both in Europe and elsewhere, that it may not be the most effective mechanism to manage the scarcity of slots or encourage competition. Critics claim that this procedure gives no guarantee that the scarce airport capacity is used by the airlines that values it most highly, it provides no guide to future investment requirements and is administratively burdensome. Also many new entrants are prevented from competing at major airports. In addition in a few cases it can result in wasteful behaviour by airlines that 'warehouse' or 'babysit' slots by operating empty or 'ghost' flights to ensure that they retain their slots. A recent example of this was a daily empty flight being flown by British Mediterranean Airways between Heathrow and Cardiff (O'Connell and Chittenden, 2007). Moreover the current system by not being based on actual use provides poor incentives for airlines to actually use slots efficiency. Thus airlines may hold onto slots by using them enough to meet the 'use it or lose it' criteria but they may waste the scarce runway resources by not making full use of the slots all of the time.

There have been lengthy debates discussing whether a better system could be introduced (e.g. see Boyfield *et al.*, 2003; DotEcon, 2006; Czerny *et al.*, 2008). Various regulatory suggestions have been put forward such as giving preference to long-haul international flights, which normally have less flexibility in scheduling than short-haul flights because of night closures and other constraints. This could potentially have an environmental benefit by shifting short-haul traffic from air to surface transport. Priority could be given to airlines which cause the least noise nuisance. Scheduled airlines could be favoured over charter airlines and passenger aircraft could have preference over cargo airlines. Alternatively, frequency caps could be placed on certain services once a daily maximum limit has been reached. Another suggestion is to give priority to large aircraft which make the most efficient use of slots. The traffic distribution rules imposed at London Heathrow airport way back in the 1980s were an example of such administrative regulation in practice. These rules restricted assess to charter, general aviation and cargo flights, although the charter rule was subsequently relaxed in 1991 (Doganis, 1992).

While such mechanisms can be useful in pursuing some economic, social, or environmental objective, they are still likely to be used in combination with grandfather rights. As a result any such system will again share the shortcomings of the traditional system, namely not ensuring that the scarce runway slots are used by the airlines who value them the most and who will most closely serve the underlying passenger demand. Therefore, market-based options have also been considered for both primary allocation, when the slots are initially allocated, and for secondary allocation, when the use of slots may be changed at some later stage. This later stage would involve setting up a system of secondary slot trading when airlines are able to buy and sell slots.

The simplest of all market-based options for primary allocation is the use of some charging mechanism, or so-called 'posted prices' to match demand and supply. A fee is attached to each slot and demand is thus reduced by raising the cost of using the slot. This either could be a set fee or could be differentiated between peak and off-peaks slots, to reflect the varying patterns of demand. However, as previously discussed, the market-clearing price would have to be set at a considerably higher rate than is the current practice with airport charges. An alternative suggestion is to use the auction mechanism as a means of allocating slots. These auctions could be held every 6 months like the scheduling committees, but this would clearly lead to considerable upheaval and disruption for both airlines and passengers. At the other extreme there could be just one auction, selling the slots rights in perpetuity and then any further changes would have to be implemented through some secondary mechanism. Somewhere in between these two options, slots allocated under long-term lease agreements could be a more attractive compromise. Individual slots or a combination of slots could be auctioned at one particular time. Alternatively lotteries for slots could be held (these have been used in a few cases in the United States). This might potentially overcome the anti-competitive problem caused by slot trading in that all airlines of all sizes would have access to slots but in practice this could cause havoc with airlines' schedules and be very disruptive. Slots obtained at one end of the route might not match up with those at the other end and in general, there would be a great deal of uncertainty. Also a major issue with all these primary allocations would be deciding who should retain the money that has been paid for the slots (e.g. the airport operator or the government?) and whether it should be stipulated that it is used at the airport for future investment to provide capacity or to reduce the environmental impacts.

The detailed study undertaken by NERA Economic Consulting (2004) for the EC considered the potential impacts of these different market-based options. The main focus of this research was on investigating whether such mechanisms would achieve a more efficient use of scarce airport capacity by assessing the effect on passenger numbers. In addition other factors such as the implementation costs, the potential for instability in airline schedules, the likelihood of increased concentration at hub airports, consistency with existing procedures and risk of international disputes, were considered. Five main options were investigated, namely secondary pricing and higher posted prices on their own, and then both of them together. The fourth option was using secondary trading with an auction of the pool slots whilst the most radical case assumed that there would be a long lease agreement with an auction of 10 per cent of all existing slots each year in a rolling programme so that each slot would come up for auction every 10 years. This was considered with secondary trading.

All the options would produce higher passenger numbers with a shift in traffic patterns because the airlines that would value and be prepared to pay the most for the slots would tend to be those offering long-haul services with larger aircraft and those with higher load factors. In addition, slot utilization is expected to improve as the airlines would be less likely to hold onto slots which they do not need. One of the disadvantages with the higher posted prices is the risk of international disputes. The same is true of the 10 per cent auction and secondary trading option because of its more radical nature. This later approach would also be the most expensive to implement and be the most disruptive to airline schedules. All scenarios are likely to lead to an increased concentration of hub carrier slots although entry barriers would be removed to allow other carriers to compete.

Looking specifically at secondary trading, officially airlines have so far been prevented from such processes, except with the case of four US airports (see 'Slot allocation' in 'The US experience' section). In Europe, slot exchanges were allowed under the EU regulation but slot trading was not until 2008. An important decision was made in 1999 by the UK High Court when it ruled that the financial payment from BA to Air UK to 'compensate' for the exchange of some highly demanded slots with some less attractive slots did not invalidate the exchange (Civil Aviation Authority, 2001). Hence this has allowed a so-called grey market for slot trading, where valuable slots are bought and very often exchanged for 'junk' or useless slots. As capacity at Heathrow has become more scarce the price for a peak slot have risen sharply (Table 5.8). Whilst the commercial nature of these transactions means that it is difficult to get accurate figures, in the early 2000s it was generally thought that airlines were paying up to £10 million (or around $20 million) for a pair of slots in peak times. However by 2007 the price seemed to have more than doubled, primarily because airlines were very keen to acquire slots at Heathrow to take advantage of the new route opportunities which had arisen because of the EU–US open skies agreement that came into effect in April 2008. Elsewhere the view towards slot trading in other European countries varied. In some places, such as Spain and Italy, it was not allowed whereas in Germany it happened in very rare occasions (Pilling, 2007).

In the research on secondary trading undertaken by Mott MacDonald (2006) for the EC a study of Heathrow found that between 2001 and 2006 499 slots a week (compared to a total of 8700) had been traded. The majority of these (73 per cent) were bought by BA but other airlines, such as Virgin, Emirates and Qantas also increased their slots. In fact over half of the slots that Virgin has at Heathrow were obtained through secondary slot trading. Overall it was concluded that the UK experience had led to a liquid and flexible market in slots, had fostered new entry, and had been supported by the industry with direct competitors being prepared to trade with each other. Moreover it had improved slot efficiency since a number of short-haul carriers

Table 5.8 Examples of slot trades at Heathrow airport

Buyer	Seller	Date	Number of slot pairs	Approximate total price	Approximate average price per daily slot pair
BA	Air UK	1998	4 per day	$25 mn	$6 mn
BA	SN Brussels	2002	7 per day	$65 mn	$9 mn
BA	Swiss	2003	8 per day	$55 mn	$7 mn
BA	United	2003	2 per day	$20 mn	$10 mn
Qantas	Flybe	2004	2 per day	$35 mn	$18 mn
Virgin	Flybe	2004	4 per day	$35 mn	$9 mn
Virgin	Air Jamaica	2007	4 per week	$10 mn	n/a
BA, Qatar Airways, Continental[a]	GB Airways	2007	4 per day	$160 mn	$40 mn
Continental[a]	GB Airways, Air France, Alitalia	2008	4 per day	$210 mn	$52 mn
Continental, US Airways, BA[a]	Alitalia	2007	3 per day	$140 mn	$47 mn

[a] There is some double counting with these 2007 trades as sale prices for individual airlines was not always available

Source: Compiled by the author from various sources.

had been replaced with long-haul carriers with larger aircraft. This research was used to help investigate the possible effects of secondary slot trading throughout Europe and to assess the overall impact in meeting the EC's four objectives of ensuring the mobility of slots, of strengthening competition at the airports, of matching the secondary trading with overall EU transport policy and of ensuring compatibility with worldwide procedures. The results of the study suggested that the objectives could be met to a large extent although it is likely that the existing dominant hub carriers would increase their market share, whilst competition on intra-EU flights would be weakened and routes to peripheral regional airports could be lost.

Whilst there is now considerable evidence to suggest that some kind of market-based mechanism could make more efficient use of scarce runway resource, there are some competition concerns (Office of Fair Trading/Civil Aviation Authority, 2005). This is because such an approach will usually increase the dominance of the major airlines at the airports (which has been demonstrated by both the NERA and the Mott MacDonald research), even though other second tier airlines will have better opportunities to compete. In addition such dominant airlines might place restrictive covenants on how the traded slots can be used to dampen the competition. These factors could be addressed by undertaking market investigations by relevant competition authorities, banning any restrictive covenants and generally increasing the amount of transparency associated with any slot sales. Moreover some argue (e.g. Starkie, 2008) that such increased concentration may not always be a negative development for passengers. Another potential issue may be reduced competition with short-haul services and perhaps a loss of regional services which tend to be served with smaller aircraft that are less full. In this case use of the European Public Service Obligation (PSO) legislation may help to improve the situation as might allowing slots to be sold to other bodies, such as regional authorities that could then safeguard slots. In general, making the best use of existing resources while at the same time encouraging or enhancing competition for all is not an easy matter. For example, it may be feasible to focus on competition but that may cause sudden disruption in schedules. Likewise, it may be possible to protect certain routes through ring fencing, but this may not produce the most effective use of the scarce runway slots.

Ground handling issues

Ground handling activities at airports are very important to airlines. They impact both on an airline's cost and the quality of service which they provide for their passengers. Ground handling services cover passenger handling, baggage handling, freight and mail handling, ramp handling, fuel and oil handling, and aircraft services and maintenance. Such activities are often divided between terminal or traffic handling, which is passenger check-in, baggage and freight handling, and airside or ramp handling, which covers activities such as aircraft loading and unloading, cleaning and servicing. Sometimes, these services are provided by the airport operators, although at most airports they are provided by airlines or handling agents. Historically, often the national airline or airport operator may have had a monopoly or near monopoly in ground handling. Within Europe, some airport operators such as Milan, Rome, Vienna and Frankfurt airports, which were heavily involved in such activities, earned very significant revenues from such activities – sometimes over half the total income of the airport. In other cases, the airport operator just earned rental fees and perhaps a small concession fee from the airlines or agents which were providing the handling services. Countries in Europe where the national airline used to have a handling monopoly included Spain with Iberia and Greece with Olympic.

A study of European airports in the early 1990s showed that 44 per cent of aircraft movements were handled by airport operators, 27 per cent were self-handled by the national carrier, 8 per cent were handled by the national carrier for other airlines, 7 per cent were handled by independent ground handlers, and the remaining 14 per cent were self-handled by other airlines. By contrast, in terms of passenger numbers, only 16 per cent were handled by the airport operator, again 7 per cent by independent ground handlers and the rest by airlines (Deutsche Bank, 1999). For operational reasons, it is far easier to have a number of airlines providing traffic handling rather than ramp handling – given capacity constraints of the equipment and space in the ramp handling areas. Providers of monopoly services claimed that providing competition, particularly for ramp handling would merely duplicate resources, lower efficiency and may also cause considerable apron congestion, particularly at airports which are already at full or near capacity.

Critics of the past situation, particularly the airlines, claimed that ground handling monopolies were pushing up prices and, in some cases, reducing service standards (Bass, 1994). In 1993, the European Commission acknowledged that it had received a number of complaints related to ground handling activities at various airports including Milan and Frankfurt and at the Spanish and Greek airports (Soames, 1997). A study in 1997 of airline turnaround costs at a number of European airports commissioned for the AEA found that the nine most expensive airports all had ramp handling monopolies whereas the next 14, in descending order of price, operated in a competitive situation (Association of European Airlines, 1998).

Thus many in Europe argued that air transport could not be fully liberalized unless the ground handling activities were offered on a full competitive basis and this resulted in the EU's adoption of the ground handling directive 96/67 in 1996. The long-term purpose of this directive was to end all ground handling monopolies and duopolies within the EU by opening up the market to third party handlers, recognizing the right of airlines to self-handle and guaranteeing at least some choice for airlines in the provision of ground handling services (European Commission, 1996). The details of the directive, which provided for phased liberalization of ground handling services, are shown in Table 5.9.

The directive took some time to have an impact as in some cases countries were as late as 1999 or 2000 in adopting the new legislation. Moreover, in some exceptional circumstances airports were granted

Table 5.9 Key features of the 1996 EU ground handling directive

From 1 January 1998	Airlines have the right to self-handling for airport terminal services
	For airports with more than 1 million passengers or 25 000 tonnes of freight, airlines have the right to self-handle for baggage, ramp, fuel, and freight services
From 1 January 1999	For airports with more than 3 million passengers or 75 000 tonnes of freight, third party handling is allowed
From 1 January 2001	For airports with more than 2 million passengers or 50 000 tonnes of freight, third party handling is allowed
	At least one handler must be independent from the airport operator or dominant airlines with more than 25% of the traffic

Source: European Commission (1996).

temporary exemptions on the basis of space or capacity constraints in order to ease the transition from a monopolistic to a competitive situation. Airports which gained exemptions until 2000 or 2001 were mostly the German airports of Frankfurt, Hamburg, Stuggart, Berlin Tegel and Düsseldorf, and Paris CDG and Funchal. By 2005, there were 95 airports above the 2 million passenger threshold and a further 49 airports had more than 1 million passengers which were covered by the directive.

A study was undertaken in 2002 to investigate the impact of the directive (SH&E, 2002). The number of third party handlers had increased although the number of self-handlers had remained the same or even decreased in some cases. It concluded that prices for ground handling services had dropped and this was particularly the case where there had previously been handling monopolies or a highly regulated market. This may have been due to the increase in competition between handlers not only because of the directive but also because of cost pressures from the airlines. However as regards quality of service levels there was a mixed picture. For this reason, the airports argued that some form of service level agreement between the airport operator and the ground handling providers should be made obligatory (ACI-Europe, 2003a, b).

In January 2007, when the European Commission adopted the proposal for the directive on airport charges, there was an expectation that there would be proposals to amend the current Ground Handling Directive which might change the traffic thresholds or introduce explicit service standards for ground handling. However instead a report was published which summarized the results of the SH&E study (European Commission, 2007c). In the end, changes were not proposed largely because of a lack of consensus between all the different stakeholders and instead the EC stated that it would focus at that time on ensuring consistent and effective enforcement of the current regulations throughout the European Union. This was not welcomed by some bodies, in particular the airlines who urgently wanted further liberalization with an increase in the number of providers, a strengthening of the role of users and a more cost efficient handling system without unnecessary charges (such as concession and access fees) and with fewer administrative burdens (Association of European Airlines, 2007).

The US experience

Airport use agreements

The relationship between airports and airlines in the United States is unique and so is worthy of special consideration. As discussed earlier, the airports and airlines enter into legally binding contracts known as airport use and lease agreements which detail the fees and rental rates which an airline has to pay, the method by which these are to be calculated and the conditions for the use of both airfield and terminal facilities. A key reason for the existence of these agreements has been because bond-holders have demanded the security of such formal relationship between the airports and the airlines before investing in the airport.

There are two basic approaches to establishing the airport charges: residual and compensatory. With the residual approach, the airlines pay the net costs of running the airport after taking account of commercial and other non-airline sources of revenue. The airlines provide a guarantee that the level of charges and rents will be such that the airport will always break even, and so they take considerable risk. Airports such as Cincinnati, Detroit, Orlando, Miami, Chicago, and San Francisco use this method. By contrast with the compensatory approach, the airlines pay agreed charges and rates based on recovery of costs allocated to the facilities and services that they occupy or use. The risk of running the airport is left to the airport operator. Examples of airports that use this method include Atlanta, Boston, Houston, Los Angeles, and the New York airports. The residual approach, therefore, is more akin to the single till practice, whereas the compensatory approach is more similar to the dual till practice. Airports have applied these two different approaches in various ways to suit their particular needs and some have adopted a hybrid approach, combining elements of both the residual and the compensatory methodologies.

Traditionally, the use agreements were long-term contracts between 20 and 50 years. In recent years, they have become shorter to reflect the more volatile, deregulated environment. The length of use agreement will normally coincide with any lease agreements, which the airlines have with the airport operator. In the United States, it is common for airlines to lease terminal space or gates, or even lease or build total terminals – as in the case of JFK airport in New York. The airlines which carry most of the airport's traffic may also play a significant role in airport investment decisions if they agree to the majority-in-interest (MII) clauses in the use agreement. These clauses, which are far more common among residual agreements, typically mean that these signatory airlines have to approve all significant planned developments or changes at the airport. The anti-competitive nature of such agreements can be a problem if other non-signatory airlines are prevented from gaining access to terminal space and gates. As a result there has been an increasing use of 'use it or lose it' clauses in which the control of assets are returned to the airport if the airline does not use the facilities as intended. Capacity improvements which may bring more opportunities for competition may also not be approved by the signatory airlines. As a result some airport operators have tried to reduce the powers of the signatory airlines by requiring MII disapproval rather than approval or have limited the airlines' influence to only major projects. Some airports have discarded MII clauses altogether.

Airport fees and taxes

The landing fees at US airports are normally very simple, being based on a fixed rate per 1000 lbs. Signatory airlines may pay less. The charges do not vary according to noise levels or peak periods, unlike the practice at some European airports. The level of landing fees tends to be relatively low partly because the airport operator provides a minimal number of services itself. The generation of aeronautical revenues at US airports is subject to a number of statutory requirements determined by Congress and policy statements issued by the Federal Aviation Administration/Department of Transportation. First, there is the Federal Government requirement for 'fair and reasonable' and not 'unjustly discriminatory' aeronautical fees based strictly on costs (Federal Aviation Administration/Department of Transportation, 1996). Secondly airports are prohibited to use airport revenues for non-airport purposes (Federal Aviation Administration/Department of Transportation, 1999). This latter requirement is one of the major obstacles in the way for any significant developments towards airport privatization in the United States (Graham, 2004).

Unlike most other airports in the world, US airports do not have passenger charges – although some of the costs associated with terminal and gate space which are normally incorporated into the passenger fee may be covered by airline lease payments. US airports are not legally allowed to levy passenger charges primarily because of fears that such revenues will be diverted from the airport to be used for non-aviation purposes. However, in 1990, the federal government approved the levying of PFCs. Although the PFCs are legally and constitutionally different from passengers charge levied elsewhere in the world, they have a similar impact on airlines. The initial PFC legislation, allowed airports to levy a US$1, US$2, or US$3 fee which had to be spent on identified airport-related projects or could be used to back bonds for the projects. In 2001, it was agreed that the maximum PFC could be raised to US$4.50. Airlines have no veto rights when it comes to PFC-funded projects nor can they have exclusive rights.

PFCs were first used in June 1992. As of 1 January 2008, 370 airports were approved to collect PFCs and it was estimated that these PFCs generated $2.7 billion in 2007. Since PFCs have been introduced, 18 per cent of this total funding has been for airside projects, 35 per cent for landside projects,

Table 5.10 Taxes at US airports (as of 1 January 2008)

Type of tax	Tax rate	Unit of taxation
Airport and airway trust fund		
Passenger ticket tax	7.5%	Domestic air fare
Passenger flight segment tax	$3.50	Domestic passengers
International departure and arrival tax	$15.40	International passengers
Frequent flyer tax	7.5%	Sale of frequent flyer miles
Cargo waybill tax	6.25%	Waybill for domestic freight
Commercial aviation jet fuel	4.3 cents	Gallons
Non-commercial jet fuel/gasoline tax	21.8/19.3 cents	Gallons
Environmental protection agency		
LUST fuel tax	0.1 cents	Gallons
Local airport projects		
Passenger facility charge	Up to $4.50	Passengers
Department of homeland security		
September 11th fee	$2.50	Passengers
Aviation security infrastructure fee	Carrier-specific	US screening costs in 2000
Animal and Plant Health Inspection Service (now CBP) passenger/aircraft fee	$5.00/$70.50	International passengers/aircraft
Customs user fee	$5.50	International passengers
Immigration user fee	$7.00	International passengers

Source: Air Transport Association of America.

5 per cent for noise projects, 7 per cent for access projects and 31 per cent for paying interest. A further 8 per cent has funded the construction costs of Denver airport. Some PFCs have been approved for a long time (longer than 30 years) whereas others will be used for as little as 3 years (Air Transport Association of America, 2008).

In addition, there are also a number of government taxes which push up the total amount paid by the airlines and their passengers (Table 5.10). There are taxes that go into the Federal Airport and Airway Trust Fund that provide the finance for airport investment grants under the Airport Improvement Program (AIP) (and finance for the air traffic control system). The most significant of the taxes is the domestic passenger ticket tax that accounts for around half of all the trust fund. Then there are also additional taxes relating to fuel, security, agriculture and health inspection, and customs and immigration services. In 2005, the ticket tax generated over $5 billion whilst the domestic segment tax, the security taxes and PFCs each generated around $2 billion. The Air Transport Association of America (2008) has estimated that for a non-stop round trip these taxes range from 27 per cent of the fare for a $100 fare to 11 per cent for a $500 fare. In recent years, however, there has been concern that these funds will not be adequate, or are not the most appropriate, to meet future airport (and air traffic control) investment needs, particularly as the downward pressure on fares and use of smaller aircraft has meant that there are more aircraft in the airport system but less revenue per aircraft. Consequently a number of changes to the PFC and AIP funds have been proposed (General Accounting Office, 2007).

Slot allocation

At most airports in the United States, there is no formal slot allocation mechanism, such as the IATA scheduling committees, since these would be in conflict with antitrust laws. This means that instead there is open access to the airports, barring any environmental constraints, and airlines design their schedules independently taking into account any expected delays. This 'first come, first served' system can result in considerable congestion at certain times of the day when many flights are scheduled around the same time.

The exception to this practice is at five airports which were subject to the 'high density airport rule'. This rule was introduced in 1969 by the Federal Aviation Administration (FAA) as a temporary measure to reduce problems of delay and congestion at JFK, La Guardia, and Newark airports in New York (although it was terminated for Newark in 1970), O'Hare airport in Chicago and Washington National airport (now Washington Reagan). The traffic was divided into three categories, namely air carriers, air taxi (now commuters) and other (primarily general aviation), with a different limit on the number of flights during restricted hours for each category. No slot allocation mechanism was defined but the relevant airlines were given antitrust immunity to discuss co-ordination of schedules.

Initially the rule worked relatively well, but the increase in traffic due to airline deregulation in 1978 and other factors, such as a major air traffic control strike, resulted in a new allocation system being introduced in 1985 (Langner, 1995). This was the 'buy–sell' rule which effectively meant that after an initial allocation process based on grandfather rights, airlines were then permitted to buy and sell their slots. Airlines were also allowed to 'lease' slots on a short-term basis. This has been the only formal secondary trading market for slots in any part of the world. This trading of slots was limited to domestic operations (international routes being more complex because of international regulation) with air carriers slot being unable to be traded for commuter slots and vice versa. Slots used for essential air services were excluded. There was a 'use it or lose it' rule requirement of 65 per cent and a slot pool was established for newly available slots. These were reallocated using a lottery – with 25 per cent initially being offered to new entrants. International slots were allowed to be co-ordinated through the IATA scheduling committees (Starkie, 1992).

Over 10 years' experience of this slot trading led to increasing criticism of the system. There had been very few outright sales of air carrier slots, very few new entrants and regional services had been reduced. The established airlines had increased their dominance at the airports, although this has to be viewed within the context of the US airline industry that itself had become more concentrated (Starkie, 1998). As a result of these concerns, the Aviation Investment and Reform Act (AIR21) of 2000 made substantial changes to the slot rules at these airports. At Chicago O'Hare airport the slot rules were to be eliminated by 2002 and at La Guardia and JFK by 2007 (they were to remain at Washington). In the interim, new entrant carriers and airlines operating to smaller communities were given slot restriction exemption. This led to major over-scheduling and congestion in La Guardia in 2000 and so the Port Authority of New York and New Jersey imposed a moratorium on peak hour flights. However, the FAA claimed that the airport authority did not have a legal right to impose this moratorium and instead it was agreed that the number of new flights would be capped and a slot lottery would be undertaken. This took place in December 2000 with the new limit starting in January 2001. This temporary solution was due to end in October 2002 but has been extended several times. In the meantime delays at JFK have also been increasing, particularly due to the fact that both Delta and JetBlue have been expanding their domestic services out the airport. This has again led to a temporary FAA order to cap movements in peak hours which was introduced in March 2008 and will operate until October 2009.

At Chicago O'Hare when the slots restrictions were relaxed in 2002, the airport rapidly became congested just as at La Guardia. In 2004, the two main carriers United and American agreed to cut peak arrivals by 5 per cent in March 2004 and an additional 2.5 per cent in June 2004. However these slots were taken up by other airlines and by the end of October the FAA was forced to impose an order which capped domestic arrivals. This order was replaced by a rule in 2006 that allowed the cap to remain until 2008 when new capacity will come on stream which should relieve the congestion. Hence the situation at Chicago is different since it is likely that the congestion problem will be resolved with additional infrastructure. However this is not the case at the two New York airports. The temporary caps at these airports have been very unpopular with the airlines and so the FAA, airlines and other interested bodies have spent a substantial amount of time considering a range of measures to reduce congestion but as yet no permanent solution has been agreed.

References and further reading

ACI-Europe (2003a). *Airport Charges in Europe*. ACI-Europe.

ACI-Europe (2003b). *ACI Europe Position on the Review of Council Directive 96/67/EC on Access to the Ground Handling Market at Community Airports*. ACI-Europe.

ACI-Europe (2005). *Building for the Future*. ACI-Europe.

ACI-Europe (2007). *ACI Europe Position on Airport Charges*. ACI-Europe.

ACI-Europe (2008). *Legislative Process for EU Directive on Airport Charges: European Airports still Concerned Following European Parliament Vote*, Press release, 15 January.

Air Transport Association of America (2008). *Taxes and fees*, available from www.airlines.org (accessed 1 February 2008).

Airports Council International (ACI) (2000). Pre-financing of airport capital expenditures. *ANSConf Working Paper 52*, ICAO.

Association of European Airlines (AEA) (2007). *AEA Policy paper on ground handling*, Position paper.

Association of European Airlines (AEA) (2008). *Airlines Want 'Level Playing Field' in Relation to Europe's Airports'*, Press release, 16 January.

Association of European Airlines (1998) *Benchmaking of Airport Charges*, AEA.

Baker, C. (2006). Taxing times. *Airline Business*, April, 66–68.

Bass, T. (1994). Infrastructure constraints and the EC. *Journal of Air Transport Management*, 1(3), 145–150.

Boyfield, K., Starkie, D., Bass, T. and Humphreys, B. (2003). *A Market for Airport Slots*. Institute of Economic Affairs.

Burns, P. (2000). The use of benchmarking in regulatory proceedings. *CAA Workshop on Benchmarking of Airports: Methodologies, Problems and Relevance to Economic Regulation*, London, September.

Citrinot, L. (2006). Airlines counting the cost. *Jane's Airport Review*, September, 9.

Civil Aviation Authority (CAA) (2000). *The use of benchmarking in airport reviews*. Consultation paper, CAA.

Civil Aviation Authority (CAA) (2001). *The Implementation of Secondary Slot Trading*. CAA.

Civil Aviation Authority (CAA) (2003a). *Economic Regulation of BAA London Airports: CAA Decision*. CAA.

Civil Aviation Authority (CAA) (2003b). *Economic Regulation of Manchester Airport: CAA Decision*. CAA.

Civil Aviation Authority (2007). *The CAA Response to DfT's Consultation Paper on European Airport Charges Directive*. CAA.

Civil Aviation Authority (2008). *Economic Regulation of Heathrow and Gatwick Airports: CAA Decision*. CAA.

Competition Commission (2002). *A Report on the economic regulation of the London airports companies*. The Stationery Office.

Copenhagen Airport (2005). *Agreement Reached on Airport Charges for the Next 3 Years*, Press release, 10 November.

Czerny, A., Forsyth, P., Gillen, D. and Neimeier, H.-M. (2008). *Airport Slots: International Experiences and Options for Reform*. Ashgate.

Department for Transport (2008a). *Decision on the regulation status of Manchester airport*, available from www.dft.gov.uk (accessed 8 March 2008).

Department for Transport (2008b). *Decision on the regulation status of Stansted airport*, available from www.dft.gov.uk (accessed 8 March 2008).

Doganis, R. (1992). *The Airport Business*. Routledge.

Doganis, R. (2006). *The Airline Business in the Twenty-First Century*. 2nd edn. Routledge.

DotEcon (2006). *Alternative Allocation Mechanisms for Slots Created by New Airport Capacity*. DotEcon.

European Commission (1993). *Council Regulation 95/93 on Common Rules for the Allocation of Slots at Community Airports*, 18 January.

European Commission (1996). Council Directive 96/67/EC on access to the groundhandling market at Community airports. *Official Journal of the European Communities*, L 272/36, App. A.

European Commission (EC) (2007a). *Proposal for a Directive of the European Parliament and of the Council on airport charges*. EC.

European Commission (2007b). *Proposal for a Directive of the European Parliament and of the Council on airport charges: Full Impact Assessment*. Commission Staff Working Document, EC.

European Commission (2007c). *Report from the Commission on the application of Council Directive 96/67/EC of 15 October 1996*, EC.

European Commission (2008) *Communication on the application of Regulation (EEC) No 95/93 on common rules for the allocation of slots at Community airports*, EC, 30 April.

European Low Fare Airline Association (2008). *European Parliament misses an opportunity to introduce robust regulation of dominant airports*, Press release, 15 January.

Federal Aviation Administration/Department of Transportation (1996). *Policy regarding airport rates and charges*, Docket No 27782, Washington DC, FAA/DOT.

Federal Aviation Administration/Department of Transportation (1999). *Policy and procedures regarding use of airport revenue*, Docket No 28472, Washington DC, FAA/DOT.

Forsyth, P. (2002). Privatisation and regulation of Australian and New Zealand airports. *Journal of Air Transport Management*, 8, 19–28.

Forsyth, P. (2004). Replacing regulation: Airport price monitoring in Australia. In P. Forsyth, D. Gillen, A. Knorr, O. Mayer, H. Niemeier and D. Starkie (Eds), *The Economic Regulation of Airports*. Ashgate.

Forsyth, P. (2008). Airport policy in Australia and New Zealand: Privatisation, light-handed regulation and performance. In C. Winston and G. de Rus (Eds), *Aviation Infrastructure Performance*. Brookings Institution Press.

Forsyth, P., Gillen, D., Knorr, A., Mayer, O., Niemeier, H. and Starkie, D. (Eds.) (2004). *The economic regulation of airports*. Ashgate.

Fraport (2002). *Fraport and airlines sign first five-year agreement on airport charges at FRA*, Press release, 30 April.

General Accounting Office (GAO) (2007). *Airport finance: Preliminary analysis indicates proposed changes in the airport improvement program may not resolve funding needs for smaller airports*. GAO.

Gillen, D. and Niemeier, H-M. (2008). The European Union: Evolution of privatization, regulation and slot reform. In C. Winston and G. de Rus (Eds), *Aviation Infrastructure Performance*. Brookings Institution Press.

Graham, A. (2004). The regulation of US airports. In P. Forsyth, D. Gillen, A. Knorr, O. Mayer, H. Niemeier and D. Starkie (Eds), *The Economic Regulation of Airports*. Ashgate.

Graham, A. (2008). Airport planning and regulation in the UK. In C. Winston and G. de Rus (Eds), *Aviation Infrastructure Performance*. Brookings Institution Press.

Helm, D. and Jenkinson, T. (Eds.) (1998). *Competition in Regulated Industries*. Oxford University Press.

International Air Transport Association (IATA) (2000). Forward pricing. *ANSConf Working Paper No. 31*, ICAO.

International Air Transport Association (IATA) (2006a). *European Aviation Taxes*. IATA Economic Briefing.

International Air Transport Association (IATA) (2006b). *Economic Regulation – Summary Europe*. IATA Economics Briefing.

International Air Transport Association (IATA) (2007). *Worldwide Scheduling Guidelines* 14th edn. IATA.

International Civil Aviation Organization (ICAO) (1992). *Statement by the Council to Contracting States on Charges for Airports and Air Navigation Services*, 9082/4. ICAO.

International Civil Aviation Organization (ICAO) (2004). *ICAO's Policies on Charges for Airports and Air Navigation Services*, 9082/7. ICAO.

International Civil Aviation Organization (ICAO) (2000) Economic regulation, *Ansconf Working Paper No 9*, ICAO.

Klenk, M. (2004). New approaches in airport/airline relations – charges framework of Frankfurt Airport. In P. Forsyth , D. Gillen, A. Knorr, O. Mayer, H. Niemeier and D. Starkie (Eds), *The Economic Regulation of Airports*. Ashgate.

Kilian, M. (2008). The development of the regulatory reform of slot allocation in the EU. In A. Czerny, P. Forsyth, D. Gillen and H.M. Neimeier (Eds), *Airport Slots: International Experiences and Options for Reform*. Ashgate.

Langner, S. (1995). Contractual aspects of transacting in slots in the United States. *Journal of Air Transport Management*, 2(3/4), 151–161.

Lu, C.-C. and Pagliari, R. (2004). Evaluating the potential impact of alternative airport pricing approaches on social welfare. *Transportation Research Part E: Logistics and Transportation Review*, 40(2), 1–17.

Mackenzie-Williams, P. (2004). A shift towards regulation – the case of New Zealand. In P. Forsyth, D. Gillen, A. Knorr, O. Mayer, H. Niemeier and D. Starkie (Eds), *The Economic Regulation of Airports*. Ashgate.

Mott MacDonald (2006). *Study of the Impact of the Introduction of Secondary Trading at Community Airport*. Mott MacDonald.

Monopolies and Mergers Commission (1996). *A Report on the Economic Regulation of the London Airport Companies*. MMC.

Niemeier, H. (2002). Regulation of airports: The case of Hamburg airport – a view from the perspective of regional policy. *Journal of Air Transport Management*, 8, 37–48.

NERA Economic Consulting (2004). *Study to Assess the Effects of Different Slot Allocation Schemes*. NERA.

O'Connell, D. and Chittenden, M. (2007). The flight now leaving Heathrow is … empty. *The Sunday Times*, 11 March.

Office of Fair Trading/Civil Aviation Authority (2005). *Competition Issues Associated with the Trading of Airport Slots*. The Stationery Office.

Oum, T., Zhang, A. and Zhang, Y. (2004). Alternative forms of economic regulation and their efficiency implications for airports. *Journal of Transport Economics and Policy*, 38(2), 217–246.

Pilling, M. (2007). Slot machines. *Airline Business*, October, 70–74.

Productivity Commission (2002). *Price regulation of airport services*, Report no. 19, Ausinfo.

Saounatsos, G. (2007). Airport charges. *Airports International*, October, 59–63.

SH&E (2002). *Study on the Quality and Efficiency of Ground Handling Services at EU Airports as a Result of the Implementation of Council Directive 96/67/EC*. SH&E.

SH&E (2006). *Capital Needs and Regulatory Oversight Arrangement: A Survey of European Airports*. SH&E.

Shuttleworth, G. (2000). Price caps, benchmarking and efficient costs. CAA, *Workshop on Benchmarking of Airports: Methodologies, Problems and Relevance to Economic Regulation*, London, September.

Soames, T. (1997). Ground handling liberalization. *Journal of Air Transport Management*, 3(2), 83–94.

Sobie, B. and Thompson, J. (2006). Time for reflection. *Airline Business*, December, 36–38.

Sorensen, F. (2008). The slot allocation philosophy at the EU. In A. Czerny, P. Forsyth, D. Gillen and H.M. Neimeier (Eds.), *Airport Slots: International Experiences and Options for Reform*. Ashgate.

Starkie, D. (1992). *Slot trading at United States airports*. Putnam, Hayes and Bartlet Ltd.

Starkie, D. (1998). Allocating airport slots: A role for the market? *Journal of Air Transport Management*, 4, 111–116.

Starkie, D. (2001). Reforming UK airport regulation. *Journal of Transport Economics and Policy*, 35(1), 119–135.

Starkie, D. (2002). Airport regulation and competition. *Journal of Air Transport Management*, 8, 63–72.

Starkie, D. (2005). Making airport regulation less imperfect. *Journal of Air Transport Management*, 11, 3–8.

Starkie, D. (2008). The dilemma of slot concentration at network hubs. In A. Czerny, P. Forsyth, D. Gillen and H.M. Neimeier (Eds), *Airport Slots: International Experiences and Options for Reform*. Ashgate.

Toms, M. (2004). UK Regulation from the perspective of the BAA. In P. Forsyth, D. Gillen, A. Knorr, O. Mayer, H. Niemeier and D. Starkie (Eds), *The Economic Regulation of Airports*. Ashgate.

Toms, M. (2003). Is airport regulation fit for purpose? In D. Helm and D. Holt (Eds), *Air Transport and Infrastructure: The Challenges Ahead*. Oxera.

CHAPTER 6

The provision of commercial facilities

The importance of commercial facilities

A key development in the evolution of the airport industry has been the increase in the dependence on non-aeronautical or commercial revenues. This chapter will discuss the generation of non-aeronautical revenues by looking at the market for commercial services and assessing how the facilities can be planned and managed. It will consider factors which influence commercial performance. The focus of this chapter will be on individual consumers who buy commercial goods/services at airports. There are, of course, other consumers such as the airlines and handling agents who also generate concession and rental revenues by paying for the use of office space, check-in-decks, lounges, in-flight kitchens, and so on. These activities are covered in Chapter 5 which considers the airport–airline relationship.

There have been a number of factors which have contributed to the growth in dependence on non-aeronautical revenues. First, moves towards commercialization and privatization within the industry have given airports greater freedom to develop their commercial policies and diversify into new areas. A more business-oriented approach to running airports has also raised the priority given to commercial facilities. Such facilities were traditionally considered to be rather secondary to providing essential air transport infrastructure for airlines. Managers are now eager to adopt more creative and imaginative strategies and to exploit all possible aeronautical and non-aeronautical revenue generating opportunities.

Moreover, the airlines have been exerting increasing pressure on the airport industry to control the level of aeronautical fees which are being levied. A more competitive environment and falling yields have forced many airlines to focus on major cost-saving initiatives such as out-sourcing, reductions in staff numbers, and the pegging of the level of wages. Increasingly, airlines are demanding that airports adopt such cost-cutting and efficiency saving measures themselves, rather than raising their charges to the airlines. Thus, airport charges have become subject to more and more scrutiny from the airlines – particularly from the low cost airlines. In addition, the ability of some airports to increase aeronautical charges is now restricted by government regulation which has often been introduced at the same time as privatization (see Chapter 5). The impact of these pressures on the level of aeronautical charges, either from the airlines themselves or regulatory bodies, has encouraged the airports to look to alternative ways of increasing their revenues and growing their businesses by giving greater attention to commercial facilities. In effect, the airports have had to broaden their horizons in managing their businesses.

At the same time, increasing numbers of people are travelling through airports and making more frequent trips. Hence, passengers are becoming more sophisticated and experienced airport shoppers, and are generally much better informed. As a result of this, airport shoppers are becoming more demanding not only in the quality of service which is provided, but also in the range and value for money of the commercial facilities on offer. This reflects not only general trends in the high street where consumers have become more discerning with quality, value and choice at the top of their priorities, but also the impact of the additional choice of internet shopping. However, it is difficult to determine entirely whether the raised expectations at airports have been caused by a genuine need or desire of the consumers for expanded facilities or whether an airport's drive to maximize its commercial income by becoming a shopping centre has merely changed passenger expectations. It is also true to say that this increased emphasis on commercial facilities has not been welcomed by all the travelling public, particularly those from the business community, that often desire a quick uncluttered route through the airport away from the distraction of numerous shops and food and beverage (F&B) outlets.

Increasing airport competition, especially between airport hubs, has also played a role in the development of non-aeronautical revenues. The main reason for why a passenger will choose a certain airport will, of course, be the nature of air services which that airport offers and the convenience of the airport's location. Consideration of the retail and other commercial facilities is bound to be secondary. Transfer passengers may, however, be more influenced by the commercial facilities if they cannot perceive any significant difference between the convenience and the quality of the choice of connecting flights at different airports. Certain airports, such as Amsterdam Schiphol and Singapore Changi, have run high-profile marketing campaigns emphasizing the quality and good value of the commercial facilities on offer to transfer passengers. Other airports have gone one stage further. In the Middle East, a number of airports such as Abu Dhabi, Dubai, and Bahrain try to use their duty- and tax-free shops as a way of capturing competing traffic, particularly by using incentives like raffles with high-value prizes, such as luxury cars.

The market for commercial facilities

Who buys at airports?

The airport environment is a unique location for shopping and other commercial facilities. The main shoppers, the passengers, make up a large captive market. They often tend to be more affluent than the average and they may have time on their hands to have a quick meal or snack. They may spend spontaneously to acquire the last minute essential or discount purchase for a holiday or souvenirs and gifts while returning. They may even spend just to dispose of the last of their foreign currency. Airport retailing is, however, fundamentally different from high street retailing since passengers who are going to the airport are going to catch a flight rather than to shop. Consequently, the passengers will be far less familiar with the airport shopping environment than with their neighbourhood shops and this, coupled with a fear of missing the flight and the stress associated with the check-in, immigration and security processes, may impose a considerable sense of anxiety on the passengers.

To fully harness the commercial development potential of the airport traffic, the range of facilities on offer and even the product selection should match very closely the preferences and needs of the specific passenger types at the airports very closely. To achieve this aim, airports, together with their retailing and F&B partners, have increasingly been devoting more resources to getting to know their customers. At the most basic level, this involves an analysis of the air services offered and the origin and destination of travellers. Even this detail of information about the market, which is automatically collected at airports, is the envy of most high street retailers. In addition, duty- and tax-free retailers can get information about travellers from their boarding passes which are shown when purchases are made (known as point of sale (POS) data). In many cases, this is supplemented by market research, of varying degrees of sophistication, which will investigate the demographic, geographic and behavioural features of the passengers. Such research will often aim to determine who shops at airports and what they buy, who does not shop at airports and why, and attitudes towards the range of facilities on offer and the value for money of the products. This type of research needs to be updated regularly as customer demands and perceptions are continuously changing.

There are different spending profiles and preferences of different types of passengers. Leisure charter passengers have traditionally been favourites for impulse buys and the use of F&B facilities. Passengers on low cost carriers are not necessarily budget spenders at the airports, tend to be more evenly spread through time and again are particularly good users of the F&B services because of the lack of free in-flight refreshments. They also tend to use car parking because of the relative remoteness of some secondary airports served by the low cost carriers, and because they are often quite time-sensitive since they are travelling on short-break trips. Long-haul leisure passengers tend to spend more time than short-haul leisure travellers, especially because they normally have more time at the airport to shop. Regular business travellers typically have a shorter dwell time and are less likely to browse in shops. Moreover, the widespread adoption of airline lounges for business and first-class customers has further discouraged these passengers from having spare time to visit the main terminal shops. As a result of this, business travellers make purchases relatively infrequently, although their average spend on a purchase tends to be high. Business travellers also tend to make high use of certain facilities, such as banks, car hire, and airport hotels and when they use F&B services their spending is less constrained as it is covered by company expenses. They may also use facilities because it is convenient to do this in their busy schedule – for example buying a new tie for work.

Then there are transfer passengers. They are unlikely to make use of facilities, such as banks and post offices, and obviously will not need car hire or car parking facilities. They may want to make some retail purchases, particularly if the duty- and tax-free prices are competitive, but this will only be possible if there is sufficient time between flights. It is hard for an airport to maximize the commercial opportunities for transfer passengers if it also wishes to maximize its efficiency as a hub by providing swift connections. At most major hubs, there will also be passengers who will spend a considerable length of time in the airside area. Various airports have developed some quite imaginative airside facilities to appear to these passengers. For example, Singapore Changi airport has a swimming pool, a sauna, a gym and a cinema, and if the transfer passengers stay for longer than 5 hours, they can arrange a bus tour of Singapore. Amsterdam airport has an art gallery and casino. Most airports have business facilities such as meeting rooms, secretarial support, internet access, and so on which are well used by transfer passengers. An increasing number of airports are also providing pampering, fitness and health services such as reflexology, massage and spa treatments which particularly appeal to passengers with time to spare when they are transferring. An interesting example here is Frankfurt airport that has the world's largest airport clinic which deals with the medical problems of both staff and passengers and in recent years has served over 30 000 patients annually.

Nationalities will also influence spending and shopping behavioural patterns. For example, Scandinavians, who have relatively high duties and taxes, are favourites for buying duty- and tax-free products at airport shops. Surveys at Heathrow show that Norwegians, who still have access to duty- and tax-free shops in Europe because they do not belong to the European Union, are particularly good spenders at these shops. The Japanese also have a same high spend per passenger which has traditionally been due to the buying of gifts to take home to friends and to relatives – although this is not so common for the more diverse, more independent and younger groups of Japanese which are now travelling. Americans, although being very fond of shopping generally, are not usually expected to do their shopping at airports and so their average spend is much lower.

Factors such as nationality, age, occupation, and socio-economic group can be used to produce different passenger classifications. For instance, BAA identified four key traveller groups associated with UK nationals – each of which had different shopping characteristics. First, there are the mass market leisure flyers who travel just once a year and are in the mood for treating themselves. They are impulse buyers and they tend to buy duty-free if they can. Then there are the young upmarket leisure flyers who travel several times a year and are high spenders. They will be brand conscious and prepared to pay for quality products. Older upmarket leisure flyers again travel several times a year and have a high disposable income. They will treat themselves at airports although they will be price-conscious buyers. They will make duty-free purchases if they can, and perfumes will be popular. Finally, there are the time-starved frequent business flyers who will be attracted by 'one-off' promotions and electronic products. They will use the airport as a convenience place to shop (Maiden, 2000). Similarly, Manchester airport has segmented its market into six different types. First, there is the airport shopaholic who typically is a young happy female on a charter holiday. Secondly, there is the agitated passenger who is a young and frustrated middle income traveller. Then, there is the unfulfilled shopper who is a young professional on business or leisure trips and the value seeker who is the student or pensioner on an annual trip to Europe. The final two categories are the unlikely shoppers, who are frequent business travellers, and the measured shoppers who are older male travellers. Each of these groups has different characteristics and spending behaviour (Agbebi, 2005). A simpler classification is suggested by Geuens *et al.* (2004), which divides airport shoppers into mood shoppers, shopping lovers and apathetic shoppers.

Concentrating on the psychographic and consuming behaviour by looking at factors such as attitudes, values, relation with brands and reaction to media is likely to be more effective than just considering the demographic- and travel-related characteristics of the passengers (Spanger, 2008). An assessment of motivation is also important because of the fact that the primary reason for passengers to come to airports will not be to shop and consequently their motivations to shop at airports will be very different from other types of shopping. For instance, distinctions can be made between entertainment shopping (gift/novelty purchasing), purposive shopping (confectionery, books, toiletries), time-pressed shopping (last minute/emergency purchases), convenience shopping (wide choice of known brand names), essential shopping (restaurants/cafeterias, foreign currency exchange, insurance) and lifestyle shopping (high-quality international brand purchases) (Institute for Retail Studies, 1997). Echevarne (2008) describes a similar classification devised by Pragma Consulting/ARC Retail Consultants. There is travel necessity (e.g. books, toys, music, confectionery), souvenirs (e.g. local produce, T-shirt, ornament), gifts for those at home or destination, personal self-treat (e.g. designer label clothing, watches, jewellery and accessories), convenience (e.g. tie for executive), exclusive opportunity to buy (e.g. reduced prices or unique merchandise in the duty-free shop) and trip enhancement (e.g. sunglasses for holiday).

Most of the airport commercial facilities have been historically provided for passengers – or perhaps their pets as in the case of the 'Park and Bark' dog kennels at Sydney airport! However, many airports have now recognized the commercial opportunities that exist with other consumer groups which use the airport and have introduced facilities wholly or partially for their needs. The airports have thus exploited their commercial potential of being business or commercial centres which generate, employ and attract a large number of visits – rather than just providing facilities for passengers who choose to use the airport. For example, staff employed by the airport operators and by the airlines, handling agents, concessionaires, and governments agencies may wish to use airport commercial facilities, particularly as they may not be able to combine a visit to their local shops and their working life at the airport. Workers from nearby office complexes, or from airport industrial estates, may find the airport facilities useful. Popular services include supermarkets, banking services, hairdressers, chemists, and dry-cleaners. Some of these services may be used by arriving passengers – another potential market sub-segment. An example here is Brisbane airport where a shopping centre with a supermarket, liquor outlet and tavern, and specialty stores such as a baker, pharmacy, grocer, newsagent and butcher are being built for the 15 000 workers at the airport.

Airports may also be attractive to the local residential community as an alternative shopping centre – especially if the airport is relatively uncongested and easily accessible with good road and rail links. Sometimes, local residents will be encouraged to go to the airport because of free parking or a certain period of free parking if a purchase is made. The growing popularity of the use of initiatives to encourage public transport use at airports, however, may be in conflict with such commercial strategies. Indeed for certain large airports with severe surface access problems, encouraging additional visits to the airport will be the last policy that they want to adopt. Opposition may also be voiced from nearby local shopping centres as has been the case at London Gatwick airport with shopping facilities at the neighbouring town of Crawley. Airports may be particularly popular as alternative shopping centres if there are legal restrictions on shopping hours imposed on the high street. For example, Frankfurt airport was one of the first airports to develop its landside shops into a shopping mall concept, benefiting from downtown shopping hour limits which were only relaxed in the mid-1990s. Amsterdam airport was also an airport to take advantage of landside shopping some time ago when it opened its Plaza area in 1995.

Meeters, greeters, farewellers and other visitors to the airport will also need F&B services, and, perhaps, additional facilities such as florists, gifts and souvenir shops. Car parking revenue can be generated from them. International and long-haul flights for passengers who are travelling for leisure purposes generally attract the most meeters, greeters and farewellers. Moreover air travel still holds a strange fascination for certain people and for these enthusiasts specialist shops and merchandise can be sold. Viewing platforms, tours, and exhibitions can also be provided on a commercial basis. They can have a dual purpose in acting as a public relations function or service to the community. For instance, Munich airport visitors park is one of Bavaria's most popular day-trip destinations, consisting of an interactive multimedia centre, an observation hill, a 'behind the scenes at the airport' display, guided bus tours, and F&B and retail facilities. Other airports, for example Düsseldorf airport, also provide airport tours. Visitors may be attracted to airports if leisure facilities are provided. A notable example is Kuala Lumpur airport where amongst the leisure facilities within the boundary of this airport there is a Formula One motor-racing track. While airports can measure their potential passenger market quite accurately, it is much more difficult to obtain meaningful figures for the other consumers at an airport. The size of this market at each airport is quite varied, which partly reflects traffic and cultural characteristics but also the methodology used to estimate the figures. At Frankfurt airport, it was estimated that 46 million passengers were joined by 7 million meeters and greeters, 8 million other visitors, and in addition, there were 60 000 employees at the airport (Middecke, 2000). In the same year, Malpensa Milan airport was predicted to handle 3.25 million meeters and greeters and 15 000 airport staff along with 13 million passengers (Amore, 1999).

For the business community, conferences and meeting facilities can be provided (Table 6.1). Most major airports offer these. The good transport links which airports generally possess can make them ideal for international business events. These facilities can be shared by business passengers, local businesses, and other customers. Many airports have also expanded beyond the boundaries of the traditional airport business by using neighbouring land for hotels, office complexes, trade centres, light industries, freight warehousing, distribution and logistics centres, and business parks. If such development occurs, the airport is often called an airport city or 'aerotropolis'. Way back in 1994, Amsterdam airport defined itself as an airport city and also later adopted this concept at Brisbane airport which it partially owned. There are numerous

Table 6.1 The different markets for commercial facilities at airports

Market segment	Facilities provided
Passengers (departing/arriving, terminal/transfer, low cost/full cost, business/leisure, different nationalities, ages, etc.)	Wide range of retail, F&B and other essential and leisure services dependent on passenger type
Workers at the airport and in the surrounding areas	Convenience shops, banks, chemists, and other essential services
Local residents	Shops, F&B, and leisure services
Visitors – meeters, greeters, farewellers	F&B, gift, and souvenir shops
Visitors – air transport enthusiasts	Specialist aviation shops, tours, visitor terraces, exhibitions, F&B
Local businesses	Office/meeting facilities, land for business development/light industry

other examples where airport cities exist or are being developed such as in Dallas Fort Worth, Washington Dulles, Baltimore and Denver in the United States, Albuquerque in Mexico, Campinas in Brazil, and Hong Kong, Kuala Lumpur and Seoul Incheon in Asia (Abeyratne, 2007). The new Dubai World Central Complex which will have at least six runways is also being planned as an aerotropolis with 50 high rise office towers and a residential, commercial, enterprise and leisure zones as well (Reiss, 2007). The Sky City programme at Gimpo airport in Korea is another interesting example where the surrounding area is being developed for shopping, conferences, leisure and entertainment with facilities such as golf courses, cinemas, convention centres, a theme park and shopping mall (Cho, 2007).

Geographical characteristics

Many of the most successful airports in terms of non-aeronautical income generation are situated within Europe. This is due to a number of general factors such as the large international traffic volumes within Europe and the relatively high income per capita. European airports have also led the way in terms of commercialization and privatization trends with the development of non-aeronautical revenues being one of the most notable outcomes of these more advanced evolutionary stages of the airport industry. The 2006 ACI airport economics survey (Airport Council International, 2007) shows that European airports as a whole generated US$12 per passenger from non-aeronautical sources in 2006 compared with a global mean of US$8 (Figure 6.1). Globally, the breakdown of these revenues is retail concession including F&B (22 per cent), car parking (18 per cent), car rental concessions (6 per cent), property or rents (19 per cent), advertsing (2 per cent) and others – such as utility recharges and visitor, IT

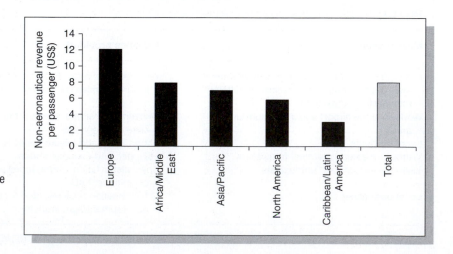

Figure 6.1
Non-aeronautical revenue per passenger at ACI airports by world region, 2006.
(*Source*: ACI, 2007.)

business and consultancy services (33 per cent). Within Europe, retail revenue is the most important single non-aeronautical source with shops being the largest revenue item (Figure 6.2).

Non-aeronautical revenue per passenger for North American airports is much less than in Europe – averaging only US$6. These airports are dominated by domestic passengers who spend less. Also at hub airports, emphasis is placed on swift efficient connections rather than providing passengers with the time to browse and shop. The dependency on the car and the lack of adequate public transport access to many airports mean that the two single most important non-aeronautical sources are car parking and car hire. Retail is much less important and within retail, F&B is much more significant. For example at airports such as Dallas Fort Worth, Indianapolis, Las Vegas, Memphis, Minneapolis St Paul, Chicago O'Hare and Seattle, more revenue is generated from F&B than from shops. Appold and Kasarda (2006) estimate that at US airports typically 54–68 per cent of passengers use F&B facilities whilst only 11–37 per cent make a non-food/drink purchase. This tends to reduce the overall concession income per square metre and per passenger as the average spend tends to be lower for F&B and more space is required for the kitchen, food storage and eating areas.

It is somewhat surprising that the United States, which is world famous for its shopping malls, only began to fully recognize the commercial potential of airports in the 1990s – well behind the European airports. Branded shops and F&B outlets were rarely found at US airports until this time, in spite of their widespread use elsewhere in the country. The turning point came about in the early 1990s at around the

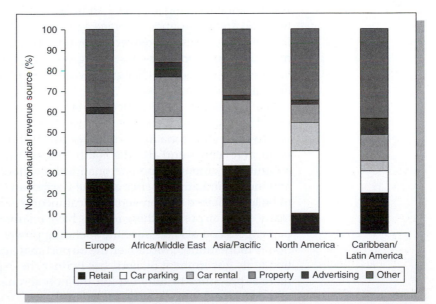

Figure 6.2
Non-aeronautical revenue at ACI airports by revenue source, 2006.
(*Source*: ACI, 2007.)

time when BAA acquired a 15-year contract to manage the commercial facilities at Pittsburgh airports. The company replaced the typical news-agent outlet and general store with well-known brands and developed other concepts which it had used with its European airports, such as pre-ordering products. Similar practices have been introduced by BAA at Indianapolis, Baltimore and Boston airports. A further forerunner in airport commercial development in the United States was Portland airport which was one of the first airports to introduce a mall concept to the airport with its 'Made in Oregon' mall. Another airport which has adopted a mall concept is the privately run Terminal 4 at JFK New York airport where a range of landside shops have been branded together under the brand 'The Shops at Terminal 4' which covers a space of $9290\,m^2$ and is one of the largest pre-security airport retail areas in the US (Holden, 2007).

Duty- and tax-free sales are not very significant at most North American airports with the exception of certain airports such as San Francisco, Los Angeles, and Honolulu, which handle a large pro-portion of Asian traffic. The situation in Asia itself is very different where duty- and tax-free income is much more important. Compared with Europe, where traditionally and especially before the abolition of EU sales in 1999, most of the sales have been associated with core products such as liquor, tobacco and fragrance; in Asia the duty- and tax-free revenue is generated from a much wider range of products. There are also arrival duty- and tax-free shops at many of the major Asian airports. Singapore Changi airport has built up a worldwide reputation for good shopping – a reputation which other relatively new airports such as Kuala Lumpur's Sepang and Hong Kong's Chek Lap Kok have also sought to acquire. However the passenger pro-file at these airports is changing with the upper-class high-spending Asian nationals being joined by an increasing volume of Asian travel-lers who are of a younger average age and are from the rapidly grow-ing middle classes. Moreover, inbound passengers are now a much more diverse, more cost-conscious group of travellers. Spending pat-terns are consequently changing, with more emphasis being placed on 'value-for-money' goods.

The Middle East and African data in Figures 6.1 and 6.2 are dis-torted to a certain degree by the fact that it includes Dubai airport where the non-aeronautical revenues are 10 times as much as aero-nautical revenues and also the South African airports which generate a significant amount of non-aeronautical revenue. Elsewhere in Africa and indeed in Latin America and the Caribbean there generally tends to be less reliance on non-aeronautical income. This is partly because many of the airports in these regions have relatively small numbers of passengers and also because the spending power of the local popula-tion is more limited. Moreover the airport management, often closely tied to its government owners, has neither the expertise nor the com-mercial pressures to fully exploit the non-aeronautical opportunities at these airports.

Approaches to the provision of commercial facilities

Most airports have come a long way since they just provided the generic newspaper, book, and gift shop, the traditional duty-free shop with its internationally branded products and the bland F&B services with no recognizable identity. In the 1980s, many European airports began to recognize the attraction of specialty retail outlets and the advantages of using familiar brand names such as the Body Shop and Tie Rack. The specialist retail chains which had grown so quickly in the high streets started to appear at airports. The branding provided reassurance for the traveller, who was aware of the quality and price level of the goods within the branded outlet. More variety was also introduced into the F&B outlets by again bringing in famous brand names as McDonald's and Burger King. The F&B area began to be split into a number of different, sometimes competing individual outlets. In most cases, the large sit-down restaurant, which took up considerable valuable floor space, became a relic of the past.

However, the widespread adoption of branding at airports has meant that there is now greater similarity in the shopping facilities at many airports and less diversity. Brand fatigue can become a problem – particularly for the frequent traveller who can find that airport shopping can become rather dull and boring. Hence, most of the airports are trying to blend together famous brand outlets with local outlets which can give the airport some kind of identity and can distinguish it from the other airports. The character and the culture of the city or the country which the airport serves can be represented by selling local merchandise or gourmet products such as cheese from Switzerland, chocolates from Belgium, or Parma ham from Italy. A flavour of the local environment can also be provided by theming the commercial facilities. For instance, at Las Vegas airport a number of the outlets are themed after hotels and entertainments in the city. In addition before space constraints became an issue, hotel developers used to place models of the new hotels in the terminal. Moreover there are slots machines everywhere (even before arriving passengers reach the baggage reclaim) and indeed gaming accounts for 14 per cent of total concession revenue (McCormick, 2006a). Likewise at Orlando airport, there are shops representing the major theme parks in the area and Memphis airport is themed around blues, rock and roll and Elvis Presley. There is even an Elvis-themed bar in Prestwick airport in Scotland which is the only place in Great Britain that Elvis visited! Vancouver airport is themed to represent the physical characteristics and cultural heritage of British Columbia, whereas Santiago airport in Chile tries to depict Chile's diverse geography from desert to Antarctic conditions. Another example is Vienna airport where the shops have been developed like a maze of streets which reflect the actual layout of Vienna.

With all these examples, the skill is in finding the correct balance between international recognized global brand retailers and local shops and F&B outlets which give the airport an individual identity. The brands also need to be appropriate for passenger spending capabilities as too expensive a brand may deter spending but, in contrast, too cheap a brand may mean that sub-optimal revenue is generated. In addition even when global F&B brands are used, local tastes should be taken into account. For example Subway increases its vegetarian offerings in Indian airports and makes greater use of chilli sauce at Changi Singapore airport. Similarly to accommodate local preferences for coffee, Caffe Ritazza focuses on strong filter coffee in Sweden, latte macciatto in Germany and strong expresso in Italy (McCormick, 2006b).

Some airports have chosen to enforce and promote an airport brand rather than the individual brands of the high street retailers. Amsterdam Schiphol and Singapore Changi airports are good illustrations of such a policy. For example, at Amsterdam airport, all the shops in the airside area are branded under the 'See Buy Fly' identity and the outlets are grouped by product type such as electronics, fragrances, confectionery and so on, rather than according to who sells them. All sold products are placed in bright yellow branded shopping bags which have become a very recognizable feature in Europe and beyond.

The development of airport terminals into shopping centres has not been universally popular. Certain passenger types, particularly business travellers who are seeking a quick transit through the terminal, favour a more streamlined airport service. Also the airlines, while welcoming the fact that non-aeronautical income can reduce an airport's reliance on aeronautical charges if a single till is adopted, have periodically expressed concerns that the shopping function of the airport has interfered with the normal flows of passengers through the airports. Clear signage to gates, for example, is difficult to achieve if the airport is cluttered with retail and F&B signage and branding. There have been claims that passengers have delayed flights because they have been lost in the duty-free shops – so many airports have now placed flight information systems in the commercial outlets as well. Some airlines have also complained that airports have been giving too much attention to developing commercial facilities while ignoring basic operational requirements. For example, in 2001, BA objected to its first-class passengers having to be routed through BAA's retail facilities on their way to their airline lounge at London Heathrow, and the former company Airtours complained that the pressure to maximize retail income at Gatwick had led to inadequate provision of passenger facilities such as seating and toilets and that additional shops had distracted passengers from making their way to the gates (Competition Commission, 2002). A correct balance between commercial and operational space is needed so that the non-aeronautical revenue is optimized without compromising the operational effectiveness – but this is no easy matter.

As well as adopting high street preferences for specialty shopping and branded products, airports have also been applying other tried and tested retail practices. This has helped by having an increasing number of airports employing professional retail managers from the high street. Airports operators such as BAA have encouraged loyalty purchases at airports by introducing loyalty cards such as BAA WorldPoints and another similar example is at Bahrain airport. As with high street shopping, the schemes not only provide the airport operators and their retailers with a mechanism to encourage repeat buying, but also enable them to find out about their customers and communicate with them when new products and services are being introduced.

Moreover, airports have also introduced value and money-back guarantees which have been commonplace on the high street for many years. These are seen as particularly important because of the perceived expensive 'rip-off' reputation of many airports. For example, Singapore Changi airport has two such guarantees:

1. The price of liquor, tobacco, perfumes, and cosmetics will be no higher than at other major airports in the Asia Pacific region. Prices for other goods will be no higher than established downtown shops. If higher prices are found at the airport, a refund of double the price difference will be given.
2. A full refund or exchange will be given for any goods whether they are faulty, inappropriate, or unwanted purchases.

No discussion about retail activities would be complete without references to the impact of the internet. In a narrow sense it can be viewed as a revenue generating opportunity at airports because internet connections can be charged for, but more generally it must clearly be seen as a threat because of the vast range of discounted goods which are now available and easy to access. It must be remembered, however, that many purchases at airports are made on impulse and form part of the 'leisure travel experience'. The internet can also bring many opportunities for airports if strategies are developed in conjunction with the terminal facilities. Most of the airport websites now give details of the commercial facilities which are available and so passengers can be more prepared when they visit the airport. They may be better able to plan their shopping in the limited time period available to them. Special offer vouchers can be made available on the internet to encourage passengers to buy at the airport. At an increasing number of airports, products and services can be pre-ordered for collection at the airport – particularly foreign currency and car parking. Moreover additional car parking services such as valeting, cleaning or repairs can be ordered.

The airport website is just one of a wide range of advertising opportunities which airports can use to generate additional non-aeronautical revenue. Advertising with airports (either at the actual physical location or website) is often seen as attractive because of the high volumes of the passengers and the cosmopolitan and higher socio-economic group of many travellers. The whole area of airport advertising has become much more varied and interactive in recent years with for example, scrolling billboards, plasma screens and the sponsorship of airport furniture such as clocks, baggage carousels, trolleys, and internet kiosks as well as the traditional billboards and light boxes. Moreover certain digital technology, for example interactive touch screens, can be used to target offers at certain passenger to make them spend more (Ross, 2007). However, it is always important with airport advertising, as with the provision of all commercial facilities, to ensure that it does not inhibit ease of movement through the airport or irritate the passengers.

The commercial contract and tender process

There are various ways in which commercial facilities can be provided at airports. Most airports have chosen to contract out these services to specialist retail and F&B companies. This lower-risk option is usually chosen because the airport operator does not have specialist skills required or a detailed understanding of the market environment. Moreover it will not have the bulk buying power and well-established supply infrastructure which the specialist companies will have. Some airports, particularly smaller ones, may opt to offer their airports as a total retail package to a master concessionaire who will then in turn seek specialist operators to run the individual outlets.

There are a few airports and operators, such as Dubai and Abu Dhabi Airport, Dublin Airport Authority and BAA, who have chosen to provide some facilities themselves, such as duty- and tax-free products, either directly or through a wholly owned subsidiary. A few others, such as Venice airport, directly manage the F&B facilities. In India the Government runs the duty-free shops and many of the airports and so again there is some link here. This situation with Dublin Airport Authority is primarily because it has built up much expertise in this area being directly involved with such operations since the first shops were opened in the 1940s. BAA only adopted this approach in the 1990s to enable it to have total control over the whole retailing process from suppliers to warehouses to customer purchases and to provide it with opportunities for international expansion. Also some very small airports run their own facilities and this makes sense with small operations where it would be difficult to attract external specialists. Car parking tends to be the only commercial activity which is provided by a substantial number of airport operators themselves since it generally requires less specialist skills and also needs greater capital investment by the airport operator. For example out of the 22 major airports in the UK (excluding BAA), 13 operated their own car parks (CRI, 2008).

The contractual details

When airport operators contract out their commercial facilities they usually enter into a concession contract with the companies providing the services. This typically involves the concessionaire paying a percentage of sales to the airport operator often in addition to agreeing a minimum annual guaranteed amount. The turnover fee or so-called retail yield may vary from as little as 5 per cent for some landside commercial activities to up to 50 per cent for facilities with higher profit margins – notably duty- and tax-free sales. The fee may vary for different products with different profit margins. The fee may also increase at a faster rate than the level of turnover in the belief that concessionaires will be in a better position to pay higher fees once all basic fixed costs have been covered (Freathy and O'Connell, 1998). On average the overall revenue yield for all retail together is in the region of 18 per cent (The Moodie Report, 2007).

The airport operator will usually only provide the shell for the outlet and it will be up to the concessionaire to provide the capital investment for fitting out the facility. A typical length for the concession will be around 5–7 years, although this can vary quite considerably and there may be options for renewal. If the contract is too short there will be no time to develop the business, whereas if the contract is too long the airport may miss out on the increased revenues and a chance to react to retail trends which the signing of a new contract may be bring. There may be longer contracts (up to 10 years) for F&B to take account of the investment required and occasionally shorter contracts may be issued for experimental facilities. Generally concession contracts will be relatively low risk for the airport operator which will tend to have little responsibility over the commercial facilities. The airport operator will be assured of a certain amount of revenues. However, since this revenue stream will be linked to the concessionaire's sales rather than profit volumes, there is no guarantee that the concessionaire will aim to maximize its sales as it may be more concerned with profit margins. An increasing number of such contracts also include service level agreements. These cover areas such as staffing levels; staff training and other policies; marketing and after sales service; store quality, maintenance and refurbishment schedules; and product innovation and pricing policies.

Alternatively, the airport operator may choose to enter into a management contract which involves greater financial risk for the airport operator. These have been used for car parking facilities at airports for many years but are not a popular approach for other commercial activities. In this case the specialist operator will be paid a monthly fee in return for maintaining certain agreed standards such as accurate financial accounts, high quality of cleanliness and professional staff appearance. The ability to build in guaranteed service levels is important especially with car parking where competition from off-airport parking providers is increasing, especially with marketing being provided on the internet. For example 40 per cent of car parks around London Heathrow airport are operated by independent firms (Bates, 2005a).

A third option is to have a joint venture arrangement when the airport operator enters into a partnership with the specialist retailer or some other organization to provide the commercial facilities. The advantages of such an approach are that the airport and retailer develop a long-term relationship and all the transaction costs and time associated with a concession contract can be avoided. Examples include the joint retail venture of Aéroports de Paris and Aelia and Hamburg airport which has a joint venture with F&B, but generally this practice is relatively rare. There are perhaps more opportunities for this type of arrangement when an airport operator is wishing to expand its involvement to other airports. Dublin Airport Authority, for example, has entered into a number of joint venture agreements in order to provide commercial facilities in the CIS and the Middle East.

Within Europe, North America, and Asia most concession contracts are automatically put out to tender when they come up for renewal. Such a practice is not so widespread in some other more developing areas but is usually the most effective way of ensuring the best contractual arrangements. Having a tendering process will give existing retailers incentives to improve their performance if they want to win the contract again. It also gives the airport a chance to introduce new concepts in retailer and F&B as fashions change and perhaps the opportunity to generate more revenue if new concessionaires are prepared to pay a higher fee.

As selection criteria will vary from airport to airport, generally the evaluation of offers will consider both the financial terms (i.e. the concession fee paid) and the more qualitative terms (i.e. quality, vision, innovation, and so on). Some airports will just choose the bid which will generate the highest revenue – indeed in some countries such as Israel they are required to do so by law. This has led to a tendency to overbid in offers, particularly in Europe, in recent years. While in the short run this will benefit the airport operator with high levels of concession revenue, such a situation will not be sustainable in the longer term. The concessionaire will lose money and will have to renegotiate conditions with the airport operator or be forced to abandon its airport operations completely. Sometimes this issue may be overcome by setting a maximum percentage fee. The problem of overbidding was one of the key reasons behind ACI Europe's attempt to develop a concession tender code in 2001, which has subsequently been developed into a best practice charter (Airport Business Communique, 2005). This covers areas such as the information which airports should collect and which retailers should provide, what should be done before and after a contract is awarded and the type of contracts which can be used and service level agreements.

Factors driving success

Choosing the right concessionaire and negotiating the most appropriate contractual agreement is crucial if an airport is going to fully exploit its commercial opportunities. However, there are many other factors which will also play a role. The airport operator may be able to influence some of these factors – but by no means all of them. Clearly, the nature of the airport traffic and its spending capability needs to be taken into account. For instance, an airport handling predominantly domestic business travellers is likely to be in a less favourable position for generating commercial income than an airport with many long-haul leisure passengers. Therefore understanding the mix of passengers and planning the facilities to match as closely as possible their needs and preferences is paramount to maximizing the revenue generating opportunities and return on investment. Market research ideally needs to be undertaken, not only of passengers but also of staff, meeters, greeters and visitors to enable their preferences and experiences to be examined.

Small airports with limited passenger traffic are at a distinct disadvantage since they will not have the critical mass, typically around five million passengers, necessary to diversify and support specialist retail and F&B outlets. Airports go through different evolutionary stages as regards their commercial income depending on their size. Small airports can only really offer the basic facilities such as a duty-free shop, newsagent, and F&B outlets especially as the volume of traffic tends to be unevenly spread with just a few flights a day. As the airport grows, more specialist shops can be added until finally the airport can be considered as a shopping centre (Jones, 2002). In fact The Airport Retail Study showed that the retail revenue per passenger at airports with more than 20 million passengers is on average twice that of airports of less than 10 million passengers (The Moodie Report, 2007).

Spending by all passengers will be influenced by the general economic climate. Factors to consider include growth in gross domestic product (GDP) and consumer expenditure, level of taxation, inflation rates, and foreign currency fluctuations. The level of sales taxation will also play a role. Moreover purchasing patterns will be affected by delays at an airport. A delay of an hour or so for a departure slot may give passengers extra time to visit the shops or F&B outlets. Such a delay may be popular with the commercial department but not with anyone else! In contrast, lengthy operational delays within the terminal, such as long queues for passport control, security or immigration will have the reverse effect, and reduce or even eliminate the dwell time that passengers have for browsing in the shops and having something to eat or drink.

Then there is a competition for airport commercial facilities, which can come from a variety of different sources. First, there are other airports. Notable examples of airports which are in a particularly competitive situation are those in the Gulf such as Dubai, Abu Dhabi, and Bahrain, and some Asian airports serving destinations such as Singapore, Kuala Lumpur, and Hong Kong. There is also a competition from the in-flight sales of airlines. Some of the airlines allow pre-booking of goods in order to catch some business before the passengers can see what the airport competitor has on offer. In addition, competition can come from downtown tax-free outlets for international travellers, which are allowed in a number of countries, particularly in Asia. In Europe and North America, competition exists with discounted electrical and other high street businesses and from the growth of factory outlets. Internet shopping, as previously discussed, is a major competitor as well and customers are now far more likely to search immediately on the internet to see what bargains they can purchase rather than wait until their next airport visit to shop. All this means that the airports need to ensure that they keep up-to-date with retail trends and fashions and that they constantly monitor competitor prices.

Just as in the high street, the outlet number, size and mix are very important. For example, too many outlets may reduce sales per outlet and create excess competition. As regards the mix this should be determined by the type of customer, the commercial viability of the outlets and the different space requirements which are needed. For example London Stansted airport which serves predominantly low cost carrier demand has much 'grab and go' F&B whereas London Heathrow terminal 3, which has a substantial amount of long-haul and transfer traffic, has many designer retail stores and sit-down restaurants. Another key factor is the location, space and design of facilities. However, a large proportion of the airports which are in use today were designed without taking sufficient account of the commercial opportunities that airport terminals can offer. All too often, concession planners get involved at a much too late stage of the terminal design and development process (Gray, 2007). This has meant that commercial facilities very often are not ideally situated or have been added on later as an afterthought.

Successful concession planning, at least when passenger purchases are being considered, is all about providing facilities close to passenger flows and not in areas which are 'dead ends' or are too far from passengers' view. Moreover a change in the flow line of passengers can have a dramatic impact on concessionaire's sales. The outlets should, ideally, be on the same floor levels as the departure gates, as having to go through the inconvenience of changing levels may deter some passengers from visiting the commercial facilities. Using the same logic, shops aimed at business travellers should be allocated near the business lounges. There is also a growing trend to have commercial facilities which require passengers to walk through them to get to the departure lounge or gates as is the case, for example, in Terminal 3 at London Heathrow, Copenhagen, Oslo and Berlin Tegel airports. These can increase 'footfall' at airports to 100 per cent but such shops are difficult to introduce into a terminal unless new infrastructure is being provided. At all times, however, the commercial facilities must not hamper the passengers ability to 'way find' themselves around the airport as this may well increase their anxiety.

Likewise when product promotions spill out of the retail units into other parts of the terminal they must not obscure the passengers' lines of sight to the next essential airport process.

Particular problems can arise from terminals which are of a linear design, such as Terminal 1 at Munich airport, because very often facilities have to be duplicated, which can be costly until there is sufficient throughput of passengers to support all the facilities. This was the situation with the fourth terminal at London Heathrow Airport when it first opened. Problems have also occurred for airports in European countries which have signed up to the Schengen agreement and have abolished immigration controls with other Schengen countries. At some airports, this has caused unnecessary duplication of facilities, resulting in reduced custom for each outlet. A similar situation exists at certain Canadian airports such as Toronto where there are three different passenger channels, namely domestic, US and other international, which have to be separated from each other. In some cases when there is more than one terminal, passenger flows can be combined to go through a central security area which is situated near a commercial area. This means that the airport can minimize the amount of duplication in its retail offer whilst at the same time giving a greater choice for passengers. This has happened at Toulouse airport where the passengers of the new Terminal 3 have been combined with the passengers of the existing Terminal 2 and hence one larger commercial area for around 4 million passengers has been constructed (Entwistle, 2007). Likewise this will happen at Hamburg airport where a walk-through shopping centre (the Plaza) is being built between Terminals 1 and 2 to accommodate all the passengers.

The amount of time a passenger has at an airport will obviously influence their shopping behaviour. This dwell time is affected by the check-in procedures and control and departure processes. Thus developments such as self-service check-in, more stringent security rules and the tendency of some low cost carriers to make early calls for their passengers to the gates, or for LCC passengers to go near the gates in order to select a good seat on the aircraft, will all have an impact on dwell time. Different types of passengers spend different average dwell times in the lounge. BAA estimated that in the domestic lounge in Terminal 3 at London Heathrow the average dwell time for economy passengers is 49 minutes compared with 27 minutes for business class and 13 minutes for first-class passengers (Toms, 2000). BAA also calculated that the incremental airport spend for each additional 10 minutes available time is £0.80 for domestic passengers and £1.60 for international passengers (Maiden, 2008). The more recent Airport Retail Study for 2006–2007 also found that on average domestic passengers spend 49 minutes in the terminal: 31 per cent of this time is spent at check-in, 12 per cent is general dwell such as seeing off friends and family and 20 per cent of this is with security. The remaining 18 minutes or 37 per cent of the time is airside dwell. In contrast on average international passengers spend 83 minutes in the terminal with 62 minutes or 75 per cent of the time spent in the landside and only 21 minutes or 25 per cent of the time spent airside. In the landside time for check-in accounted for 23 per cent, general dwell 25 per cent, customs and immigration 16 per cent and security 12 per cent (Moodie, 2007). These figures were however collected before the recent LAG developments which have generally increased time spent in the security process.

Passengers also need to feel relaxed when they shop and so they tend to have a preference in buying from outlets which are situated within the vicinity of the departure gates – once all essential processes such as check-in and security screening have been completed. They also will not want to walk long distances to be able to shop. Throughout their time at the airport, passenger stress levels will fluctuate, depending on where they are within all the airport processes, and this will have a direct impact on their spending patterns. Their stress levels will vary according to other factors, for example whether they are travelling alone or with their family. If they are travelling for leisure purposes, their excitement levels will often increase as well as they go through the airport which should encourage spending in the airside area (Bork, 2006). Boredom levels also need to be considered.

Landside shopping is different to plan than airside shopping as convenient locations not only for passengers, but also for staff, meeters, greeters, farewellers and local residents, must be found. If there is too much landside shopping, passengers may spend too much time in this area which can reduce their purchases in the airside area, where average spend tends to be higher. On average 55 per cent of retail space is in the departures airside area and a further 34 per cent in the departures landside area. Only 10 per cent is in the arrivals area (3 per cent airside and 7 per cent landside) and 1 per cent outside the terminal (The Moodie Report, 2007). The split between airside and landside varies significantly, however, with Dubai airport for instance, having very few landside facilities whereas the split at Zürich is almost equal because this latter airport has been very active in developing facilities for non-travelling customers. At most airports it is the sales in the airside area of the airport which still brings in the most revenue for the airport operator. Some landside facilities such as post offices, travel agents, or booking agencies may not bring in huge amounts of revenues to the airport but may be perceived as adding value to the airport product from the point of view of the passenger and other consumers.

A few airports have developed very successful arrival duty- and tax-free shops. This has tended to happen in developing countries where there are large numbers of returning expatriate workers For example, in Colombo in Sri Lanka, two arrivals stores generate half of all duty- and tax-free sales due to spending from returning nationals from the Middle East. Likewise in Manila over 60 per cent of duty- and tax-free sales are from arrivals shops (Bates, 2004). Oslo airport in Norway also has substantial sales from its arrivals shops but this is because it is the only Scandinavian country to still sell duty- and tax-free goods within Europe since it is not a member of the European Union. Arrivals shops overcome the recent security problems related to liquids and also can be considered to be more environmentally acceptable as, unlike goods from departure shops, they do not increase the overall weight on the aircraft and consequently cause comparatively less emissions. However it is usually very difficult to get passengers to shop on arrival because they are anxious to get through the airport as quickly as possible and to focus on the essential processes such as baggage reclaim. For this reason Buenas Aires Ezeiza airport has TV screens in their arrivals shop which show when the baggage is ready to be collected.

F&B outlets can compete with passengers' dwell time in shops and so they need to be positioned near the retail facilities but must not interrupt the flow. This is particularly important as most shop purchases are made on impulse, whereas this tends not to be the case with F&B. Shops and F&B outlets have to be large enough so as not to give a congested and overcrowded image, but they must not be so large that consumers may be deterred by an appearance of inactivity and empty space. Whilst F&B tends to account for a fairly small share of total airport commercial revenues and profit levels, more passengers tend to use F&B facilities than shops and so they can have a major impact on a passengers image and perception of the airport. The Airport Retail Study 2006–2007 (The Moodie Report, 2007) found that average penetration rate for F&B was over 40 per cent compared with around 30 per cent for duty-free and news/gifts and less than 10 per cent for bureau de change for international passengers. Thus if the F&B is considered to offer poor value for money, the customer may assume that the same is true for the shops. Indeed Select Service Partner found that typically F&B income accounts for 2–3 per cent of airport income but 20–25 per cent of perceived image (Allett, 2001).

Finally the commercial performance of an airport will be influenced by a wide range of laws and regulations. These will include the duty- and tax-free limits which are set by governments and also any regulations related to the legal contracts and the bidding process. There may also be local planning regulations, particularly if the airport is competing with nearby shopping centres. Then there are security rules which have increasingly had a major influence on airport retail – these are discussed elsewhere.

Measuring non-aeronautical performance

Airports, with their concessionaire partners, have become increasingly active in monitoring their non-aeronautical performance. This is partly due to a drive for better performance monitoring of all aspects of the industry and also because retail experts, with experience of assessing retail performance at other locations, are being bought in to manage airport facilities. Consumer satisfaction levels and perceptions of value for money are assessed by many airports through customer surveys (as described in Chapter 4). In addition, airports use indicators such as sales per passenger, passenger penetration levels and sales per square metre to analyse the economic performance of their commercial facilities. The latter measure has the advantage in that it can be used to compare airport performance with other retail facilities at other sites such as shopping malls.

Making inter-airport comparisons is difficult because of the commercially sensitive nature of the information required and lack of reliable industry-wide data. One of the most comprehensive benchmarking studies is The Airport Retail Study which has been undertaken since 1998. In the 2006/2007 research 46 major airports in Europe, Asia Pacific, and North America (plus Dubai and Santiago) were investigated (The Moodie Report, 2007). The study looked at performance indicators such as gross sales and retail revenue per passenger and gross sales and retail revenue per square metre both airside and landside, departures and arrivals and by different segment or different type of retail. In addition it also had a number of management indicators examining how the airports manage and control the retail function which considered factors such as concession structures, dwell time and the marketing which is undertaken (Table 6.2). The study also analysed various factors which helped explain the comparative results that were obtained such as the volume and nature of traffic, and the location, mix, and density of outlets.

Table 6.3 shows the average revenue per passenger and per square metre and per passenger from The Airport Retail Study. Duty-free generates by far the largest amount of revenue per passenger and square metre, and there is a relative small amount of revenue per square metre which is generated from F&B facilities which is typical for most airports. The revenue yield (revenue to the airport as a percentage of gross revenue) is in the region of 19–20 per cent. Figure 6.3 shows that the BAA airports, Brisbane and Hong Kong airports generate the most revenue related to sales space whereas Louisville, Calgary and Munich generate the least. Most of the Canadian and US airports generate quite low revenues which must in part be related to the high proportion of domestic traffic and the greater importance of F&B facilities.

Ultimately, however, it is the profits from the commercial facilities rather than the revenues which are the key interest to the airport operator. Their contribution to overall profit levels will, of course, depend on whether the airport has adopted a single or dual till and the range of other activities (such as handling) which the airport may provide. In most cases, however, airport operators will have no direct costs associated with retail and little capital investment which will be

Table 6.2 Indicators used in the Airport Retail Study

Performance indicators

Base series	Per passenger and per square metre series	Space and precinct series	Segment series
Source of revenue Gross sales and retail revenue Retail yield (income as % sales) Passenger number and mix Number & location of outlets Outlets by segment and location Square metres by location Square metres by precinct Square metres by segment & location	Gross sales per passenger Retail revenue per passenger Gross retail sales per square metre Retail income per square metre Low cost carrier passenger spend	Square metres of retail floor space per 1000 passengers Gross sales by precinct and region Retail revenue by precinct and region	Gross sales per passenger by segment Gross sales per square metre by segment Retail revenue per passenger by segment Retail revenue per square metre by segment Retail yield by segment Penetration rates by segment

Management indicators

Structured series	Performance variable series	Marketing series	Organization structure series
Lease structures Rental structures Concession structures Typical concession length Concession performance audit tools	Average dwell time by precinct Average penetration rates Passenger segmentation Meeters, greeters and farewellers Contribution of airport workers to retail	% Gross sales spent on marketing Areas of marketing spend Contribution of internet sales	Management reporting structures Staff numbers devoted to retail

mainly limited to refurbishment of terminal surfaces, and so profit margins tend to be high. For example, on average, Credit Suisse (2006) found that whilst retail revenues account for only 13 per cent of total revenues, they represent a much higher share of the EBITDA, namely 41 per cent. More specifically Table 6.4 clearly demonstrates the relatively high profit margins of retail and other commercial facilities compared to airport charges and property for London Heathrow and Gatwick.

A more qualitative study examined the views of 12 experts in airport concessions. The research found that location, price level, brand name and image, product quality, and service levels are the most important characteristics of commercial operations for both profit maximization and customers' satisfaction. However too much

Table 6.3   Average revenue from different retail sources 2006

	Revenue per m²	Revenue per passenger
Gross revenue (SDR)		
Duty-free	23 950	3.14
Specialty retail	8070	1.40
News/Gifts	9940	0.69
F&B	4570	1.44
All retail	11 221	7.95
Revenue to airport (SDR)		
All retail	2101	1.62

Notes: SDR = Special Drawing Right = $US1.54 at time of calculation.
Different airport samples used for the two measures.
Source: Moodie (2007).

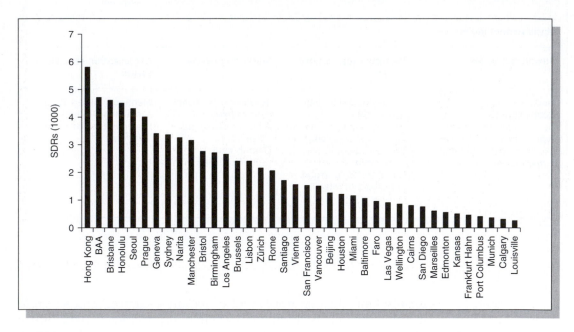

Figure 6.3
Airport retail revenue per square metre.
(*Source*: The Airport Retail Study, 2006/2007.)

product diversity could have a detrimental impact on profitability and excess advertising could negatively affect the customers' satisfaction levels (Kim and Shin, 2001). Whilst these findings are not that surprising or striking, the study is of interest as it is one of the few examples of published research which has investigated this area of airport operations.

Table 6.4 Revenues and profits at London Heathrow and London Gatwick 2005/2006

Heathrow	Revenue (£mn)	Profit (£mn)	Profit Margin (%)	Gatwick	Revenue (£mn)	Profit (£mn)	Profit Margin (%)
Airport charges	560.2	219.6	38.7		152.9	−26.9	−17.6
Retail	206.5	156.9	76.0		98.5	75.0	76.1
Car parking	67.1	42.4	63.2		38.1	27.2	71.4
Car rental	9.9	7.9	79.8		3.1	2.5	80.6
Terminal	47.9	7.5	15.7		10.6	−4.1	−38.7
Property Advertising	24.6	21.8	88.6		4.8	4.7	97.9

Source: Competition Commission (2007).

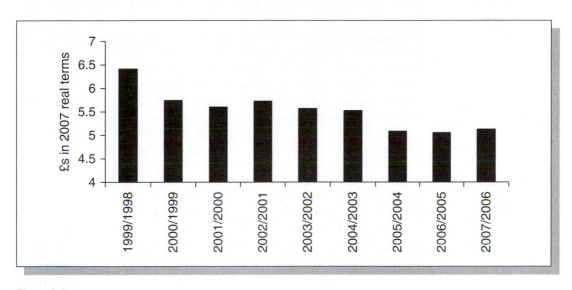

Figure 6.4
Non-aeronautical revenue per passenger 1998–2007 at UK airports.
(*Source*: CRI.)

Recent developments and future trends

Generating commercial revenues at airports over the last few years has become much more challenging. Whilst global traffic growth has ensured that absolute commercial revenue levels have continued to rise, for many airports, particularly in mature markers, the real spend per passenger has actually been decreasing. For example, Figure 6.4 shows that for an average of 17 UK airports real non-aeronautical revenue per passenger (in 2007 terms) has decreased from £6.43

in 1998/1999 to £5.14 in 2006/2007. This has also been reflected in the trends in non-aeronautical revenues as a share of total revenue, which in Europe as discussed in Chapter 3, has actually reduced slightly in recent years. Globally as well the commercial share increased from 46 per cent in 1995 and 1996 to 52 per cent in 1997 and 1998 and peaked in 2001 at 54 per cent. Since then it has dropped back to 47 per cent in 2005 and 48 per cent in 2006 (ACI, 2007). Whilst it is difficult to precisely identify the cause and effects of these trends, undoubtedly there are certain events such as the abolition of EU duty and tax-free, 9/11 and the LAG restrictions which have played a key role.

The ending of EU duty- and tax-free sales in 1999 and other EU developments

Duty- and tax-free shops have been in existence for many decades. The first duty- and tax-free airport outlet was opened in 1947 at Shannon airport in Ireland. In 1951, another shop was opened in Prestwick airport in Scotland. These shops were designed to be attractive to transatlantic passengers on refuelling stops (Freathy and O'Connell, 1998). The shops sold a small range of alcohol, tobacco, and perfumes and a few other items. By the 1960s, other airports had opened similar shops and had started to expand the range of merchandise on offer. For example in 1957 shops were opened in Amsterdam and Tel Aviv, in 1958 in Brussels and Miami, in 1959 in London Heathrow, Frankfurt and Düsseldorf and in 1960 in Osaka and Oslo. This was primarily in response to the rapid increase in passenger traffic at that time and particularly the growth in package holidays and other forms of leisure travel. Amsterdam Schiphol airport was one of the first airports to offer tax-free electronics and photographic material. Then came a retail boom in duty- and tax-free shopping with many airports substantially increasing the area dedicated to such shops and offering a much more diverse and varied product selection, ranging from the traditional alcohol, tobacco and perfume products to camcorders, watches and jewellery, sports clothing, and other fashion accessories.

The 1990s were a period of uncertainty for most EU airports. It was originally intended that all EU duty- and tax-free sales would be abolished on 1 January 1993 as the single market was 'born'. The rationale was that it was illogical and incompatible to have such a system when the EU should be behaving as a single market with open borders. In addition, these shopping privileges were considered to distort competition between modes of transport with no access to these sales, such as rail, and to be unfair trading in relation to downtown shopping. It was argued that EU consumers were subsidizing not only duty- and tax-free outlets but also air and ferry travellers. In response, the airports, charter airlines, ferry companies, and associated manufacturing industries collectively argued that duty-free privileges did not distort or hamper the development of the single market and that abolition would result in millions of jobs being lost. It was claimed that the cost of travel would have to rise substantially to compensate for the loss of income, which would have a knock-on effect throughout entire national economies. Through active lobbying of government ministers, the proponents to the abolition managed to achieve a six-and a-half-year extension of these sales until 30 June 1999 when eventually these sales were abolished.

In the first few months after the abolition of duty- and tax-free sales, it quickly became apparent that the airport industry had focused too much of its attention on fighting the campaign to save the sales, with not enough effort being channelled into preparing for change if abolition were to occur. The immediate impact of loss of EU duty- and tax-free sales in many cases was much greater than was expected. This was largely the result of airports being victims of their own very successful awareness campaigns. The travelling public was sold the message that duty- and tax-free shopping would no longer be available after 30 June 1999, and hence stayed away from all airport shops – even those passengers who could still use them. While for many airports, the situation improved in a few months after the initial reaction to abolition, the loss of revenue within the first year of operation after this development was in many cases considerable as can be seen from Figure 6.3 in the UK. Examples elsewhere include Amsterdam, Brussels and Düsseldorf airports where duty- and tax-free revenue was down by 12, 22 and 20 per cent respectively in 1999 compared to 1998. To address the confusion among passengers, a number of airports launched major marketing campaigns, explaining what passengers travelling to EU destinations and beyond could and could not buy at airport shops.

Many of the EU airports, in partnerships with their retail concessionaires, have absorbed the value added or sales tax themselves – effectively offering the merchandise still at 'tax-free' prices. A few airports are also selling a selection of liquor products at duty-free prices but at most airports cheaper tobacco is no longer available to EU passengers. At many airports passengers for both EU and non-EU destinations share the same retail terminal area and so the airports in Spain, Portugal, Greece and the Netherlands, for example, have dual pricing. Elsewhere for instance in Denmark and Sweden there are different facilities for these different types of passengers. Moreover European airports in Austria, Belgium and Germany, for example, have joined together with concessionaires and ferry companies to form the Travel Value Association. All these organizations have adopted the common and recognizable 'Travel Value' trade mark on their shops, merchandising and advertising in order to indicate to the travelling public that there are still good savings to be made while travelling (Freathy and O'Connell, 2000).

More recently in May 2004, 10 new European countries joined the EU which reduced the potential for duty- and tax-free sales to and from these countries. This must be one of the key reasons for the drop in non-aeronautical revenue per passenger in Figure 6.3 for 2005/2004. Then in January 2006, Bulgaria and Romania also joined the EU which had the same effect. In the future if other countries such as Turkey become members of the Union, clearly the opportunities for duty- and tax-free sales to and from these countries will also be reduced. In addition, a further EU development has been the adoption of the euro in 2002 by the majority of the EU countries. This has decreased the need for currency exchange outlets at the airport and combined with the widespread use of automatic teller machines (ATMs) to access cash, has reduced the prospects of generating revenue from exchanging money.

The impact of 9/11, the Iraq War and SARS

Shortly after the abolition of EU duty-free, airport commercial managers had to face a new challenge, namely the impact of 9/11. This had a number of different effects on the airport industry. First, there were comparatively less passengers to generate commercial revenues. However, the overall impact of this decline depended very much on the type of passengers using the airport. For example, post 9/11, the actual concession revenue per passenger from retail facilities at BAA airports went up from £4.12 to £4.19 because of the decline in US passengers who typically spend relatively little at airports (BAA, 2002). Revenues also declined because of the additional time being spent during check-in and other processes involving of more stringent security requirements. However, in some cases passengers arrived earlier at the airports because of security requirements and actually had more time to shop. Some airports were quite innovative in providing F&B kiosks and carts for passengers who are waiting in long security queues. However, these security queues at some airports blocked important retail areas which previously had been in prime locations.

In the United States where the impact of 9/11 was the greatest, it was estimated that overall non-aeronautical revenues declined by 4.5 per cent in 2002 compared to 2001 for the whole airport industry (ACI-North America, 2002). Moreover many of the US airports had to redesign many of their commercial facilities in order to conform with new security measures. For example, previously meeters, greeters and farewellers had been permitted to accompany passengers right up until the gates but this practice was then stopped. Most of the commercial facilities were near the gates and so this caused a reduction in the commercial revenue generated by non-passengers. Also certain car parks near the terminal which generated large amounts of income had to be closed or reallocated for security reasons since the FAA brought in a 300-foot rule which prevented any vehicle being parked within that distance of the terminals (Pilling, 2002).

The events of 9/11 were followed in 2003 by the Iraq War and the outbreak of SARS. This latter development had a very significant impact on traffic levels in Asia and led to price reductions in both the aeronautical and non-aeronautical areas. All this has meant that the last few years have produced more uncertain passenger growth and has thus also created a much more volatile trading environment for concessionaires-with more focus on ensuring commercial viability. Indeed, in some cases this has led to a more flexible risk sharing concessionaire–airport operator relationships to cope with the more unpredictable passenger flows which, for example, has involved abolishing the minimum guarantees in the contracts or linking them instead to passenger numbers.

LAG restrictions

The latest event which has had an impact on the commercial performance of airports has been the initial banning of LAGs on aircraft in August 2006 in certain countries due to the terrorism threat and then the subsequent regulations which have been introduced to take account of this situation. Chapter 4 has outlined the operational issues related to this development and so the focus here is purely on the commercial impacts. Originally when all LAGs were banned, it was feared that the sales of liquids from airport shops would no longer be an option. Whilst the EU regulation 1546/2006 partially overcame this problem by allowing liquid items bought from an airport side from another EU/EEA airport in a tamper evident bag, it does not allow liquid items that are purchased at airports outside EU/EEA. Moreover some third countries, for example Australia, do not recognize the security of items purchased in the EU.

This has led to many unsuspecting passengers from outside the EU having their LAG purchases being confiscated at EU airports if they are transferring onto a different flight. For example in 2007 Frankfurt airport was confiscating 2500 liquids a day, and Amsterdam and Madrid airport were removing around 1000. Zürich estimated that it was taking away $29 540 worth of alcohol and perfume from passengers daily, whilst at Heathrow this figure was around $211 000. Whilst ICAO and the European Commission are working towards reducing this complex situation, the current inconsistencies are leaving passengers very confused and has damaged the overall consumer confidence in airport shopping (Jane's Airport Review, 2007). In addition the 100 ml rule is encouraging passengers to buy lower value and essential travel items airside which they previously would have bought landside or packed in their hand luggage, and this reduces the money and dwell time which they have airside to make more high value and impulsive purchases. This is occurring at the same time when more stringent and more time-consuming security measures at many airports are causing congestion, taking up more space and reducing dwell time for shopping.

Future Strategies

These recent developments, combined with continuing privatization and pressures on airport charges, are having a major influence on modern day airport commercial performance and the prospects for the future. There are, of course, many other factors which have to be considered such as the role that greater airport congestion plays on the airport shopping experience and changing customers' preferences, which means that cheap price no longer plays a dominant role in influencing purchasing decisions. There are also health issues, particularly related to tobacco (as well as actual bans in public places and more restrictive advertising) and alcohol, which are likely to cause a continuation in the reduction of the purchase of these duty-free goods in favour of other products such as perfume and cosmetic (Freathy, 2004). Personnel and pampering services such as manicures, pedicures and massages are becoming more popular. F&B is also increasing in importance, partly because of the trend to serve less F&B on board. Many of these factors demonstrate one of the key issues which is fundamental to the generation of commercial revenue. This is that whilst in some sense airports can be considered as just another place where consumers can do their shopping and be refreshed, their primary aim is not to act as shopping centres and hence the external influences affecting commercial success of an airport are much more numerous and complex than with other types of shopping. These future challenges can and no doubt will be approached by airport operators and their concessionaires in different ways. Some may try to improve the performance of the current retail offer by focusing on improving customer satisfaction and penetration levels (with walk-through shops for instance) whilst others may reassess the appropriateness of the retail mix which is on offer. Other airports may opt for more diversification with the aim of becoming an airport city or aetropolis. Elsewhere, a change in customer characteristics, for example an increase in long-haul passengers due to further airline deregulation, may also create a shift in commercial focus in the future.

Dublin Airport Authority and Aer Rianta International: An international airport retailer

Dublin Airport Authority (DAA) (formerly known as Aer Rianta) is an interesting example as it was one of the first airport companies to expand beyond national boundaries and get involved with the management and operations of commercial facilities at other international airports. DAA is the Irish state-owned airport company which has been responsible for managing the country's three major airports, namely Dublin, Shannon, and Cork since 1937. It has a long history with the provision of commercial facilities, as the world's first duty-free shop was opened at Shannon airport in 1947. It continues to operate its own duty-free and travel-value shops at the three airports.

In 1988, Aer Rianta International (ARI) was set up as a wholly owned subsidiary of Aer Rianta. With a population of less than 4 million, Aer Rianta recognized the limits of its own market and aimed to use ARI to promote commercial activities in locations outside Ireland. The first undertaking was a joint venture company Aerofist with Aeroflot Russia, the Moscow Airport Authority and ARI each having a one-third interest in the company. Aer Rianta had originally developed links with the Soviet Union in the early 1970s with an agreement whereby Aeroflot would trade airport charges for fuel at Shannon airport. In 1988, Aerofist opened the first duty-free shop at Moscow airport. It also began offering in-flight duty-free sales on international flights operated by Aeroflot out of Moscow. In the next few years, joint venture companies with ARI involvement were also set up to manage duty-free shops at St Petersburg and Kiev airports as well as downtown shops in Moscow and two shops, which are now closed, on the Russian–Finnish border.

In 1991, ARI expanded its involvement into the Middle East area with the setting up of a joint venture company with local investors in Bahrain to be responsible for designing the duty-free shops, overseeing their fitting out and their day-to-day management. ARI further expanded operations in this region by getting involved in the management of the duty-free shops at Karachi airport in 1992 and at Kuwait airport in 1994. In 1997, other new duty-free shop contracts were awarded in Beirut, Qatar (in-flight F&B for Qatar airways), Damascus, and Egypt. In Europe, ARI's first retail operation outside Ireland in Europe was at the terminals of the Channel tunnel. The organization provided duty-free facilities from the tunnel opening in 1994 until the abolition of duty-free sales in 1999. In addition ARI opened two shops in Cyprus in the late 1990s – one at Larnaca airport in 1997 and one in Paphos in 1998. Then, in 1998, ARI expanded into North America for the first time by acquiring the duty-free division of Canada's United Cigar Stores and the concession for duty-free shops at Montreal, Winnipeg, Edmonton, and Ottawa airports. In 2002 ARI took over the duty-free concession at Halifax airport as well. Since then contracts have been won in Oman, New York and most recently in Barbados. This means that ARI currently has over 20 retail operations in over 10 countries (Table 6.5). With the contracts which it has, it offers its so-called 'Runway'

Table 6.5 Aer Rianta International's involvement in international retailing activities, 2008

Region	Location
Europe	Larnaca Airport
	Paphos Airport
CIS	Sheremetyevo and Domodedovo Airports, Moscow
	Pulkova International Airport, St Petersburg
	Borispol Airport, Kiev
Middle East	Bahrain International Airport
	Kuwait International Airport
	Beirut International Airport
	Sharm el Sheikh Airport
	Muscat International Airport
	Qatar Airways (in-flight)
America	Montreal Airports
	Winnipeg Airport
	Edmonton Airport
	Ottawa Airport
	Halifax Airport
	New York
	Barbados Airport

Source: Aer Rianta/Dublin Airport Authority annual reports.

brand concept which includes a number of different individual brands such as Runway Duty Free, Runway Beauty, Runway Fashion, Runway Voyager, Runway Beach Hut and so on.

To cover all these global businesses it has four main business divisions based in Ireland (Europe), Canada (North America), Bahrain (Middle East) and Kosovo (Eastern Europe). These are managed through a combination of management contracts and joint ventures. Overall ARI employs around 2200 people. In addition to providing duty-free retailing, ARI has a 40 per cent share in Airport Partners GmbH which owns 50 per cent of Düsseldorf airports. It also previously had partial ownership of Hamburg and Birmingham airports but these stakes were disposed of in 2006 and 2007 respectively. In 2006, ARI had a turnover of €90 million. This was 15 per cent of DAA's total turnover with the commercial area accounting for a further 50 per cent of DAA's turnover and the aeronautical area only 29 per cent (the remaining 6 per cent came from Great Southern Hotels which was sold in 2006). However ARI is more important to DAA in terms of profitability having generated €16.8 million in 2006 which accounted for 24 per cent of all profits (Dublin Airport Authority, 2007).

BAA: Retail developments of a major airport group

Much of BAA's current practice as regards commercial facilities can be traced back to 1990 when a new retail strategy was launched. There were various elements to this strategy. An improved system of market research and customer satisfaction was introduced by replacing the original passenger opinion survey at the airport with the QSM. In addition, Egon Ronay, the renowned food critic, and his team of inspectors began to monitor the quality of all the F&B outlets at Heathrow and Gatwick airports. Moreover to overcome the problem of being regarded as a 'rip-off' airport by many of its customers, BAA launched its value guarantee in 1991. The key message with this was that all tax-paid goods sold at the airport were guaranteed to be of the same price as equivalent goods in the high street. Savings of up to 50 per cent were assured for duty-free goods such as liquor and tobacco, and 30 per cent for fragrances. (Whilst this policy over the years has been successful, recently it has come into criticism because some of the 'high street' prices which have been involved with comparisons were West End or City of London prices which are higher than elsewhere (Webster, 2007)) The next stage of the value guarantee was introduced in 1994 after BAA had undertaken further extensive market research into its commercial operations. This promised a full refund on goods bought at BAA airports to passengers from any region of the world, with a freepost address in the United Kingdom and refunded postage elsewhere. BAA also introduced a free telephone enquiry number for shopping facilities, pre-ordering possibilities and help desks, and personal shopping consultants at its airports.

A year later, at Gatwick airport the bonus points scheme was launched, whereby points could be earned for car parking, eating, drinking, shopping and currency exchange, and could be traded for money off certain goods and services such as car parking and shopping at the airports or points on some airlines' frequent-flyer programmes. The bonus point initiative was subsequently adopted at all the airports in 1996 and re-launched in 1999 as world points. The early 1990s also saw BAA progressively introducing more and more international brand names to its airports and offering increased competition with many of the services on offer particularly in areas such as F&B, banking, and car parking. The total floor space allocated to retail activities has increased substantially from a mere 41 000 square metres in 1990 to over 106 000 square metres by 2006 (Figure 6.5). A key feature of the retail strategy in recent years has been the development of the internet as a marketing and distribution medium. The retail site gives information about the commercial

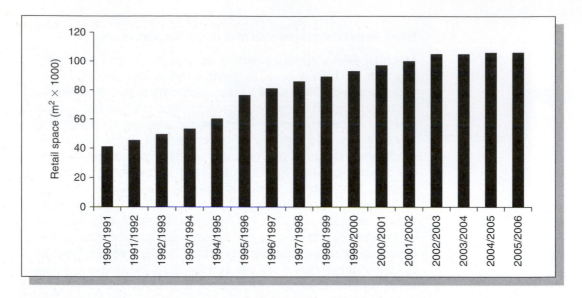

Figure 6.5
Retail space at BAA UK airports, 1990–2006.
(*Source*: Annual reports.)

facilities on offer and enables the pre-ordering of retail goods, currency, and car parking to take place. Discount vouchers to be used at the airport shops are also available. Another relatively new aspect of the retail strategy was the introduction of 'Retail Academy' for the retail businesses at the Heathrow airport in 2004. This helps retailers recruit, train and retain their staff, which has always been a difficult issue at this airport.

BAA undertakes a continuous departing passenger retail survey called the retail profiler. The passengers are asked about the outlets they have visited and the amount they have spent – both landside and airside. Information about the key characteristics of the passengers, such as nationality, frequency, and reason for travel, is also gathered. There are also regular 'Flyer Panels' to find out about the needs of different nationalities and focus groups to particularly investigate product positioning and promotion. BAA has also undertaken passenger-tracking surveys to understand where departing passengers spend their time in the terminal and how available time influences retail spend. They do this by planting a sticker on passengers at check-in and tracking their passage to the gate by recording the time at various points on the way.

In 1996 BAA launched World Duty Free, a wholly owned subsidiary of BAA, which it established to run airport duty- and tax-free shops. BAA claimed that this would give it complete control over the duty-free business and its airports and would enable the company to introduce more effective warehousing and distribution systems, and obtain procurement discounts. Gradually BAA started to replace the management contracts at its own UK airports. This process was completed in 1999. The establishment of World Duty Free was also seen as a way to give BAA opportunities to expand its commercial activities to non-BAA locations, either through commercial management contracts or as part of an overall privatization package to operate the whole airport. Subsequently in 1997, BAA acquired the US retail chain Duty Free International which had around 200 outlets, mainly in the United States at airports and border crossings. It was also involved in diplomatic and in-flight business. This subsidiary was renamed World Duty Free Americas with BAA's original duty-free company being renamed World Duty Free Europe. The acquisition was undertaken to provide greater geographical strength away from Europe, where the abolition of sales appeared imminent and to increase the company's purchasing power.

In a parallel development in the 1990s, BAA began to manage commercial facilities at non-BAA airports. The first main contract was for Greater Pittsburgh International airport. This was a 15-year agreement signed in 1991 – which has subsequently been extended until 2017. The new facilities were grouped together in what was called 'The AirMall' which had over 100 outlets and 60 companies – many of which have famous branded names – and covered an area of around 10 000 square metres. The AirMall was opened in 1992. With this arrangement the airport operator was guaranteed an index-linked US$0.40 per passenger. BAA received a certain share of income above this amount, and if further income were generated, the revenue was to be split. Consequently, BAA has been involved in the management of commercial facilities at Boston and Baltimore airports and in 2008 another contract was awarded for Cleveland airport. A further area of retail diversification was with discount designer outlet centres. BAA entered into a joint venture scheme with the US retail developer McArthur/Glen to develop a chain of outlets in the UK and continental Europe with the first centre opening in 1995.

Table 6.6 summarizes the key retail developments which have taken place since 1990. As with most airports in Europe, the abolition of intra-EU duty- and tax-free sales had a major impact on the financial performance of the company. Consequently BAA introduced a number of strategies to address this problem. To overcome the confusion among passengers, it reconfigured passenger flows in its major terminals so that passengers were

Table 6.6 Key developments in BAA's retail strategy since 1990

Date	Development
1990	Launch of new retail strategy; QSM introduced
1991	Value guarantee launched; Egon Ronay became F&B inspector
1991	First retail airport contract awarded at Pittsburgh
1994	Worldwide guarantee launched
1995	First BAA McArthur/Glen outlet opened
1996	BAA bonus points launched at all BAA airports; World Duty Free established
1997	Acquisition of Duty Free International (renamed World Duty Free Americas)
1998	New website launched enabling pre-ordering
1999	Abolition of EU duty/tax free; bonus points re-launched as WorldPoints
2000	Boston Airport contract awarded
2001	World Duty Free Americas sold
2002	BAA McArthur/Glen joint venture dissolved
2004	Baltimore Airport contract awarded; Retail Academy set up
2008	Cleveland Airport contracted awarded; World Duty Free sold

Source: BAA Annual reports.

channelled through the shops where they could still make purchases. It also launched a major advertising campaign telling consumers that they could still shop at airports and provided arrivals duty-paid shops and collection-on-arrival facilities. Its strategy for recovery was to refocus on what it saw as its core airport business by disposing of World Duty Free Americas and BAA–McArthur/Glen. The in-flight business of World Duty Free was sold in 2000 and World Duty Free Americas was sold in 2001, leaving BAA to focus on the 58 World Duty Free outlets at UK airports. In 2002, the BAA–McArthur/Glen joint venture was dissolved. BAA also terminated the contract which it had with Eurotunnel which lost the company £20 million in 2000. BAA also sold off World Duty Free in 2008 primarily to reduce the debt levels of the company.

The more external recent events, which have been described above, such as EU enlargement and more stricter security, have also meant that overall in real terms retail revenue per passenger at BAA airports has declined (Donaldson, 2006; Competition Commission, 2007). This is demonstrated in detail in Table 6.7. This table also reflects general trends which have been observed at other airports with a growth in F&B revenues (primarily because of less in-flight catering) and a drop in 'other' retail – which is

Table 6.7 Retail revenue at BAA London airports per passenger 2000–2007 (£ in real 2007 terms)

	2000/2001	2006/2007	% Change
Airside shops	1.83	1.87	2.2
Bureau de change	0.44	0.43	−2.3
F&B	0.28	0.39	39.3
Car parking	1.00	0.87	−13.0
Other retail	1.22	1.10	−26.5
Total retail	4.77	4.66	−2.3

Source: Competition Commission (2007).

mostly landside shops (largely because of stricter security rules). In 2008 BAA opened Terminal 5 at Heathrow airport which will have over 160 retail and F&B outlets. Whilst it is expected that this will have a positive effect on retail revenues, the overall impact of this new development will be difficult to assess as at the same time Terminals 1 and 2 will begin to be redeveloped as 'Terminal East' which could temporarily cause a corresponding reduction in sales.

Dubai airport: non-aeronautical strategies for a competing airport

Many of the Gulf airports are in fierce competition for transit and transfer traffic – albeit to a lesser extent nowadays because of more non-stop long-haul flights. They are very interesting airports as regards non-aeronautical strategies as they have probably done more than any other airports in the world to attract passengers by promoting the duty-free facilities on offer. Dubai airport is the largest airport in the region. In 2006, it handled 29 million passengers compared with just 4.5 million in 1989. The airport is forecast to handle 40 million passengers in 2010 – although it only has a national population of 1.3 million (only around 20 per cent of these are nationals). It works closely with the national airline, Emirates, which is based at the airport. The airport serves Dubai, which has become the major trading base of the Gulf region as well as being used as a transit stop for intercontinental services.

The airport is owned and operated by the Dubai Department of Civil Aviation. The duty-free shop operator Dubai Duty Free (DDF) is also run by this department. This state ownership enables the prices to be kept low and very competitive compared with other airports. DDF works very closely with the airport management and this enables it to get involved with the master planning process at a very early stage. The first DDF shop was introduced in December 1983 and then, in 1987, arrival duty-free shopping was added. In 2007 sales totalled US$880 million and gold accounted for around 12 per cent of these sales! The average penetration rate is claimed to be 45 per cent which is much higher than average (Bates, 2005b). The shops cover an area of over $7000\,m^2$ and the airport will open Terminal 3 and Concourse 2 in 2008 which will increase the retail space to around $15\,000\,m^2$.

In November 1989, the DDF launched its 'Dubai Duty Free Finest Surprise' to mark the expansion of its shopping complex. This promotion offered a Rolls-Royce Bentley Mulsanne car to the winner of a raffle and had been undertaken ever since with a continuous high-profile display of luxury cars in the airport concourse. The tickets, which are sold exclusively at the airport or on-line at over $100 a ticket, are limited to 1000 per draw. By 2007, 1190 travellers from 66 countries had won luxury cars. Other competing airports in the Middle East, such as Abu Dhabi and Bahrain, have also undertaken similar promotions. In 2000, a new duty-free area was opened at the airport and to commemorate this and the millennium, the airport launched another promotion called the 'Dubai Duty Free Finest Cyber Surprise'. This promotion offered US$1 million to winners of the 'Millennium Millionaire Draw'. Originally this was planned as a one-off event but it has now become an on-going promotion. Tickets for this draw can only be bought at the airport or on-line for nearly $300 a ticket and are limited in number (5000 this time) to increase the chances of winning ticket. By 2007, 78 passengers had been made millionaires! Also to promote the company, DDF organizes the Dubai Tennis Championship and sponsors various events such as the Dubai Duty Free World Cup.

In the future a new airport known as Dubai World Central International Airport will be a main part of Dubai World Central which will be a major residential, commercial, enterprise and logistics centre or airport city-with tourist and entertainment facilities as well as a golf resort. It will cover an area of $140\,km^2$ and will be 40 km away from the current airport. This new airport will have six parallel runways and will be capable of handling 120 million passengers (Sheikh Ahmed bin Saeed Al Maktoum, 2007). DDF is planning to offer very substantial facilities in this new airport.

Singapore airport: aiming to maintain its position as a leading Asian/Pacific hub

Singapore Changi airport, which is owned by the Civil Aviation Authority of Singapore, has developed some interesting strategies in order to maintain its position as a hub in the very competitive Asia and Pacific market where it competes, particularly for transfer traffic, with airports in Hong Kong, Kuala Lumpur and Bangkok. In 2006 the airport handled 33 million passengers compared to 30 million at Bangkok, 43 million at Hong Kong, and 24 million at Kuala Lumpur. This compares with 13 million passengers at Changi airport in 1989. To cope with the traffic growth, in 2006 the airport opened its 'Budget Terminal' designed specifically for low cost airlines and further expansion occurred at the beginning of 2008, when the new Terminal 3 became operational.

To compete with the nearby airports, since 2003 the airport has had an Air Hub Development Fund to attract airlines to the airport. Moreover it has a sophisticated commercial strategy which is designed to give it a competitive edge. It offers a very wide range of commercial facilities and has pre-shopping facilities and price guarantees like BAA and some other airports. To appeal to transfer passengers it lists on its website activities for transfer passengers divided into different time periods (0.5–1 hour, 1–2 hours, 2–3 hours, 3–5 hours, 5 hours or more). For long waits it organizes bus tours of Singapore. There are also hotels situated in the transit area, which have many facilities including a swimming pool, gym, sauna, hairdresser and aromatheraphy massage, foot reflexology, facial, manicure, pedicure and waxing services. One of its unusual features is its gardens. It has a Cactus Garden located in Terminal 1, which has more than 20 varieties of cacti which are native to North and South America. It also has a Bamboo and Heliconia Garden in Terminal 1. In Terminal 2 it has an Orchid Garden which covers an area of over 600 square metres and has over 20 different varieties of orchids. The terminal also had a Fern Garden and outdoor Sunflower Garden. The Orchid and Fern Gardens have Koi Ponds.

The airport aims to ensure that it provides the latest technological and communication services – particularly for its business travellers. In 1996 it was one of the first airports to offer internet services to passengers and now it has over 300 internet-ready terminals and wi-fi access. It also has a science discovery area called the Explorer's Lounge and a cinema, Microsoft X-box stations and TV lounges. Live music performances are organized. There is also a family zone which provides essential services and entertainment for travellers with young children. It has an e-newsletter called 'Friends of Changi' which gives details of all the recent commercial developments and events at the airport. One recent unique event for the airport was a live gameshow 'What's Your Range?' which ran for 3 months within the departure/transit mall (Long, 2007). In addition to all these commercial services for passengers, the airport has a Changi Airfreight centre and a logistics park to ensure that it is a leading air cargo centre in South East Asia.

References and further reading

Abeyratne, R. (2007). Bustling aerotropolis has arisen at many leading airports. *ICAO Journal*, 3, 22–23.

Agbebi, Y. (2005). *How Do Traffic Structure and Leisure Preferences Drive Airport Retail and Investment Strategies*, Hamburg Aviation Conference, Hamburg.

Airport Business Communique (2005). *ACI-Europe Best Practice Charter*. Chennai: ACI Europe, May.

ACI-North America (ACI-NA) (2002). *State of the industry report*, ACI-NA.

Airport Council International (ACI) (2007). *ACI Airport economics survey* 2006.

Amore, M. (1999). New airport, new opportunities. *Marketing and Commercial Strategy Handbook, vol. 7*, ACI-Europe.

Allett, T. (2001). Food and beverage. *Airports International*, December, 50–52.

Appold, S. and Kasarda, J. (2006). The appropriate scale of US airport retail activities. *Journal of Air Transport Management*, 12, 277–287.

BAA (2000). *Annual Report 2000/2001*. BAA.

Bates, J. (2004). Shops tempt on arrival. *Jane's Airport Review*, December, 33.

Bates, J. (2005a). Making car parks pay. *Jane's Airport Review*, February, 40–41.

Bates, J. (2005b). Dubai shares its retail vision. *Jane's Airport Review*, May, 31.

Bork, A. (2006). Developing a retail marketing strategy to promote both airport and retailers. *Journal of Airport Management*, 1(4), 348–356.

Centre for the Study of Regulated Industries (2008). *Airport Statistics 2006/2007*. University of Bath.

Cho, S-S (2007). Sky City program at Gimpo airport: Making the airport a tourist attraction, *2nd ACI Asia-Pacific Regional Assembly, Conference and Exhibition*, Seoul, May.

Credit Suisse (2006). *European Airports: No Rush to Board*. London: Credit Suisse.

Competition Commission (2002). *A Report on the economic regulation of the London airport companies*. Competition Commission.

Competition Commission (2007). *A report on the economic regulation of the London Airport Companies*. Competition Commission.

Donaldson (2006). *Scrutinising trends in commercial revenue at BAA's designated airports*, Supporting paper VIII in CAA, Airports Price Control Review-Initial proposals for Heathrow, Gatwick and Stansted, CAA.

Dublin Airport Authority (2007). *Annual Report 2006*. Chennai: Dublin Airport Authority.

Entwistle, M. (2007). Customer service and airport retail: Stimulate passenger spending. *Journal of Airport Management*, 1(2), 151–157.

Echevarne, R. (2008). The impact of attracting low cost carriers to airports. In Graham, A. Papatheodorou, A. and Forsyth, P. (Eds), *Aviation and tourism, Implications for leisure travel*. Ashgate.

Freathy, P. (2004). The commercialization of European airports: Successful strategies in a decade of turbulence? *Journal of Air Transport Management*, 10, 191–197.

Freathy, P. and O'Connell, F. (1998). *European airport retailing*. Macmillan.

Freathy, P. and O'Connell, F. (2000). Strategic reactions to the abolition of duty free: Examples from the European airport sector. *European Management Journal*, 18(6), 638–645.

Geuens, M., Vantomme, D. and Brengman, M. (2004). Developing a typology of airport shoppers. *Tourism Management*, 25, 615–622.

Gray, F. (2007). Maximisation of the commercial potential from a new airport terminal development. *University of Westminster Airport Economics and Finance Symposium*, London, April.

Holden, J. (2007). The shops at terminal 4. *Airports International*, March, 36–37.

Institute for Retail Studies (1997). *Airport Retail Economics*. University of Stirling.

Jane's Airport Review (2007). Duty-free industry fears security restrictions pose risk to revenues. *Jane's Airport Review*, May, 4.

Jones, R. (2002). A retailer's perspective. *Cranfield University Airport Commercial Revenues Course*, Cranfield, May.

Kim, H. and Shin, J. (2001). A contextual investigation of the operation and management of airport concessions. *Tourism Management*, 22, 149–155.

Long, Goh Yong. (2007). Premier aviation hub of the region. *International Airport Review*, 3, 11–14.

Maiden, S. (2000). Getting to know the market at airports. *University of Westminster Marketing and Market Research Seminar*, London, December.

Maiden, S. (2008). How BAA uses its market research, *University of Westminster Marketing and Market Research Seminar*, London, February.

McCormick, C. (2006a). A sense of place for play and pay. *Airports International*, April, 28–29.

McCormick, C. (2006b). Bringing home the global brand. *Airports International*, March, 34–35.

Middecke, R. (2000). Designing the perfect airport to optimise retail revenue: a retailers point of view. *Ninth ACI-Europe Airport Trading Conference*, London, February.

The Moodie Report (2007). *The Airport Retail Study 2006–07*, The Moodie Report, Brentford.

Moodie, M. (2007). Analysing airport commercial revenues in Airport Council International (ACI) *ACI Airport Economics Survey 2006*.

Pilling, M. (2002). Airports seek parking revival. *Airport World*, October–November, 55–57.

Reiss, B. (2007). Maximising non-aviation revenue for airports: Developing airport cities to optimize real estate and capitalize on land development opportunities. *Journal of Airport Management*, 1(3), 284–293.

Ross, J. (2007). Retail: The digital age. *Airport World*, 12(2), 36–37.

Sheikh Ahmed bin Saeed Al Maktoum (2007). Dubai, the world's aviation hub in the making. *International Airport Review*, 4, 19–26.

Spanger, R. (2008). The future of airport retailing, *11th Hamburg Aviation Conference*, Hamburg.

Toms, M. (2000). Critique of cost benchmarking. *CAA Workshop on Benchmarking of Airports: Methodologies, Problems and Relevance to Economic Regulation*, London, September.

Webster, B. (2007). Millions misled over airport prices. *The Times*, *August 29*, 8.

CHAPTER 7

Airport competition and the role of marketing

It used to be commonly believed that most major airports were monopolies with their precise role being determined by the passenger demand in the catchment area. Moreover, airline choice was considered to be limited to particular airports because of bilateral agreements. While this may still be true in a few markets, there are now many opportunities for airports to compete for passengers, freight, and airlines. The modern-day airline industry, which has been transformed in many places from a regulated and public sector controlled activity into a liberalized and commercially orientated business, has played a major role in this changing airport situation. Certain airline developments such as the formation of global alliances have been particularly important, as have been the development of the low-cost sector, to create new views on airport competition.

Airport competition is a complex area to examine because there are different aspects which can be considered (Graham, 2006). There is the competition between airports and competition within airport groups. Then there is the competition inside airports, such as the competition for the provision of a certain service or competition between airport terminals. The chapter begins by discussing all of these. They have major consequences for many key areas of the airport business such as pricing and quality management which have been considered elsewhere in this book. However another important issue related to competition, which is yet to be covered is the role of marketing. This is investigated in the second part of this chapter.

Airport competition

Competition between airports

There are a number of key ways in which airports can compete (ACI-Europe, 1999; Cranfield University, 2002; Starkie, 2002). Clearly if airports are physically close, their catchment areas may overlap for certain types of traffic. For short-haul routes, passengers tend to choose the most convenient, nearest airport that has suitable services. For long-haul flights passengers may be more willing to travel further distances to an airport that they regard as offering a more desirable or superior long-haul service. If airports are located on small islands or remote regions, there will be very little competition.

In some major urban areas or cities there are a number of situations when more than one airport serves the population. Notable examples are the European cities of London and Paris, and the American cities of New York and Washington. Sometimes the airports may be under the same ownership as with Aéroports de Paris (AdP), which owns Charles de Gaulle, Orly, and Le Bourget airports, and the Port Authority of New York and New Jersey, which owns JFK, La Guardia, and Newark airports. Such common ownership may clearly reduce the amount of potential competition. Elsewhere in London, for instance, the BAA airports of Heathrow, Gatwick, and Stansted compete with the independently run London City and London Luton airports, whereas in Washington the Metropolitan Washington Airports Authority airports of Dulles and National compete to a certain degree with Baltimore airport, which is owned by the State of Maryland. The San Francisco bay area also has three airport which compete for domestic traffic. Another example of an area where neighbouring airports compete for large volumes of traffic is the Pearl River delta region of China and the airports of Hong Kong, Guangzhou and Macau.

In many cases when there are overlapping catchment areas, one airport tends to become the dominant player in a preferred location with the other airports playing a more secondary role. In the London area, for example, the Heathrow airport is considered by many passengers, particularly those travelling on business, to be the 'London airport' in spite of a range of services being offered at the other London airports. The secondary airports tend to fulfil more specialized roles. They may act as an over-spill airport when the major airport has inadequate capacity, which has happened to a certain extent in London when airlines that cannot get into Heathrow go to Gatwick or Stansted instead. Alternatively, centrally located secondary airports may be able to attract a certain amount of domestic or short-haul traffic, particularly business-related traffic. These types of passengers favour the convenience and generally less congested environment that a city centre airport such as London City may offer. Other airports may choose to specialize in charter operations (e.g. Rome Ciampino airport).

Then there are the airports which market themselves as low-cost alternatives to the major airports – having been encouraged by the rapid development of European LCCs (Table 7.1). Outside Europe, there are similar airports such as Avalon which acts as an alternative for Melbourne and Hamilton for Toronto, although this use of secondary airports is not so widespread. In general these airports offer faster turnarounds, short walking distances from the terminal to the aircraft, and fewer delays, which are all vital elements of the low-cost model. They are also usually in a position to be more flexible on pricing and maybe to enter into long-term pricing agreements if desired by the LCCs. In many cases they are situated substantially further from the town or city they are serving compared with the competing airports. Sometimes these airports may be owned by the same operator who has control of the competing airports; for example, Frankfurt airports owns Hahn airport. Elsewhere separate ownership patterns exist. Some low-cost airlines, such as Ryanair, have suggested that there ought to be competing terminals at airports, especially Dublin, run by different operators.

Problems can arise when a new airport is built and is perceived as providing an inferior service to the old one, perhaps being in a less conveniently situated location. A notable much quoted example is Montreal Mirabel's airport that was built in the 1970s to provide extra

Table 7.1   Example of alternative low-cost airports within Europe

Low-cost airport	Competing major airport	Under same ownership?
Beauvais	Paris – CDG/Orly	No
Charleroi	Brussels National	No
Girona	Barcelona	Yes
Hahn	Frankfurt	Yes
London – Luton	London – Heathrow	No
London – Stansted	London – Heathrow	Yes
Lubeck	Hamburg	No
Orio al Serio	Milan – Linate/Malpensa	No
Prestwick	Glasgow International	No
Reus	Barcelona	Yes
Rome – Ciampino	Rome – Fiumicino	Yes
Sandefjord – Torp	Oslo – Gardermoen	No
Skavsta	Stockholm – Arlanda	No
Weeze	Düsseldorf	No

capacity in addition to Dorval airport but never managed to attract the volume of traffic that was forecast. Milan is a more recent case where there was considerable reluctance among carriers to transfer from Linate airport, which is closer to the city centre, to the expanded Malpensa airport (now Alitalia has chosen to concentrate more of its flights in Rome). Unless effective regulation is introduced, the only feasible way of ensuring that traffic will transfer to the new airport is by actually closing the old one, which has happened in locations such as Munich, Hong Kong, Oslo, and Denver (Caves and Gosling, 1999). Competition for the new Athens airport is even more limited as not only has the old airport closed down but also no new airport development within the same catchment area is allowed.

Competition tends to be weak at airports which have a high concentration of both short- and long-haul services. These airports appeal most to the traditional scheduled carriers who have networked services. In these cases it is difficult for other airports to provide effective competition. This is unless the airport is competing as a hub by providing good flight connectivity and efficient passenger transfers. Key prerequisites for a hub are a central geographic position and an adequate runway/terminal capacity enabling a 'wave' system of arriving and departing flights to take place. Certain airports can compete as hubs for cargo operations especially for express parcel services, particularly if they are open all night and have a good weather record. New infrastructure, notably at Asian destinations such as Kuala Lumpur, Hong Kong, Bangkok, and Macao, has provided the impetus for more intense competition for hub traffic in this region as is also the case in certain Middle Eastern countries such as the United Arab Emirates. Ultimately all hub airports are, however, very much dependent on the operating strategies of airlines. While many medium- and large-sized airports aspire to become a hub, in reality there is now less opportunity for this to happen as a result of the growing concentration within the airline industry through developments such as global alliances and code sharing. An alternative may be just to try to encourage airlines to base themselves at an airport because this will be normally mean that the airline will offer more flights and make better use of all the other airport facilities.

In most cases, passengers will have a specific destination in mind when they travel. The exception may be with some intercontinental traffic when passengers might be more indifferent. For example, Americans visiting Europe may not have a strong preference as to whether they start their European tour from Paris, London, or Frankfurt. Airports serving these cities can, therefore, compete for this traffic. The same can be true with cargo traffic. This is particularly the case within Europe where most long-haul freight is trucked to its final destination. A rather similar passenger example in North America is airports which compete as embarkation points for cruise holidays.

When an airport's relative competitiveness is being assessed, the substitution possibilities need to be considered. First the prospect of new competing airports emerging has to be investigated. This is generally low because of the large investment that is needed for the new infrastructure and because of the long and complex planning and regulatory processes which frequently have to be followed in order for approval of any new development to be given. Secondly in many areas of the world it is increasingly difficult to find suitable locations for new competing sites, although in some regions, such as Europe, the existence of a number of obsolete military airfields (e.g. Finningley and Manston in the United Kingdom), have provided some opportunities for new airport development. Thirdly barriers to entry for new airports may also be high because of the existence of cost economies of scale although as discussed in Chapter 3, these may disappear once the airport reaches around three million passengers and then at some stage diseconomies of scale may actually develop.

At a broader level, the amount of substitution from other transport modes needs to be considered. High speed rail is probably the greatest threat. For regional airports, the introduction of high speed rail services can have a significant impact on air services to major airports. However at major capacity constrained airports increased usage of high speed rail for short-haul trips may free up capacity for other long-haul services, although this may have a detrimental impact on the airport's ability to act as a hub and attract transfer passengers. Improvements to the road and rail infrastructure to major airports may also reduce the necessity for feeder services from regional airports.

Clearly the amount of substitution that exists depends on the type of traffic which is being served. For example as discussed in Chapter 5, different types of airlines have varying degrees of sensitivity to price. Airport charges can be substantially more important for short-haul operations as they are levied more frequency. For low-cost and charter operations they can be even more significant because these airlines will have minimized many of the other airline costs. In these cases, airport price competition can be very real particularly if additional pricing incentives (which are discussed below) are offered. As regards passengers, those on leisure trips are usually the most willing to shift between origin airports because of airline price or product differences. Those on holiday may even have a choice of destination and hence a choice of airport, whereas those travelling for business or VFR purposes will probably be more limited in their ability or desire to shift destination airports.

When the price monitoring process in Australia was being reviewed, the Productivity Commission (2007) considered these three substitution issues (i.e. airport, modal and destination). By way of illustration these findings are summarized in Table 7.2. The substitution possibilities generally seemed low with the exception at Canberra airport because of surface transport competition and Darwin which competes with other airports for holiday passengers. An additional element for the airport operator which is not covered here is the competition for commercial facilities. Some airports with a large share of transfer traffic, such as Dubai and Singapore, may compete directly with their retail offering. Moreover whilst airports have the advantages of having a captive and often fairly affluent passenger market, the substitution possibilities with high street and internet shopping are quite considerable.

As discussed in Chapter 5, price regulation is often introduced even when competition is not considered strong enough to deter airports from abusing their position of market power. This is most relevant for large city airports as smaller regional airports especially in high population density countries, will tend to have overlapping catchment areas and be in a sufficiently competitive environment so as to not need regulatory intervention. One of the key issues, however, is determining which airports have substantial market power. Clearly it cannot simply be related to the airport size but also has to take account of competitive factors such as market share, pricing, quality of service, capacity provision and substitutions possibilities. This is why a number of stakeholders have criticized the adoption of a traffic throughput threshold for airports covered by the EU airport charges directive (see Chapter 5).

An interesting example here is the United Kingdom where the two price regulated airports of Stansted and Manchester have just been investigated by the government with a view of possibly having the price control removed. The criteria currently being used in the United Kingdom for price regulated airports is that they must possess substantial market power, that EU and domestic law will provide an insufficient tool to remedy any abuse and that the incremental net benefits of regulation can be shown to outweigh its costs. In the

Table 7.2 Substitution possibilities at Australian airports

Airport	Main market segments	Substitution possibilities		
		Airport	**Modal**	**Destination**
Adelaide	Domestic: Business 49%, VFR 29% International: Holiday 41%, VFR 34%	Low with no nearby airports	Low for business travellers but some for VFR and holiday travel	Relatively low since mostly business and VFR traffic
Brisbane	Domestic: Business 33%, VFR 27% International: Holiday 61%, VFR 25% International: Holiday 61%, VFR 21%	Low but increasing with airports in the Gold Coast and Maroochydore	Low for business travellers but some for VFR and holiday travel	Relatively low since mostly business and VFR traffic
Canberra	Domestic: Business 64%, VFR 25%	Low with no nearby airports	High since three quarters of visitors to Canberra arrive by car and go by surface to Sydney and then fly from there to a holiday destinations	Relatively low since mostly business and VFR traffic
Darwin	Domestic: Holiday 40%, Business 37% International: Holiday 59%	Various by market segment being low for visits to the 'Top End' but higher for those visiting several areas within the Territory.	Low for business travellers but significant holiday for travel	High as mostly holiday traffic Can choose to go to other tourist destinations
Melbourne	Domestic: Business 48%, VFR 27% International: Holiday 42%, VFR 26%	Generally low but Avalon airport used by Jetstar for some of its flights	Low for business travellers but some for VFR and holiday travel	Relatively low since mostly business and VFR traffic
Perth	Domestic: Business 42%, VFR 31% International: Holiday 51%, VFR 27%	Low with no nearby airports	Low since Perth is relatively isolated	Relatively low since mostly business and VFR traffic
Sydney	Domestic: Business 52%, VFR 24% International: Holiday 51%, VFR 21%	Low with no nearby airports	Low for business travellers but some for VFR and holiday travel	Relatively low since mostly business and VFR traffic

Source: Productivity Commission (2007).

Manchester case it was decided that the airport did not currently hold a position of substantial market power since local airports such as Liverpool airport provided a meaningful substitute; there was spare capacity at Manchester and competing airports; the market share of Manchester was declining; high service quality was provided at Manchester; the airport and the airlines effectively and constructively engaged with one another; and finally that pricing and quality of service decisions appeared to have been determined more by competitive forces than by the price cap. This was not, however, the view of Liverpool airport and International Air Transport Association (IATA) (Department for Transport, 2008a). Meanwhile for Stansted, it was concluded that the airport already had substantial market power by virtue of BAA's common ownership and that it was likely to acquire more market power in the future (Department for Transport, 2008b). Consideration of this market power criterion together with the other two criteria resulted in the government deciding to remove the price control for Manchester but not for Stansted.

Competition within airport groups

When airports are operated as a system or a group rather than individually, there is an important issue as to whether this inhibits competition (Forsyth, 2006). As discussed in Chapter 2, particularly when privatization of groups takes place, decisions have to be made as to whether the group should be privatized in its entirety or split up. Arguments for keeping the group include the ability to share resources and expertise, reduce costs due to scale effects and adopt a strategic as well as co-ordinated approach to airport development. In Australia, the government decided on individual privatizations for the major international airports (even though most of them were at least 800 km apart), in Argentina the airports were privatized as a group and in Mexico the airports were divided into four different groups with a mixture of small and large airports in each group.

In the United Kingdom, BAA was privatized as a single entity but this has remained a controversial issue ever since. At the time of the privatization of BAA, the arguments in favour of the retention of this single airport group, as opposed to separation, included the existence of very limited competitive pressures because of product diversity at the airports and the dominance of Heathrow; the small effect of airport charges on airline costs; economies of scale in airport operations; less uncertainty and a higher share price; and less risk of under-investment with an overall investment strategy (Foster, 1984). Moreover it was claimed that group ownership was needed to enforce the Government's Traffic Distribution Rules (TDRs) which redirected traffic from congested Heathrow to elsewhere, and to fund investment at Stansted airport. Opponents, however, argued that Gatwick and Stansted could compete for charter traffic as the former was developing into a credible alternative airport to Heathrow, and that the group sale would give BAA much less incentive to provide any extra capacity than would have been the case with individual airport sales (Starkie and Thompson, 1984).

Since the privatization of BAA, the airline regulatory environment has become progressively more liberal providing more opportunities for airport competition. Consequently there have been various governmental reviews investigating whether BAA should be split up but these have generally concluded that the additional benefits of competition would be more than offset by the disbenefits of loss of economies of scale and fragmentation of financial strength together with the dispersion of expertise (Toms, 2004). Interestingly, however, this UK policy does seem entirely consistent as a few years after BAA privatization, Belfast International airport wanted to buy the neighbouring Belfast City airport but was prohibited from doing so by the government as it was seen as anti-competitive. More recently in 2005 the owners of Bristol airport (Ferrovial/Macquarie) were selected as preferred bidders for the nearby Exeter airport, but pulled out when it was announced that there would be a detailed investigation to ensure that this situation did not have a negative impact on competition in the region.

In 2006, the UK airports market was investigated again this time by the Office of Fair Trading (OFT). By then BAA was just under new ownership and was coming under increasing criticism from both airlines and passengers regarding its responsiveness to customer needs. As a result the OFT enquiry concluded that the BAA group should be referred to the Competition Commission for more detailed investigation as the OFT identified joint ownership might be a factor which could be preventing, restricting or distorting competition (OFT, 2006). The Competition Commission is expected to reach its own conclusions in late 2008 and this could ultimately lead to a demand for BAA to divest in one or more of its airports.

Whilst issues related to competition and airport groups tend especially to be raised when airport privatization is taking place, clearly it is an on-going issue which is relevant to both public and private airports alike. An interesting example of this as regards a public sector group is the Dublin Airport Authority (DAA) which is discussed below.

Competing facilities and terminals

As already discussed in Chapter 3, many airport services, such as air traffic control, security, ground handling and the provision of commercial facilities, can be provided either by the airport operator or by a third party. The way in which they are offered, and whether there are competing services, can have a major impact on an airport's competitive situation in both price and service quality terms. Competing services tend to be the most established in the commercial areas such as airport retail outlets, restaurants, hotels and car parks.

A key airport service for airlines is ground handling and the issue of competition with the provision of handling services has always been controversial as traditionally it has been quite common for the national airline or airport operator to have a monopoly or near monopoly in providing these services. This resulted in the introduction in 1996 of the ground handling directive in Europe (see Chapter 5). However elsewhere the extent to which ground handling services are offered on a competitive basis varies from country to country.

Potentially the greatest competition within airports could be achieved by having competing terminals under different ownership offering competition in terms of price and service quality. Varying quality standards and facilities could be offered to serve different services such as low cost, short haul, long haul or business – although the more specialized the terminal, the less scope for competition with other terminals. However strategic planning could be much more difficult with the lack of a single ownership and economies of scale could be lost. Also competing terminals might not always bring about the best use of capacity which for many of today's airports is a crucial consideration as they have limited space to expand. There could also potentially be an anti-competitive issue, if the airlines control the competing terminal and limit the access to rival airlines.

There is only limited and insufficient industry evidence to conclude whether it is possible to have successfully competing airport terminals. In 1986, Terminal 3 at Toronto airport was handed over to a private consortium to provide new investment. However in 1996 it was bought back under the responsibility of the Greater Toronto Airport Authority to allow for the development of the airport master plan. Elsewhere at Birmingham airport, the Eurohub terminal was at one stage operated separately but has now been brought back under single management at the airport. In Brussels there were not competing terminals but the management of the airside and the terminal was split. However in 1998 this division of management was reversed with the establishment of the Brussels International Airport Company. These cases suggest that the experience of competing terminals or split management was not too favourable. In contrast, in the United States and particularly at JFK airport in New York, there are permanent examples of competing terminals being operated by airlines. Likewise in Australia, some of the domestic terminals have been run directly by the airlines.

In the last two regulatory reviews in the United Kingdom, the introduction of competing terminals has been discussed. In 2003 the Civil Aviation Authority (CAA) concluded that the benefits of regulatory intervention to stimulate intra-airport competition were most likely to be outweighed by the operational and regulatory disbenefits. In the more recent review, the issue was again considered and whilst some stakeholders, such as the airlines at Stansted, very much favoured competition between terminals, there was no overall consensus of views and consequently this idea was again not developed any further (CAA, 2007). The country where competing terminals have probably been given the most consideration is Ireland and this is discussed in greater detail below. Experience here has shown that attempts to introduce competition can also significantly lengthen the process of planning and constructing additional capacity.

The birth of airport marketing

Having debated the extent of competition which exists at airport, the rest of this chapter now focuses on airport marketing. However it needs to be acknowledged that airport marketing as a concept at most airports did not really exist until the 1980s. Prior to this, the role of the airport as a public service meant that very often airport management would merely respond to airline requests for new slots by providing published charging and use-of-facility information rather than initiating talks to attract new services. In most cases, the airports considered it was solely the role of the airline to identify opportunities for new or expanded services. It was up to the airport to provide an efficient and safe airport with good facilities for aircraft and travellers. Promoting the air services at the airport was also not considered to be a responsibility of the airport, with the view being that the airlines and travel agents selling the products should undertake this. It was rare to find airport marketing managers and, generally, the resources allocated to marketing activities were very small. Airport promotion tended to be very basic, typically consisting of the production of a timetable and publicity leaflets, and reactive responses to press enquiries about the airport. In essence, even if there was some potential for competition between airports, even at this early stage of the evolution of the airport industry, there were very few airports that recognized and exploited this.

This passive approach has long since gone at most airports. Airports have become much more proactive in their approach and have developed a wide range of increasingly sophisticated techniques for meeting the demands of their complex mix of customers such as passengers, airlines, freight forwarders, tour operators and so on. Within any commercially run business, marketing is considered to be a core activity and one which is a vital ingredient for success. The airport sector is no longer an exception and marketing is increasingly being seen as an integral part of the airport business.

Deregulation of air transport markets has of course made the airport business much more competitive. Airlines in Europe, for example, are much freer to operate out of any airport they choose without being constrained by bilateral restrictions. They are thus much more susceptible to aggressive marketing by airports. Many airports have actively sought to attract the new LCCs through a range of marketing techniques. The increase in demand for air transport due to deregulation and other more general factors, such as economic growth, has meant that there have been enhanced opportunities for more airports to share in this expansion of the market. This has provided airports with greater incentives to develop innovative and aggressive market strategies so that they can reap some of the benefits from this growth. Moreover, a number of airports are close to capacity and unable to offer attractive slots for new services. This means that there may be attractive prospects for other airports to promote themselves as alternative uncongested airports.

The travelling public has also become more demanding and more sophisticated in their travel-making decisions and their expectations of the airport product. Airports have had to develop more sophisticated marketing strategies and tactics to meet the needs of the traveller. In addition, deregulation, privatization, and globalization trends within the airline industry have increased the commercial pressures being faced by airlines, which, in turn, have encouraged airports to recognize the need for a professional marketing-orientated approach when dealing with their airline customers.

By the late 1990s, the majority of airports were devoting considerable resources to marketing activities. It is difficult to accurately quantify this increased emphasis on the role of marketing but some indication of this trend can be gleaned from an analysis of staff employed in the marketing area. For example, with UK regional airports the number of passengers per marketing staff decreased significantly between 1991 and 1997. For instance the number of marketing staff at Manchester airport increased from 16 to 27 and at Birmingham airport from 10 to 24. This meant that the number of passengers per marketing staff decreased from 631 000 to 562 000 at Manchester and from 325 000 to 227 000 at Birmingham (Humphreys, 1999).

If marketing is defined in its broadest sense of satisfying customer needs, there are various other activities (which have been discussed in other chapters) that also can be considered as airport marketing. These activities include quality assessment and improvement, and environmental neighbourhood communication initiatives. The development of non-aeronautical activities can also be treated as a marketing role. However this chapter takes a more narrow consideration of satisfying customer needs by assessing how general marketing concepts and techniques can be applied to the airport industry.

Marketing concepts

The market for airport services

The focal point of any marketing system is always the consumer of the services. For the airport product, demand comes from a variety of markets each with their own specific requirements. From a marketing perspective, it is useful to divide this demand into two, namely the trade such as airlines who buy the airport facilities direct and the general public or travellers who merely consume or utilize the airport product. The marketing techniques used for these two types are very different. Most airports would probably agree that both airlines and passengers are key customers, whereas airlines tend to think of passengers as their customers and themselves as customers of the airports.

In addition, there are the other market segments such as local residents and businesses whose needs must also be met. Obviously these types of demand do not impact directly on the amount of aeronautical revenue and traffic throughput at an airport but their presence at the airport can have a significant impact on the level of non-aeronautical revenue. They can also help airports in acting as a catalyst for economic development. Concessionaires, tenants, and other organizations such as handling agents can also be considered customers of the airport. Table 7.3 shows some of the major market segments at an airport. Each of these needs to be further subdivided into much smaller discreet segments so that they can be targeted appropriately and so that the airport's marketing efforts can be the most effective.

A common way to segment demand is by airline product type. For example, with passenger travel this would include a full-cost traditional service, a low-cost service, and a charter service. Airline alliances could well be given special consideration. In the cargo area, the market may be segmented into integrators, cargo airlines, passenger airlines, and other freight companies.

Rather than considering the demand by product type or purpose of travel, it can sometimes be more useful to consider it by travel behaviour in order to match more closely the needs of each market segment. For example, there are 'Agoraphobics' who have the lowest level of need, have a fear of flying and of missing the plane, and do not want to be distracted from the departure monitor. Then there are the 'Euphorics' who are the once-a-year holidaymakers who arrive early at the airport and spend money as part of the holiday experience. Next in the order of needs are the 'Confident indulgers' who are frequent leisure fliers who are familiar with the airport product and want

Table 7.3   The airport's customers

Trade	Passengers	Others
Airlines	Traditional scheduled (also	Tenants and
Tour operators	know as network/legacy/full	concessionaires
Travel agents	cost carriers)	Visitors
Freight forwarders	Low cost	Employees
General aviation	Charter	Local residents
	Business	Local businesses
	Leisure	
	Transfer	

to be pampered. Most complaints come from 'Airport controllers' who are typically frequent business passengers flying economy with their families on holiday and feel aggrieved that they do not have the privileges that they normally experience when flying business class. Then, finally, there are the 'Self-controllers' who are frequent business fliers who just want to be processed through the airport as quickly and as efficiently as possible. The amount of time that these types of passenger spend at the airport varies from considerable in the case of the Agoraphobics down to the minimum possible for the Self-controllers (Young, 1996). Another useful way to segment the market is also by loyalty to the airport. Freathy and O'Connell (2000) discuss such a classification devised by Ballini which identifies the passengers as loyalists, defectors, mercenaries and hostages.

For each type of customer, choosing an airport is the result of an amalgam of many decision processes (Table 7.4). For passengers, for example, clearly the nature of air services on offer (in terms of fares, destinations, schedules etc) – in effect the airline product – will be the key factor as no one will choose to fly from an airport unless it offers the required travel opportunities. Hence in this case this often means that what seems like airport competition is in effect competition between airlines. For example, two airports may be described as being in strong competition with each other but this may be since they are served by airlines which themselves are in fierce competition. Hence from a passenger viewpoint airport competition will be closely linked to the amount of airline competition which exists (Morrell, 2003).

Factors such as the distance, cost, and ease of surface access to a certain airport as well as cost and convenience of car parking at the airport can also be very important to passengers. The quality of the airport product can have a marginal impact but only after these other factors have been taken into account. For business passengers, facilities such as fast-track processes and airline lounges may affect choice,

Table 7.4 Factors affecting the choice of airports

Passengers	Airlines
Destinations of flights	Catchment area and potential demand
Flight fare	Slot availability
Flight availability and timings	Competition
Frequency of service	Network compatibility
Image and reliability of airline	Airport fees and availability of discounts
Airline alliance policy and frequent-flyer programme	Other airport costs (e.g. fuel, handling)
Surface access cost to airport	Marketing support
Ease of access to airport	Range and quality of facilities
Car parking cost	Ease of transfer connections
Range and quality of shops, catering and other commercial facilities	Maintenance facilities

whereas for customers with special needs, for example, disabled passengers, the quality of the provision of wheelchair, lifts, and general assistance may be important. Then there are other factors that are more difficult to explain and quantify. For example, in many European countries there will be a preference for the established capital city airport even if there are alternative airports that offer a comparable service. This is especially the case among the business community. In some instances, this may be because of better flight availability and frequency at the main airport, but not always. Often it might be because of ignorance about the other airports, especially among travel agents, or because of some other factor such as the traveller's choice of a certain airline in order to add to their frequent flyer points.

For the airline and other trade customers such as tour operators, it is clearly the nature of the catchment area rather than design details of the airport facilities that are of paramount importance. Depending on the type of route being considered, key factors are business and tourist appeal of the catchment area for incoming passengers, and the characteristics and purchasing power of those residing in the catchment area (Favotto, 1998). Other important elements include the availability of attractive slot times, the presence of competitors, and the network performance of the airport. The marketing assistance that the airport is prepared to give, not only in terms of pricing incentives but also with the funding of activities such as market research and promotional campaigns can also be crucial. Other customers will take into account different factors. For example, retailers will only wish to operate at an airport if they have proof that the passenger profile is attractive enough and that the airport has a sufficient traffic throughput.

Passenger surveys at five UK airports, namely Heathrow, Gatwick, Manchester, Birmingham and Newcastle in 1998/1999 gave some insight into the reasons for the choice of airport (CAA, 1999; 2000). The location of airport and flights on offer were the key factors determining choice. For the London airports, the most important was the nature of flights on offer – at Heathrow for both local and connecting flights. Half the passengers at the regional airport of Manchester, however, chose the airport because it was close to their home, with an additional 13 per cent picking it because it was near to their business or leisure destination. Similarly locational factors were very important for the regional airports of Birmingham and Newcastle. The timing of flights appeared to be a more influential factor at Heathrow, because of its higher share of business passengers, than at the other airports.

The airport product

The airport product consists of a supply of services, both tangible and intangible, to meet the needs of different market segments. Marketing

243

theory often divides the product into the core, actual or physical, and augmented elements. The core product is the essential benefit that the consumer is seeking, while the actual product delivers the benefit. Product features, quality level, brand name, design, and packaging will all make up the physical product. The augmented product is then additional consumer services and benefits that will be built around the core and actual products, and will distinguish the product from others. Much of the competition will typically take place at the augmented level (Kotler and Armstrong, 2006). Sometimes the physical product is referred to as the 'generic' product with the 'wide' product representing the augmented elements (Jarach, 2005).

Each market segment will perceive these product levels very differently. For the airline, the core is the ability to land and take off an aircraft, whereas for the passenger it will be the ability to board or disembark an aircraft. For freight forwarders it will be the ability to load and unload the freight on the aircraft. In order to provide the core product for the airline, the actual product will need to consist of the runway, the terminal building, the freight warehouses, the equipment, and so on – and the expertise to provide all these facilities efficiently and safely. For the passenger, the actual product will include check-in desks, baggage handling, and other features such as immigration control that will enable the passenger to fulfil his/her need of boarding or disembarking the aircraft. The actual product will also include adequate transport services to and from airport, and the provision of outlets selling essential travel goods, as well as other facilities such as information desks and toilets. At the augmented level the airport may, for example, offer marketing support or pricing incentives to the airlines or may formalize some agreement about the exact service levels to be expected. For the passenger the range and diversity of shops, catering, and other commercial facilities as well as other features such as ease of transfer between different aircraft could all be considered to be part of the augmented product.

It is difficult to apply this marketing concept to the airport sector because of the composite nature of the airport product. From a passenger viewpoint, the airport product includes the airline product as well as the product of the concessionaire, handling agent, and so on. Another way of looking at the airport product is by considering its 'raw' and 'refined' features. The raw product consists of both physical tangible elements (such as the runway, buildings, apron, lighting, navigation aids, fuel, fire, and rescue) and intangible service elements provided by the airport operator's own staff and those of the customs, immigration, and security agencies. To produce the refined product involves adding the services provided by concessionaires and other tenants and the air travel elements, both tangible and intangible, provided by the airlines.

At the broadest level, the airport product can be considered to be a large commercial centre, which meets the needs of travellers, visitors, and residents. In this case the airport can be defined as an 'Airport City' or 'Aerotropolis' as discussed in Chapter 6. Other airports may look at the product in a different way. For example, there is London City airport in the United Kingdom that targets the business market. According to the airport, since time is money in the business world, the main product feature is time. This is achieved by having a 10-minute check-in and a 5-minute arrival time from plane to terminal. Valet parking is also provided to speed up the departure process. In addition, there are service features specifically designed for the business traveller and which range from leather seats in the departure lounge, shoe shining in the terminal concourse, travel and hotels reservation desk, taxi-account services and a range of different meeting facilities. Corporate jet aircraft have also been encouraged and there are dedicated facilities for these.

Related to the concept of the airport product is the idea of an airport brand. In marketing theory a brand is represented by a name, logos, design, signing, merchandising, and advertising, all of which give the product an identity. These tangible and intangible features of the identity differentiate the product from its competitors. Within the airport sector it is certainly true that there are widespread attempts to create a corporate identity with the use of catchy publicity slogans, and eye-catching logos as well as designs on promotional information and within the terminal itself. For airport operators who own more than one airport, use of similar signposting, colour schemes, and interior design may also be used for all its airports. For example, BAA has traditionally used a common and constant brand image for its seven UK airports. Whether such 'branding' actually gives an airport any competitive edge is, however, very debatable although it may make the customer feel more at ease because of the familiar surroundings. Many airports use a number of sub-brands for different areas, especially retail zones. Too many brands may confuse passengers, however, particularly as airlines and their alliance groupings are also becoming increasingly keen to have their own identity represented in the area of the terminal where their passengers are handled.

Marketers often give considerable attention to the name of the airport. Many regional airports like to be called 'international' airports to demonstrate that they serve international as well as domestic destinations – even if in some cases there may be only one international route! In contrast, as airports become more developed and more well known for their range of services, they may choose to drop the international name as Manchester airport did way back in 1986. Other airports will include the name of the nearest large city or town, even if it may not be particularly close, and there may be more conveniently located airports. For example, with the London area there is now not only London Heathrow, London Gatwick, and London Stansted but also London Luton, London Manston, London Southend, London Biggin Hill, and London Ashford. Charleroi is known as Brussels South, Sandefjord-Torp as Oslo South, and Skavsta as Stockholm South. Other airports include Frankfurt Hahn which is 70 miles from Frankfurt and Chicago Rockford which is 90 miles from Chicago. One of the most extreme examples is the new Madrid Sur Ciudad airport which is 125 miles from Madrid (Catan, 2007). Including the nearby city name may well make the airport easier to market and will give routes served by it better placing in the airline computer reservation systems. However it can also be misleading to passengers and disliked by rival airports. A relevant example here is in 2003 when the German court ordered Ryanair not to call Weeze airport 'Düsseldorf' airport as it was more than 70 km away from the city.

An example of an airport which has had a particular problem with its name and geographical position is the airport in the UK which up until 2003 was called East Midlands airport. In 2003 it decided to change its name to Nottingham East Midlands to make its location seem more specific. However there are two other towns, Leicester and Derby, which are nearer to the airport than Nottingham, and the new name was therefore not popular there. Eventually in 2006 the airport was given another new name, East Midlands airport – Nottingham, Leicester and Derby.

Giving an airport a name which is based on geographical characteristics, natural or man-made attractions or aspects of historical importance may raise the visibility and profile of the airport. For instance the name EuroAirport for Basel-Mulhouse airport has been devised to reflect its central European location and bi-national ownership characteristics. Knock airport in Ireland was re-branded as Ireland West Airport Knock in 2005 to emphasize its importance as an access point to the West of Ireland. Other interesting examples include Zürich airport which was re-branded as 'Unique Zürich Airport' in 2000 to reflect a new management structure, partial privatization, and expanded facilities. In the UK there are also now 'John Lennon' Liverpool airport, 'Robin Hood' Doncaster airport and 'George Best' Belfast City airport. However there can be a problem if the name is too distinctive and encourages certain traffic types. For example Rovaniemi airport in Finland became known as Santa Claus airport in order to contribute to the 'Santa-based' tourism in Finnish Lapland, after British Airways (BA) took a Concorde flight of 100 passengers there in 1994. However this type of traffic is very seasonal and is dominated by charters and so this name may discourage other airlines which might provide a more regular service (Halpern, 2008).

Ultimately most decisions concerning the choice of airport will be based primarily on the air services available at the airport (i.e. the airline product) and the proximity of the airport to the potential customer. It is very important for the airport to remember this and to focus its marketing on the air services on offer and the airport's convenience rather than giving every fact about the facilities on offer. Similarly, when marketing to airlines, it is information about the nature of catchment area and potential demand rather than small details about the airport infrastructure that will most probably sell the airport. No amount of money spent on improving facilities will attract airlines to the airport unless they consider that there is a market for their services.

Airport marketing techniques

Successful airport marketing involves focusing on understanding and responding to the needs of the various customer segments. Clearly every airport is unique and needs to be marketed in its own specific way. At small airports, all marketing tasks may be undertaken by a couple of staff, whereas at larger airports there may be separate departments for coping with different customers such as the passengers and airlines, and different teams looking at different marketing activities such as market research, sales, and public relations. Once an airport gets to a certain size, the marketing focus is likely to change. Small airports may concentrate on growing specific services that appear to offer opportunities for the airport. Larger airports, which already have a reasonably developed route network, may be more concerned with putting forward a good positive image for the airport and trying to build on a corporate identity. The marketing of airports aiming to be hub or feeder points is totally different from marketing an airport that relies on point-to-point services such as charter or low-cost services. Airports with considerable spare capacity will adopt different strategies to congested airports. Smaller airports competing with major capital city airports will probably find that they are facing an uphill struggle but nevertheless a considerable amount of proactive and aggressive marketing may achieve results.

Airlines

At the most basic level, airports promote themselves to airlines by producing general publicity information, by placing advertisements in trade journals, and by being represented at exhibitions, travel trade seminars and workshops, roadshows, and other similar events. The aim here is to increase awareness amongst the airlines. Sometimes simple messages may be used to sell the airport. Vienna airport, for instance, has promoted itself as being 'Europe's best address', Nice airport has described itself as the 'Greatway to Europe' and Brussels airport as 'At the crossroads of Europe'. With other airports the key message may be more specific. Large hub airports may focus on their size to demonstrate that the airport is popular and has connecting traffic possibilities. For instance, Atlanta airport has invited airlines to become 'Members of the busiest airport in the world', Bahrain airport has said that 'All routes lead to Bahrain', whilst Rome airport has used the message 'With more than 150 destinations we help half of the world to reach the other half. And vice versa'. Cologne airport's location was made to look like an electric circuit with an instruction 'Plug in to connect'.

Other airports try to emphasize different product characteristics such as uncongested facilities and quick processing times. Kansas airport told airlines not to 'Get drawn into a congested hub', whilst the small Palm Beach airport's slogan was 'Touch Down 11:00, Towel

Down 11:45'. Kent international airport was promoted as 'The best kept secret in South East England'. Price sometimes features in such advertising. Geneva airport, for example, has sold itself as being 'The high yield airport with surprising low costs', while Macau airport advertised half price landing fees at night with the message 'Our night fall brings sweet dreams … 50 per cent off at night'. Other airports adopt much more vague and less specific messages. For instance, Incheon Airport was promoted as the 'The Winged City' and was described as the '21st century airport of your dreams'. An alternative approach is to sell the destination which the airport is serving. For example Bermuda airport used the message 'Share the success of a world class destination', Macau had 'Land on the doorstep of culture and entertainment', Baltimore used 'One great airport serving two great cities' and Oslo promoted itself as the 'Gateway to Scandinavia'. It must be borne in mind, however, that this advertising will usually only reach a general audience and will tend to be very costly.

Developing regular contact with key airlines through visits by airport sales staff, or with regular mail shots and other promotional activities, may also be effective. Often airports deal with potential airline customers in a much more direct and personal way as well. This hard-selling approach, called route or air service development, was developed in the 1980s owing to the realization that airports were actually in a good position to identify new route opportunities for airlines. This was a task previously left solely to the airlines. The airport marketers analysed passenger and catchment area data that gave them adequate information to suggest new route opportunities to potential operators. Many of the airports had the advantage that they already kept at least some of these data for their own passenger marketing and forecasting. They also benefited from certain cost economies by being able to consider all different markets and routes simultaneously. For a small airline interested in operating just one or two new routes, the cost of undertaking such research could well have been too prohibitive.

So the airports started to take a leading role in initiating interest from airlines with this more direct route development approach. From their databases, they would provide airlines with information about potential routes and the size of the market and perhaps other factors such as the likely requirements for frequency and aircraft size, and route cost and yield considerations. By the 1990s, airline presentations from the marketing departments of airports to route planners in airlines had become commonplace. Typically, the presentation would give a detailed analysis of the new route or routes and usually an approximate financial evaluation. This would be supplemented by information about the catchment area, in terms of the characteristics of residents and its tourist and business appeal for incoming passengers. Information would also be given about the airport's facilities and accessibility by transport links.

The airports that first adopted this more reactive approach to marketing to airlines, such as Manchester and Vienna, claimed many success stories. Times have now moved on in the air transport industry and both the airports and the airlines have developed more sophisticated marketing techniques. The airline presentation is still an important element of an airport's marketing but it has to be highly focused. The emphasis must be very much on the potential demand at the airport (including an assessment of any newly stimulated traffic and the impact on existing routes) and the level of services which is needed in terms of frequency and capacity with the quality of facilities taking a second place. Emphasis on architectural excellence and best-quality facilities could even have a negative impact, with airlines being concerned that the cost of such infrastructure may be passed on to them. The airlines themselves have become awash with route studies from numerous airports and therefore have become much more skilled in using this information to back-up and verify the own research.

At the same time as detailing the opportunities for route development, the airport operator will also explain the incentives which will be offered to encourage the airline to serve the airport. These are usually both financial and non-financial. Many airports offer reduced fees over a certain period of time (Table 7.5). These can be particularly important and can be crucial particularly for LCCs. Such discounts will usually diminish as traffic grows and the service becomes sustainable – they are actually required to do so in the European Union (for publicly owned airports). One of the most popular methods is to waive or reduce the landing fee in the first few years of operation so that the airline only pays for the passengers it carries. If demand

Table 7.5 Types of airport charges discounts

Discount	Objective
Landing charge discount on flights to new destinations	Encourages new routes
Landing charge discount on all additional flights or larger aircraft	Encourages new frequencies or additional capacity
Landing charge discount for replacing one-stop service by non-stop	Encourages new direct routes
Landing charge discount for positioning flights	Encourages airlines to base aircraft at the airport
Transfer passenger discount	Encourages growth of transfer passengers
Passenger charge discount	Encourages new routes and more frequencies/capacity
Passenger and landing charge discounts for off-peak/daytime flights	Encourages new routes and frequencies/capacity while avoiding congestion and night noise
Aircraft parking charges discount	Encourages new routes and more frequencies/capacities and basing of aircraft

Source: Adapted from STRAIR (2005).

at the start of a service is initially low, the airline will pay very little. This means that the airport will share more of the risk when the airline is developing the route. There may also be discounts on the passenger and parking charges. Alternatively the three charges may be replaced with a set charge per passenger, which again is a more risky option for the airport as it has the effect of relating the charge solely to passenger numbers which drive airline revenues. Apart from these new routes incentives to encourage greater connectivity for the airport, there may be incentives to persuade airlines to offer more capacity or increase frequencies or to operate non-stop services. Incentives may be offered to support airlines to use the airport as a base and in this case very often in return the airline will make commitments themselves to the airport operator to base a certain numbers of aircraft at the airports, to achieve a certain volume of traffic, and to remain at the airport for a minimum period.

Not all of these incentive schemes are published but Table 7.6 contains a sample of those which are to give an indication of the range of incentives which are on offer. Some of these are very general and simple such as at Geneva, Hong Kong and Kuala Lumpur whereas elsewhere, for example at Stockholm, Manchester and the Airports of Thailand, a more complicated scheme exists with differentials between various types of traffic. Other more focused initiatives (not shown in the table) include incentives specifically to promote non-EU traffic at Dublin airport or to promote the development of Casablanca airport in Morocco as a regional hub.

Airports may be able to make themselves appear particularly attractive if they guarantee that the overall package of costs that an airline is faced with at the airport will be reasonable. In many cases, airports will be able to offer discounted airport charges but will have no control over handling or fuel charges. However, a few airports such as Abu Dhabi in the Middle East offer a one-stop approach when there is a single contract for all ground services at the airport. Since all the facilities, including aircraft fuelling, are owned by the government, the airport is in a position to do this and to have complete control over what it offers to the airlines. Bahrain airport also operates a comprehensive package of incentives which includes reduction in fees, discounts on hotel accommodation for crews and low fuel prices. All the promotional efforts are channelled through the 'Single Co-ordinated Group' which includes Bahrain Airport Services, Bahrain Petroleum Company, Air BP and Bahrain Duty Free (STRAIR, 2005). A number of smaller regional airports are also able to offer low-cost airlines deals which include the handling charges as well, as they provide these services themselves.

Apart from offering reductions on charges, airports very often provide financial help for marketing or will pool resources so that joint advertising and promotional campaigns may be run to promote the new services. Costs may also be shared for exhibitions and trade fairs. Very often stakeholders such as regional agencies and tourism boards can get involved at this stage (See Chapter 8). In addition

Table 7.6 Examples of airport discount schemes 2007–2008

Airport	Scheme
Airports of Thailand (Chiang Mai, Chiang Rai, Hat Yai and Phuket (summer) only)	*New international route discount on landing charge*: More than one weekly flight (95%); One weekly flight (75%) *New airlines discount on landing charge on international routes already served by Airports of Thailand*: More than one weekly flight (75%); One weekly flight (50%) *Discount on landing for increased frequencies*: More than one weekly flight (75%); One weekly flight (50%) (Different discounts apply for domestic routes)
Berlin Schonefeld	*Passenger volume rebates*: >500 000 (5%); >100 000 (10%); >250 000 (15 %); > 500 000 (20%); > 1 million (30%); > 2 million (40%) *New route discount on landing charge*: First 6 months (80%); 2nd 6 months (60%); 3rd 6 months (40%); 4th 6 months (20%); 5th 6 months (10%) There is also a growth discount for increases in tonnage and passengers per flight
Düsseldorf	*Passenger volume rebates*: 500 000 – 1 million (2%); 1–2 million (3%); 2–3 million (3.5%); 3–4 million (4.0%); 5–6 million (5.0%); > 6 million (5.5%) There are also incentives to encourage better use of runway capacity and to increase intercontinental services
Glasgow, Edinburgh, Aberdeen	*New route discount on airport charges*: Year 1 – International (50%); Domestic (30%) Year 2 – International (30%); Domestic (20%) Year 3 – International (10%); Domestic (10%) *Increased capacity/frequency growth and replacement of multi-sector with non-stop service discount on airport charges*: Year 1 (30%); Year 2 (20%); Year 3 (10%)
Geneva	*New route discount on landing charge*: Year 1 – 100%; Year 2 – 50%
Hong Kong	*New route discount on landing charge*: First 6 months – 75%; Next 6 months 25%
Hamburg	*New route discount on landing charge*: Year 1 – Intercontinental (100%); Europe (75%) Year 2 – Intercontinental (75%); Europe (50%) Next 6 months – Intercontinental (50%); Europe (25%) A passenger growth bonus is also paid
Kuala Lumpur	*New routes and increased frequencies discount on landing fees*: Year 1–3 (100%); Year 4 (75%); Year 5 (50%)
Manchester	*New routes – All inclusive passenger charge instead of a landing, passenger and parking charge*: Standard – Year 1 (£3); Year 2 (£4); Year 3 (£5) Off-peak – Year 1–3 (£3); Year 4 (£5); Year 5 (£7) *Capacity growth discount*: The bigger aircraft pays the same landing charges as the original aircraft Non-stop replacing multi-stop service landing charge discount: Year 1 (40%); Year 2–3 (20%)

(continued)

Table 7.6 (Continued)

Airport	Scheme
Stockholm Arlanda	*New routes discount on landing and passenger charges*: Year 1 – Intercontinental (50% landing, 100% passenger); Tricontinental (50% landing, 100% passenger); Europe (70% passenger) Year 2 – Intercontinental (25% landing, 50% passenger); Tricontinental (50% landing, 50% passenger); Europe (30% passenger) Year 3 – Intercontinental (50% landing) *Bonus for passenger growth*: Intercontinental (SEK 50 for each new passenger); European (SEK 20)

Note: Some of the 'discounts' may be described as 'rebates' by individual airports but for clarity they have all been presented as 'discounts' in the table. *Sources*: Airport websites.

non-financial incentives can be offered, such as information provision, for example regarding the regulatory situation and market characteristics or useful contacts lists for local travel agent, tour operation, ground handling, recruitment agencies and media sectors. Airports may give advice on scheduling decisions, particularly if an airline is to benefit from connecting traffic from other airlines. The airport may also promise to help to lobby government to remove environmental or traffic rights regulatory obstacles. Finally another way in which an airport can put together an attractive deal for an airline and be cost-effective in its marketing is by pairing up and co-operating with the airport at the other end of a route that has been identified as having potential.

An interesting development as regards airline marketing has been the 'Routes' conference. This has been held annually since 1995 and is an opportunity for airport marketers and airline route planners to get together to discuss future market opportunities. In one-to-one meetings airlines explain their expansion strategies to airports, who in turn try to sell the virtues of their catchment areas and facilities and services. The airline network planners, who are fewer in number than the airport staff, sit at desks whilst the airport representatives move from desk to desk in allocated 15–20 minutes periods – rather like speed dating! This type of conference has proved so popular that there are now regional as well as global routes meetings and other similar events such as Network USA and French Connect. The 2007 global routes meeting attracted around 2300 delegates who had more than 30 000 meetings.

A very visible indication of what LCCs are looking for from an airport was illustrated in 2005 when easyJet took the unusual step of advertising on their website the criteria which they use for airport selection (easyJet, 2005). These were:

● Does the airport serve a large population of people within 1 hour; or serve an attractive destination?

- Does the airport support rapid aircraft turnarounds?
- Can the airport support services to other easyJet destinations?
- Is low-cost part of the airport strategy?
- Is the airport seeking to improve the efficiency of it's business?

If the airport could answer yes to all these questions, it was invited to send detailed information about the demand characteristics and facilities at the airport. This helped easyJet in choosing some of its newer bases.

The most common airlines to benefit from a total package of measures are the LCCs. Airports are willing to enter into such agreements due to the additional commercial revenues that hopefully the extra passengers will bring and the impact that such services will have on raising the profile of the airport and encouraging other new carriers. For a number of regional airports, this may also be a way of filling airport capacity which was under utilized. Moreover if the airport is under regional public ownership, the new services may be supported because of the potential broader economic benefit that they could have on the whole region – for example in terms of encouraging tourism and inward investment. However this raises the issue of whether state aid should be used in this way to support certain airlines. For example as a result of a complaint by Air France in 2003 the Strasbourg court ruled that the marketing support given by the publicly owned Strasbourg airport to Ryanair was illegal. Ryanair pulled off the route and opened a route from Baden-Karlsruhe in Germany instead which had a very negative impact on the traffic levels at Strasbourg. A similar but in the end much more significant example, which has had wide-ranging impacts in Europe, is the Brussels South Charleroi airport (BSCA) case.

The Brussels South Charleroi Airport case

Charleroi airport is a regional airport owned by the Walloon regional government which is 46 km south of Brussels. Between 1990 and 1996, its passenger levels fluctuated at around 50 000. Then, in 1997, Ryanair began to operate two flights a day to Dublin and the airport passenger numbers increased dramatically to 200 000. Ryanair's passenger numbers increased from 86 000 in 1997 to 178 000 in 2000 but the airport still remained very much a small regional airport. The most significant change came in 2001 when Ryanair decided to make Charleroi its first continental base and began operating 10 routes with 19 daily frequencies. This changed its status from that of a regional airport serving passengers on charter airlines originating from the Walloon region to a larger secondary airport with a much greater traffic base in the whole of Belgium and also cross-border regions in France and Germany. It was at this time that the name was changed from Charleroi Airport to Brussels South Charleroi Airport (BSCA) (Jossart, 2006).

The airport offered Ryanair a very favourable deal because it felt that the presence of Ryanair could substantially grow its non-aeronautical revenues and attract other airlines to the airport. For example, it transformed the coach shuttle from the Airport to Brussels City from a loss making into a profitable activity and generated a substantial amount of revenue from car parking since it introduced parking charges in 1999. It also expanded the duty free and catering outlets to cope with the additional passengers and increase the overall non-aeronautical revenues.

Table 7.7 shows the reported details of the arrangement made between BSCA and Ryanair. Ryanair paid very low landing and handling charges starting at €1 per passenger which was planned to go up to €1.13 in 2006 and €1.3 in 2010. In addition, BSCA contributed towards other expenses incurred by Ryanair, which together with the low charges resulted in a net benefit to Ryanair. The expenses covered by BSCA included marketing support, incentive payments for each route started, and Ryanair's costs for local crew hiring and training. Office and hangar space was also provided for a minimal cost. For this support from BSCA Ryanair agreed to base two to four aircraft at the airport and to operate at least three departing flights for each aircraft over a period of 15 years – if not it would have to repay the incentives.

However in 2001 a complaint was lodged with the European Commission concerning these incentives and whether they were

Table 7.7   Elements of agreement between Ryanair and BSCA

Annual Payments	Amount (€)	Cost assumptions (€)	Other assumptions (€)
Ryanair to BSCA		Landing fees/	Annual pax: 1 million
Landing fees	1 000 000	pax: 1.00	New routes: 12
Handling fees	1 000 000	Handling fees/	
Total	2 000 000	pax: 1.00	
BSCA to Ryanair		Marketing	
Marketing fees	2 000 000	contribution/pax: 2.00	
Hotel costs	250 000	Hotels costs/year:	
New route	1 920 000	250 000	
payment		Payment/new route:	
Recruitment	768 000	160 000	
payment		Recruitment/training	
Office costs	250 000	(one-off): 768 000	
Hangar costs	250 000	Estimated office	
Total	5 438 000	costs/year: 250 000	
Net benefit	3 438 000	Estimated hangar	
		costs/year: 250 000	

Source: Aviation Strategy (2001).

anti-competitive and hence an investigation was undertaken concerning this state aid which had been given by the Walloon region to Ryanair. Two issues were considered. First, according to Article 87 of the Treaty of Rome and European transport policy, aid is allowed if it encourages the development and use of under-utilized secondary airport infrastructure. Secondly, state aid is not allowed when it can be proved that a private airport operator would not behave in the same manner, the so-called private market investor principle. A decision was reached in 2004 when it was decided that Ryanair could keep some of the aid, but the remaining amount had to be paid back (European Commission, 2004). The Commission determined that no private operator in the same circumstances as Charleroi Airport would have granted the same advantages to the airline and hence the private market investor principle had not been followed. However, the Commission took the view that some aspects of the aid could be compatible with European transport policy. Hence the Commission allowed Ryanair to keep some of the aid intended for the launch of new air routes (such as marketing and publicity) and other one-off incentives, such as recruitments payments. However other aid which took no account of the actual costs of launching such routes was not allowed. Nor were the fee discounts because they had not been allocated in a non-discriminatory and fully transparent manner and were planned for a very long period of operation. Ryanair launched an appeal against this judgement, the outcome of which is yet to be decided.

Following on from this case, and to clarify the application of state aid principles to airports, the European Commission issued guidelines on financing of airports and start-up aid to airlines departing from regional airports in 2005 (European Commission, 2005). This stipulates that the aid can only be offered by airports of less than five million passengers and it must in most cases be limited to 3 years and be degressive (Table 7.8). However these are not law, but only guidelines of the EC's interpretation of how the law should be applied. Since the issuance of the guideline the European Commission has investigated a number of airports and their incentives schemes for airlines. Also it is important to emphasis that it only applies to publicly owned airports in Europe, whereas the growing numbers of private airports are free to offer whatever incentives they feel are suitable.

Travel trade

Airports also need to promote themselves to the travel trade such as travel agents, tour operators and freight forwarders. Again this can be done by producing general publicity information, by placing advertisements in trade journals, and going to trade exhibitions such as ITB Berlin and the World Travel Market in London. In spite of

Table 7.8 Key features of the 2005 EU guidelines on financing of airports and start-up aid to airlines departing from regional airports

Supported routes must usually be between EU airports of less than 5 million passengers.

The aid must only apply to new routes or to increased frequencies which lead to an increase in passengers.

The aid must be linked to the net development of the number of passengers carried.

The route must be shown to be viable after the aid has expired.

The aid must be linked directly to the start-up costs or increased costs of the airline in operating the new route or increased frequencies.

The aid must be digressive and granted for maximum period of 3 years (5 years for remote airports).

The aid must not exceed 50% of the total eligible costs in one year and the total aid must not exceed an average of 30% of all eligible costs.

Source: European Commission (2005).

the increased use of the internet and other direct-booking methods, travel agents can still be highly influential in some cases when passengers go through the process of selecting and assessing possible travel options. Some of the general sales promotions directed at the airlines may be targeted at the travel agency sector as well, and may help to give exposure to the airport and the services that it offers. Regular mail shots by post and electronically to agents may enhance that awareness.

In many cases, however, this is not enough. Numerous airports, particularly the regional and smaller ones, have found that it is particularly important to spend some time and effort in developing close and personalized links with travel agents serving the direct catchment area. This usually involves regularly sending out a sales representative who can talk to the agents about new developments at the airport and explore the agents' knowledge and views of the services on offer. This one-to-one contact can be supplemented with frequent, personalized mail shots giving details of promotions, new facilities, up-to-date timetables, and other information. Very often airports will also organize competitions, airport tours, and other social events to encourage greater interest in the airport and to forge closer links with the agency sector. Familiarization trips and launch parties for new routes for key business and travel trade representatives are particularly important. There are many stories of regional airports discovering that all their neighbouring travel agents are completely unaware of any local air flights. Instead, the agents will have automatically advised passengers to travel via a larger airport further away. Cardiff airport in the United Kingdom overcame this problem by buying a chain of 22 local travel agents in an attempt to promote flights from its airport (Humphreys, 1998).

Norwich airport, also in the United Kingdom, went even further to encourage passengers and the travel trade to use the airport. In 1988, it opened its own travel agency in the terminal building to persuade passengers to buy flights and package tours departing from Norwich. The success of the agency encouraged the airport to open another five outlets in the surrounding area of the airport in 1998 to further promote the sales of flights from Norwich airport. Another decision by the airport was to operate its own charter flights. This move came about because the airport had been unable to persuade the large tour operators to operate programmes from Norwich airport. In 1995, a weekly service at a total annual cost of £400 000 was operated from the airport to Alicante. This destination was chosen because it was apparent from passenger surveys that there was considerable demand, not only for package holidays, but also because there was a large number of British-owned villas in this area. The service was a success, bringing in a profit in the region of around £150 000 directly from aeronautical charges and associated increases in non-aeronautical revenue from sources such as car parking, retail, and F&B. Some of the seats were sold to tour operators and some direct to passengers. The airport added summer services to Malaga and Faro in 1996 and a winter service to Malaga in 1997. By 2000, it was offering services to Malaga, Faro, Minorca, Alicante, and Malta and had allocations on flights to Corfu and Cyprus. By 2002, however, the airport was down to offering allocations on only four destinations, namely Alicante, Cyprus, Faro, and Malaga and by 2006 there were no more in-house services. This was because the airport had proved successful in persuading the tour operators and airlines that there was a demand for direct services and they had therefore taken over the destinations themselves (Eady, 2007).

Passengers and the local community

Generally, a much more soft-sell approach is adopted for passengers. Airport timetables with details of airport services, facilities and surface access, and other promotional literature is commonly distributed to travel agents, libraries, shopping centres, tourist information offices, and so on. Travel brochures, produced jointly with tour operators or airlines, can be circulated. This not only has this advantage of sharing the cost but also has the benefit of having the operators' brand associated with the airport. Loyalty schemes can also be encouraged. For example Birmingham airport has its 'Flight Club' which provides discounts of travel products and facilities and services at the airport. A quarterly magazine is also sent out to the 100 000 members of this relational database.

At the airport itself, information services are provided for passengers and visitors, as are maps and other information about the facilities and services. To increase awareness of the airport and improve relations with the community, open days, air shows, exhibitions, and educational visits are also often organized. Branded giveaways to reinforce the airports image and identity, such as badges, key rings, T-shirts, and stationery items are frequently distributed. Sponsorship of key events is also quite common in the airport business.

Airport information is now available on airport websites that have been set up by most airports, with various degrees of sophistication. The type of information usually on offer includes airport location details, car parking, and local transport details, with perhaps opportunities for pre-booking car parking space or buying public transport tickets online. Tourist and other information about the airport's catchment area might be included. There may also be links to airlines and other products such as car hire, hotels and tourist boards. There may even be the possibility to book flights directly with the websites acting as a distribution channel itself – as is the case for example with London City and Norwich airport. Nearly all the websites, even the most basic ones, include terminal maps and a list of facilities, such as shops and F&B, on offer. Pre-ordering from these may be possible. Many of the major airports have real-time flight information and flight-delay details on offer 24-hours a day. Many other opportunities exist. For example, three pieces of information that travellers usually require is local weather details, local time and exchanges rates but these simple facts are often not always provided (Gillen and Lall, 2002). The internet can offer potentially numerous marketing and revenue opportunities, and an increasing number of airports are taking full advantage of this. Customer profile and preference information can automatically be collected from users of the website and the pre-ordering purchases, online shopping, and advertising can increase non-aeronautical revenues.

However, the internet clearly has a much greater role to play than merely providing information for the traveller. The local community can find out about achievements, for example, in environmental protection. Shareholders can track the performance of their shares and have instant access to the airports' financial reports. Airlines should be able to retrieve traffic statistics and catchment area information, while details about customs requirements, and handling and warehousing facilities should be available to cargo customers.

Airports advertise to the public through the internet and all the other usual media channels such as television, radio, newspapers, magazines, and posters. The choice of media, as with all marketing, clearly depends on the relative costs, the target audience, and the message that the organization wants to put across. A basic message or idea can be successfully communicated with radio or television media (although in practice this is rare), whereas more detailed information, for example, timetable or flights material, needs to be presented in the written form. As with the marketing to airlines, airports adopt various approaches to woo passenger to their airports. Most commonly, airports try to increase the consumer's awareness of flights and closeness of the airport by listing the destinations on offer or by focusing on the convenience of the public transport links. More specific messages may relate to a certain service or facility at the airport, particularly airport shopping, or a certain market segment, such as business travellers.

The ultimate aim of promotional and advertising activities is usually to sell a product, but the airport has a rather unique relationship with its passengers as it is not directly selling a product to them. The passenger will not go to the airport unless the required airline service is there and marketing communication techniques can usually only encourage use at the margins. Similarly, the quality of commercial facilities is unlikely to have an impact over a passenger's choice of airport unless perhaps the passenger is transferring flights or the incentives are very considerable – as with the high-value raffles at the airports serving Dubai, Bahrain, and Abu Dhabi.

Airports, of course, have a major impact on the local community not only by providing local flights for the residents, but also by generating jobs and other economic benefits. However, the environmental impacts such as noise and pollution are of major concern. Generally, the aviation industry being the newest of all transport modes still holds a fascination and wonder for some and a fear for others. For all these reasons, airports tend to receive extensive coverage, both favourable and otherwise in the press. It is worthwhile for airports to put reasonable effort into trying to capitalize on the general interest that people have with airports and to create a degree of goodwill between the airports and the community, particularly should anything go wrong. Developing good links with local, regional, national, and, in some cases, foreign media is crucial, and hosting events for journalists and travel writers can increase interest in the airport and stimulate press coverage. Arranging school visits and other trips will also be an essential public relations activity.

Market research

A fundamental element of marketing is market research in order that organizations can have a thorough understanding of the characteristics and needs of their market. Most research will cover two areas, namely market characteristics in terms of market size, share, segmentation, and trends, and the more subjective area of passenger satisfaction. Chapter 4 has already considered passenger satisfaction and so the emphasis of the discussion here is very much on the first area. In practice, many small airports will not have the resources to undertake all the market research which is needed and so strategic partnerships with tourism and regional development agencies may be vital so that resources can be pooled.

When any airport is considering route development prospects such as the identification of new routes or enhanced frequency opportunities, there are a number of data sources which may be consulted (Table 7.9). Passenger volume data is easily available from the airport itself, and

Table 7.9 Types of data used for route development research

Type of data	Typical sources	Information obtained
Airport traffic data	Airport or government departments	Passenger, freight and aircraft volumes
Airport passenger survey data	Airport or government departments	Passenger characteristics such as origin/destination, purpose and frequency of travel, socio-economic group, etc.
Tourism data	United Nations World Tourism Organization (UNWTO), tourist boards or government departments	Tourist numbers and tourist/trip characteristics
Airline booking and sales data	Computer Reservation System Market Information Data Tapes (CRS-MIDT)	Travel details such as passenger origin/destination, connecting airports, routing patterns
Airline schedule data	Official airline guide (OAG), airlines	Current routes, frequencies/schedules and seat capacity data

in addition many airports undertake periodic surveys of their passengers to find out details such as origin and destination, age, sex, socio-economic group, flying frequency, and so on (these surveys may be tied in with the quality surveys described in Chapter 4 so that correlations between passenger profiles and levels of satisfaction can be made). In some countries, surveys may be undertaken by the national civil aviation authorities or government transport departments instead of, or in addition, to those carried out by the airport operators. For example, in the United Kingdom, the CAA regularly surveys passengers at all main airports. This has the advantage in producing survey data that are directly comparable for different airports.

Information about the characteristics of existing travellers may also be obtained from tourism statistics which may be available from local or national government agencies or from the United Nations World Tourism Organization (UNWTO). Whilst these can give an indication of the volume of tourists and current trends, they may have limited use if they are not available by mode of transport and if they are not available for outbound as well as inbound flows. Booking data from the Computer Reservation System Market Information Data Tapes (MIDT) can be useful in picking up the true origin and destination of passengers which may not be possible from other sources but there are a number of shortcomings with this data. It does not cover tickets sold through direct distribution channels such as airline call centres and internet sites and so does not provide a complete coverage – particularly with the trend towards more direct internet selling. Also with MIDT data it is assumed the place of issuance of the ticket represents the passenger's residency but in many cases now travel agencies process bookings through a centralized office which will invalidate this assumption. Moreover the cost of obtaining such information may be beyond the reach of many airport marketing department budgets.

Most of the market analysis that is undertaken is based on revealed preference techniques, that is, by assessing the passenger's current behaviour to determine future travel patterns. The alternative is to use stated preference techniques when passengers are asked to state their preference between a number of different scenarios. The techniques have been used to look at airport choice and also transport modal choice for surface access. For instance, passengers might be asked how they would trade-off higher journey cost to an airport compared with journey time. Such information can give airports invaluable insight into how passengers rate the factors that influence passenger choice. While stated preference techniques are widely used for other transport modes, their application within the airport industry is more limited. Manchester airport was one of the first airports to use such techniques in the mid-1980s (Swanson, 1998). More recently the UK CAA undertook a stated preference survey at Stansted airport which helped to estimate the price elasticities of these passengers (CAA, 2005).

More in-depth information about current services and particularly any underserved destinations can also be gleaned from passengers and other organizations such as travel agents, local businesses, and freight forwarders. For example the marketing department at Southampton airport formed a group of frequent business travellers called 'High Flyers' which met at least four times a year to discuss future developments at the airport. It also had periodic meetings with the travel and aviation press (the 'Scoops' group) and the local corporate travel agents (the 'Dirty Dozen') as well as current and prospective airlines.

Most airports, particularly in the regions, refer to the surrounding population and economy that they serve as their catchment area. This is the area where most of the local traffic comes from and so will be where airports concentrate their marketing effort. The most basic approach to define a catchment area is by using a certain drive time period criteria – typically 1 hour. This area can be called the primary catchment area where most travellers are likely to consider the airport their first choice based on proximity. Isochromes of longer times may represent weaker or secondary catchment areas where the airport will not necessarily this time be the first choice. The size of the catchment area and the proportion of it which is likely to fly will depend on factors such as the quality of the road network, the economic, business, and tourist activity within the area, the demographic characteristics of the residents and past immigration patterns, and the competing services at other airports. Improvements in the road infrastructure or public transport, or new or additional services at neighbouring airports, can significantly alter the catchment size. The catchment area is a dynamic rather than static measure that has to be constantly reviewed and revised. It also changes depending on the destination being assessed. Many regional airports have overlapping catchment areas. Usually for short-haul travel to popular destinations there may be considerable competition from other airports and so the catchment area will probably be comparatively small. For less popular or longer distance destinations there is likely to be less competition and so the catchment area will be extended over a greater area. The notion of catchment areas for large capital city airports is not generally so applicable since in many cases these airports may offer the only link to the destination under question in the whole country.

A number of LCCs have been particularly successful in attracting passengers from much wider catchment areas than other airlines because of the lower prices which they offer. For example, Dennis (2004) describes how Stansted originally operated as a regional airport for East Anglia but has now been transformed into a major airport serving the London area. Another example cited is Charleroi where only 16 per cent of Ryanair passengers resident at the Charleroi end of services come from the natural catchment area of the airport. Pantazis and Liefner (2006) also observe how LCCs have enlarged the catchment area of Hanover. However Dennis observes how catctment areas can contract as the provision of low-cost services increases – giving the example of the low-cost service to Barcelona from East Midlands which began in 2002 but two years later had competing services from the nearby airports of Leeds/Bradford, Birmingham and Manchester.

For airports that attract many business travellers, market research related to the size of nearby businesses and any new developments can prove very useful in helping to assess the levels of future demand. For example, at London City in 2006, 64 per cent of all passengers through the airport travelled for business purposes, with 59 per cent of the passengers working for banking and finance organizations. Thirty per cent of all passengers had full economy/business/first tickets as opposed to only 22 per cent at Heathrow and 4 per cent at Gatwick. The passenger profile of these business travellers with the majority being male travellers of high socio-economic group traveling alone is very different from the profile of the more leisure focused Luton airport which is not that far away (Tables 7.10 and 7.11). Table 7.12 shows the main originating areas of the passengers and shows the reasons why the airport thinks the demand for business travel – both currently and in the future – will be so strong.

Once airport operators are able to define the catchment area they are then able to quantify the market size and assess the traffic leakages or diversions. Leakages occur when passengers use neighbouring airports or indirect services to get to a destination rather than flying direct due to factors such as insufficient airline capacity or frequencies, higher air fares, or a lack of non-stop services at the airport in question. As discussed this may be able to be measured from airport surveys or MIDT data. For example Aeroporti di Roma

Table 7.10 Passenger profile at London City airport, 2006

	%			%			%
Journey purpose			**Socio economic group –**			**Sex**	
UK residents business	40		**UK business passengers**			Male	66
Foreign residents	24		A/B		85	Female	34
business			C1		14		
UK residents leisure	21		C2		1	**Group size**	
Foreign residents	15		D/E		0	Alone	78
Leisure			Total		100	2	17
Total	100					3–4	3
			Socio economic group – UK			Other	2
Flight type			**leisure passengers**			Total	100
Scheduled International	74		A/B		63		
Charter International	0		C1		26		
Domestic	26		C2		6		
Total	100		D/E		5		
			Total		100		

Source: Civil Aviation Authority (2007).

Table 7.11 Passenger profile at London Luton airport, 2006

	%			%			%
Journey purpose			**Socio economic group –**			**Sex**	
UK residents business	15		**UK business passengers**			Male	50
Foreign residents business	5		A/B		67	Female	50
UK residents leisure	58		C1		28		
Foreign residents leisure	21		C2		4	**Group size**	
Total	100		D/E		1	Alone	54
			Total		100	2	32
Flight type						3–4	6
Scheduled International	76		**Socio economic group –**			Other	8
Charter International	8		**UK leisure passengers**			Total	100
Domestic	16		A/B		38		
Total	100		C1		37		
			C2		12		
			D/E		13		
			Total		100		

Source: Civil Aviation Authority (2007).

calculated that 2.8 million passengers flew towards their final destination through other European hubs as there were no direct flights from Rome. For North America this leakage rate was 52 per cent (1.6 million passengers) for the Far East 25 per cent (0.4 million passengers) for Central/South America 59 per cent (0.4 million passengers), Africa 78 per cent (0.2 million passengers) and for the Middle East

Table 7.12 Main catchment areas of London City airport, 2006

Docklands/Canary Wharf	City of London/Westminster
28% originating passengers in 2006	**16% (City of London), 14% (Westminster) originating passengers in 2006**

Canary Wharf

- London's new business and financial district
- 10 minutes from City and LCY
- 738 000 m^2 of offices and shops
- 500 000 m^2 being built
- 180 000 currently in design stage
- 400 000 available for future use
- 3.1 million workers lie within 1 hours' commute of Canary Whalf and LCY
- Working population 90 000

Docklands

- Canary Wharf just one part of Docklands
- Millennium quarter (500 000 m^2 office space)
- Royal's business park (150 000 m^2 office space)
- Excel 65 000 m^2 exhibition hall (55 000 m^2 additional space to be developed)
- Silvertown Quays 92 000 m^2 commercial development and 14 000 m^2 aquarium (expected to be a major international tourist attraction)
- Other developments include Galleons Reach (major new shopping centre), Peruvian Wharf (100 000 m^2 office, retail and hotel space)

City of London

- 331 000 people work in City 80% in financial services
- 264 foreign banks
- 8 million m^2 office space exists
- 327 000 m^2 under construction
- 1 107 000 m^2 awaiting planning approval

Westminster

- 565 000 people employed – largest UK employment district
- 32% in business and financial services
- 47 000 businesses

Source: Lavelle (2008).

29 per cent (0.2 million passengers) (Aeroporti di Roma, 2008). More detailed analysis on a route by route basis would then enable the airport to identify potential routes, assess their feasibility and prioritize route development opportunities.

Competition and marketing issues at the Irish airports

There have been a number of interesting competition and marketing issues at the Irish airports which make it a valid case study. In 1937, the Irish state owned company Aer Rianta was established as a holding company for the national carrier Aer Lingus. It also took control of Dublin airport with this becoming a statutory responsibility in 1950. Then in 1969 it also took over the management of Cork and Shannon airport and in 1988 Aer Rianta International was established to pursue international projects (see Chapter 6). The three airports handle over 95 per cent of all air traffic to, from and within the Irish Republic and Dublin airport accounts for around 80 per cent of all the traffic of the three airports. Traffic rose rapidly in the late 1990s, very much helped by the economic boom which was occurring at the time (Figure 7.1) (McLay and Reynolds-Feighan, 2006).

During these early years, Aer Rianta had one of the most complex published discount schemes in existence at the time (Table 7.13). The airport operator gave discounts on new routes and growth on existing routes, which reduced over time. In the initial years, airlines could be paying as little as 10 per cent of the standard landing and passenger charge. Various airlines, especially Ryanair, benefited significantly from this scheme – particularly because of the short-haul nature of their services and the price sensitivity of their leisure passengers (Table 7.14). However Aer Rianta terminated their discount scheme at the end of 1999, largely in preparation for the demise of EU duty- and tax-free sales. This was greeted with considerable opposition from the airlines, particularly Ryanair who announced that it would abandon any new route development from Dublin. As a consequence the Commission for Aviation Regulation was established in 2001 and the level of fees are now controlled with an RPI-X single till approach. However the level of fees has continued to be a very controversial area with both the airport operator and the airlines (particularly Ryanair) being critical of the Regulator's decisions.

This unsatisfactory situation has played a major role in encouraging the government to explore market-based alternatives to this heavy handed regulation. Whilst privatization has been discussed at various times, this option has not become a reality. However a less radical move was introduced by the State Airports Act of 2004 which created the Dublin Airport Authority (DAA) to replace Aer Rianta and also established new authorities for Shannon and Cork. These two airports now have separate boards of directors and have been authorized under the Act to prepare business plans which will lead to full separation from DAA but as yet this has not happened as a number of issues, particularly as regards debt restructuring, need to be resolved. The split was welcomed by a number of the airlines including Ryanair, but heavily criticized by management and the trade unions who feared it would weaken the company and lead to job losses in Cork and Shannon.

At the same time, for a number of years there has been the issue of a second terminal at Dublin. Ryanair argued that it should have the right to run its own separate terminal rather than to put up with what it claimed to be the costly and inefficient operation of Aer Rianta, which had led to the unjustified high charges. Partly as a result of this pressure and because of the need for extra capacity due to the high growth rates, in

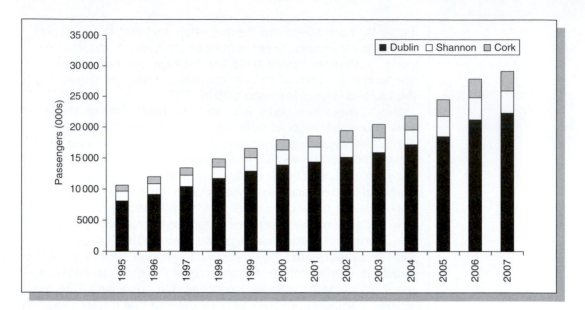

Figure 7.1
Passenger traffic at Irish airports 1995–2007.
(*Source*: Annual Reports.)

Table 7.13   New growth and new route discounts available at Aer Rianta airports, 1994–1999

	Discount rate (%)					
	1994	**1995**	**1996**	**1997**	**1998**	**1999**
New growth – landing and Passenger fees						
93–94 growth	80a	70	60	50	40	30
95–94 growth		80	70	60	50	40
96–95 growth			90	90	70	70
97–96 growth				90	90	70
98–97 growth					90	90
99–98 growth						90
New route – passenger, landing, and parking fees	80	80	90	90	90	90

aPassenger fees only.
Source: Aer Rianta.

2002 the Irish Government asked for expressions of interest from organizations which might wish to develop an independent/competing terminal at Dublin airport. Thirteen companies responded including international airport groups and airlines.

Table 7.14   Discounts given to each airline at Aer Rianta airports, 1998–2001

	% of initial calculated charges			
	1998	**1999**	**2000**	**2001 (to October)**
Dublin				
Aer Lingus	32.5	30.2	9.6	7.7
Ryanair	50.3	44.0	13.3	11.8
British Midland	34.0	32.4	8.0	7.0
Lufthansa	29.7	20.7	6.6	2.5
Shannon				
Aer Lingus		40.4	14.6	14.3
Ryanair			23.8	30.7
Cork				
Aer Lingus		45.8	21.6	4.9
Ryanair		28.3	3.5	16.7

Source: Doganis (2002).

Table 7.15   New route discounts available at Shannon and Cork airports on passenger, landing and parking fees in 2008

	Year 1	**Year 2**	**Year 3**	**Year 4**	**Year 5**
Shannon	70	60	40	20	0
Cork	100	80	60	40	20

Source: Shannon and Cork Airport.

The government appointed an independent panel to scrutinize these proposals and advise on the feasibility of the concept and in 2003 this panel decided in favour of an independent terminal. It concluded that this could bring effective competition at Dublin through increased capacity and quality of service (Department of Transport, 2003).

This was followed by the Irish Government approving the building of a new terminal in 2005 which would be commissioned by the DAA and would have a tender process to select an operator for the new terminal. So although the principle of having the second terminal being operated on a competitive process was accepted, the recommendation of the panel of 2003 to also have this terminal designed, built and owned

Table 7.16 Cork airport marketing support development criteria 2008

1. Network development potential	New market
	Existing market
2.	New country 1st applicant
	New country 2nd applicant
	Country already served
3.	New region within country
	Region within a country already served
4.	New route 1st applicant
	New country 2nd applicant
	Existing route
5.	Direct routing
	Indirect routing
6. Operator commitment to Shannon/Cork	Single route
	Double route
	Group of routes (over 3)
	Aircraft based at Shannon/Cork
	Predatory route entry
7. Commercial potential	Long-haul
	Short-haul
8.	EU
	Non-EU
9. Aircraft capacity	> 200 seats
	101–199
	50–100
	0–49
10. Capacity origin	Redeployed from another route
	New capacity
	Traffic switching from another airline
11. Congestion effect	All peak operations
	Some peak operations
	No peak operations
12. Route support	Receiving discounts
	Not receiving discounts
13. Seasonality	Year round
	Seasonal
14. Tourism potential	High (over 60% foreign originating)
	Medium (between 36% and 59%)
	Low (35% and under foreign originating)

Source: Cork airport.

separately was not adopted. Whilst DAA welcomed this decision, Ryanair opposed it claiming that this would mean that the terminal would be too costly and badly designed. This meant that when planning approval was granted in October 2006, a number of parties, including Ryanair appealed against this decision. In August 2007 planning permission for the terminal was confirmed (although only for the first phase) but Ryanair appealed against this decision to the High Court. This appeal was rejected in January 2008 and the terminal is now in the process of being built for a planned opening in 2010.

After 9/11 new discount schemes were introduced to stimulate new routes and they are still in existence today at Cork and Shannon. Discounts on all charges are given for 4 years at Shannon airport and 5 years at Cork (Table 7.15). Marketing support is also offered on routes that meet certain criteria which are shown in Table 7.16. Three levels of support are possible related to this criteria at Shannon airport (€10 000–€25 000; €25 000–€50 000; over €50 000) and four levels are available at Cork (up to €10 000; €10 000–€25 000; €25 000–€50 000; over €50 000). Elsewhere at Dublin a decision was made in 2005 to focus the route support scheme on the development of non-EU routes. However in 2007 this was suspended pending a review because of uncertainties relating to the operation of the airport, including the construction of the second terminal.

References and further reading

ACI-Europe (1999). *ACI Europe Policy Paper on Airport Competition.* ACI-Europe.

Aeroporti di Roma (2008). *Aviation marketing*, available from www.adr.it (accessed 5 March 2008).

Aviation Strategy (2001). *Ryanair, Just Too Good a Negotiator*, July–August, 3.

Catan, T. (2007). Budget flyers face the long haul – but only after they have landed. *The Times*, August 29, 27.

Caves, R. and Gosling, G. (1999). *Strategic Airport Planning.* Elsevier.

Civil Aviation Authority (CAA) (1999). *Passengers at Gatwick, Heathrow and Manchester airports.* CAA, CAP 703.

Civil Aviation Authority (CAA) (2001). Passengers at Gatwick, Heathrow, London City, Luton, Stansted, Manchester, Bournemouth, Bristol, Cardiff, Exeter and Southampton airports in 2000, CR00, I: CAA.

Civil Aviation Authority (CAA) (2005). *Demand for Outbound Leisure Air Travel and Its Key Drivers.* CAA.

Civil Aviation Authority (CAA) (2006). *Airports Review – Policy Update.* CAA.

Civil Aviation Authority (CAA) (2007). *CAA Passenger Survey Report 2006*. CAA.

Competition Commission (2002). *A Report on the Economic Regulation of Manchester Airport plc*. The Stationery Office.

Cranfield University (2002). *Study on Competition Between Airports and the Application of State Aid Rules*. Cranfield University.

Dennis, N. (2004). Can the European low cost airline boom continue? Implications for regional airports, 44th European Congress of the Regional Science Association, Porto, August.

Department for Transport (2008a). *Decision on the regulatory status of Manchester airport*, available from www.dft.gov.uk (accessed 8 March 2008).

Department for Transport (2008b). *Decision on the regulatory status of Stansted airport*, available from www.dft.gov.uk (accessed 8 March 2008).

Department of Transport (2003). *Dublin Airport – Review of Expressions of Interest for an Independent Terminal – Panel Report to Minister for Transport*. Department of Transport.

Eady, T. (2007). *Developing a Travel Product for Regional Airports*. London: University of Westminster Regional and Low Cost Air Transport, July.

easyJet (2005). *easyJet just keeps getting bigger and bigger!* Available from www.easyjet.com/en/newairports (accessed 21 September 2005).

European Commission (2004). Commission's decision of 12 February 2004 concerning advantages granted by the Walloon region and Brussels South Charleroi airport to the airline Ryanair in connection with its establishment at Charleroi. OJ L 137, 30 April.

European Commission (2005). Community guidelines on financing of airports and start-up aid to airlines departing from regional airports. OJ C 312, 9 December.

Favotto, I. (1998). Not all airports are created equal. *Airports World*, December, 17–18.

Freathy, P. and O'Connell, F. (2000). Market segmentation in the European airport sector. *Marketing Intelligence and Planning*, 18(3), 102–111.

Forsyth, P. (2006). Airport competition: Regulatory issues and policy implications Lee, D. (Ed.), *Competition Policy and Anti-trust*. Elsevier.

Foster, C. (1984). Privatising British airports: What's to be gained? *Public Money*, March, 19–23.

Graham, A. (2006). Competition in airports, Papatheodorou, A. (Ed.), *Corporate Rivalry and Market Power: Competition Issues in the Tourism Industry*. I.B.Tauris.

Gillen, D. and Lall, A. (2002). The economics of the internet, the new economy and opportunities for airports. *Journal of Air Transport Management*, 8, 49–62.

Halpern, N. (2008). Lapland's airports: facilitating the development of international tourism in a peripheral region. *Scandinavian Journal of Hospitality and Tourism*, 8(2).

Humphreys, I. (1998). *Commercialization and privatization: the experience of Cardiff Airport. Department of Maritime Studies and International Transport Occasional Paper No 49*. University of Wales.

Humphreys, I. (1999). Privatization and commercialization: changes in UK airport ownership patterns. *Journal of Transport Geography*, 7, 121–134.

Jarach, D. (2005). *Airport Marketing*. Ashgate.

Jossart, L. (2006). *The airport's relationship with low cost carriers*. University of Westminster/Cranfield University Airport Economics and Finance Symposium, April.

Kotler, P. and Armstrong, G. (2006). *Principles of Marketing* 11th edn. Pearson Prentice Hall.

Lavelle, B. (2008). *Airport marketing*. University of Westminster Marketing and Market Research for Air Transport London, February.

McLay, P. and Reynolds-Feighan, A. (2006). *Competition between airport terminals: The issues facing Dublin airport*, Transportation Research Part A 40, 181–203.

Morrell, P. (2003). *Airport competition or network access?* A European perspective, German Aviation Research Seminar, Leipzig, November.

Office of Fair Trading (OFT) (2006). *UK Airports: Report on the Market Study and Proposed Decision to Make a Market Investigation Reference*. OFT.

Pantazis, N., and Liefner, I. (2006). The impact of low-cost carriers on catchment areas of established international airports: The case of Hanover airport. *Germany. Journal of Transport Geography*, 14, 265–272.

Productivity Commission (2007). *Review of Price Regulation of Airport Services*. Productivity Commission.

Starkie, D. (2002). Airport regulation and competition. *Journal of Air Transport Management*, 8, 37–48.

Starkie, D. and Thompson, D. (1984). Privatising London airports, London: Institute for Fiscal Studies.

STRAIR (2005). *Air Service Development for Regional Development Agencies*. STRAIR.

Swanson, J. (1998). *The Use of Stated Preference Techniques*. London: University of Westminster Demand Analysis and Capacity Management Seminar, October.

Toms, M. (2004). UK regulation from the perspective of BAA plc, Forsyth, P., Gillen, D., Knorr, A., Mayer, O., Niemeier, H. and Starkie, D. (Eds.), *The Economic Regulation of Airports*. Ashgate: Aldershot.

Weatherill, J. (2006). North American airline incentives: Best practices and emerging trends. *Journal of Airport Management*, 1(1), 25–37.

Young, D. (1996). *Knowing your customer*. ACI Europe Good Communication and Better Airport Marketing, April.

CHAPTER 8

The economic and social impact of airports

The wider picture

The focus of this book now shifts in the next two chapters from the internal environment within which the airport operates to considering the wider consequences of the airport business. This chapter looks at the economic and social impact of airports while the next chapter discusses the environmental effects. A key issue for any airport operator is how to optimize the economic potential of an airport while providing acceptable environmental protection. This may be a particular problem when the economic benefits of airport development may be perceived as being the most relevant within a regional or national context, whereas the negative environmental impacts may be mostly felt by the local community.

An increasing number of airports are now undertaking economic impact studies. They are doing this for a number of reasons. They want to inform debates about strategic economic investment and to make the economic case for investment in new airport facilities or off-site infrastructure such as roads or rail links. Alternative expansion options may be evaluated with consideration of the relative economic benefits, which they will bring. Impact studies may be used for planning purposes to assess whether there is enough land for new commercial projects in the vicinity of the airport or whether there is sufficient supply of labour and associated housing to support such developments. Impact information may also be used for lobbying purposes, to gain regulatory approval, for example, for more direct services. Moreover such studies can have an important public relations role in educating policy-makers, airport users, and the general public of the economic value of airports.

There are basically two types of economic impacts on airports. First, there is income, employment, capital investment, and tax revenues which airport operations can bring by nature of the fact that they are significant generators of economic activity. Second, there are the wider catalytic or spin-off benefits, such as inward investment or the development of tourism, which can occur as the result of the presence of the airport. This can contribute to the economic development of the area surrounding the airport. Thus, within an economic context airports have a role to play both by being a significant economic activity in their own right and by supporting business and tourism activity.

Economic impacts are measured in a various ways. A key indicator is the number of jobs generated. This is the most readily understandable measure and can easily be used to determine an airport's relative importance within an economy. In addition, there is the 'income', 'earnings', or 'gross value added' measure. This is the value that the airport dependent activities add to the economy in terms of wages, salaries, interest, and profits. This indicator can be related to an area's total income or GDP to assess the relative contribution that the airport has on wealth generation. Then there is the economic/business activity or output measure which is the sum of the gross revenues of all the businesses which depend on the airport. Indicators related to capital investment and tax revenues can also be considered.

Airports as generators of economic activity

Economic effects can be classified as direct, indirect, and induced impacts. The direct or primary impact is the employment and income generated by the direct operation of the airport. This is the most obvious economic impact and is the most easily measured one. This impact is associated with the activities of the airport operator itself, the airlines, the concessionaires providing commercial facilities, the handling agents and other agencies, which provide services such as air traffic control, customs and immigration, and security. Some of these activities, such as car parking, car hire, in-flight catering, freight forwarders, and hotels may actually be located off-site, in the surrounding area of the airport.

However, the economic impact of an airport is not just limited to these direct, airport-related effects – although this is the impact which is most frequently quantified and studied. The role of the suppliers to the airport industry also needs to be considered. This requires an examination of the indirect impact, which is defined as the employment and income generated in the chain of suppliers of goods and services to the direct activities that are located both at and in the vicinity of the airport. These types of activities include the utilities and fuel suppliers, construction and cleaning companies, and food and retail good suppliers. In addition, the impact that these direct and indirect activities have on personal spending also needs to be taken into account. This so-called induced impact can be defined as the employment and income generated by the spending of incomes by the direct and indirect employees on local goods and services such as retail, food, transport, and housing. The indirect and induced effects are combined often known as the secondary effects (Figure 8.1).

These indirect and induced impacts are clearly much more difficult to measure, involving an understanding of how the airport interacts with other sectors within the economy. Their combined impact can be measured by the economic multiplier. This concept takes account of the successive rounds of spending that arise from the stimulus of the direct impacts and assumes that one individual's or organization's spending becomes another individual's or organization's income in the next round. Some of the money spent on airport-related activities will be re-spent on purchases from suppliers of goods and services – the indirect effect – with a proportion of this leaking out of the economy as imports. Much of the remainder will be spent on labour or will go to the government in the form of taxes. The suppliers will then make purchases locally, import goods and services, distribute wages and salaries, and pay government taxes. During each round of

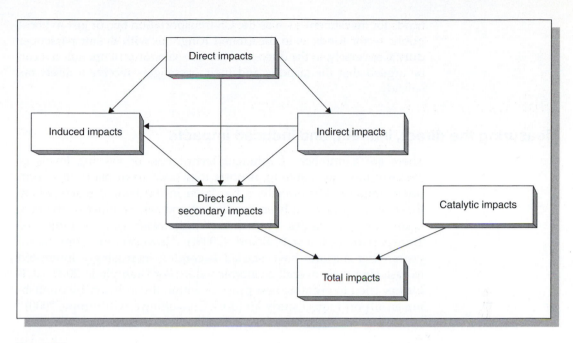

Figure 8.1
The economic impact of airports.

spending, a certain proportion of the money will accrue to local residents in the form of wages, salaries, and profits. Some of this money will then be re-spent again producing the induced effects. The rest will be saved and not re-circulated within the economy. Eventually, the successive rounds of spending will become so small that they will be considered negligible. The multiplier analysis thus quantifies the economic value and jobs of the financial transactions, which take place within any economy.

There will be new investment associated with these direct, indirect, and induced activities in the form of airport facilities, computer systems, maintenance facilities, offices, and so on. Airport activities can also have a significant impact on local, regional, and national government revenues. Employees will pay income tax, and sales transactions will be subject to sales or value added taxes. Airports, particularly in the private sector, will probably also be subject to other taxes such as property or land taxes and business or corporation taxes. Some airports in the public sector may be exempt from these but instead they may pass over a considerable share of their profits to their government owners. In return, of course, many government owners have traditionally allocated considerable public sector funds to aid airport development. Then there are the taxes collected through airport charges. These may be required to cover some specific airport service such as immigration and public health inspection as in the United States, to provide funds for investment such as the US transportation tax, or just to boost public sector funds as in the United Kingdom with the air passenger duty. Conversely, in the duty- and tax-free sales area of operation it can be argued that the airports and their passengers receive a direct tax subsidy.

Measuring the direct, indirect, and induced impacts

There are a number of different techniques, of varying levels of sophistication, available to airports that want to measure their economic impacts. Historically, it has been in the United States where these techniques have been developed and where most of the economic impact studies have been undertaken (for example see Transportation Research Board (2008)). However, in more recent years other airports have started becoming increasingly interested in assessing their overall economic value. For example in 2000, ACI-Europe tried to promote best practice within the industry by publishing an airport impact study kit (York Consulting/ACI-Europe, 2000).

Direct impacts

Direct impacts are clearly the easiest of all the impacts to measure. Employers at the airport can be asked to provide details of their employees, how much they earn and where they live. Details concerning purchases of goods and services, location of suppliers, revenues, expenditures, and capital expenditure also need to be gathered. While such a process for on-site airport activities should not pose too many difficulties, the off-site data collection may be more difficult. First, a definition of 'off-site' needs to be established – a rule-of-thumb figure is an area within a 20-minute drive time (York Consulting/ACI-Europe, 2000). Then the relevant companies within this area need to be identified by taking into account the knowledge of the airport operator and other industrial bodies and, perhaps, by direct visual inspection. Many airports systematically measure the direct economic impacts, particularly the employment effects. For example, at London Heathrow airport, there is an annual spring census of all airport-related employers (the 'employer' survey), which produces total numbers of staff by type of employer. Then every few years BAA also undertakes a survey (the 'employee' survey) to find out the details of employee's characteristics such as home address, travel to work mode and nature of job undertaken.

The direct employment at an airport will vary according to a combination of factors such as the volume and structure of passenger traffic, the amount of freight and the actual capacity utilization of the airport. The role of the airport also has to be considered, for example, whether it is a major hub, whether it acts as a base for airline activity and whether it provides other opportunities such as office or other commercial development. A study of employment at European airports in 2001 showed that the airline and handling agents were, on average the largest employers at the airport, followed by the airport operators and concessionaires (York Aviation, 2004) (Figure 8.2). This was similar to the results of the previous study in 1996 which additionally found out that 80 per cent of the employees were male, although women made up 60 per cent of the part-time workforce (ACI-Europe, 1998).

For meaningful airport comparisons to be made, direct employment in the airport is related to the traffic throughput of an airport to produce an employment density figure. This is usually equivalent to the number of employees per million passengers per annum (jobs per mppa) or per WLU if freight is an important activity at the airport. A figure of 1000 jobs for every million passengers or WLUs equal to a density figure of 1000 tends to be the rule-of-thumb figure generally accepted by the industry, although it obviously masks wide variations in employment at different airports. Globally, in 2006 it has been estimated that there were 405 000 airport operator employees and a total of over 4 500 000 employed at the airport. This gave an overall employment density figure of 972 – the equivalent number in 2001 was 1616. For every person employed by an airport operator, there were another ten working for other companies at the airport. This ratio was much higher for the North American airports since many more activities are outsourced (Airports Council International, 2002, 2007).

Within Europe in 2001, jobs per million WLUs averaged around 950 compared with around 1120 in 1998. For the smaller airports in

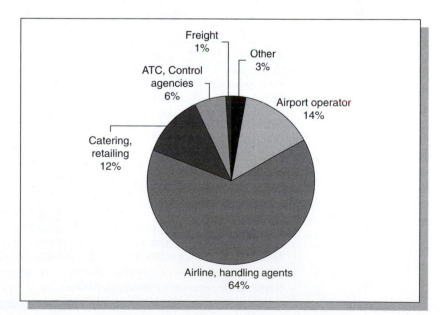

Figure 8.2
Employment at European airports in 2001.
(*Source*: York Aviation.)

2001, the average employment density was higher than the larger airports, which may be because they are unable to achieve economies of scale and also they may have airline or aircraft maintenance bases not directly related to the traffic at the airport. For example for airports of less than 1 million WLUs the figure was 1724 and for airports of 1–4 million it was 1034. By contrast for airports of 10–19 million WLUs it was 934 and for 20–49 million, it was 867. In general, three of the key factors affecting employment density are capacity utilization, the existence of airline bases, and development opportunities. This means that airports such as Malaga, Edinburgh, Gothenburg, Nice, and Cork have much lower values of employment density (350–600) because of limited development at the airports, high utilization, and no base airlines. In contrast, Paris CDG, Amsterdam, Frankfurt, and Copenhagen airports have high values of employment density (900–1200) because they are major airlines bases and have substantial development. The values at Cardiff and Hamburg airport are even higher mostly because of major maintenance facilities being located at these two airports (York Aviation, 2004). Also airports serving low cost carriers tend to have lower values of employment density because the number of airline staff employed by LCCs at the airport is kept to a minimum. Table 8.1 shows direct employment density for UK airports and although there is quite a considerable variation in the values, the average figure is 865 which is fairly close to the rule of thumb figure of 950–1000.

Table 8.1   Direct employment at UK airports

	Passengers (mn)	Direct employment	Jobs per 1 mn passengers
Aberdeen	2.64	2716	1029
Belfast City	2.13	807	379
Birmingham	8.86	9071	1024
Bristol	4.65	4747	1021
Cardiff	1.89	1932	1022
East Midlands	4.38	4512	1030
Edinburgh	8.02	2300	287
Gatwick	31.47	23761	755
Glasgow	8.58	5442	634
Heathrow	67.34	68427	1016
Luton	7.54	7756	1029
Manchester	21.25	18000	847
Newcastle	4.72	4855	1029
Stansted	20.91	10592	507
Other	20.63	21116	1024
Total	214.98	185900	865

Source: Oxford Economic Forecasting (2006).

Very often in using economic impact studies to support proposals for future development, airport operators will have to project their employment figures into the future. This will involve some assessment of the productivity gains, which are likely to occur. These productivity improvements are already occurring, with the global density shifting from 1616 to 972 and the European figure reducing from 1120 to 950. Future forecasts should be derived from historical trends and experiences elsewhere and should also take account of the changing demands on airport employment due to more stringent security and quality requirements but also technological developments such as self-service check-in. In addition reduction in airline employee numbers, not only because of more LCCs but also because of pressure on all airlines to decrease costs, needs to be considered as well as less labour involved with services such as in-flight catering because of a reduction in meal services being provided on aircraft. Any economies of scale that apply to labour productivity should be taken into account as well. For example, aircraft size may rise with traffic growth, which will increase staff productivity in certain areas, or alternatively low factors may rise without any increase in cabin crew being needed.

Irrespective of what assumptions are made for the future, it should be borne in mind, that whilst the promise of greater employment may be seen as a positive outcome of airport expansion in relatively underdeveloped areas; the views on airport employment may be different at a major established airport. In this case, the presence of the airport may very well mean that there is full employment in the region and hence extra job vacancies would be hard to fill. This may be the case especially as many of the jobs are not seen as being very attractive as they tend to be low skilled and may very well involve anti-social hours because of the 24-hour operations schedule at most of the airports.

Indirect and induced impacts

There are two main approaches for estimating the multiplier effect and measuring the indirect and induced impacts. The first method involves using multiplier values that have been calculated by using information which has been gathered from surveys of on-site and off-site employers and by making assumptions about the tax rate and the share of purchases which are imported.

A more sophisticated approach involves using an input–output model. This model looks at the linkages, which exist within any economy by considering the relationships between the different economic sectors (e.g. agriculture, manufacturing, construction, and services) within a certain area. This methodology involves constructing a transaction table which shows, in money terms, the input–output relationships for the sectors in the economy. Each sector is shown as a column representing purchases from other sectors and as a row representing sales to the other sectors. From this table, coefficients or multiplier values can be obtained for each economic activity. This technique will thus allow the impact of additional spending in any one specific economic activity to be identified sector by sector as well as for the area as a whole. One country which has extensive experience of using the input–output method to measure impacts is the United States. Since the 1980s, the Bureau of Economic Analysis in the Department of Commerce has been developing their regional input–output modelling system, RIMS II. This has been used widely to estimate regional impacts in both the public and private sector and forms the basis of many of the airport economic impact studies. The input and output structure of nearly 500 US industries is contained within the model (US Department of Commerce, 1997).

The choice of method will usually depend on the amount of data, which is available, and the resources which can be utilized. Clearly, the data requirements will be greatest for the input–output models, and this technique tends to be used only at a national or regional level. If a more local situation is being assessed, the other approach may be more appropriate, or there may be the option, with a considerable degree of caution, of adapting the national or regional input–output model.

At a global level for the overall air transport industry, it has been suggested that for every 1000 direct jobs, there are 1160 indirect jobs and 540 induced jobs. In addition it is estimated that these direct, indirect and induced impacts contribute to 2.4 per cent of GDP (Air Transport Action Group, 2005). More specifically within the European airport sector, it has been found that 1000 direct jobs support 2100 jobs nationally, 1100 jobs regionally or 500 jobs sub-regionally; the contribution to the economy was in the range of 1.4–2.5 per cent of GDP (York Aviation, 2004).

Clearly, these aggregate figures will hide significant variations, which exist between different airports. Individual values will depend on many factors such as the nature of the traffic at the airport, propensity to travel characteristics, employment sector mixes, and the role of the airport. They will also be related to the size of the economy under consideration, depending on whether the national, regional, or local situation is being assessed. The indirect impacts tend to increase with the size of the study area as this increases the likelihood of goods and services required by airport-related companies being supplied within the area, rather than being imported from outside. The choice of study area will depend primarily on the role and size of the airport and the reason for measuring the impact. Large capital city and main international airports tend to have such an important impact on the overall economy, that it makes sense to assess their impact within a national context. Specific issues, however, particularly related to the employment market, may be more appropriately considered at a regional or local level. The impacts of smaller airports clearly need to be considered within a narrower context.

Estimates for airports may vary quite widely because of the use of different terminology and methodology or the adoption of models of varying levels of sophistication. Even, in the United States where the FAA recommends procedures for identifying and quantifying the economic impacts of airports, there are substantial differences in the detailed methodologies used. Studies adopt different definitions of multipliers and interpret direct and indirect impacts in a number of ways. For example, sometimes all off-site impacts are considered as indirect impacts, irrespective of whether the activities are directly airport related or not. This makes it very difficult to compare multiplier values. Then there is the problem of how to treat any activities which are based at the airport but not actually related to airport operations. Very often the split of activities on and off-site will depend on whether the actual site is constrained or not.

One of the major areas of discrepancy is in the treatment of jobs associated with leisure and business tourists who arrive via the airport. These jobs in tourism industry activities are such as hotels, restaurants, attractions, conferences, and exhibitions. Some airports, particularly in the United States, treat these as indirect jobs, which can have a dramatic effect on the overall magnitude of indirect impacts. Other studies separately identify the visitor impacts, or adopt more qualitative approach to assessing this effect. Another area of inconsistency between airports occurs with the treatment of construction activities. Sometimes the temporary staff employed in the construction industry will be included in the impact figures and sometimes they are left out. When there is a major capital investment programme, such as a new runway or terminal, airports tend to identify the impacts separately to add additional support to the case for new capacity.

Using the United Kingdom as an example, it has been found that most regions support around 500 secondary jobs for each 1000 direct jobs, with the ratio of direct: secondary gross added value being closer to 3:1. However, for each region this relationship between direct and secondary effects can vary quite considerably – for both employment and gross value added – as can be seen from Table 8.2. As regards the split between indirect and induced impacts, overall in the United Kingdom it is estimated that the relationship between direct/indirect/induced jobs is 1/0.90/0.47. Travel agents are not included here and it is estimated that 1000 direct jobs additionally generate 440 travel agency jobs (Oxford Economic Forecasting, 2006). Around the world the relative share of direct/indirect/induced jobs varies considerably, which is probably as much to do with different methodologies and assumptions as it is to do with the different characteristics of airports and their surrounding regions. For example, recent studies at Singapore show these multipliers figures to be 1/0.82/0.76 as opposed to Houston and Vancouver airport where values 1/0.66/2.33 and 1/0.49/0.47 respectively have been calculated. At London Gatwick and Stansted airports the multiplier

Table 8.2 Employment and income impacts of UK airports on their 'home' regions in 2004

	Direct jobs	Secondary jobs	Direct: secondary jobs	Direct GVA[a] (£m)	Secondary GVA[a] (£m)	Direct: secondary GVA[a]
North East	4100	2800	1.46	246	78	3.15
North West	21800	20500	1.06	1306	580	2.25
Yorkshire	2100	1400	1.50	128	41	3.12
West Midlands	7200	2600	2.77	430	73	5.89
East Midlands	6500	4000	1.63	390	114	3.42
East England	20000	13900	1.44	1201	392	3.06
London	70000	47300	1.48	4260	1347	3.16
South East	26800	18100	1.48	1610	513	3.14
South West	6800	4600	1.48	410	131	3.13

[a] GVA = Gross value added.
Source: York Aviation (2005).

effects are estimated as being much smaller namely 1/0.06/0.25 and 1/0.1/0.27 respectively, which is more similar to the values at Louisville (1/0.20/0.48). At the small airport of Carcassone, indirect and induced employment of 5 and 10 times the direct impacts has been estimated. This clearly demonstrates the inappropriateness of generalizing and adopting some kind of rule of thumb measure in most cases since every airport is very different from each other.

Airports and economic development

As well as being a generator of economic activities in its own right, an airport can also play a role in attracting and sustaining wider economic activities in the surrounding area – both in terms of business and tourism development. This is the catalytic, magnetic, or spin-off impact. This impact can be defined as the employment, income, investment, and tax revenues generated by the wider role, which an airport can play by being an economic magnet for the region it serves. Airports can give a company easy assess to other parts of the company as well as to suppliers and customers, and can offer speed and security for goods being transported. Hence, airports can play an important role in influencing company location decisions. They can encourage inward investment and the relocations of businesses by attracting industries which rely on quick and convenient access to air services for both people and goods. These businesses will not rely directly on the airport for their operation, but they will prefer a location near an airport because of the accessibility benefits which can be gained. The existence of a business park or Airport City which exist in the surrounding area of a number of airports may be an additional factor that companies will take into account when choosing their location.

Airports can also help retain current businesses or encourage them to expand. Moreover, by providing access to a wide range of both passenger and freight services, an airport can enhance the competitiveness of the economy and can contribute to the success of the businesses located in the vicinity of the airport. In some cases, the airport can be the lifeline to local economies, as has been the situation in some developing countries in Africa and Latin America where air travel has enabled the export of fresh and perishable fruits and flowers to Western countries.

The trend towards globalization, both in terms of multinational companies and also in terms of increased reliance on imported components and products, has increased the importance of finding a location in the vicinity of an international airport. Some of the fastest growing knowledge-based industrial sectors such as computing, electronics, communications, and pharmaceuticals are the most international and are heavily reliant on air travel for the transportation of their high-value/low-weight products. The increasing reliance on just-in-time inventory systems for these expanding industries and more traditional sectors, such as car manufacturing, has meant that air travel has become a critical element for a quick and efficient distribution system and rapid delivery times. In short, airports have become increasingly more important for businesses operating in global marketplace.

In economically disadvantaged areas, where unemployment is high and there is a narrow declining economic base, airport development is often seen as a way of generating new employment, creating wealth and regenerating the area. These arguments are frequently used to gain approval for airport expansion or development. Airports undoubtedly play an integral part in economic development, and areas which are relatively inaccessible by air will be at a distinct economic drawback. Certain regions will find it difficult to attract inward investment if their airports have not reached the critical mass needed to provide an adequate range of services. Thus airports are often considered as a vital component of a regional development policy and can be viewed as giving a real advantage to competing regions. However, it is very difficult to formally establish the causality between the expansion of an airport and wider economic development (Caves and Gosling, 1999). Indeed in many cases it is impossible to establish whether it is the nature of the surrounding economy of an airport, in terms of wealth and population size and distribution, which has encouraged airlines to operate from the airport, rather or is it development of air services that have influenced the economy.

It is certainly true that investment in airport infrastructure is not usually sufficient in itself to generate sustained increases in economic growth. The ability of airports to generate jobs and attract new business should never be used as the main justification for new airport construction. The wider economic benefits will depend very much on the scale of the airport and, very critically, its ability to attract air services. In the end, it will be the airlines that will determine the success of an airport and its broader economic impacts, in choosing whether to operate from the airport or not. Their primary concerns will be whether sufficient passenger demand exists and the suitability of the airport's strategic and geographic location, and not the quality of the infrastructure (Graham and Guyer, 2000).

It is extremely difficult to isolate and quantify the economic effects which are caused by the presence of the airport from the wide range of other factors which affect a company's location decision. The exact location of any business activity will be only partially related to the existence of any nearby airport services, with other factors being the availability, quality and cost of any potential development sites, the nature of the local labour market, tax incentives, trade policies the supporting communications, and transport infrastructure. The situation is also made more complex by the fact that many economic regions are served by a number of airports, with either complementary or competing roles.

Airports can play a role in encouraging both business and leisure visitors to the surrounding area. There are many examples of countries, particularly in developing areas such as the Caribbean, Asia, and Pacific, where the tourism potential of a destination has only been realized after direct services and suitable airport infrastructure have been provided. The increase in the number of visitors may then have a spin-off effect on the income and employment generation in places related to the tourism industry, such as hotels, restaurants, attractions, conferences, and exhibitions. Tourism markets which are particularly dependent on air travel include package holiday travel, city break tourism, long-haul travel, and conference business. Also the low cost airlines, particularly in Europe, by flying to airports in relatively unknown regions have had the effect of transforming some of these into new tourism destinations. Table 8.3 shows some of these airports which have been served by LCCs.

Causality between airport growth and tourism development, as with business development, is very difficult to prove. For example, is it new air services at a resort which encourage new hotel development, or do more bed spaces encourage more frequent flights? Some impact studies, particularly in the United States, have a separate visitor impact category. An estimate of spending is often calculated by multiplying the numbers of visitors by average daily spend and length of stay. Other airports choose to categorize the visitors' impact as indirect. Admittedly, many of these tourism businesses will be reliant on air services for their tourism demand, but it is unlikely, except in an isolated island situation, that this tourism industry would not exist if a certain airport was not present. It thus seems rather inappropriate to include these tourism impacts as indirect impacts. Instead,

Table 8.3 European airports served by LCCs that have encouraged new international tourism flows

Country	Airport served
Austria	Graz, Linz, Klagenfurt
Belgium	Charleroi
Denmark	Esbjerg
Finland	Tampere
France	Bergerac, Rodez, Limogez, Carcassonne, Pau, La Rochelle, Nimes, St. Etienne, Tours, Poitiers, Dinard,
Germany	Karlsrhue-Baden, Altenburg, Hahn, Tempelhof, Münster (Osnabrück), Erfurt
Ireland	Knock, Derry, Kerry
Italy	Bari, Pescara, Ancona, Brindisi, Palermo, Alghero, Trieste
Norway	Haugesund
Poland	Gdansk, Poznan
Slovakia	Kosice
Spain	Bilbao, Girona, Jerez, Murcia, Santander, Valladolid, Zaragoza
Sweden	Malmo, Nyköping
United Kingdom	Blackpool, Bournemouth, Newquay

Source: European Low Fares Airline Association (2004).

it is more preferable to consider them alongside the catalytic impacts causing business development.

Since it is very difficult to prove any direct causality between airports and broader business and tourism development, it is not usually feasible or suitable to identify with any certainty the exact number of jobs, or the amount of income which is generated from these catalytic or spin-off impacts. Some studies have made some estimates by usually assuming that a certain proportion of jobs within the business and tourism industries in the vicinity of the airport exist because of the airport. Globally it is estimated that every 1000 direct jobs bring 3100 catalytic jobs with 1340 of these being tourism related (Air Transport Action Group, 2005). Within Europe such estimates have ranged from below 1000 jobs per mppa for airports such as Amsterdam, Birmingham, Brussels, and Oslo to above 2000 at Barcelona, Düsseldorf, and Newcastle airport in the United Kingdom. Therefore, the average figure comes to 1800 jobs per mppa (ACI-Europe, 1998). There is a danger, however, that by including crude estimates for these catalytic impacts, there is a possibility of reducing the credibility of the more accurate direct, indirect and induced impact measurements (York Consulting/ACI-Europe, 2000).

A more qualitative approach is often adopted which involves investigating factors such as the significance of the airport to location decision, competitiveness and business performance by surveying and holding discussions with relevant businesses. This is done in order to gain a closer understanding of the nature of the interaction between the airport and the wider elements in the local economy. For example, in a survey on the views of 500 European companies on leading business cities in 2007, 52 per cent stated that transport links with other cities and internationally were an absolutely essential factor for locating a business. Only three other factors, namely availability of qualified staff (62%), easy access to markets, customers and clients (58%), and quality of telecommunications (55%) were selected by a higher percentage of companies. Also the top five cities for external transport links with other cities, namely London, Paris, Frankfurt, Amsterdam, and Brussels, were rated as 1, 2, 3, 5, and 6 in terms of best cities for locating a business (Cushman and Wakefield, 2007). Likewise, a survey of 165 UK companies examined the most important factors in determining the country in which the organization chooses to invest and around 40 per cent stated that the air transport network was vital. Again only three other factors were selected by more organizations – size of local market, availability of skilled labour and the extent of government regulations on business (Oxford Economic Forecasting, 2006). Other more specific surveys have found that 31 per cent of companies relocating to the airport around Munich airport cited the airport as the primary factor in their location decision and 80 per cent of businesses in the Hamburg area reported air service connections as important to getting customers to look at their products. At London City airport, 70 per cent of businesses stated that air services were critical for business travel (York Aviation, 2004).

Trends in business and leisure tourism can be investigated in a similar manner with the importance of the role of the airport discussed among industry experts. A difficulty with this interview approach is to ensure that respondents give genuine comments. They will often have a very positive but perhaps not totally realistic view of the value of new air services, for example, since the respondents will bear no direct costs associated with the new services but may benefit from the gains. Alternatively, the impact of opening up specific new routes can be considered in order to see how air services directly impact on business or tourism development (Button and Taylor, 2000). For example in the San Diego region it has been estimated that a new domestic flight would produce an additional annual visitor spending about $1.7 million which would not have occurred if there was no new flight (i.e. these visitors would not have used other means such as connecting flights or other modes to travel to the region). For an international flight, this figure is $5.4 million (San Diego International Airport, 2008).

In assessing the impact that airports have on the wider economy, it is the net benefits which should be considered (Caves and Gosling, 1999). For example, airports cannot only encourage visitors to the local region but can also enable local residents to holidays abroad rather than staying in their own locality. Similarly, the availability of nearby direct air services may increase the use of imported goods and services at the expense of local products. The impacts should also ideally be compared with possible alternative, non-airport-related, economic activities with an assessment being made of the comparative economic benefits and opportunity costs. Alternative developments could have a better overall impact on the economy. The crossover effects on other industries, for example, the impact on other modes of transport, also needs to be considered. Increased industrial and economic activity around an airport may merely be draining resources from other areas, such as city centres. The negative or adverse potential impacts of airport development, such as extensive urbanization and industrialization, overheating of the economy and consequences of local labour shortages, also need to be taken into account. The overall impact on the local community of tourism development related to aviation activity also needs to be assessed. The positive effects may not be very substantial if the tourism industry has to be supported by a substantial level of imports and foreign investment.

Table 8.4 illustrates a selection of economic impact measures for the two Washington airports and the airports of Miami. The two studies have been undertaken separately so the methods may not be totally consistent and for comparative purposes, the measures have been divided by passenger throughput. Washington National airport has the least jobs per mppa primarily because of the domestic nature of the passengers and less involvement in other activities such as freight. Between 1998 and 2005, the direct jobs per mppa at Dulles and National airports of Washington have reduced from 992 to 719 and 646 to 514 respectively – which again demonstrates the labour productivity gains in recent years. The visitor activities in theses airports are identified separately and so the impact of including them in the economic assessment is apparent. However as explained previously, if the airport was not there these places would still likely to be a considerable tourism industry and therefore these figures need to be viewed with caution. Likewise it is not known how many of the 1.9 million international tourists who used Nice Airport in France and generated €1.46 billion in 2001 would have visited the area if the airport had not been there (Nice Airport, 2008).

Aviation can clearly have a multitude of impacts on society as well. In the broadest context, it is often claimed that air travel brings wider benefits to society in the form of strengthening ethnic and cultural links between countries, enhancing opportunities for travel and increasing consumer choices for foodstuffs and other products. These are all very general impacts, which are extremely difficult to quantify or contribute to any one airport. In acting as a catalyst for economic development, airports will also have a major social impact on the surrounding area. Employment and living patterns will change with implications for housing, health, education, and other social needs. An over-heated economy associated with a successful airport development may bring problems of labour shortages, insufficient housing, and rising prices.

Table 8.4 Economic impacts at Washington Dulles, Washington Reagan National, and Miami International airports

	Jobs	Income (million US$)	Business revenue (million US$)	State and local taxes (million US$)	Jobs per mppa[a]	Income per ppa[b] (US$)	Business revenue per ppa[b] (US$)	State and local taxes per ppa[b] (US$)
Washington Dulles (2005) 27.0 million passengers								
Direct	19414	872	4626	224	719	32	171	9
Indirect	4077	1016	n/a	n/a	151	38	n/a	n/a
Induced	12076	194	n/a	n/a	447	7	n/a	n/a
Total	35567	2081	4626	224	1317	77	171	9
Visitors	194837	3902	7166	419	7216	145	265	16
Total	230404	5983	11792	643	8533	222	437	24
Washington Reagan National (2005) 17.8 million passengers								
Direct	9155	411	1845	102	514	23	103	6
Indirect	930	479	n/a	n/a	52	27	n/a	n/a
Induced	5696	43	n/a	n/a	320	2	n/a	n/a
Total	15781	933	1845	102	886	52	104	6
Visitors	122113	2446	4491	268	6860	137	252	15
Total	137894	3379	6336	370	7747	190	356	21
Miami International (2006) 32.5 million passengers								
Direct	35522	1593	11557	472	1093	49	356	15
Indirect	20828	746	n/a	n/a	641	23	n/a	n/a
Induced	23873	2379	n/a	n/a	735	73	n/a	n/a
Total	80223	4718	11557	472	2468	145	356	15
Visitors	187690	4850	13745	485	5775	149	423	15
Total	267913	9568	25302	957	8243	294	779	29

[a] mppa = million passengers per annum.
[b] ppa = passengers per annum.
Sources: Airport economic impact studies.

In addition to all these impacts, it must also be remembered that since airports can provide accessibility and mobility, they can have a major role in promoting social inclusion – especially for remote and island communities. These social impacts are very difficult to quantify but undoubtedly without such airports, certain communities would suffer and have a reduced quality of life. Airports can enable remote regions to have access to essential services such as hospitals and higher education. They can also make the communities more attractive places to work and can contribute to attracting and retaining skilled labour in the area. For example a survey of residents in the Highlands of Scotland found that 50 per cent felt that the existence of air services made the area a better place to live with 75 per cent agreeing that it made it less remote and 40 per cent saying that it made it more like that they would remain there (York Aviation, 2004).

Overall there is little doubt that airports have a substantial economic and social effect on the region in which they are located. Whilst concepts such as the multiplier or the catalytic effects are reasonably straightforward to understand, they are very difficult to actually quantify with any degree of confidence and there are still considerable inconsistencies in the terminologies and methodologies used. However, there is a growing need to develop more effective and accurate measures, not only so that airports can justify their existence when facing increasing pressure from the environmental lobby, but also so that incentives which are used to encourage economic development through air transport growth, can be used in the most effective way. The remaining part of this chapter now considers the nature of these incentives.

Incentives to encourage economic development

Chapter 7 has already described how various airport operators may offer financial and other incentives to encourage new carriers or more services. This may be undertaken purely to grow the airport business – particularly if the airport is privately owned. However if the airport is publicly owned such incentives may be adopted because of the broader catalytic impacts which additional services to the surrounding region may bring. Alternatively regional development agencies, chambers of commerce or tourists boards may directly contribute to supporting airline services. For example, Ryanair has developed a number of such arrangements with the regional and local authorities in Spain. In 2004 in Gerona, the Generalitat (local government), through its Departments of Commerce, Tourism and Consumer Affairs and Public Land and Development; the Gerona Government Council; the Gerona Chamber of Commerce, Industry and Navigation; and the Hotel Federation of the province signed an agreement for 2 years when €6.2 million was provided to the airline to help promote the Gerona region. Nearby in Reus €2 million was provided by a group of municipalities and the chamber of commerce. In Granada, it was agreed that €300 000 would be paid to the airline for a publicity and promotion campaign in 2005, rising to €700 000 in 2006 and €1 million in 2007. In return Ryanair guaranteed the arrival of a minimum of 90 000, 240 000, and 370 000 passengers in these 3 years respectively. This type of marketing aid, where the airline commits itself to promoting the destination – for example with links on its website, has the advantage of not being covered by the EC guides for state aid for airlines from regional airports (Travel Trade Gazette, 2005).

It is common practice for public bodies in North America to provide marketing support to airlines that offer new services. These so-called 'Co-op marketing funds' are used to promote the new air service at the same time as the region. Risk sharing mechanisms, such as revenue guarantees are also used. In this case public and private institutions as well as local businesses in a region raise a minimum amount of money as a guarantee to an airline to cover the costs associated with the provision of the service during a limited period of time. There are also community ticket trusts or travel banks which require the airport operator and/or public institutions to persuade the major airline customers in their region to commit to book a minimum number of tickets during the early stages of operation of a new service. Companies may be prepared to do this is and it means that the local air services will improve. Again, this will reduce the risk for the carrier and will not necessarily involve any extra cost from the public authorities. However many airlines are not in favour of trust funds as they find them cumbersome to administer and difficult to ensure that the pledged funds are actually used on the air services (STRAIR 2005; Weatherill, 2006). In spite of this a study of small airports in the United States found that travel backs had recently been used by a number of airports such as Stockton (California), Pensacola (Florida), Augusta (Georgia), and Wichita (Kansas). Revenue guarantees had also been used by airports of Durango, Gunnison, Montrose, and Telluride in Colorado; New Haven in Connecticut; Tallahassee in Florida; and again Wichita in Kansas (General Accounting Office, 2003).

Since airlines have different economic impacts, the incentives must be designed to appeal to the airlines which will bring the public agencies the specific economic benefits that they desire. For example network or legacy carriers can bring much business traffic to an area and often link the region to their global air service networks through hubs. In contrast, LCCs may be able to encourage inward tourism but may also promote outbound tourism – which in the end might have a net negative economic impact. Charter carriers can also bring in extra tourists, but they may have the disadvantage of being highly seasonal.

The UK route development funds (RDFs) are an interesting example of funds provided by regional development bodies to support new services that were deemed beneficial to the region's overall economic development by encouraging better business links or inbound tourism. Moreover, such funds were designed to have a catalytic impact so that airlines could potentially share the same aircraft on these supported routes which bring inbound benefits, with using them on additional non-subsidized outbound leisure services. The funds need to comply with UK and EU laws especially in respect with state aid and competition policy. The EC guidelines on start-up aid to airlines departing from regional airports are particularly relevant here (see Chapter 7). These guidelines resulted in a protocol for the RDFs being agreed in 2006 with the EC which allowed the funding allocated before the guidelines were established to continue until June 2007. After that, however, the guidelines have been applied which has meant that the funding is now limited in most cases to airports supporting 5 million passengers, can only be granted to EU carriers on EU routes and can only represent 30 per cent of the start-up costs (Department for Transport, 2006)

The first RDF, which ran from November 2002 to May 2007, amounted to £6.4 million and was created by the Scottish Executive and managed on a partnership basis by Scottish Enterprise, Highlands and Islands Enterprise and Visit Scotland (Pagliari, 2005). This was followed in 2003 by a £3.6 million fund which was set up by the Northern Ireland Department of Enterprise, Trade and Investment and was managed by Invest Northern Ireland. Then in the UK Airports White Paper of December 2003, other regional development agencies and the Welsh Assembly Government were invited to consider such funds. Subsequently the Welsh Assembly Government and One Northeast (the regional development agency of the Northeast) set up RDFs in June 2006.

In order to examine the likely benefit to the economy as a whole of the route proposals, an economic appraisal framework was established. The first stage of this was to undertake the net user benefits of the new route. This involved looking at the net present value to users by considering generalized cost savings from journey time savings and air fare savings. It also involved calculating the benefit/cost ratio by considering the benefits to users compared to the cost of funding support. If either the net present value was negative or the benefits cost ratio was less than 1, the proposal was rejected. Otherwise it was then assessed according to a route appraisal score. This was calculated by quantifying the business efficiency benefits (in terms of service frequency, hub connectivity, business centre links) the tourism impacts (in terms of net additional tourism employment), the direct employment impact, the social impacts (in terms of connectivity) and the environmental impacts (in terms of aircraft noise and carbon dioxide emissions). The final appraisal score was calculated by weighting these impacts according to the strategic priorities and the primary drivers for the route development funding. A risk assessment was also undertaken to investigate the risk that the route would not be sustained by the airline in the long term by considering the airline's financial position and route network. If this score was greater than some threshold or calibrated score, the route proposal was then recommended for support (STRAIR 2005; Mason, 2007).

Table 8.5 shows the routes, which were set up as a result of the RDFs – although a number of these are no longer operated. In general, the RDFs do seem to have helped improve the connectivity of the more peripheral UK regions but experience has been varied according to whether each specific region has decided to adopt such a fund or not. The more restriction conditions which have been applied since June 2007 have meant that all these funds are now closed, particularly as in a number of cases airports which previously were entitled for aid (such as Edinburgh, Glasgow, and Newcastle) are not longer eligible (except in exceptional circumstances) because they have grown beyond the 5 million passenger threshold. The regional development agency for the Northwest has considered setting up of a fund but has again found the EC's guidelines too restrictive. It seems more likely

Table 8.5 Services funded by the UK route development funds (as of August 2007)

Airport	Routes
Scottish route development fund	
Aberdeen	Bristol, Liverpool, Southampton, Stornoway, Brussels, Copenhagen, Groningen, Kristiansand, Oslo
Dundee	Belfast City, Birmingham
Edinburgh	*Jersey, Atlanta*, Barcelona, Cologne, Dortmund, Gdansk, Geneva, Katowice, Krakow, Madrid, Milan (Malpensa), Munich, Newark, *Oslo*, Zürich
Glasgow	Barcelona, Berlin, Boston, Dubai, *Prague*, Toronto (Hamilton)
Inverness	Birmingham, Bristol, East Midlands, Leeds Bradford, Liverpool, *Newcastle*, Dublin, *Stockholm*
Kirkwall	*Bergen*
Prestwick	Barcelona (Girona), Berlin, Düsseldorf (N'rhein), Gdansk, Gothenburg (Save), *Hamburg* (*Lubeck*), Milan (Orio), Pisa, Rome (Ciampino), Stockholm (Skavsta), Warsaw, Wroclaw
Sumburgh	Stansted, *Faroe Islands*, Oslo
Northern Ireland route development fund	
Belfast City	*Norwich*
Belfast International	Berlin, Geneva, Newark, Nice, Paris (CDG), *Rome (Ciampino)*
City of Derry	Birmingham, Manchester
Welsh route development fund	
Cardiff	Barcelona, *Brussels*, Paris (CDG), *Manchester*
North East air route development programme	
Durham T.V.	*Brussels*, Warsaw
Newcastle	Bergen, Copenhagen, *Inverness*, Krakow

Note: Routes in italic are no longer operated.
Source: Civil Aviation Authority (2007).

that the UK regional development agencies will instead be turning their attention to providing more general marketing initiatives to help support new routes (Civil Aviation Authority, 2007).

References and further reading

ACI-Europe (1998). *Creating Employment and Prosperity in Europe.* Europe: ACI.

Air Transport Action Group (ATAG) (2005). *The Economic and Social Benefits of Air Transport*. ATAG.

Airports Council International (ACI) (2002). *ACI Airport Economics Survey 2001*. ACI.

Airports Council International (ACI) (2007). *ACI Airport Economics Survey 2006*. ACI.

Button, K. and Taylor, S. (2000). International air transportation and economic development. *Journal of Air Transport Management*, 6, 209–222.

Caves, R. and Gosling, G. (1999). *Strategic Airport Planning*. Pergamon.

Civil Aviation Authority (CAA) (2007). *Air Services at UK Regional Airports: An Update on Developments*, CAP 775. CAA.

Cushman and Wakefield (2007). *European Cities Monitor 2007*. Cushman and Wakefield.

Department for Transport (DfT) (2006). *A National Protocol for UK Route Development Funds*. DfT.

European Low Fares Airline Association (ELFAA) (2004). *Liberalisation of European Air Transport: The Benefits of Low Fares Airlines to Consumers, Airports, Regions and the Environment*. ELFAA.

Graham, B. and Guyer, C. (2000). The role of regional airports and air services in the United Kingdom. *Journal of Transport Geography*, 8, 249–262.

General Accounting Office (GAO) (2003). *Factors affecting efforts to improve air service at small community airports*, GAO-03-330.

Mason, N. (2007). The economic impacts of airports. *University of Westminster Airport Economics and Finance Symposium*, April.

Nice Airport (2008). *Impact economique*, available from www.nice.aeroport.fr (accessed 30 June 2007).

Oxford Economic Forecasting (OEF) (2006). *The Contribution of the Aviation Industry to the UK Economy*. OEF.

Pagliari, R. (2005). Developments in the supply of direct international air services from airports in Scotland. *Journal of Air Transport Management*, 11, 249–257.

San Diego International Airport (2008). *Economic impact*, available from www.san.org (accessed 1 March 2008).

STRAIR (2005). *Air Service Development for Regional Development Agencies*. STRAIR.

Transportation Research Board (TRB) (2008) *Airport economic impact methods and model*, ACRB Synthesis 7, TRB.

Travel Trade Gazette (TTG) (2005). Ryanair's cushy number: Over 20 million euros in grants, *World Travel Market TTG edition*, November.

US Department of Commerce (DOC) (1997). *A User Handbook for the Regional Input–Output Modelling System (RIMS II)* 3rd edn. DOC.

Weatherill, J. (2006). North American airline incentives: Best practices and emerging trends. *Journal of Airport Management*, 1(1), 25–37.

Wilbur Smith Associates (2000). *The Economic Impact of Civil Aviation on the US Economy 2000*. Wilbur Smith Associates.

York Consulting/ACI-Europe (2000). *Europe's Airports: Creating Employment and Prosperity an Economic Impact Study Kit*. ACI-Europe.

York Aviation (2004). *The economic and social impact of airports in Europe*, available from www.aci-europe.org (accessed 20 November 2006).

York Aviation (2005). *Airport Operators Association: The economic and social impact of airports*, available from www.aoa.org.uk (accessed 20 November 2006).

York Aviation (2007). *Social benefits of low fares airlines in Europe*, available from www.elfaa.com (accessed 15 February 2008).

CHAPTER 9

The environmental impact of airports

Growing concerns for the environment

The airport industry, like all other industries, is facing the effects of increasing environmental pressure. The level of environmental concern varies from country to country or indeed from one airport to another, depending on views about aviation and other social and political attitudes. In many countries increased prosperity has led to greater expectation for the quality of life and more sensitivity to the environmental impacts of airports. For this reason it has become increasingly difficult to substantially expand airport operations or to build new airports. All indications are that this will become even more difficult in the future as concern for the environment grows. At the same time, continual growth in demand is putting greater commercial pressures on airports to develop activities. The problems are particularly acute for airports which are popular because of their proximity to local population centres but this means that a significant proportion of the community is affected by airport operators. In short, environmental issues must be seen as one of the greatest challenges to, and possible constraints upon, the future activities of the air transport industry.

The environmental impacts have to be considered at two levels, namely global and local. Within a global context, the role that aviation plays in contributing to world problems such as global warming and ozone depletion is increasingly coming under scrutiny. These are long-term issues which society as a whole has to address. The meeting of governments in Kyoto in 1997 was one of the first attempts to introduce constraints upon environmental impacts at a global level – although international aviation was excluded from this. At a local level, impacts due, for example, to aircraft noise and air quality have to be considered. In some areas of operation airport managers may be legally required to minimize the adverse effects, whereas elsewhere many airport operators are increasingly voluntarily introducing measures to mitigate the impacts. It is the more local problems which the airport operators mostly have to address on a day-to-day basis. The focus of this chapter, therefore, is very much at this level, although some investigation of the global developments have also been made to put the local issues into a broader context.

Consideration of the environmental impacts at airports is made much more difficult because of the many different bodies involved in, or affected by, airport operations. These include the airport operator, the airlines, governments and statutory organizations, amenity and conservation groups, and local residents. These will have a complexity of different, and often conflicting, interests. Issues such as resident safety or loss of wildlife habitat can cause anxiety among certain sectors of society and generate considerable emotive concern. Other impacts may require complex technical data to be assessed, which may be difficult for all interested parties to fully understand. Some impacts cannot be measured adequately. Then, when mitigation measures are considered, most standard procedures have to be adapted to suit each airport's individual circumstances because of variation in aircraft use, night flights, land-use rules, closeness to residential areas, and overall environmental sensitivity of the community.

The main impacts

The main environmental impacts can be divided into five categories:

1. Noise
2. Emissions
3. Water pollution and use
4. Waste and energy management
5. Wildlife, heritage, and landscape.

Noise

Aircraft noise has traditionally been considered the most important environmental problem at airports and, in many cases, public tolerance of aircraft noise has been diminishing. This is in spite of the fact that over the years the noise levels associated with aircraft movements have been declining. This reduction has been primarily due to the development of less noisy aircraft and the pressure of more stringent requirements for noise certification of new aircraft types. Current aircraft types are typically 20 dB quieter than aircraft of 40 years ago (Air Transport Action Group, 2008). Noise certification was first introduced in 1969 by the United States in the Federal Aviation Regulations Part 36 (FAR Part 36). The International Civil Aviation Organization (ICAO) adopted similar international standards in 1971. These standards were included in the Environmental Protection Annex 16 of the Chicago Convention. The initial standards for jet aircraft, based on the maximum noise level given a certain flight procedure, became known as 'chapter' 2 or 'stage' 2 in the United States. In 1977, more stringent standards, known as chapter 3 or stage 3, to be applied to all new aircraft designs, were adopted by ICAO. Chapter 2 aircraft include the Boeing 727, DC-9, and older types of Boeing 737 and 747. Newer aircraft certificated under chapter 3 included the Boeing 757, 767, 777, and all the airbus family of aircraft.

Since 1990, the first generation of noisy aircraft (i.e. chapter or stage 1), such as the Boeing 707, have been prohibited. After that, the second generation chapter 2 aircraft were the noisiest types. They were phased out completely in the United States at the end of 1999 and worldwide in 2002. An issue which has complicated this noise certification process is the treatment of hushkitted or re-engined jets. These are chapter 2 jets which have been modified to comply with the chapter 3 rules. They are, however, the noisiest of chapter 3 aircraft and so there have been pressures, particularly in Europe, for phasing them out. This was in fact the cause of a very major dispute between

European and American authorities a few years ago, particularly as the United States was the sole supplier of hushkit technology and US airlines had a higher proportion of hushkitted equipment than many other countries. Since there was no agreed standard from ICAO concerning these marginally compliant chapter 3 aircraft the European Union (EU) introduced its own regulation that banned all these types of aircraft from 2002.

It was decided by ICAO in 2001 that a new chapter 4 standard would apply to all new aircraft designs beginning in 2006, which have to cumulatively be 10 dB quieter than chapter 3. However, these standards were already achieved by some existing designs and so the EU and most airports were disappointed that their demands for a much tighter cumulative 14 dB reduction were not met. At the same time, ICAO agreed the concept of a 'balanced approach' to noise management which comprised of four principal elements:

1. reduction of aircraft noise at source,
2. land-use planning and management measures,
3. noise abatement operational procedures,
4. local noise-related operating restrictions.

The acceptance of this integrated approach meant that in 2002 the European regulation regarding hushkits was repealed following the adoption of a new directive which incorporated ICAO's balanced programme as the directive allowed for operating restrictions to be placed on marginally compliant aircraft, such as hushkitted aircraft, at individual airports (European Commission, 2002).

Undoubtedly, reduction of aircraft noise at source which has been brought about by international certification has an impact on reducing overall aircraft noise levels. The newest generation of aircraft such as the A380 and Boeing 787 are the quietest yet and research continues into researching new technology solutions in reducing noise from jet engines. However such reductions of noise at source can take a considerable length of time to achieve – given the heavy investment needed by both aircraft manufacturers and airlines, and the long lifetime of an aircraft. Hence this is why other measures, detailed in the balanced approach, are also needed.

The appropriate control of land use near the airport is vital when the mitigation of the noise impacts is being considered. This is in order to prevent the gains which have to be achieved by using quieter aircraft being offset by people living closer to the airport. To overcome this problem, noise zoning is often applied to airports. This involves defining a certain area, or noise buffer, around an airport where the construction of new houses and other noise-sensitive buildings is not allowed. In a study of European practice, it was found that 33 out of 52 airports had some land-use planning or management controls including airports such as London Gatwick, London Heathrow, Vienna, and Athens (MPD Group Ltd, 2007).

Individual airports can also introduce unilateral noise abatement operating measures which can reduce the annoyance caused by aircraft noise. For example, many airports have introduced preferred noise routes (PNRs) (or noise preferential routes, NPRs) to minimize the noise impact on the surrounding population. This is usually done by directing aircraft away from the most densely populated areas. Airports may also choose to place restrictions on flight procedures by requiring, for example, reduced power and flap settings for take-off or approach. Other noise abatement procedures may involve having favoured runways with flight paths over uninhabited areas and continuous descent approach (CDA) which entails having a continuous steady descent to a runway rather than a number of short descents to set cleared altitudes as is traditionally required by air traffic control (ATC).

Flight-track monitoring equipment, when combined with airport surveillance radar, is used to improve airline departure and arrival procedures and to monitor the adherence to the PNRs. In some cases, airport operators may impose financial penalties on airlines that deviate from their required flight track. For example, there is a £500 fine during the day and £750 at night at Manchester. There may be difficulties with this, however, because airlines quite legitimately may be required to depart from their preferred route for ATC reasons. Money from penalties may be used for soundproofing or other community projects. Many airports also use noise-monitoring equipment. This can be used to measure local noise levels and calculate noise contours, or to enforce noise limits. The information gathered from the noise- and track-monitoring procedures can be provided for the airlines, local community, governments and other interested parties, and a growing number of airports actually publish the results.

There is also the noise from airline engines running, especially during maintenance. To reduce the noise emission levels, a number of airports have introduced mufflers or noise attenuating walls and special noise attenuating hangars. Restrictions have been placed on when and how engine tests can be undertaken. Restrictions have also been imposed on the use of reverse thrust by airlines. However, the noise problem is not just limited to the aircraft landing, taking-off, taxiing, or engine testing. There is the noise from ground vehicles and auxiliary power units. Noise has been reduced at a number of US airports which have mostly fixed rather than auxiliary power units, as is the case of some European airports such as Zürich and Copenhagen.

The fourth aspect of the balanced approach is local noise-related operating restrictions. A common measure is a night curfew or limitations on night flights. This may involve a blanket ban on all aircraft, such as at London City and Wellington airport, or a limit on the noisier aircraft, such as at Manchester, Lisbon, Brussels, and Toronto. At a number of Australian airports such as Sydney and Adelaide the airport is closed at night to all aircraft except very small ones. Night constraints may significantly impact on the development of freight or charter traffic which often rely on night movements, and make scheduling long-haul services more difficult.

The application of a 'noise budget' is also a noise-related operating restriction. In this case the budget will restrict the overall noise during a certain period of time at night such as a season or year. For example at the UK airports such as Heathrow, Gatwick, and Stansted use a noise budget called a Quota Count (QC) system. The QC is based on the aircraft's noise performance with noisy aircraft receiving a higher QC than a quieter one. For example, a 747-400 has a QC count of 4 on departure and 2 on arrival compared with a 777-200 aircraft which has a QC count of 1 and 0.5. The sum of all the QCs is then the noise budget or noise limit for the specified time (British Airways, 2008). At Amsterdam airport the noise budget is based on different standards for the night and day, and there are a number of enforcement points on the ground (35 for the entire 24-hour period, 25 for the night) where the noise levels must not exceed the standard set (Schiphol Group, 2007). A similar budget exists at Hamburg airport. In most cases, restrictions on noisier aircraft only apply at night but in some cases they have been imposed during the day as well. Specifically, the EU directive allows for the marginally compliant chapter 3 hushkitted aircraft to be banned but very few airports have introduced such restrictions. Madrid is a rare example which expects to have all these aircraft gone by 2012. At a few other airports (e.g. Schiphol, Toulouse, and Paris CDG) such aircraft are banned at night.

Many airports also impose noise surcharges for noisier aircraft and an incentive to use quieter aircraft. These charging policies are, however, unlikely to influence an airline's choice of aircraft unless the fee differential is very large. Frankfurt airport was one of the first airports to introduce such charges in 1974. It now has a basic landing charge, a noise charge which all airlines pay depending on their aircraft type and additional charges at night (Table 9.1). Noise charges are now used in many countries particularly in Europe but also in Gimpo in South Korea, Toronto in Canada and in a number of Australian and Japanese airports. There is, however, no consistency in the way that these noise charges are structured. At many airports such as Brussels, Oslo, Amsterdam and those in Germany, the landing charges are higher at night as well. A survey in Europe found that around half of the airports used landing charges which differentiated by noise category and around half also had day/night time differentiated charges (MPD Group Ltd, 2007).

In spite of all these measures to reduce the noise levels, there will always be some residents who will be subject to noise annoyance, and for this reason many airport operators will fund or assist in the financing of noise insulation for properties in the vicinity of the airport – either voluntarily or because it is a legal requirement. Housing and also buildings such as schools and hospitals may be insulated. In most cases the cost of insulation will be covered by the airport operator alone but sometimes national or regional governments will

Table 9.1 Landing and noise charges at Frankfurt airport 2008

Category	Typical aircraft	Landing charge per tonne (€)	Noise charge per landing/take-off	Additional night charge (22.00–22.59 and 05.00–05.59)	Additional night charge (23.00–04.59)
0.	B737-600, Avro RJ	0.88	0.00	35.00	43.75
1.	A318/319/320, 757-200/300	0.88	12.00	35.00	43.75
2.	A300/310/321, B767	0.88	31.00	90.00	112.50
3.	A330/340, B777	0.88	75.00	170.00	212.50
4.	B747-400	0.88	270.00	310.00	387.50
5.	B747-100/200/300	0.88	610.00	1250.00	1562.50
6.	–	0.88	6750.00	13 500.00	16 785.00
7.	AN124, IL76	0.88	14 250.00	28 500.00	35 625.00

Source: Frankfurt airport.

also contribute as is the case at Copenhagen and Milan. Sometimes the funds may come from specific noise taxes as at Amsterdam airport. There is also a noise tax in France where the costs of house insulation are primarily financed by the state, but unlike at Amsterdam these tax revenues are not directly earmarked for the insulation costs. Some of the insulation programmes are quite substantial. For example, 26 000 domestic properties are covered in Manchester and 18 000 at Cologne. The scheme at Frankfurt includes 14 000 housing units, 20 Kindergartens, 5 schools, and 7 nursing homes (SEO Amsterdam Economics, 2003; MPD Group Ltd, 2007).

Emissions

Through the combination of the development of quieter aircraft and noise abatement operating procedures, most airports have managed to contain many of the problems arising from aircraft noise. However, there is a 'new' environmental threat which has been growing in recent years – that of aircraft emissions. By consuming fuel, the aircraft are producing emissions of carbon dioxide (CO_2), nitrogen oxides (NO_x) particles (mainly soot) of sulphur oxides, carbon monoxide, and various hydrocarbons. CO_2 is the most important of all the greenhouse gases.

One of the most comprehensive studies of aviation emissions, albeit rather old now, found that globally aviation's contribution to the world total of human-made CO_2 was fairly small in the 1990s, at around 2 per cent. If other less scientifically certain effects are also taken into account such as the NO_x emissions (which have an impact on methane and ozone particularly when emitted at cruise altitudes) and the creation of condensation trails, it was estimated that the radiative forcing or global warming effect of all aircraft emissions would be around 3.5 per cent (This excluded possible damaging unknown changes in cirrus clouds). However, because of the growth of air transport and the relative ability of other industrial sectors to reduce their emissions, by 2050 this global share was predicted to rise to around 4–15 per cent, depending on different growth scenarios and other assumptions. This research was updated in 2005, and it was found that because of more developed scientific knowledge total radiative forcing was estimated to be 3 per cent of the global total – with CO_2 emissions accounting for 2 per cent and being forecast to increase by 3–4 per cent per annum (Intergovernmental Panel on Climate Change, 2007). Specifically within the EU between 1990 and 2003 whilst all greenhouse gas emissions fell by 5.5 per cent, international aviation emissions increased by 73 per cent, corresponding to annual growth of 4.5 per cent. If that growth were to continue by 2012, emissions will have increased by 150 per cent since 1990 (European Commission, 2005).

Emissions from international flights (but not domestic flights) are excluded from the Kyoto Protocol which was adopted in 1997 and came into force in 2005 – and instead ICAO through its Committee on Aviation Environmental Protection (CAEP) has been given the responsibility for developing proposals on international aviation emissions. In addition to considering the most appropriate standards and the best operating practices to reduce emissions, ICAO has been looking at various market-based options. These include voluntary programmes, taxes and levies (e.g. fuel tax, en route emission charges), and emissions trading options whereby airlines would buy licences to pollute that can be traded with other industries.

It is generally agreed that future global air traffic will increase at growth rates which will outperform the impact of any technology improvements which will reduce engine emissions. Aircraft in the 1990s were 70 per cent more fuel efficient than 40 years before. It is also projected that there will be a 20 per cent improvement in fuel efficiency by 2015 and a 40–50 per cent improvement by 2050 (Intergovernmental Panel on Climate Change, 1999). Lighter materials and more efficient engines will help improve fuel efficiency. However, the scale of these developments will only be sufficient to partially offset the growth effect. In addition, while greater fuel-efficient aircraft may produce less emissions such as CO_2, the higher combustion temperatures needed for greater efficiency may actually produce more NO_x emissions. All these also have to be viewed within the global context where major CO_2 reduction efforts are taking place in other industrial sectors.

At present there does not appear to be a viable alternative to jet fuel. There has been some experimentation with biomass fuels, most notably with a Virgin flight from London to Paris in early 2008, but it is still very unclear as to whether this could be a feasible option. Hence the aviation industry is looking at other ways to mitigate aviation emissions. Improved operational procedures, such as more efficient air traffic management and flight operations, coupled with reduced airport and airspace congestion, could bring about a further reduction in fuel burn of around 8–18 per cent over 20 years – but still these developments by the themselves are not likely to reduce emissions to an acceptable level (Intergovernmental Panel on Climate Change, 1999).

Market-based options are another alternative. These options include a kerosene tax. Currently, aviation kerosene fuel is exempt from tax on international flights under the 1944 Chicago Convention, and also many bilateral air service agreements between countries prohibit such a tax (domestic fuel taxes are allowed and are in fact levied in a few countries such as the US, India, Japan, and the Netherlands). In the late 1990s, the European Commission (EC) expressed significant interest in the introduction of a EU-wide fuel tax. It considered two options, first, just taxing EU carriers on intra-EU flights and, second, taxing all flights of all carriers operating within the EU. It was estimated that, if such a tax was introduced in 1998, the first option would reduce fuel consumption by 0.5 per cent between 1992 and 2005. The second option would bring a greater saving of 2.5 per cent.

The subsequent effect on the operating result of the airlines with the first option was predicted to be a reduction of 12 per cent for EU carriers and a 4 per cent increase for other carriers. The alternative of taxing all flights was estimated to bring down the results of EU carriers by 15 per cent and other carriers by 4 per cent. The taxing of EU carriers would therefore give them a distinct competitive disadvantage and produce fairly marginal emission savings. This was not considered to be acceptable. The environmental effectiveness of taxing all routes would be far greater but this option would be very difficult to implement since this would involve complicated reworking of bilateral agreements or amending global Chicago Convention policies – most probably through agreement with ICAO. It was concluded that this it was not a feasible option in the short term (European Commission, 1999).

Within this context, it is noteworthy that a few countries have introduced a more general government tax to reflect the environmental costs of flying. For example, in the United Kingdom, a departure tax called the Air Passenger Duty (APD), which goes directly to the Treasury, was introduced in 1994. Originally this was just really considered as a passenger airport tax and only recently as the environmental effects have become much more of an issue has the tax been labelled an 'environmental' tax and been substantially increased. However, it is considered to be a very blunt instrument in tackling the environmental problem as each passenger category (i.e. economy/business on short- or long-haul flights) pays the same regardless of the level of emissions from the aircraft and how full it is. The money is also not used on any environmental projects. However, it has recently been announced that it will be replaced with a tax payable per plane rather than per passenger from November 2009, which will take account of the carbon impact of each aircraft type and its occupancy. Meanwhile at Amsterdam airport in 2008 a new environmental passenger tax is due to be introduced which again has been heavily criticized by the airlines.

An alternative to a fuel tax is an emission charge, which could be levied as part of the airport or ATC charge. In the United Kingdom, the environmental costs have been estimated to range from £3 to £35 per passenger for a single trip (Royal Commission on Environmental Pollution, 2002). It has also been estimated that demand would decrease by 10 per cent if environmental costs are passed onto passengers (DfT, 2003). The EC has also been looking at a more broader-application of emission charges as an alternative to a fuel tax having commissioned a major study of this option in 2002 (CE Delft, 2002). This research concluded that emissions charges, unlike fuel taxes, if limited to flights within EU airspace would not give rise to legal objections from third countries, nor would they create any distortions of competition. Such charges would be levied through the ATC system and the research explored two main alternatives. The first was a charge proportional to the volume of greenhouse gas emissions discharged in EU airspace. It was estimated that this could produce annual revenues of 1–9 billion euros, depending on the exact valuations which were used. If charges of 30 euros per tonne of CO_2 and 3.6 euros per kg of NO_x were used, it was estimated that emissions could be reduced by 9 per cent in 2010. About half of this reduction would be due to technical and operational changes introduced by the airlines, and about half would be due to a reduction in air travel demand because of the rise in ticket prices. It was estimated that ticket prices would rise by roughly 3–5 euros for short-haul one-way flights and 10–16 euros for long-haul flights. The additional revenue generated could be allocated to individual EU member states or to a supranational fund for financing emission abatement measures. The second alternative which the research explored was a revenue-neutral charge or performance standard incentive (PSI). With this option if an aircraft performed better than a performance standard it would receive money but if it performed worse it would pay money. It was estimated that this would cause a 5 per cent reduction in emissions coming almost entirely from technical and operational measures introduced by the airlines and, as such a scheme would be revenue-neutral, there would be no additional funds to distribute.

A few airports have introduced emission charges. This happened initially in the late 1990s at the Stockholm airports of Arlanda and Bromma, some other Swedish airports and the Swiss airports of Zürich, Basel-Mulhouse, Bern, and Geneva airports (Table 9.2). Heathrow, Gatwick, Munich, and Frankfurt also have such charges

Table 9.2   Emission charges at Geneva airport 2008

Class of aircraft	Typical aircraft type	Increase in landing charge (%)
1.	B747-100	40
2.	B747-200 (some engines)	20
3.	A310-200	10
4.	B757-200	5
5.	A320-200	0

Source: Geneva airport.

now. Clearly they are generally mainly aimed at improving local air quality, but could also have a positive impact on cruising emissions. However very few airports have chosen to use emission charges.

The third option after fuel taxes and emission charges, which generally seems to be considered by the industry to be the most attractive option, is emissions trading. In this case an overall target for emissions is set and then individual participants can choose to meet the target; reduce their emissions below the target and sell excessive emissions allowance; or keep their emissions above the target and buy more emissions allowance. There is either a closed system when individual companies just buy or sell emission certificates from others in the same sector or a more radical open system when companies can buy or sell from other industries. Overall it is felt that this gives a much greater incentive to monitor and regulate emissions than the other options.

In 2005 a multi-sector emission trading scheme has been applied in the EU to fixed source energy-intensive installations. The EC is also now planning to include aviation in the ETS. The EC proposed that this should be applied to flights within the EU from 2011 and to and from EU airports from 2012. The allowances would be capped at the average emission levels for 2004–2006 and mostly issued free based on the historical share of traffic (Ezard, 2007). However, the European Parliament has proposed making the limits stricter with allowances being capped at 90 per cent the average level for 2004–2006 and with 25 per cent of these being auctioned. Also it wants all flights covered from 2011. Final agreement on the ETS is expected in 2008. This unilateral European approach has proved to be very controversial and unpopular with many states outside of Europe who believe that if a scheme is introduced it should be co-ordinated globally by ICAO. Potentially this could result in trade and legal battles between these countries and the EU in the future.

While the global impacts of aircraft emissions have attracted a great deal of attention in recent years, clearly they are not the only impacts which need to be considered. At a regional level the emissions from aviation are thought to contribute to acid rain. At a local level the air quality of the area in the immediate vicinity of the airport can be affected – primarily due to emissions of hydrocarbons, carbon monoxide, and nitrogen oxides. An increasing number of airports monitor local air quality at airports. Very often independent companies will undertake the monitoring. The monitoring systems vary considerably in their level of sophistication and accuracy. Some airports use these systems to help them model predicted air quality in the future. Since 1981, ICAO has laid down standards for four categories of engine emissions, namely smoke, hydrocarbons, carbon monoxide, and nitrogen oxides. These standards are aimed at local air pollution problems, since they are based on the aircraft landing and take-off (LTO) cycle and do not cover emissions during the cruise phase. Over the years these standards have been strengthened with the latest 2008 standards being 12 per cent lower than the previous standards. However, they are not legally binding and it is up to member states to include these standards into their law.

Whilst these standards particularly related to NO_x, like the emission charges, are mainly aimed at improving local air quality, they could also have a positive impact on reducing emissions during cruising. Local air quality may also be regulated by general national or international laws related to air quality. For example, within Europe there is the 1996 Framework Directive on Ambient Air Quality that has limits for NO_x which become binding after 2010. These standards may be breached by some airports as traffic grows and, for example, there has been considerable debate as to whether this would occur if there were a third runway at London Heathrow.

Whilst local emission standards can have an influence over aircraft emissions at airports, the actual airport operators have very little control over this matter. Encouraging more fuel-efficient operating procedures such as CDA may help a little. The operator can also seek to reduce the impact of running engines while the aircraft are on the ground or by minimizing taxiing times and taxiing with single engines or by seeking to use fixed ground power. As with the noise issue, the problem at airports is not just limited to aircraft operations since the local air quality may also be affected by the ground service vehicles, which tend to be fuel powered. At some airports, electric vehicles which are more economically and environmentally favourable have been used. Then there are emissions from maintenance and cleaning processes, auxiliary power units and from the cars and other surface transport modes.

It may be seen from Figure 9.1 that only 56 per cent of all ground-level NO_x at Heathrow airport were actually from aircraft followed by landside vehicles. Eight per cent of emissions come from airside vehicles and for this reason in 2002 BAA established its so-called Clean Vehicles programme. This has 45 members and encourages them to use lower emission vehicles and to increase fuel efficiency.

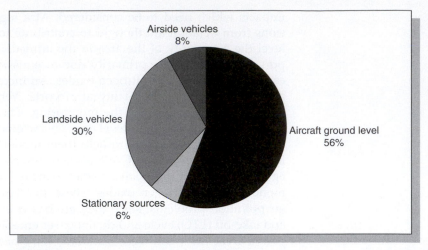

Figure 9.1
Estimated 2002 ground-level airport-related NO_x emissions.
Source: BAA Heathrow (2007).

In 2006 it launched an incentive scheme with a total fund value of £100 000 in response to calls from members for financial assistance with implementing technologies such as replacing old diesel vehicles with electric alternatives or fitting cleaner technologies to existing vehicles. Elsewhere at Phoenix airport in the US, the airport uses compressed natural gas for its car and bus fleet, and Fraport has been undertaking tests on hydrogen-powered vehicles. Bristol airport has converted its airport fleet to biodiesel. Hong Kong airport has a Green Apron Policy which includes having fixed ground power and aims to replace its existing 43 vehicle fleet with alternative fuel or low emissions vehicles. Dallas/Fort Worth airport has also replaced most of its vehicles to reduce emissions. At Gatwick and San Francisco airport, Virgin Atlantic has been experimenting with towing the aircraft closer to the runway to reduce the time that the engines were running on the taxiway. Boiler plants also create emission (they are included in the six per cent stationary emissions at Heathrow). Therefore airports are looking at ways to produce cleaner electrical power, for example at Toronto where the airport has been developing natural gas turbine facilities.

Water pollution and use

Water pollution at airports can occur for a number of different reasons. Surface water discharge or run-off which goes into local watercourses from runways, aprons, car parks, and other land development may be contaminated by anti-icing and de-icing fluids such as glycol which are used during the winter months. The chemicals used in maintaining and washing aircraft and vehicles, as well as fire training activities and fuel spillages, can also contribute to this pollution. Leakages from underground tanks and pipes, and grass fertilizers used in landscaping activities can contaminate the soil. Then there is the normal wastewater from buildings and facilities such as domestic sewerage. An increasing number of airports now monitor water quality as well as air quality and have adopted various measures to minimize this water pollution. These include revised operational practices to reduce the use of the harmful chemicals, to improve cleaning processes and to minimize the spillage and leakages. For example at Hamburg airport de-icing takes place only on sealed apron surfaces to ensure that the fluid run-off does not leak elsewhere whilst at Munich airport this is done at a specially designated remote area so that the de-icing fluids can be recovered for recycling. A by-product of this recycling process is heat which can be used to help warm the terminal. Many other airports such as Detroit, Seattle, and Dallas/Fort Worth also recycle de-icing fluid. Balancing reservoir treatment may be undertaken before the surface water joins local watercourses such as at Auckland airport.

Waste and energy management

Waste pollution is also an issue, as it is with most other industrial activities (Pitt *et al.*, 2002). In many cases there may be general legislation related to waste management. However, airports are also faced with specific operating restrictions because of the nature of the aviation business. For example, airports need to incinerate or send to a controlled landfill site all 'international' food waste from aircraft. In addition, the transfer of waste from airside to landsite at airports is problematic because of security, customs, and insurance restrictions.

The waste at airports is generated by airlines, airport operators, and other airport-related companies. While most of the waste comes from the airlines, it is usually the airport operators that have overall responsibility for waste management for the entire airport activities. Most of the individual companies, especially the airlines, do not have enough space for waste management facilities and there are cost economies of scale to be gained by having communal recycling and other waste management procedures. Improvements can usually be brought about by an assessment of on-airport treatment methods and the scope for reducing, reusing, or recycling waste. In-flight catering waste, with the disposable nature of most of the packaging, is considered to be a particular problem. Off-airport disposal methods which typically involve incineration and landfill also need to be considered.

Many airports now have recycling initiatives. One of the earliest airports to undertake this was Zürich airport which introduced an airport wide waste management concept in 1992. Other examples range from concrete recycling at Jersey airport, recycling food waste at Hong Kong airport to produce compost for airport landscaping, reusing cut grass instead of fertilizer at Stansted airport, airline pillow recycling at Oakland airport, and reuse of excavated soil at Dallas/ Fort Worth airport. At Los Angeles airport the food waste is used to produce methane gas which is turned into electricity and at Seattle it is given to a food bank in the city. Other airports, such as Canberra, recycle their water (Airports Council International, 2008).

Energy management, associated with the provision of heating, ventilation, air conditioning, and lighting, is also very important. Many airports undertake energy audits. With energy conservation, as with waste and water management, there are good financial reasons for why airports should address these issues since environmental improvements may bring about considerable cost savings. Some airports such as Vancouver, Chicago, and San Francisco have installed solar panels whereas La Palma airport in Spain has wind power generators. The LFV group which operates the Swedish airports has achieved carbon neutral operations and East Midlands airport is aiming for this in 2012.

Wildlife, heritage, and landscape

There is also a need to protect the wildlife, heritage, and the landscape of the local environment and there are many examples of how specific airport operators in the past have tackled the disturbance of certain wildlife habitats – particularly during the construction of a new airport or during airport expansion. While the new Chek Lap Kok airport in Hong Kong was being built, a 1-km exclusion zone for dolphins was set up to ensure that their sensitive hearing was not harmed during blasting work. At Indianapolis airport, 3000 new bat homes for the Indiana bat had to be installed due to a new maintenance building which displaced the bats. At Perth airport, development was halted when a rare western swamp tortoise colony was discovered. At Miami airport, the death of four manatees beneath the runway forced the airport operator to take action to protect this endangered species. At Manchester airport, badger sets had to be relocated, and a rare breed of newt had to be protected when the second runway was being built. At Oslo Gardermoen airport, a bridge had to be built to prevent the 1000 moose who annually migrate across the region from wandering onto the airport approach roads (Anker, 1997). There are many more recent examples – such as the movement of Great Crested Newts for an airside location to a habitat especially created by the airport operator at Stansted airport in 2002. Heritage may also be affected by airport development. For example, historic buildings may be situated within the area which has been allocated for airport expansion. In the case of Manchester and Copenhagen airports, this has meant that such buildings have been moved to other locations.

Landscapes can be radically changed by airport development, which can disturb the ecosystem and can be visually intrusive. To compensate for this some airports have established 'green areas' such as Athens airport where there are five such projects which cover a total area of 6 hectares and include features such as walking paths, playgrounds, and planted areas. Detroit airport has developed a wetlands area whereas at Southwest Florida airport a nature reserve has been established.

Community issues

Clearly airport environmental impacts can have a detrimental impact on the quality of life of residents in the vicinity of the airport. The major areas of concern are aircraft noise, air pollution, fuel odour, ecological damage, and the safety of aircraft. While the exact relationship between human health and well-being and these factors is still not entirely clear, an area which has received particular attention is the problem of sleep disturbance due to night flying. It is for this reason that many airports restrict aircraft movements at nights or ban noisier aircraft types. The rising number of aircraft movements has also increased concerns about aircraft safety and has resulted in some airports establishing risk contours around airports associated with third party death and injury.

Many airports address some of the social issues raised by airport operations within the framework of a broader environmental or sustainability strategy. For airport employees, this may involve consideration of other issues as well such as equal opportunities, ethics policies, skills training, and workplace safety and security. Moreover, forging strong links with the community and ensuring continual public dialogue with all interested parties is often considered an important role. Most airports get involved in community relations such as the provision of information about environmental and other developments, offering a complaints-handling service, supporting and sponsoring local arts, culture and sports events, and developing educational links. Some airports set up residents' forums. Many airports also have consultative committees with representatives from local government, amenity groups, local commerce and industry, and airport users. These may be a legal requirement.

The role of other transport modes

There are two ways in which the use of other transport modes can affect the direct and indirect environmental impacts of airports. First, there may be some opportunity for passengers on short- and medium-distance flights to be diverted on to high-speed rail services. In Europe, it has been estimated that around 10 per cent of passengers could be transferred from aircraft to high-speed trains (Intergovernmental Panel on Climate Change, 1999). In the 1980s and 1990s there was a continuing growth in the number of high-speed rail services notably in France and Germany. Various studies have shown that a quick city centre to city centre rail service can be quite successful in attracting a certain share of the population away from competing air services. For example, it was estimated that the rail share of traffic on the Frankfurt–Munich route increased from 30 to 37 per cent in the first year of operation with a drop in airline share from 27 to 23 per cent. On the Stockholm–Gothenburg route, the rail share was estimated to have increased from 40 to 55 per cent in the first 4 years of operation and the first TGV route in France between Paris and Lyons was claimed to have gained a 90 per cent market share (CAA, 1998).

However, switching from air to rail is only feasible when dense routes are being considered. Such rail links also require huge capital investment. In the end passengers will choose the rail option when the time, fare, frequency and access characteristics of the service offer them an advantage (International Air Transport Association, 2003). Moreover, rail services are not usually an attractive option for transfer traffic unless the high-speed network is linked to airports and the appeal of the rail alternative will also depend very much on the comparable level of fares and the quality of service on offer. An interesting development occurred in Germany when, in 1998, Lufthansa and the railway company, Deutsche Bahn (DB) signed a memorandum of understanding which enabled them to produce their AIRail product upon completion of the high-speed train link. This involved a partnership on the high-speed routes of Frankfurt–Stuggart from 2001 and Frankfurt–Cologne from 2003. There was a code-sharing agreement between Lufthansa and DB and similar agreements now exist with other airlines such as American Airlines, ANA, and TAP Portugal. (At Paris CDG, at least nine airlines have similar agreements with the French railways, SNCF.) The services are also operated with thorough baggage check-in and the same transfer times as at the air terminal. This initiative has switched passengers to high-speed trains and reduced the use of feeder flights as well as shifting some demand from cars and local urban rail services (Fakiner, 2005).

The individual airport operator has far greater control in influencing the mode of surface travel used by passengers and employees to reach the airport, which is the other aspect of surface transport that needs to be considered. Ground transport makes a major contribution to the overall noise levels and air pollution at an airport, with the impacts rising as the transport system becomes congested. Many airports are trying to develop more effective public transport alternatives to the car for accessing the airport. They have also introduced many initiatives to encourage passengers and airport employees to use public transport.

Historically, most passengers arrived at airports by private car or taxi, with only a small proportion using bus or coach transport. With airport growth in the 1970s and 1980s, some existing suburban or local rail services were extended to reach the airport. They are still the most common form of rail link today, with many examples being found in North America (e.g. Cleveland, Boston, Atlanta, and

Chicago) and other airports such as Munich, Stuttgart, Barcelona, Malaga, Rome Fiumicino, London Luton, Changi Singapore, and Shanghai. There are also underground or light rail links at some airports such London Heathrow, Madrid, Newcastle, Nuremberg, Bremen, London City, Portland Oregon, and Baltimore. More are being planned at Edinburgh, Lyon, Manchester, and Copenhagen (Sharp, 2007).

Many of these services are relatively slow, with a rather basic quality of service, and are not dedicated links to the airport. They may be popular with employees but are less attractive to passengers. This has meant that a number of airports, particularly those with large traffic volumes or a long journey away from the city centre, have instead developed high-speed dedicated links. Such links bring environmental benefits and alleviate road congestion as well as bringing extra convenience for passengers. Indeed, Arlanda, Stockholm airport's third runway was only approved subject to a rail link being built. Other dedicated airport rail link examples include Gardermoen in Oslo, Heathrow in London, Chek Lap Kok in Hong Kong, Milan in Italy, Nagoya and Narita in Japan, Inchoen in Korea, and Sepang in Kuala Lumpur. A number of airports have also developed high-speed links connecting airport terminals to international routes such as Charles de Gaulle in Paris, Lyon, Frankfurt, Zürich, Cologne, and Düsseldorf. Some airports also have integrated regional and high-speed rail links – Paris Charles de Gaulle being a good example. Frankfurt airport has three railway interfaces. There is a regional train station below Terminal 1, the AIRail terminal for the long distance services and a rail connection to Cargo City South. Other airports as well are looking at rail links for the carriage of freight. This is a relatively new idea since, historically, the only freight transported has been aviation fuel. Airports particularly interested in developing rail freight include Liege, Leipzig/Hall Amsterdam, Paris Charles de Gaulle, Milan, and London Heathrow (IARO/ATAG/ACI, 1998; Janic, 2003).

There are many more rail links in Europe than in North America as they are considered to be a much more acceptable and attractive surface access option in Europe. Few of the North American links integrate effectively with other rail services as is the case with a growing number of links in Europe. Remote baggage services are also frequently available in Europe but not in North America. The most developed service of this type is the Fly Rail baggage system in Switzerland which provides two-way check-in for Zürich, Basel, and Geneva at 116 rail stations. At 23 rail stations, complete check-in can be made for flights of Swiss and partner airlines. These factors plus the greater car dependency in North America explain why the rail modal share and the actual number of rail links is far less common there than in Europe.

A growing number of airport operators have recognized that encouraging passengers onto public transport involves much more

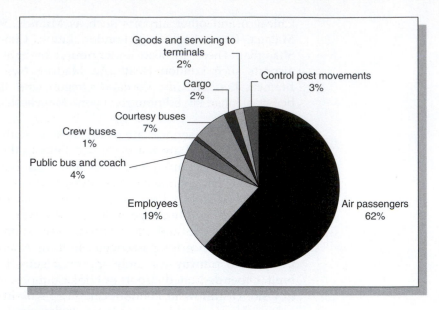

Figure 9.2
Average daily split of airport-related vehicle trips on landside roads.
Source: BAA Gatwick (2007).

Table 9.3 Surface transport use by passengers at UK airports 2006

	Private car	Hire car	Taxi	Tube	Rail	Bus/coach	Other	Total
Belfast City	61.7	6.5	25.2	0.0	0.4	5.7	0.6	100
Belfast International	76.7	7.0	8.8	0.0	0.0	7.2	0.4	100
Birmingham	54.2	3.4	23.7	0.0	9.8	8.7	0.4	100
East Midlands	68.6	2.8	19.2	0.0	4.5	4.6	0.4	100
London City	16.8	1.3	39.4	0.0	40.2	1.6	0.6	100
London Gatwick	48.2	2.2	14.0	0.0	29.1	6.3	0.3	100
London Heathrow	34.4	2.5	27.5	13.4	9.1	13.1	0.0	100
London Luton	52.9	3.0	13.7	0.0	0.3	29.8	0.3	100
London Stansted	46.9	3.1	8.8	0.0	23.3	16.3	1.5	100
Manchester	58.2	2.5	29.1	0.0	7.4	2.2	0.6	100

Source: Civil Aviation Authority (2006).

than just consideration of journey time. It also includes looking at the accessibility of the surface modes, ease of transfer to the airport and arrangements for baggage. Some airports are designing better interchange processes between public transport and the airport, and offering more remote check-in. Others have tried making improvements in marketing, signage, and the availability of information.

Table 9.3 shows the modes of surface transport used at a range of UK airports. Private car use is greatest at the smaller airports in

Belfast and East Midlands where there is no direct rail link. Private car use is low at London City airport but the taxi use is high because of the dominance of business travellers. The surface transport share for the London airports (excluding Heathrow) is in range of 30–40 per cent. At Frankfurt airport the equivalent figure is 33 per cent, at Amsterdam 47 per cent, and at Zürich 59 per cent. In the United States, public transport use tends to be much lower, typically around 10–15 per cent.

It may be seen from Figure 9.2 that employees at Gatwick airport contribute to 19 per cent of all vehicle trips. Hence airport operators at Gatwick and numerous other airports have also been trying to encourage more airport employees to use public transport. Inherently there are a number of characteristics of airport employment which encourage the use of private car. Many of the jobs tend to be on a shift basis, often at unsociable times when public transport services are inadequate. Employees' residences tend to be dispersed around the vicinity of the airport which makes it much more difficult to provide an effective public transport system. Moreover, airport employees have traditionally been provided with free parking spaces at airports – thus increasing the attractiveness of car transport. As a result of these factors, car use tends to be even higher for employees than for passengers. For example, at Manchester airport in 2005, around 80 per cent of employees used private cars compared to around 60 per cent of passengers using them. At Amsterdam staff using so-called collective transport which is mostly public transport is around 40 per cent of the total compared to 47 per cent for passengers and at Zürich staff use of public transport is only 28 per cent compared to 59 per cent for passengers. However Frankfurt is a rare example where employee use is greater than passenger use (39 per cent as opposed to 33 per cent). This is also the situation at London City airport because of the location of the airport and the nature of the employees compared to the passengers.

Staff initiatives to encourage public transport use include discounted bus and rail travel, dedicated airport workers' buses, the development of cycling networks, and park and ride schemes. When car use is still necessary, car sharing has been encouraged at some airports. Restrictions on car use within the airport area have also been introduced. One of the many examples of a staff travel plan is the 'lift' plan at Auckland airport which has an overall initial goal of encouraging staff to car pool once a week or use public transport once a fortnight. As a result of such plans, at some airports the transport use by employees has been increasing. For instance, at Gatwick airport in 2007 employees travelling by car represented 70 per cent of the total which was down from 78 per cent in 1997. Use of the train and bus/coach has increased from 8 to 11 and 3 to 9 per cent, respectively (BAA Gatwick, 2007).

Since 1998 in the United Kingdom all airports with scheduled services have been required to form airport transport forums (ATFs) and

Table 9.4 Bristol airport staff travel plan

Targets

To reduce the proportion of staff who commute on their own from 93% to 75%
To increase the level of those who commute as a car passenger approximately fourfold to 15.5%
To treble the proportion of staff who use bus based services from 2.5% to 7.5%
To achieve 1% cycle modal share
To achieve 1% powered two wheeler mode share
Measures to achieve targets
Easy-to-use car sharing scheme
Extension to the Flyer airport express coach service
Staff only minibuses serving wide area and shift times
Improved secure staff car park with fairer charging policy
Staff travel incentive scheme
Better information and promotion of travel options
Staff travel website with information and live travel news
Travel plan co-ordinator to help with travel needs and journey planning
Cycle facility improvements and cycle purchase scheme
Initiatives to reduce business travel impact

Source: Bristol airport (2007).

prepare airport surface access strategies (ASASs) as part of a national policy framework for integrated transport (DETR, 1998). The ATFs have three specific objectives (DETR, 1999):

1. To agree to short- and long-term targets for decreasing the private car usage to and from airports.
2. To devise a strategy for achieving these targets.
3. To oversee implementation of the strategy.

The ATF consists of the airport operator and representatives from local businesses, local government, transport operators, the local community, and other interested parties. In preparing the ASASs the forum has to ensure that the proposals are consistent with the broader integrated transport plans for the area (Humphreys *et al.*, 2005). By way of illustration, the targets and policies for one specific aspect of these strategies, namely staff travel, are shown in Table 9.4 for Bristol airport.

Environmental management

For many airport operators, environmental policies are increasingly becoming a core component of their overall business strategy. Environmental pressures from governments, users and other bodies have made it essential for airports to address environmental issues very seriously. In some areas, such as air or water quality, airports often have to comply with environmental legislation. Airports have recognized, though, that sound environmental practice can also bring financial benefits through the effective management of resources such as energy, waste, and water. As a result, most major airports in the Western world now have well-established environmental strategies and relatively sophisticated policies which typically seek to reduce noise and emissions, control pollution, reduce waste and energy use, and encourage the use of renewables and public transport. Increased technology and new mitigation methods are constantly enabling improvements in the efficiencies of such policies. Smaller airports and airports in the developing world have more basic approaches – but few have managed to escape the whole issue of environmental management entirely. Since airport operators themselves produce relatively little of the direct environmental impacts, a key to any successful environmental strategy is a partnership approach between all the different interests on the airport site.

Many airports have seen their environmental control processes develop into comprehensive environment management systems. These systems provide the framework for airport operators to develop an effective and co-ordinated response to all the environmental issues. Within any system, clearly defined objectives and targets are set for reducing the impacts and the most appropriate mitigation methods are identified. Through adopting such an approach the airport operator also sends messages to the outside world that it is tackling the environmental issues in a responsible manner. In addition, when an airport is planning a major extension of its facilities, it is usually required by law to undertake an environmental impact assessment (EIA) as part of the planning approval process. This will examine the potential impacts of the proposed development during the construction and operational stages. The results of this assessment are summarized in an environmental impact statement (EIS).

Some airports choose to formalize their environmental management system by conforming to the International Environmental Management system standards ISO 14001. This is equivalent to the ISO 9001 standard for quality management (see Chapter 4). To meet the requirements of ISO 14001, airports need to review their environmental impacts, formulate an environmental policy, ensure that their practices comply with all relevance legislation, set objectives and targets to improve environment performance and demonstrate that appropriate measures have been introduced so that environmental practice can be monitored and targets can be reached. Dublin airport became one of the first European airports to receive ISO 14001 certification in 1999 and many other European airports such as Zürich, Rome, Athens, and Paris have subsequently been certified (Hooper et al., 2003). Toronto Lester B. Pearson was the first airport in North America to achieve this standard in 1998. Within the EU, there is an additional system called the Eco Management and Audit Scheme (EMAS) which is based on 1993 European regulation. The EMAS takes the ISO 14001 standard that much further by requiring companies to report to the public about their environmental performance. This report, as well as the implementation of the management system, is subject to external scrutiny. Airport companies such as Schiphol and Fraport have reached these standards.

One of the key elements of any environmental management system is the identification of suitable environmental indicators which can be used to monitor performance and set targets. The indicators should provide a representative picture of the issue under consideration and it must be possible to obtain relatively easily and accurately the data required for such indicators. The indicators need to be fairly simple, easy to interpret and able to show time trends. The results should be available to everybody who has an interest in the airport, including the local community.

Some airports, such as BAA and Amsterdam, now view environmental performance as an aspect of corporate responsibility and so report environmental measures alongside policies such as human resource management, health and safety, and community relations in corporate responsibility documents. Other airports such as Zürich, Copenhagen, and Helsinki have retained environmental reports which solely cover environmental measures and issues. However in whatever manner the environmental measures are presented, there does tend to be a lack of comparability between the indicators which makes any comparison between different airports very difficult to achieve (Upham and Mills, 2005). In 2000, a survey of 200 of the world's largest airports was undertaken by Loughborough University and the UK Open University to investigate how airports themselves were measuring their performance (Francis *et al.*, 2001). Some of the most popular environmental measures used were found to be the number of complaints which were used by 84 per cent of the airports, the population within a specified noise (67 per cent), passengers using public transport (53 per cent), and waste recycled (50 per cent) but overall there was an inconsistency in the measures used. This could be overcome with the adoption of a set of standardized indicators as detailed in Table 9.5. This shows both absolute values of resources used and wastes emitted as well as relating these to performance targets or limits.

In conclusion, this chapter has identified the major environmental impacts associated with airport operations and has described various environmental management approaches designed to reduce these effects. Environmental issues affect most aspects of airport operations and undoubtedly will become even more important in the future. In spite of technological, operational, and other mitigation measures to minimize the environmental impacts, the growth rates being predicted for air transport, if allowed to take place, will mean that the environmental impacts will increase.

This means that the concept of environmental capacity will become a key issue. In a purely physical sense, an airport's capacity can be

Table 9.5 Core environmental performance indicators and measures at airports

Indicator	Absolute measures	Threshold-related measures
Number of surface access vehicles by type	Number arriving/departing (monthly, annually)	Movement number relative to hourly maxima
Aircraft movements	Number arriving/departing (hourly, monthly, yearly)	Movement number relative to hourly maxima
Static power consumption	Fossil-fuelled electricity/gas consumption plus wind/solar or bio-generated electricity consumption (monthly, yearly)	Consumption relative to any relative hourly maxima
Gaseous pollutant emissions (from surface vehicles, aircraft and static power)	Emissions per source and ambient concentrations	Ambient concentrations relative to any set limits
Aircraft noise	Day, evening and night values	People and area within noise contour relative to any set limit
Terminal passengers	Number arriving/departing at gates	Gate arrival/departure relative to hourly maxima
Surface access passengers	Number arriving/departing	Number arriving/departing relative to hourly maxima
Water consumption and waste water	Monthly volume consumed. Effluent concentrations and ambient concentrations of water pollutants	Volume consumed relative to hourly maximum
		Pollutant concentrations relative to any set limit
Solid waste	Monthly volume (total and hazardous). Monthly recycled	Absolute volume relative to set targets
Land take and biodiversity	Area paved. Area of high/medium biodiversity	Absolute areas relative to set targets

Source: Adapted from Upham and Mills (2005).

defined in a variety of ways, such as the number of runway slots, or capacity of terminals, gates, or apron areas. However, it is likely that in the future environmental capacity, which is set by consideration of the impacts of an airport's operation upon the local environment and the lives of residents of local communities, will determine the ultimate overall capacity of an airport. Hence it may well be the environmental capacity of airports which is likely to constrain growth, rather than any physical or financial considerations. In many cases, airports will reach their environmental capacity before making full use of existing infrastructure and they may also not be able to make changes to the physical infrastructure if this involves exceeding the environmental capacity limits. In effect, airports will only be able to grow if they minimize the impact of these expanding activities on the environment and the community. Therefore, the aviation industry clearly faces a major challenge in the future. In essence, this challenge is how to maintain economic and social benefits from air transport, encourage economic development through mobility and yet respond to the increasing environmental pressures being placed on the industry. There is still a great deal of uncertainty as to how this can be achieved.

References and further reading

Air Transport Action Group (ATAG) (2008) *enviro.aero facts and figures*, 23 January, available from www.enviro.aero (accessed 20 March 2008).

Airports Council International (ACI) (2008) *Worldwide airport environmental initiatives tracker file*, available from www.aci.aero (accessed 1 April 2008).

Anker, R. (1997). *Airports and the Environment*. University of Westminster Airport Policy and Planning Seminar, London, May.

British Airways (BA) (2008) *Quota Count (QC) night restrictions classification scheme*, available from www.ba.com (accessed 1 April 2008).

BAA Gatwick (2007). *Gatwick Surface Access Strategy*. BAA Gatwick.

BAA Heathrow (2007). *Local Air Quality Action Plan 2007–2011*. BAA Heathrow.

CE Delft (2002). *Economic Incentives to Mitigate Green House Gas Emissions from Air Transport in Europe*. CE Delft.

Civil Aviation Authority (CAA) (1998). *The Single European Aviation Market: The First Five Years*, CAP 685. CAA.

Civil Aviation Authority (CAA) (2006). *Survey of Passengers at Belfast City, Belfast International, Birmingham, Gatwick, Heathrow, London City, Luton, Manchester, Nottingham East Midlands and Stansted*. CAA.

Department of the Environment, Transport and the Regions (DETR) (1998) *A New deal for transport*. White Paper, The Stationery Office.

Department of the Environment, Transport and the Regions (DETR) (1999). *Guidance on Airport Transport Forums and Airport Surface Access*. DETR.

Dft (2003) *Aviation and the environment: Using economic instruments*, DfT.

European Commission (1999) *Air Transport and the Environment: Towards Meeting the Challenges of Sustainable Development*, COM (1999) 640 final, EC.

European Commission (2002) *Council Directive 2002/30/EC on the establishment of rules and procedures with regard to the introduction of noise-related operating restrictions at Community airports*, OJ L 85, 28 March.

European Commission (EC) (2005) *Reducing the Climate Change Impact of Aviation*, COM (2005) 459 final, EC.

European Commission (2008) *Noise Operation Restrictions at EU Airports: Report on the Application of Directive 2002/32/EC*, EC.

Ezard, K (2007) Emissionary positions, *Airline Business*, November, 52–54.

Fakiner, H. (2005). The role of intermodal transportation in airport management: The perspective of Frankfurt airport. In W. Delfmann, H. Baum, S. Auerbach, & S. Albers (Eds), *Strategic Management in the Aviation Industry*. Aldershot, Ashgate.

Francis, G., Fry, J. and Humphreys, I. (2001). *An International Survey of Performance Measurement in Airports*. Open University Business School Research Paper 01/4.

Hooper, P., Heath, B. and Maughan, J. (2003). Environmental management and the aviation industry, Upham, P., Maughan, J., Raper, D. and Thomas C. (Eds), *Towards Sustainable Aviation*. London, Earthscan.

Humphreys, I., Ison, S., Francis, G. and Aldridge, K. (2005). UK airport surface access targets. *Journal of Air Transport Management*, 11(2), 117–124.

IARO/ATAG/ACI (1998). *Air Rail Links: Guide to Best Practice*. IARO/ATAG/ACI.

Intergovernmental Panel on Climate Change (1999). *Aviation and the Global Atmosphere: Summary for Policymakers*. IPCC.

Intergovernmental Panel on Climate Change (2007). *Climate Change 2007: Fourth Assessment Report*. IPCC.

International Air Transport Association (IATA) (2003). *Air/Rail Intermodality*. IATA.

Janic, M. (2003). The potential for modal substitutions, Upham, P., Maughan, J., Raper D. and Thomas C. (Eds), *Towards Sustainable Aviation*. Earthscan.

MPD Group Ltd (2007). *Study of Aircraft Noise Exposure at and Around Community Airports: Evaluation of the Effect of Measures to Reduce Noise*. MPD Group Ltd.

Pitt, M., Brown, A. and Smith, A. (2002). Waste management at airports. *Facilities*, 20(5/6), 198–207.

Royal Commission on Environmental Pollution (2002). *The Environmental Effects of Civil Aviation in Flight*. RCEP.

Schiphol Group (2007). *Corporate Responsibility Report 2006*. Schiphol Group.

SEO Amsterdam Economics (2003). *Benchmark: Government Influence on Aeronautical Charges*. SEO Amsterdam Economics.

Sharp, A. (2007). Airport rail links, *CILT Focus*, February, 42–44.

Upham, P. and Mills, J. (2005). Environmental and operational sustainability of airports. *Benchmarking: An International Journal*, 12(2), 166–179.

CHAPTER 10

Future prospects

A dominant theme running through this book is that the airports are going through a period of unprecedented change. Enhanced competitive pressures from airline deregulation and airport privatization coupled with increased demands for a more sustainable and quality conscious industry have brought many new challenges for the airports. New airline models and groupings have emerged. In addition, airports have had to face the unparalleled consequences of a number of unpredictable events – notably 9/11, SARS, and the LAGS security issue. All of these mean that the industry has been operating in a much more volatile and uncertain environment than ever before and all indications are that this is not going to change in the future, particularly with the current high fuel prices and economic slowdown. This is likely to lead to more flexibility and adaptability in the way that airports are operated and will see the industry becoming more experienced and knowledgeable in areas such as crisis and recovery management strategies.

One of the most important changes that has occurred within the airport sector is privatization. Whilst a number of significant airport privatizations have taken place, currently the degree of concentration and private sector involvement within the airport industry is fairly small – much less than in the airline industry. However, all indications are that more privatizations are planned for the future – albeit that the effect of the current credit crunch remains uncertain. Possible airport privatisations from various corners of the world include Amsterdam, Lisbon, Bucharest, Milan, Munich, Hong Kong, Narita, Kansai, Inchoen, and Abu Dhabi. Investors are, however, much more cautious than they were in the 'gold rush' days of the late 1990s and particularly the number of traditional airport operators who may be interested in getting involved with other airports do not seem likely to expand dramatically. At the same time, though, new investors that were not present in these early stages of privatization, most notably from the financial sector, are now emerging as dominant players. As the industry further evolves, more secondary sales are likely. All this raises the fundamental question-are airports really any different from any other business once the technical and operations know-how has been acquired? It is probably still too early in the evolutionary stage of airport privatization to answer this question with any degree of certainty or to identify the factors which will determine the most successful type of airport management in the long run in this new global environment, or which will bring the greatest value addition.

The impact of such fundamental structural changes within the airport industry cannot be assessed without considering the parallel airline developments towards deregulation and privatization. The post-deregulation environment in many countries has meant that airlines are trying hard to control costs to improve their operating margins and are consequently exerting greater demands on the airports to control their costs and keep down their level of airport charges. Slower and maturing traffic in some markets, coupled with unprecedented fuel price increases, has resulted in such pressures becoming very much greater. Moreover, the evolution of airline alliances at one extreme and the low cost carrier (LCC) sector at the other is producing new challenges for airport operators to cope with different types of customers. Such developments are irreversibly changing the traditional airline–airport roles and interactions that have existed for many years.

The creation of airline alliances has meant that airlines are no longer automatically linked to the national airport of the country and airports can no longer, as before, be guaranteed of their custom. Moreover, even if they retain the business of such airlines, the needs and requirements of the customers will be different. Alliance members want to be able to share and get cost economies and brand benefits from operating joint facilities at the airports. For other airports, it is the emergence of the LCC sector that has been the key driver of change. Airports have devised different strategies to cope with these airlines which operate in a much more cost conscious environment than most other airlines and hence place different demands on airport management. Some airports have tried to offer the same level of service to all their airline customers whereas at the other extreme some have built purpose built low cost terminals. The experience of the low cost terminals to date had only been very limited and so it is difficult to draw any conclusions about these – albeit that both Kuala Lumpur and Singapore have announced plans to expand these facilities. A particular issue is the impact on non-aeronautical revenues. Hence it seems likely to assume that in the near future there is not going to a wide spread shift to the two tier airport terminal product (full service and low cost) although a selection of airports may choose to follow this strategy.

Undoubtedly the airline and airport industries are operating in a more competitive environment nowadays and this trend is likely to continue particularly with the deregulation of the north Atlantic market in 2008 and the knock-on effect that this will have elsewhere in the world. The actual extent of competition which each airport will face, however, will always remain variable depending on location, the nature of the airlines and their services and other factors. A major issue within the industry, however, which is becoming more important than before, is consideration of whether airports possess sufficient market power to warrant economic regulation. Experience particularly in Europe, Australia, and New Zealand have shown that different stakeholders have very different views about this. These debates are not likely to go away in the future and are likely to be intensified as more airports become privatized. At the same time the merits and disadvantages of different regulatory structures, for example single versus dual till regulation, and price cap versus reserve regulation, will no doubt continue to be argued at length.

Technology developments for essential processes such as check-in, security and border control can potentially offer considerable advantages to passengers, airlines and airports. Passengers will have simpler and quicker services, airlines will reduce their costs and airports will be able to use their scarce terminal space more effectively to provide a better quality product. Ultimately how far these technologies can go in producing an overall simplified and integrated processes rather than the cumbersome and discrete ones which exist today will depend on many factors and hurdles such as the cost of the technology, the ability of the different stakeholders to work together and co-ordinate their efforts, and the ability of governments to reach agreements on very sensitive and important matters concerning national security and immigration. One area of certainty is that the days are long gone since everyone at the airport queued up at a traditional airline desk to check-in. There are many other technological developments (too many to cover in this book) associated with airports and airlines which will also have an impact in the future. The introduction of new aircraft types, such as the A380, has had and will continue to have major infrastructure and capacity implications for airports. Technological improvements to airfield and airspace infrastructure and aircraft may improve efficiency and at the same time reduce some of the undesirable environmental impacts of airports. The evolving e-economy will also continue to have a major impact on the nature of freight operations at airports just as e-procurement policies will play an ever-increasing role.

The more uncertain airport environment makes it increasingly difficult to produce accurate forecasts but overall most stakeholders are of the view that demand, if accommodated, will grow significantly. Forecasting in the short term with the current economic difficulties is particularly challenging, but the passenger forecasts produced by International Air Transport Association (IATA) in 2007 showed that international passenger numbers were expected to grow at an average annual growth rate of 5.1 per cent between 2007 and 2011 which was slightly lower than the average of 7.4 per cent which was experienced between 2002 and 2006 as traffic recovered from 9/11. It was expected that the forecast slower global economic growth would weaken demand but traffic would also be boosted by the liberalization of markets and the emergence of new routes and services. The Asia Pacific and Middle Eastern regions were forecast to grow the most, 5.9 and 6.8 per cent respectively, and high growth was also expected in Eastern Europe. Eight individual countries were forecast to have growth rates above 8 per cent, namely Latvia, the Russian Federation, Poland, Ukraine, China, India, and the United Arab Emirates. Domestic passenger traffic was forecast to grow at a marginally faster rate (5.3 per cent), very much helped by strong growth in the Chinese and Indian domestic markets. International freight demand was expected to grow by 4.8 per cent per annum with the greatest growth happening in fast-growing economies especially in Asia Pacific with growth rates of 10.8, 8.3, and 8.2 per cent respectively for China, India and the Republic of Korea (International Air Transport Association, 2007).

Table 10.1   Long-term forecasts of global traffic growth

Organization	Time period	Traffic measure	Average annual growth rate (%)
Passengers			
Boeing	2007–2026	Passengers-kilometres	5.0
		Passengers	4.5
Airbus	2007–2026	Passengers-kilometres	4.9
Rolls-Royce	2007–2026	Passenger-kilometres	4.9
ICAO	2006–2025	Scheduled-passenger kilometers	6.6
		Scheduled passengers	4.1
ACI	2006–2025	Passengers	4.0
Freight			
Boeing	2007–2026	Freight tonne-kilometres	6.1
Airbus	2007–2026	Freight tonne-kilometres	5.8
ICAO	2006–2025	Scheduled freight tonnes-kilometers	6.6
		Scheduled freight tones	5.5
ACI	2006–2025	Freight tonnes	5.4
Aircraft movements			
ICAO	2006–2025	Aircraft departures	3.6
ACI	2006–2025	Commercial ATMs	2.8

Source: Boeing (2007), Airbus (2007), Rolls-Royce (2007), ICAO (2007), ACI (2007).

In the longer-term, Airports Council International (ACI) is predicting that passenger numbers will increase by around four per cent per annum (Table 10.1). International Civil Aviation Organization (ICAO) and Boeing have similar forecasts of passenger volume. The manufacturers and ICAO also produce forecasts of passenger-kilometres which are actually more relevant to airlines than airports. This tends to push up forecasts by up to 1 per cent per annum as the average distance flown is predicted to increase and so overall these forecasts are fairly similar to those of ACI. Growth in aircraft movements is likely to be less than passengers as larger aircraft such as the A380 will be used and as also the airlines will continue to fly with higher load factors.

As in the past, economic growth, which reflects business activity and personal wealth, and the cost of travel, will continue to play a major role in shaping the growth of passenger demand. For certain markets, particularly within the United States and Europe, the responsiveness of demand to changes in income may be weakening as demand maturity sets in. Elsewhere, particularly in developing areas of the world, the relative immature market and higher than average predicted economic growth will ensure high growth rates. For example, ACI predicts that the relatively mature US and European markets will

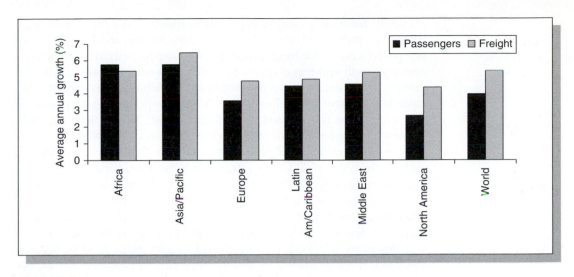

Figure 10.1
Average annual airport passenger forecasts by regional 2006–2025.
(*Source*: ACI, 2007.)

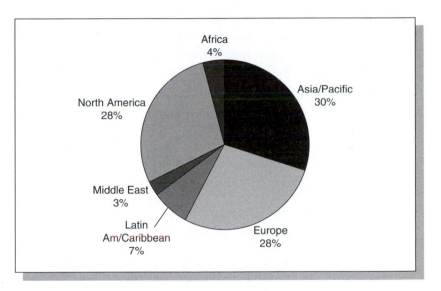

Figure 10.2
Forecast airport passengers by world region, 2025.
(*Source*: ACI, 2007.)

grow by only 2.7 and 3.6 per cent respectively compared with higher growth rates for the more developing markets of Africa and Asia Pacific (Figure 10.1). The highest growth rates are expected to occur in India (10.4 per cent) and China (8.1 per cent). Overall by 2025 it is expected that the Asia Pacific market will be the largest having taken over from North America (Figure. 10.2). Similarly, Boeing is predicting that nearly 40 per cent of air travel will be to, from, or within Asia Pacific by 2026 (Boeing, 2007).

Freight traffic is generally expected to increase at a faster rate than passenger traffic with Asia Pacific markets having the highest average growth rates. Air freight demand is also primarily driven by economic growth and travel cost – as well as international trade. Higher growth is generally expected because of globalization trends that have led to increased reliance on global components and products that need to be transported around the world. The rapidly expanding knowledge-based industrial sectors such as computing, electronics, communications, and pharmaceuticals are the most international and are heavily reliant on air travel for the transportation of their high-value/low-weight products. Increasing reliance on just in-time inventory systems favours air freight. E-commerce has also brought substantial reductions in the distribution costs of air freight and increased demand for the integrators and the express mail sector.

If this growth in both passenger and freight traffic is to be accommodated, there is a need for much more airport capacity. For example in Europe it is estimated that if capacity levels are not drastically increased, over 60 airports will be heavily congested by 2025 and the top 20 airports will be saturated at least 8–10 hours a day (ECAC/ Eurocontrol, 2004). In the short term, a more effective slot allocation process might alleviate some of the capacity bottlenecks. Secondary and regional airports could also take some of the growth away from major airports as they have already done, and so could high-speed rail. In the long term, however, the problem of capacity shortages at major European airports is not going to disappear. Similarly in the United States, it has been estimated that 18 airports will need additional capacity by 2015 and 27 by 2025 (Federal Aviation Administration, 2007). In many other areas of the world, there is also a pressing need for new capacity, especially in the areas where high growth is being predicted, such as India and China. Worldwide ACI estimated that with the current pace of construction, airport capacity would accommodate 6 billion passengers in 2020 – although it was forecasting 7 billion passenger demand.

Expanding airport capacity can be very challenging due to a number of reasons. First, the finance for such development needs to be found. Traditionally many funds came from public sources, but increasingly this sector is unable or unwilling to provide such support. Internal funds will not be sufficient in most cases and hence this is one of the key reasons why privatization has become an important trend in the airport sector. In Europe it is predicted that capital expenditure of €82.6 billion will be needed in the next 10 years (SH&E, 2006). In the United States, it is estimated that the capital investment just needed for 2007–2011 is around $87.4 billion (ACI-North America, 2007). It is uncertain whether the current main forms of financing in the United States (i.e. aviation trust funds, passenger facility charges, and commercial bonds) will be sufficient to cover this needed investment.

In some cases, where there is a strong political will to develop air transport as in China for instance, airport expansion can be agreed swiftly and with little trouble. The building of the Dubai World Central International airport with six runways is another example. However in other regions, it can take years for airports to gain approval through the planning process which can be excessively long and costly. It can often take over 10 years for the process to expanded airport facilities and even longer, if a new greenfield site airport is being considered. The London Heathrow Terminal 5 inquiry in the late 1990s in the United Kingdom lasted more than 4 years and was one of the longest planning enquiries in UK history. Overall the whole planning process took 14 years and cost €550 million which is 12 per cent of the total cost. Likewise the planning process for Munich airport took 22 years and cost €800 million (20 per cent of the total cost) (Jankovec, 2007). Other examples include the construction of a parallel runway at Seattle airport which because of environmental constraints and a number of lawsuits filed by local residents will be opening in late 2008, which is 20 years later from receiving initial approval by the local authorities. Very few new airports or fully expanded airports have been built in the United States or Europe in recent years with Denver, Munich, Oslo, Athens, and Milan being the only examples. Elsewhere in Narita in Toyko, the second runway was opposed for over 10 years by local politicians and farmers and eventually was approved but with a shorter length. Meanwhile in Auckland, it took 7 years to get the second runway approved.

Without doubt, the greatest challenge that the airport sector, and indeed the whole air transport industry faces, is to cope with the expected traffic growth whilst at the same time living with the huge pressures for greater sustainability and environmental capacity constraints. It is an extremely difficult problem balancing out the needs for quality of life and sustainability against desires for greater mobility. The more extreme environmentalists will continue to argue that there is no way that the potential demand for air transport in the future should be met, and that the solution is to constrain growth. Others hold less radical views but most agree that the industry has to focus much of its effort and resources on developing sustainable solutions if the industry is to be allowed to grow at all to meet the increasing traffic levels.

In conclusion, airport operators have a challenging time ahead. They are confronted with conflicting demands from their different stakeholders. Different airline groupings and types of airlines are favouring more differentiated facilities and services and putting increasing pressures on airport costs. Passenger expectations in terms of service quality are rising. Regional authorities want to ensure that airports generate maximum economic benefits whilst not harming the well-being of the population in the region. National governments want to ensure that the environment and society is adequately protected and may also want to guarantee, perhaps through regulation, that airports are not abusing any excessive market power and are not acting in an anti-competitive manner. Then there are the financial demands from the airport owners or shareholders, which are increasingly being driven by private sector motives. Finally everyone wants the airport to provide a secure, safe and healthy environment which has become increasingly difficult to achieve in recent years because of the new security and health risks that now exist. This book has considered all these important interrelated issues and has aimed to provide some insight into how airport operators might address the challenges of the future.

References and further reading

Airbus (2007). *Global Market Forecast 2006–2025*. Airbus.

Airports Council International (ACI) (2007). *Global Traffic Forecast 2006–2025*. ACI.

ACI-North America (2007). *Airport Capital Development Costs*. ACI-North America.

Boeing (2007). *Current Market Outlook 2006–2026*. Boeing.

ECAC/Eurocontrol (2004). *Challenges to Growth*. ECAC/Eurocontrol.

Federal Aviation Administration (FAA) (2007). *Capacity Needs in the National Airspace System 2007–2025*. FAA.

International Air Transport Association (IATA) (2007). *Passenger and Freight Forecasts 2007 to 2011*. IATA Economic briefing paper.

International Civil Aviation Organization (ICAO) (2007). *Growth in Air Traffic Projected to Continue to 2025*, news release, 18 September.

Jankovec, O. (2007). How to address the capacity challenge, presentation given to the European Aviation Club, 19 June, available from www.aci-europe.org, (accessed 25 March 2008).

Rolls-Royce (2007). *Market Outlook 2007*. Rolls-Royce.

SH&E (2006). *Capital Needs and Regulatory Oversight Arrangements*. SH&E.

Index